OXFORD **READERS**

War

Lawrence Freedman is Professor of War Studies at King's College, London. His most recent publications include *The Atlas of Global Strategy* (1985), *The Price of Peace* (1986), *Britain in the World* (1988), *Britain and the Falklands War* (with Michael Clarke, 1991), and *The Gulf Conflict, 1990–91* (with Efraim Karsh, 1993).

D0834866

OXFORD **READERS**

The Oxford Readers series represents a unique interdisciplinary resource, offering authoritative collections of primary and secondary sources on the core issues which have shaped history and continue to affect current events.

OXFORD **READERS**

War

Edited by Lawrence Freedman

OXFORD
UNIVERSITY PRESS

OXFORD
UNIVERSITY PRESS

Great Clarendon Street, Oxford OX2 6DP

Oxford University Press is a department of the University of Oxford.
It furthers the University's objective of excellence in research, scholarship,
and education by publishing worldwide in

Oxford New York

Athens Auckland Bangkok Bogotá Buenos Aires Calcutta
Cape Town Chennai Dar es Salaam Delhi Florence Hong Kong Istanbul
Karachi Kuala Lumpur Madrid Melbourne Mexico City Mumbai
Nairobi Paris São Paulo Singapore Taipei Tokyo Toronto Warsaw

with associated companies in Berlin Ibadan

Oxford is a registered trade mark of Oxford University Press
in the UK and in certain other countries

Published in the United States
by Oxford University Press Inc., New York

Selection and editorial matter © Lawrence Freedman 1994

The moral rights of the author have been asserted

Database right Oxford University Press (maker)

First published as an Oxford Reader 1994

British Library Cataloguing in Publication Data

Data available

Library of Congress Cataloging in Publication Data

War / edited by Lawrence Freedman.
p. cm.—(Oxford readers)
Includes bibliographical references and index.
1. War. I. Freedman, Lawrence. II. Series.
U21.2.W357 1994 355.02—dc20 93-21348

ISBN 0-19-289254-1

10 9 8 7 6

Printed in Great Britain
on acid-free paper by
Biddles Ltd,
Guildford and King's Lynn

Preface

While I have taken the responsibility of editing this volume, and for the final choices of materials, it would not have been possible to put this reader together without the hard work and support of my colleagues in the Department of War Studies at King's College London. The Department has taught an MA course for many years and has recently supplemented this with an undergraduate degree. In compiling materials for individual sections my colleagues took account of the interests of students. However, they also considered a more general reader and the need to address the basic questions which tend to be asked by all those interested in the origins of wars and the way they are fought. I would like to take the opportunity to thank all members of my Department, including those whose names do not appear in this book, for their co-operation and friendship over the past decade. It is always surprising to those who join the War Studies Department how an institution with such a forbidding name can sustain such cheery collegiality. I would also like to thank Catherine Clarke of OUP for encouraging me to take on this project and her patience in waiting for its completion. As ever, my wife Judith deserves my gratitude not only for putting up with another book, but for everything else.

Contents

B. The Causes of War

C. War And the Military Establishment

F. Total War and the Great Powers

G. Limited War and Developing Countries

War

General Introduction

LAWRENCE FREEDMAN

Wars have taken place from the beginning of recorded time and in all parts of the world. They are prominent, and sometimes dominant, both in history books and in today's headlines. They have shaped the international system and prompted social change. They have inspired literature, art, and music. They are at the same time products of social and economic development, and threats to continuing progress. In recent years it has even been possible to describe how an uncontrolled nuclear confrontation could trigger an ecological chain reaction that would leave little life on earth. On a more personal scale, wars provide some of the most intense as well as brutal of human experiences, bringing out the best as well as the worst in people—heroism, comradeship, and self-sacrifice as well as cruelty and viciousness. In the process they raise the most fundamental questions of ethics.

War is a function of ambiguities in the state system. If the world's land mass was all distributed between groups of people, each homogeneous in make-up, occupying territory sufficiently rich for its needs and blessed with a popular government, then there would be little war. Unfortunately people, territory, resources, and power are distributed unevenly. It is often uncertain where some states end and others begin. Sometimes significant sections of the population believe that they should be part of another state or question the legitimacy of their government. At other times, the power and intentions of another state pose a direct challenge.

By definition a state should enjoy a monopoly of legitimate and organized violence within its territorial boundaries. When that monopoly is seriously challenged, by external aggression or by an internal threat such as a rebellion or secessionist movement, or when it sees opportunities to expand its territory by using force, it can consider itself at war. It is the severity of the threat, rather than the scale of violence, which makes the difference. Urban rioting in the United States may be vicious but it is essentially a police matter: it does not take on the characteristics of a civil war until an attempt is made to take over the basic functions of the state. Equally there may be border skirmishes, perhaps connected with smuggling or illegal immigration. Considerable force may be applied but the threats to security are comparatively slight and indirect.

States do not only go to war because of an immediate threat to their own survival. They are often part of alliances, such as the North Atlantic Treaty Organization, or collective security arrangements, such as the United

Nations, through which they accept some obligation to act to defend others. The unifying concept here is that of security, which is normally taken to refer to an absence of threat. Security is a combination of a physical condition, in the sense of being able to prevent others inflicting harm, and a mental condition, in the sense of confidence that this is indeed the case. A threat to security may be imagined—which might be regarded as paranoia—or disregarded as complacency. Much of the assessment will be dependent not only on identifying hostility in the external or internal environments but on an awareness of a vulnerability within the society that the hostile might target and exploit. A state with long open borders is liable to feel more insecure than one protected by mountains or with expanses of ocean separating it from any likely enemy. Self-sufficiency in key raw materials provides for more security than dependence upon distant suppliers and lines of communication, as does a homogeneous and satisfied population as against one that is divided within itself, perhaps on ethnic lines.

Because of these vulnerabilities there are aspects of security which have nothing to do with armed force. A government which senses that its people are getting restless may be better advised to look to economic conditions or means of free political expression than to physical repression. Over-dependence on a particular source of energy might be mitigated by a range of measures from developing alternative suppliers, to substituting alternative energies, to measures of conservation. Even where there is awareness of a potential enemy, preparation for war is not the only option. There may be a deal to be done or a shared interest to be jointly developed which might deflect attention from more divisive matters, or a display of reassurance to convince this potential enemy that there is no reason to be suspicious.

Wars tend to occur when there is a doubt about the outcome. If the power relations are clear-cut then the weak may recognize that they have little choice but to comply with the wishes of the strongest. However, when the stakes are high and both sides see a possibility of winning (or at least of emerging from the fight in a relatively stronger position) then battle may be joined. It is not just the quantity and quality of the armies and equipment that will be decisive; it will be the strategic imagination with which they are deployed, the nerve of the leaders in the face of set-backs and their readiness to exploit breakthroughs and, often most crucial, their ability to forge and sustain alliances and disrupt those of the other side. Needless to say, history is full of examples of misplaced confidence in all these attributes as well as in the decisive potential of war itself.

The miseries produced by war, and the general social and political up-heavals it normally generates, encourage the view that 'wars never solve anything'. It would be better if this were true, because it would provide a powerful argument against initiating hostilities. Yet war has shaped too many states in the modern world to justify such a generalization, however true it undoubtedly is in many cases. Wars have toppled dictators and liberated oppressed peoples. They have also been fought and won to protect ways of life and cherished values.

Sometimes it is said that wars are the product of a particular sort of society—bellicist as opposed to pacifist—in which they are seen as a vital proving ground for young men and even whole societies, and on occasion necessary to avoid the onset of decadence. Others point the finger at those connected with the military Establishment, who are seen to have a stake in sustaining an exaggerated sense of threat to keep their budgets and their profiles high. Others note how democracies may be slow to respond to an overt challenge but become ferocious and uncompromising when roused, or that an unpopular regime can be tempted by a military adventure to distract attention from its domestic failings. All these issues underline the difficulty of any attempt to study war without addressing its broader social and political context.

A detached, unsentimental approach to the study of war can be justified. If nothing is said about war, other than that it is absolutely awful, then there can be no attempt to contain it and reduce its role in human affairs. One would not expect a physician to speak of little but the traumas of a particular disease in its terminal stages: rather, one would hope for systematic enquiry geared to a level of understanding that can at most produce cures and at least reduce pain. Even those who describe themselves as students of peace tend to find themselves drawn to the analysis of the causes and conduct of war. Certainly plans to eliminate war based on simplistic notions of its likely origins rarely prosper and can be counter-productive. Yet to insist that the study of war is a prerequisite for its prevention is too easy. There are other motives which draw people to the topic. The first, and the most long-standing, is the need to prepare to fight more efficiently. Until recently this accounted for the bulk of the literature on the topic, much of which was written by military commanders, generalizing on their experience and producing collections of principles to guide their successors, or by shrewd observers who saw patterns and regularities where the men of action saw little more than brute strength and a determined will.

A second reason for studying war is that very little else in human affairs can be understood without reference to it. Anyone who is curious about how people, organizations, and states adjust to great changes in their environment, cope with severe stress, and respond to fundamental challenges, finds in war their case studies. Historians would have to choose their time-frame and their subjects in an extremely restrictive manner if they wished to avoid war. Every speculation on the future depends in large measure on a judgement as to whether a major war can be avoided.

So the study of war can be both instrumental and instructive. It can also be extremely interesting and for many this is a sufficient justification. Wars occur when at least one party has determined that a dispute cannot be settled through negotiation. It is a trial of strength. As such, it can be a compelling spectacle, as each side searches for ruses and manœuvres to ensure that any fighting takes place under the most favourable conditions, drawing on the inventiveness of its scientists and the fortitude of its people as well as the courage and fighting prowess of its troops. The uncertainty over the outcome adds to the excitement. 'It is well that war is so terrible; we would grow too fond of it', the Confederate General Robert E. Lee is said to have commented in 1862 after the battle of Fredericksburg in the American Civil War.

There is a thrill and drama associated with war, which every news editor and most publishers understand. Trade negotiations and environmental initiatives may be just as critical to the health of the world community, but they generally attract only a specialist audience. The General Agreement on Trade and Tariffs is unlikely to stimulate great novels or popular magazines with blow-by-blow accounts of negotiations over market access for textiles. The green agenda gains general approval but low attention spans. War is the deadliest of sins, and unfortunately sin fascinates while good deeds bore. 'War makes rattling good history', observed Thomas Hardy, 'but Peace is poor reading.'

War is in fact often boring for those involved. Much time is spent exercising familiar routines, organizing the basics of life, watching where nothing is moving and waiting when little is about to happen. The moments of action are often short and extremely confusing for those in the middle of a battle, who are often the worst informed as to what is actually going on. It is usually those moments upon which historians and reporters seize, compressing the long periods of waiting and preparation into a few sentences, and often perceiving a logic in the progression of events that would surprise those who had lived through them.

In the West the most recent experience of major war, the allied action to liberate Kuwait from Iraq in the early months of 1991, was turned by the media coverage into something of a colossal sporting event. There was footage of encounters from both sides, with reporters talking to airmen who were about to strike Iraqi targets, and their colleagues then describing the results from Baghdad. The military was expected to provide full briefings on each day's events. Those aspects of the preparation for war which the military know to be crucial—such as the setting-up of supply lines and the consumption of food, fuel, and ammunitions, as well as thorough staff work—produced few enquiries. In what was a comparatively short campaign, patience could wear thin. After a few days the air bombardment of Iraq lost its novelty. 'Why are things dragging on?', a reporter asked of a senior American official. To keep the media content they were offered replays of key moments and images of 'clean kills' of command centres and aircraft bunkers rather than people (who tended to appear moving forward or surrendering but rarely fighting). Evidence of death became an unpleasant distraction. The story ended with a decisive victory and the evil dictator defeated, though not quite receiving his full comeuppance.

It took perhaps the subsequent war in the former Yugoslavia, with its political, as well as moral, confusion to remind Western audiences of the pity and suffering of war. There is no glamour or daring in innocents being turned out of their homes, or in continued bombardment of cities because the military manpower is not there to take them by force.

War grips our attention because even the vicarious experience provided is intense. To be complete, that experience should cover the range of emotions, from fear and horror to excitement and pride. There is no need for the student of war to deny these emotions. Precisely because they are so intense and so perplexing in their cumulative impact, there are few better ways of coping than to look hard at the evidence and then analyse it with candour and rigour.

The ubiquitous, contradictory, and multi-faceted character of war poses enormous problems for the editor of a reader. This book could be an anthology of writing or a collection of anecdotes and quotations. It could concentrate on the most modern period or go back to classical times. It could be very much longer. So what factors have influenced the choice of extracts for this collection?

First, it starts with the early nineteenth century. The debates of today can be traced back to those of classical times, so that Thucydides' account of the Peloponnesian wars from 400 BC can still serve as a starting-point for analyses of the causes of war while Machiavelli can still be read with profit by aspiring strategists. None the less, the Napoleonic wars still represent a clear break with those of the past in both their scope and intensity, introducing the nation in arms and leading to what remains the most important single text on the theory of war by Carl von Clausewitz.

A second feature of the selection is that it focuses on Anglo-Saxon perspectives. There is a rich body of literature, as well as a profound experience of war, in Britain and the United States. For reasons of both coherence and convenience, materials have been drawn disproportionately from these two countries. However, care has been taken to prevent this bias from becoming overwhelming by including materials from the other major powers, and also from those who have been on the receiving end of their campaigns in the Third World.

Third, the selection has a documentary bias. It contains first-hand accounts of fighting but not imaginative fiction. The intention is to serve those who are both puzzled and intrigued by the phenomenon of war, and to demonstrate the range of possible answers to the basic questions consistently asked: What are the causes of war? How have they been fought in the past and what are the prospects for the future? Are there basic principles which should shape the conduct of war if it is to be successfully prosecuted? In what ways, if at all, can this conduct be moral?

An exploration of these questions leads naturally to an interdisciplinary approach. This volume includes contributions from historians, political scientists, philosophers, sociologists and economists, as well as practitioners. This academic bias is qualified by a first section which contains first-hand accounts. They convey the character of war in the raw, and in so doing illuminate the complex sensations it triggers.

Where possible, original texts have been provided, especially in the case of the key figures in strategic thought as well as personal memoirs of combat. No précis or extract can ever do full justice to the original expression. Inevitably many writers have had to be omitted, but the extracts which have been chosen are here because they represent particularly lucid and concise statements and analyses, though they might not always be the best or the most subtle pieces of writing on particular topics. Even then, editing has proved necessary if there was to be any hope of including sufficient pieces to do justice to the wealth of material available. This book should be seen as a taster, a starting-point for the serious student of war.

As with all such collections, this will infuriate those who miss their favourites and are surprised at the editor's choice. A truly balanced collection, catering for all tastes and interests, would be superficial and bland. But war is not a 'balanced' activity. It takes place at the extremes of human behaviour, social organization, and political relations.

There is a degree of overlap in the various sections. The volume opens with a series of memoirs of war, from the perspective of the trooper on the ground to the senior commander and the civilian, the defeated as well as the victorious. Section B considers the various theories on the causes of war and sections C & D the phenomenon from sociological and ethical perspectives. Section E consists of a series of extracts from leading strategists whose ideas form a backdrop for the general discussions of the history of warfare in sections F and G. The first of these looks at total war as it has affected the great powers; the second considers limited war, which has often seemed total enough to those on the receiving end.

Section A

The Experience of War

MICHAEL DOCKRILL

The documents in this section are all concerned with the experiences of human beings caught up in warfare, normally as combatants, from the Napoleonic wars until the conflict in Bosnia, which was still under way as this reader was being prepared. This period of nearly two centuries witnessed a massive increase in the technology of war. There was also a huge expansion in the numbers of personnel fighting in the front line, and also in the proportion of the populations of belligerent countries who were directly involved, either in activities in the rear of the battlefield—communications, supply, etc.—or as munitions and factory workers on the home front and scientists and technologists engaged in perfecting new military techniques. With the coming of air power and the growing importance of the industrial and financial base of a country in sustaining a war effort, the entire civilian population of an enemy country could be regarded as potential belligerents, liable to be attacked directly from the air in their homes, factories, or offices or starved by the imposition of a naval blockade. After 1914 one could genuinely describe warfare as having become 'total'.

However, despite these awesome developments in the technology and comprehensiveness of warfare, human beings remain in 1993 as vulnerable to death and injury from destructive projectiles as they did in 1800. Missiles have become much more accurate and protective measures in the shape of armour and entrenchments are more sophisticated, but the human frame has not changed. The feelings and emotions of those exposed to firepower, whether as civilians or combatants, have remained constant throughout history. Barea noted during the Spanish Civil War that 'when you are in danger of death you feel fear, beforehand, or while it lasts, or afterwards' (7). This sensation is evident in many other documents, yet others also acknowledge the thrill of combat. As the German sailor admits as he approaches his baptism of fire in the Battle of Jutland in 1916, 'If I said that I was afraid, I would be lying. No, it was an undefinable mixture of joy, fear, curiosity, apathy and . . . love of battle' (5). Even Londoners caught in the Blitz could savour the excitement of a near miss (9), though the utter destruction of an atom bombing precluded any emotion but horror (14). Those mounting air raids faced their own dangers. Bomber crews, setting out night after night on their deadly missions, suffered an astonishing rate of attrition, 55,500 being killed during the Second World War, equal to the number of British officers killed on the Western front during the First World War (13).

This section thus attempts to provide the reader with a sense of the range of ways in which war has been endured and perceived by those involved. They tell stories of heroism at the lower ranks and the utter dejection of senior commanders contemplating defeat. Compare, for example, the diary entries of General Pownall as the British Expeditionary Forces face defeat in France in 1940 (8) with that of Field Marshal Rommel two years later as Hitler demanded the impossible from his troops at Alamein (11).

Inevitably the collection is Western orientated, for all the major wars of the nineteenth and twentieth centuries originated either in Europe or from the actions of Europeans and Americans in regions far from their native soil. However, the post-1945 extracts provide a broader range, including an Argentinian in the Falklands (18) and a Russian in Afghanistan (21).

The first entries deal with the Napoleonic wars, after which Europe enjoyed a century of relative peace. Most of the energies of the British army were concentrated on fighting in India and Africa, as reflected in the account of fighting in the Sudan (4). To the British after 1918 this was 'real soldiering' as opposed to the bloody trench deadlock in Flanders during the First World War. The American Civil War (1861–5) has been seen by many writers as a savage precursor of the First World War; the carnage is described in 3. By contrast, the Franco-Prussian War of 1870–1, which resulted in the rise of Germany to paramountcy in Europe, was regarded by European military thinkers as a paradigm of future wars—short and overwhelmingly successful, at least for the victor. Basil Liddell Hart's account of his experience of the Somme in 1916 (6) combines reminiscence with a historian's perspective, and provides an insight into the source of many of his own strategic ideas, which are briefly outlined in the later section on strategy (66).

During the period of the cold war two major wars were fought by the West—by the United Nations forces in Korea between 1950 and 1953 and by the Americans in Vietnam from 1965 to 1975. The first resulted in a stalemate along the 38th Parallel after the Chinese had surprised the UN forces as they approached the Yalu River (15), while the second was a devastating defeat for the American Army (17). The post-1945 section also reveals the great variety of conflict in recent decades, from the demoralized Soviet soldier in Afghanistan (21) to the curiously old-fashioned conflict over the Falklands (18 and 19). Even in the post-cold-war 1990s a stark contrast is provided by the high-tech opening to Desert Storm, the operation which began in January 1991 to liberate Kuwait (22) and the cruelty of a brutal civil war in Bosnia (23). Despite what had been feared, no nuclear weapons were used in anger after Nagasaki. In the transcript from one of the key meetings during the 1962 Cuban Missile Crisis (16) we find President Kennedy wrestling with the dilemma of a potential compromise with Moscow though at the expense of relations with a key NATO ally.

After beating about the Channel for some time, we were ordered to proceed along the Spanish coast to look after the combined fleet of France and Spain. Having heard that Sir Robert Calder had fallen in with them a few days previous, we pursued our course, looking in at Ferrol and other ports, until we arrived off Cadiz, where we found they had got safe in. Here we continued to blockade them, until Nelson joined us with five sail of the line. In order to decoy the enemy out, stratagem was resorted to, and five sail were sent to Gibraltar to victual and water, whilst Nelson with his five sail kept out of sight of the enemy, and thus they thought we were only twenty-two sail of the line, whilst their fleet consisted of thirty-three sail. With this superior force they put to sea, with the intention, as we afterwards learned, of taking our fleet; and if they had succeeded, possessed of so great a force they were to occupy the Channel, and assist in the invasion of England by the troops then encamped along the French coast, with an immense number of flat bottomed boats, with which the French ports swarmed. But here, as in many other instances, they reckoned without their host. British valour and seamanship frustrated their design and destroyed their hopes; for on the memorable 21st of October 1805, as the day began to dawn, a man at the topmost head called out 'A sail on the starboard bow', and in two or three minutes more he gave another call, that there was more than one sail, for indeed they looked like a forest of masts rising from the ocean, and as morning got light we could plainly discern them from the deck, and were satisfied it was the enemy, for the Admiral began to telegraph to that effect. They saw us and would gladly have got away when they discovered we counted 27 sail of the line, but it was too late and situated as they were hemmed in by Cape Trafalgar on the one side and not being able to get back to Cadiz on the other.

As the enemy was thus driven to risk a battle, he exhibited a specimen of their naval tactics by forming themselves into a crescent, or half-moon, waiting for our approach, which did not take place until ten minutes of twelve o'clock, so that there was nearly six hours to prepare for battle; while we glided down to them under the influence of a gentle breeze, cheering to every seaman's heart, that Providence took us in tow, and from a signal made by Lord Nelson, our ships were soon formed into two lines, weather and lee.

During this time each ship was making the usual preparations such as breaking away the Captain's and officers' cabins, and sending all the lumber below—the doctors, parson, purser and loblolly men, were also busy getting the medicine chests and bandages out, and sails prepared for the wounded to be placed on, that they might be dressed in rotation as they were taken down to the aft-cockpit. In such a bustling and, it may be said, trying as well as serious time, it is curious to notice the different dispositions of the British Sailor. Some would be offering a guinea for a glass of grog, whilst others were making a kind of mutual verbal will, such as: 'If one of Johnny Crapeau's shots (a term given to the French) knocks my head off, you will take all my effects, and if you are killed and I am not, why, I will have yours and this is generally agreed to.' During this momentous preparation the human mind had ample time for meditation and conjecture, for it was evident that the fate of England rested on this battle; therefore well might Lord Nelson make the signal 'England expects each man will do his duty'. Here, if I may be indulged the observation, I will say that could England but have seen her sons about to attack the inhabitants of Spain with an inferior force, our number of men being not quite twenty thousand whilst theirs was upwards of thirty thousand; from the zeal which animated every man in the fleet, the bosom of every inhabitant of England would have glowed with indescribable patriotic pride; for such a number of line-of-battle ships have never met together and engaged, either before or since. As we drew near, we discovered the enemy line was formed with a Spanish ship between two French ones nearly all through their line, as I suppose, to make them fight better; and it must be admitted that the Dons fought as well as the French in that battle; and, if praise was due for seamanship and valour, they were well entitled to an equal share. We now began to hear the enemy's cannon opening on the *Royal Sovereign*, commanded by Lord Collingwood, who commenced the action, and a signal being made by the Admiral to some of our senior captains to break the enemy's line at different points, it fell to our lot to cut off the five sternmost ships; and, while we were running down to them, of course we were favoured with several shots and some of our men were wounded. Upon being thus pressed, many of our men thought it hard that the firing should all be on one side and became impatient to return the compliment; but our captain had given orders not to fire until we got close in with them, so that all our shot might tell—indeed these were his words: 'We shall want all our shot when we get close in. Never mind their firing: when I fire a carronade from the quarter deck, that will be the signal for you to begin, and I know you will do your duty as Englishmen.' In a few minutes the gun was fired and our ship bore in and broke the line, but we paid dear for our temerity, as those ships we had thrown into disorder turned round and made an attempt to board. A Spanish three-decker ran her bowsprit over our poop, with a number of her crew in it, and, in the fore rigging, two or three hundred men were ready to follow; but they caught a Tartar, for their design was discovered and our marines with their small arms, and carronades on the poop, loaded with canister shot, swept them off so fast, some into the water and some on the decks, that they were glad to sheer off. While this was going on aft, we were engaged with a French two-deck ship on our starboard side, and on our larboard bow, another, so that many of their shots must have struck their own ships, and done severe execution. After being engaged about an hour, two other ships fortunately came up, received some of the fire intended for us and we were now enabled to get at some of the shot-holes between wind and water and plug them up. This is a duty performed by the carpenter and his crew. We were now unable to work the ship, our yards, sails, and masts being disabled, and the braces completely shot away. In this condition we lay by the side of the enemy, firing away, and now and then we received a good raking from them passing under our stern. This was a busy time with us for we had not only to endeavour to repair our damage, but also to keep to our duty. Often during the battle we could not see for the smoke whether we were firing at a foe or a friend, and as to hearing, the noise of the guns had so completely made us deaf, that we were obliged to look only to the motions that were made. In this manner we continued the battle till near five o'clock when it ceased.

It was shortly made known by one of our boat's crew that Lord Nelson had received a fatal shot; had this news been communicated through the fleet before the conflict was over, what effect it might have had on the hearts of our seamen I know not, for he was adored, and in fighting under him, every man thought himself sure of success; a momentary but naturally melancholy pause among the survivors of our brave crew ensued.

We were now called to clear the decks, and here might be witnessed an awful and interesting scene, for as each officer and seaman would meet (oh! what an opportunity for the Christian and man of feeling to meditate on the casualty of fate in this life) they were inquiring for their mess mates. Orders were now given to fetch the dead bodies from the after cockpit and throw them overboard; these were the bodies of men who were taken down to the doctor during the battle, badly wounded and who, by the time the engagement was ended, were dead. Some of these perhaps could not have recovered while others might, had timely assistance been rendered which was impossible, for the rule is as to order is requisite [sic], that every person shall be dressed in rotation as they are brought down wounded and in many instances some have bled to death.

The next call was 'all hands to splice the main brace', which is the giving out a gill of rum to each man, and indeed they much needed it, for they had not ate or drank from breakfast time. We had now a good night's work before us; all our yards, masts, and sails were sadly cut, indeed the whole of the sails were obliged to be unbent, being rendered completely useless, and by the next morning we were partly jury-rigged. We now began to look for our prizes, as it was coming on to blow hard on the land, and Admiral

Collingwood made signals for each ship that was able to take a prize in tow, to prevent them drifting into their own harbour as they were complete wrecks and unmanageable.

[From 'Jack NastyFace', cited in Henry Baynham, *From the Lower Deck: The Navy 1700–1840* (London: Arrow Books, 1972), 55–9.]

2   A French Infantryman at Waterloo, 18 June 1815

We marched forward at 3.0 p.m. crossed the three bridges and attacked Wavre. Horse and foot performed prodigies of valour. General Vandamme finally made himself master of the position. The battle was of little use to us, and made us lose 1,100 men. It did little honour to our generals, who seemed to be groping in the dark; and all day long we heard the cannon on our left, in the direction of Waterloo. We ceased to hear it about 10.0 p.m. Nothing can describe the uneasiness this cannonade caused us. The soldiers were melancholy, and had the presentiment of a misfortune. They boldly declared that the Emperor was beaten, because the sound of the cannon was always in the same direction. Contrary to my custom, I was sad also, but inwardly I was raging. (June 19th). We of the 30th at the outposts, were attacked at three in the morning by the troops of the Prussian General Thielmann. General Pecheux sent us forward, and we surprised a Prussian guard of about 300 men, some of whom we bayoneted, and the rest we took prisoners. I was the last to cut and slash in the enemy's ranks, being enraged, and wanting to avenge myself, I did not know on whom, whilst cursing most of our generals, whom I considered traitors. This affair being over, we advanced noiselessly, and when daylight came, formed a line of skirmishers; then we fired on Messieurs the Prussians, who retired without making great resistance, towards Wavre and the woods, to draw us on. These boasters seemed to know of the disaster at Waterloo. Many of them, after having fired, retired, crying in German; 'Come along with us, brave Frenchmen. You have no army left; Napoleon is dead.' I, and several of my comrades who understood German, did not know what to think of these rumours.

Our generals gave few orders, and let the men shoot if they liked. Their conduct puzzled us. We took and retook Wavre several times, without being able to keep it. The Prussians came out of the woods, and our sharpshooters fell back. Many of the officers had retired to the divisions, and the men were fighting without any leaders. About 1 o'clock in the afternoon, the generals sent for the superior officers, for the soldiers were grumbling, saying they had been betrayed, for they had noticed that, since the previous evening, no cannon had been heard in the direction of Brussels. Was the Emperor beaten?

At 2.30 p.m. orders were given to cease firing. The enemy's fire also ceased.

[From R. H. McGuffie (ed.), *Rank and File: The Common Soldier at Peace and War 1642–1914* (London: Hutchinson & Co., 1964), 358–9.]

3 A Union–Confederate Infantry Skirmish at Gettysburg, 1863

The conflict opens. I know not who gave the first fire, or which line received the first lead. I only know that the carnage began. Our regiment was mantled in fire and smoke. I wish that I could picture with my pen the awful details of that hour—how rapidly the cartridges were torn from the boxes and stuffed in the smoking muzzles of the guns; how the steel rammers clashed and clanged in the heated barrels; how the men's hands and faces grew grim and black with burning powder; how our little line, baptized with fire, reeled to and fro as it advanced or was pressed back; how our officers bravely encouraged the men to hold on and recklessly exposed themselves to the enemy's fire—a terrible medley of cries, shouts, cheers, groans, prayers, curses, bursting shells, whizzing rifle bullets and clanging steel. And if that was all, my heart would not be so sad and heavy as I write. But the enemy was pouring a terrible fire upon us, his superior forces giving him a great advantage. Ten to one are fearful odds where men are contending for so great a prize. The air seemed to be alive with lead. The lines at times were so near each other that the hostile gun barrels almost touched. As the contest continued, the rebels grew desperate that so insignificant a force should so long hold them in check. At one time there was a brief lull in the carnage, and our shattered line was closed up, but soon the contest raged again with renewed fierceness. The rebels had been reinforced, and were now determined to sweep our regiment from the crest of Little Round Top. . . .

Our line is pressed so far that our dead are within the lines of the enemy. The pressure made by the superior weight of the enemy's line is severely felt. Our ammunition is nearly all gone, and we are using the cartridges from the boxes of our wounded comrades. A critical moment has arrived, and we can remain as we are no longer; we must advance or retreat. It must not be the latter, but how can it be the former? Colonel Chamberlain understands how it can be done. The order is given 'Fix bayonets!' and the steel shanks of the bayonets rattle upon the rifle barrels. 'Charge bayonets, charge!' Every man understood in a moment that the movement was our only salvation, but there is a limit to human endurance, and I do not dishonor those brave men when I write that for a brief moment the order was not obeyed, and the little line seemed to quail under the fearful fire that was being poured upon it. O for some man reckless of life, and all else save his country's honor and safety, who would rush far out to the front, lead the way, and inspire the hearts of his exhausted comrades! In that moment of supreme need the want was supplied. Lieut. H. S. Melcher, an officer who had worked his way up from the ranks, and was then in command of Co. F., at that time the color company, saw the situation and did not hesitate, and for his gallant act deserved as much as any other man of the honor of the victory on Round Top. With a cheer, and a flash of his sword, that sent an inspiration along the line, full ten paces to the front he sprang—ten paces—more than half the distance between the hostile lines. 'Come on! Come on! Come on, boys!' he shouts. The color sergeant and the brave color guard follow, and with one wild yell of anguish wrung from its tortured heart, the regiment charged.

The rebels were confounded at the movement. We struck them with a fearful shock. They recoil, stagger, break and run, and like avenging demons our men pursue. The rebels rush toward a stone wall, but, to our mutual surprise, two scores of rifle barrels gleam over the rocks, and a murderous volley was poured in upon them at close quarters. A band of men leap over the wall and capture at least a hundred prisoners. This unlooked-for reinforcement was Company B whom we supposed were all captured.

Our Colonel's commands were simply to hold the hill, and we did not follow the retreating rebels but a short distance. After dark an order came to advance and capture a hill in our front. Through the trees, among the rocks, up the steep hillside, we made our way, captured the position, and also a number of prisoners.

On the morning of July 3d we were relieved by the Pennsylvania reserves, and went back to the rear. Of our three hundred and fifty men, one hundred and thirty-five had been killed and wounded. We captured over three hundred prisoners, and a detachment sent out to bury the dead found fifty dead rebels upon the ground where we had fought.

[From R. H. McGuffie (ed.), *Rank and File: The Common Soldier at Peace and War 1642–1914* (London: Hutchinson & Co., 1964), 324–5.]

4 A British Soldier Fighting the Mahdists in the Sudan, 1885

On January 16th we approached Abu Klea Wells, which are situated in a defile between some low hills. We brought up for dinner three miles off in the desert, and sent forward a party of Hussars to see if the wells were occupied. As they did not return, General Stewart ordered an advance, when all at once there were shouts of 'Dismount! Undo ammunition!' and we saw the Hussars riding back for their lives, and announcing that the Mahdists were thousands strong at the wells.

We were at once formed into a three-sided square, with the camels in the middle; one man being told off to look after six camels. Then we began to advance over the broken ground. About two miles from the wells it became dusk, and just as the sun was setting on the skyline, we saw the gleam of hundreds of native spears on the brow of a low hill. Some sharp shooting followed, but we were too far off to do any good, and in a few minutes it was dark.

Then commenced a night of terror. We formed a zereba of bushes and crouched behind it; many a man prayed that night who was not in the habit of doing so, I can assure you. You see it is one thing to face a foe in the field, and quite another to lie awake at night expecting to be killed every minute. All the while the Mahdists kept up a desultory firing—for they had two thousand Remingtons, captured from Hicks Pacha—and we lost several men and a number of camels.

All night long we could hear the native tom-toms beating, and every moment we expected a charge. I was told off for outpost duty, which was not very pleasant under the circumstances, but we did not go more than a hundred yards from the column. My regiment was in the rear, the heavy Camel corps being in front. Colonel Burnaby came round to us all, and said, 'Don't strike a light, and don't fire on any account, or you will show the enemy where you are; wait till you see the white of their eyes, and then bayonet them.'

By this time we were almost maddened with thirst, for our supply of water was nearly exhausted and we had only a pint per man left. Hence it was absolutely necessary that we should capture the wells before we went any farther.

The next morning we had one of those glorious sunrises that are only seen in the tropics. At eight o'clock we again formed square, for the Mahdists were beginning to descend from the hills. We sent out skirmishers to attack them, and Lieutenant de Lisle was shot while we were forming square.

The enemy then formed in three columns of five thousand men each, with riflemen on each side, the rest being armed with spears, and all thoroughly well disciplined.

We were only two deep in square till within fifty yards of the enemy, when our skirmishers retired, and we opened square to let them in. At that moment the Mahdists charged, but were repulsed. A second charge failed, but at the third they succeeded in breaking one corner of the square, and then the position became very serious indeed. Probably their success was due to the fact that our men at that corner were not used to the bayonet but to the sword. Anyhow, the Soudanese broke a British square, and that is something to their credit.

Our seven-pounders were thus left outside, and Colonel Burnaby rushed out of the square to recapture them. He fought like a hero, but was thrust in the throat by a Mahdist spearman and killed. We dragged him back to the square, but it was too late.

It was at this point that Gunner Smith won the only Victoria Cross of the campaign. When the square was broken, Major Guthrie stuck to the guns, and fought till he fell wounded. Then Gunner Smith rushed to the rescue. He had lost his rifle, but he caught up a gun spike, beat off the Soudanese, and dragged the Major back into the square.

When the square was re-formed a lot of the Mahdists were inside, but you may be sure that none of them lived to get out again. One odd incident happened inside the square. We were carrying a number of chests of bullion for Gordon, and these were knocked open in mistake for ammunition, so that the ground was literally strewn with sovereigns.

At last the Gatling guns were got into action, and that practically ended the battle. The Soudanese were simply mown down. Their bodies flew up into the air like grass from a lawn-mower. But their pluck was astonishing. I saw some of the natives dash up to the Gatling guns, and thrust their arms down the muzzles, trying to extract the bullets which were destroying their comrades! Of course, they were simply blown to atoms.

The battle lasted off and on from eight in the morning till five in the afternoon, when the Soudanese finally fled. We did not pursue them, but with a ringing cheer we dashed to the wells, for we had drunk nothing all day, and were nearly maddened with thirst. Altogether sixty-five of our men were killed, and a hundred and eighty wounded, while about two thousand natives lay dead upon the sand.

We buried Colonel Burnaby where he fell, and every uninjured man brought the biggest stone he could find, and so we built a great cairn over the man who died as a volunteer in the service of his country.

[From R. H. McGuffie (ed.), *Rank and File: The Common Soldier at Peace and War 1642–1914* (London: Hutchinson & Co., 1964), 269–72.]

5   A German Seaman at the Battle of Jutland, June 1916

I took the lookout on the forward bridge at four o'clock. It was apparent that something was approaching; the signalmen ran all around and removed the canvas bridge-rail covering. The Captain informed the lookouts that the enemy would be sighted in half an hour. Our battle cruisers had already engaged six large English ships.

Gradually our speed rose to 19 sea miles. How beautiful it was to see our twenty-one primeval elephants charging forward! Forward, forward, quickly toward the roar of the guns! Everything within me stormed and tossed in happy excitement. My mind already visualized the trained guns and the exploding shells all around. I was burning with impatience and it seemed to me that everything was happening much too slowly. Quickly, quickly staunch ship, up ahead our brave cruisers are already fighting and bleeding. If you don't hurry they will sacrifice themselves.

'There they are!' shouted the Adjutant. Sure enough, dim lightning could be seen through the fog off port. Clouds of smoke rose in the air. One, two, three, four, five, six, seven of them! 'Bugler! Battle Stations! Clear for Action. Ta, ta, ta, ta.' The men ran around like mad. In a minute and a half everyone was ready. 'Lookouts down! Battle Stations!' yelled the First Officer. Pretending not to hear, I continued to look feverishly through the binoculars. I noticed that the lead ship had a triple mast. 'Get going,' came a yell from the command tower. I yielded and made my way down the ladder to the munition chamber of B Gun.

It was six o'clock. Down there the heat was already unbearable. With cheeks flushed with joy and excitement everyone was at work carrying shells to the elevator. 'Don't be impatient,' I said, 'the enemy is still far off.' Someone shouted back, 'Did you see something?' The battle would start soon, I told them. At last count we had been thirty kilometers apart.

All of us were hungry. Hence the port side was ordered to leave stations to get supper. They obeyed with unprecedented speed. Everyone jumped to the upper deck or a porthole to catch a quick glimpse before going. It was still completely light. Because the English sailed in the fog, the light was against us at that point. Soon, however, we outmaneuvered them and had the evening sun ahead of us.

'Enemy has commenced firing. First volley 1,000 meters short. Third Squadron replying slowly,' the bridge reported. We felt immeasurably relieved at these words. 'We shall get to fight today!' 'Pay attention, something is happening!' Long range fire off port! Damn it, why not on our side? Once again a shot—a cruiser—9,300 meters. Why don't we answer? There—our trained ear told us plainly—the forward gun had fired. A violent wind flew through the chamber, the gun tower shook. 'Bang, bang!' Our first broadside was off. At first we thought that our B Gun had fired with the rest, but no. Bang, bang, another volley. We had hit a cruiser and a destroyer and they were burning. Both tilted over and sank.

What kind of a strange sound was this? 'Crash, crash,' the sound reverberated. Ah! It was the death cry of an English shell! I fell down on the deck and listened. I noticed that the floor vibrated slowly and sang at each crash. It was loud or quiet, depending on the distance from the point of impact. The engines shook like a machine gun. Before I left the bridge, I heard the captain tell the engine room, 'In an emergency, use oil.' Now I understood. As our tensions rose to the breaking point, our thirst became terrific.

Fortunately we had a bucket of water and when it became empty we drank the water from the fire buckets. Later on these buckets served another, less pleasant, but nevertheless very important function.

The battle had already lasted half an hour. It was eight o'clock. Won't the enemy come to starboard? After all, this was the customary side for battle. We had practiced long-range firing from starboard for many years and now everything was different from what we expected. Slowly the battle veered to starboard. The enemy tried to turn our point! At last! Our gun tower turned slowly but our joy was short-lived. The ship suddenly shifted to one side. My first reaction was that we had hit a mine or something, although there was no loud explosion. But it was something else. We had turned hard rudder and the engines puffed their usual rhythm.

Once again the battle stood off port. We had nothing to do, so we yelled and carried on without restraint. Deep in our hearts we were all afraid and tried to still our fear by making noise. Once more I put my ear to the deck to listen to the crash, crash, crash. Suddenly I got a terrific slap. All at once everything became still. It was 9.19 p.m. The ship had been hit. 'Thank God!' someone called out, 'now we'll get leave to go home.' He was silenced at once. 'Shut up! Who knows how many got killed!'

'A hit in Compartment 15 above the waterline. No dead,' reported the bridge at last. Everyone felt relieved. Then we began to discuss how long it would take to repair, whether we would get leave, and so on. The shells rained down like hail on the outside while the splinters dashed themselves to pieces against the armored sides of the ship.

'A lull in the battle! Enemy too far away. . . . But no one to leave stations because it can start once more any minute. . . .' And so it was. The guns began to roar again in less than five minutes. We fired very slowly with deliberation while the *Kaiser*-class ships in front of us shot like mad. Compared with the past, the range [of fire] was incredible. It fluctuated between 18 and 23 kilometers. Now the English were in an unfavorable position. The shining sun stood behind their backs while we had the dark Danish coastline in our rear. Before long, however, the firing ceased and the night lowered its merciful veil over the horror of the day.

While the others played cards I managed to doze off for an hour and three quarters. The most dangerous time for both us and the enemy had arrived: torpedo attacks. Perhaps at this very moment our famous black fleet [the torpedo boats] are engaging the enemy to demonstrate how German boats ride to the attack. Our friends on the torpedo boats who had thus far been denied an opportunity to demonstrate their offensive spirit and love of battle, will now be unleashed. As they passed by us during the first days of the war they had shouted triumphantly, vainly hoping that they would have a chance to fire their torpedoes at something that very night. 6 June 1916.

However they had to be patient like all of us. There were some people who insisted that torpedo boats had no value at all. Undoubtedly up until this time the submarine has been much more successful. Now, however, they [the torpedo boats] have had their day. Their attack delivered the death blow to a number of Dreadnoughts and caused the enemy much damage. The Ninth Flotilla attacked three times and fired all of its torpedoes.

At 12.30 I was placed on lookout duty once more. I wish I could describe my inner feelings as the grandiose drama unfolded before my eyes. A picture like that would have to be painted in the most brilliant of colors. It would have to record the most contradictory thoughts. Hence I am convinced that it is impossible for any human being to describe his feelings and thoughts as they actually race through his mind in the course of the baptism of fire. If I said that I was afraid, I would be lying. No, it was an undefinable mixture of joy, fear, curiosity, apathy and . . . love of battle.

[From *The Private War of Seaman Stumpf: The Unique Diaries of a Young German in the Great War* (London: Leslie Frewin, 1969), 197–200.]

B. H. LIDDELL HART

6 An Infantry Officer at the Battle of the Somme, July 1916

[T]he race was lost before it started. The barrage moved on, the infantry could not go on, the barrage could not be brought back, and reinforcements were pushed in just where no infantry could push on—a compound tragedy of errors. No scope was allowed for flexibility and initiative in exploiting penetration at particular weak spots, nor in adjusting the artillery arrangements. It is not surprising that the Fourth Army staff subsequently tried to recall and burn the booklet of tactical instructions—known as 'the Little Red Book'—which they had issued for the battle. I have one of the few surviving copies, as I became a casualty before they were recalled, and was thus able to preserve it.

In the last stage of preparation for the attack, three cavalry divisions began to move up close to the front ready to pass through 'the G in Gap'—the current phrase used to express their cherished aim and hope. In Haig's optimistic instructions, they were to ride through on the first morning to Bapaume, a ten-mile bound beyond the British front line. (Five months later, when the offensive petered out, Haig's armies were still three miles short of Bapaume and over 400,000 of his men had been lost.)

The assault was originally planned for delivery on June 29, and our battalion marched up to the take-off trenches on the afternoon of the 27th. Before starting, the officers assembled at the headquarters mess, in a typical Picardy farmhouse. Recent strain between the commanding officer and some of the others led to an embarrassing pause when the senior company commander was called on to propose a toast to the CO. On a sudden inspiration, he raised his glass and gave the toast with the words: 'Gentlemen: when the barrage lifts.' That toast, unforgettable to those who were present, has been repeated ever since in a memorial notice that appears in *The Times* on each anniversary of the attack.

Then the battalion set off, singing 'Pack up your troubles in your old kit bag', the principal marching song of that year. When on the way to the division's assault sector, between Fricourt and La Boisselle, news came that 'Z Day' had been put off until July I because of a bad turn in the weather—which meant that the battalion had to wait for about sixty hours in trenches that were partially flooded by a torrential downpour, deafened by the noise of our own bombardment and under counter-shelling from the German batteries.

In view of experience in 1915, it had been ordered that a small proportion of the officers and of the other ranks in the leading battalions should be held back as a nucleus on which to rebuild the units in case of severe casualties—although no such eventuality was expected. So officers who were second-in-command of companies, as I was, were kept in immediate reserve, along with the adjutant and a few others.

'Zero hour' on July I was 7.30 a.m. and the assaulting waves 'went over the top' in full daylight under a cloudless blue sky. The first vague rumours which came back were delusively optimistic, but before long we heard that the CO and all four company commanders had been killed before the enemy's front trench was reached, and that most of the other officers and men had been either killed or wounded. That brought a speedy call for us. After running the gauntlet of enemy snipers and other fire, with the moans and cries of many badly wounded men ringing in our ears, we reached a slightly sunken road half a mile beyond the enemy's front trench, and there found what survived of the battalion. Only two officers were left, and one of them was wounded. Casualties went on increasing that evening and during the night, as the low bank beside the road provided little cover. The neighbouring battalion had no officers left, and I took charge of it temporarily until some fresh ones arrived. But the expected counter-attack did not come, and it became evident that the enemy were in as much confusion as we were.

That night the leading troops of the division's reserve brigade came up to strengthen the narrow wedge that had been driven into the German position, but did not attempt to push on farther. We wondered why there was no sign of the reserve divisions which we had been told, beforehand, were coming through to carry on the advance. Some of us had the feeling that a strong fresh infusion that night would have been able to push forward with little difficulty, and achieve a breakthrough, before the enemy had recovered their balance. But the second day passed without any such initiative by the Higher Command.

As the division's left flank was 'in the air' I took out a bombing party on the third morning to explore the situation and cover that flank. The worst difficulty in this expedition was to be sure of one's location, as the German trenches had been flattened out and landmarks obliterated. Everywhere was an arid waste of tumbled earth, with here and there a limb or face protruding—of men who had been buried by our shells. During this reconnaissance I had a 'grandstand' view of a renewed attack that was launched by the 34th Division on the La Boisselle sector. It was strangely different from any picture of battle sketched by war artists in the illustrated Press. Instead of the dramatic charge of cheering troops which they depicted, one saw thin chains of khaki-clad dots plodding slowly forward, and becoming thinner under a hail of fire until they looked merely a few specks on the landscape.

That night the division was relieved, and withdrawn to rest. The remains of our battalion, which had been more than eight hundred strong at the outset, set off back across no-man's-land in three small parties—in all less than seventy men, with four officers. We were so weary after six nights with scarcely any sleep that we moved in a stupor, stumbling along painfully, until we reached 'Happy Valley'—a sheltered hollow filled with dumps—half a mile behind the old front line, where later our dead were buried. Here we were revived by tea laced with rum—and also rejoined by a number of 'strays' who had missed their way during these confused days. On reaching the road, the remnant of the battalion formed into column of route. We marched back singing 'Pack up your troubles in your old kit bag.'

Meeting survivors of other battalions in the days that followed, we found that our losses were not at all exceptional. On the first day the total casualties had been nearly 60,000—the heaviest day's loss in the whole history of Britain's wars.

[From Captain B. H. Liddell Hart, *Memoirs*, 2 vols. (London: Cassell & Co., 1967), i. 20–3.]

ARTURO BAREA

7 A Spanish Republican Official at the Siege of Madrid, November 1936

When you are in danger of death you feel fear, beforehand, or while it lasts, or afterwards. But in the moment of danger itself you attain something I might call power of sight: the percipience of your senses and instincts becomes so sharpened and clarified that they see into the depth of your life. If the danger of death persists over a long, unbroken period, not as a personal, isolated sensation, but as a collective and shared experience, you either lose your power of imagination to the point of insentient bravery or numb passivity, or else that power of sight grows more sensitive in you until it is as though it had burst the boundaries of life and death.

In those days of November 1936, the people of Madrid, all of them together, and every single individual by himself, lived in constant danger of death.

The enemy stood at the gates of the city and could break in at any moment. Shells fell in the streets. Bombers flew over the roofs and dropped their deadly loads, unpunished. We were in a war and in a besieged town; but the war was a civil war and the besieged town held enemies in its midst. No one knew for certain who was a loyal friend and who a dangerous hidden enemy. No one was safe from denunciation and error, from the shot of an over-excited Miliciano or of a masked assassin dashing past in a car and spraying the pavement with machine-gun bullets. What food there was might disappear overnight. The air of the town was laden with tension, unrest, distrust, physical fear, and challenge, as it was laden with the unreasoning, embittered will to fight on. We walked side by side, arm in arm, with Death.

November was cold, damp, and hung with fogs. Death was filthy.

The shell which killed the old street seller at the corner of the Telefónica flung one of her legs far away from the body into the middle of the street. November caught it, smeared its slime and mud on what had been a woman's leg, and turned it into the dirty tatters of a beggar.

The fires dripped soot. It dissolved in the dampness and became a black, viscous liquid that stuck to one's soles, clung to one's hands, hair, face, and shirt collar, and stayed there.

Buildings slit open by bombs exhibited shattered, fog-soaked rooms with swelling, shapeless furniture and fabrics, their dyes oozing out in turgid dribbles, as though the catastrophe had happened years before and the ruins stayed abandoned ever since. In the houses of the living, the fog billowed through the broken window panes in chill wads.

Have you ever leaned by night over the curbstone of an old well where the waters sleep far down? Everything is black and silent and you cannot see the bottom. The silence is dense, it rises from the bowels of the earth and smells of mold. When you speak a word, a hoarse echo answers from the deep. If you go on watching and listening, you will hear the velvet padding of slimy beasts on the walls of the shaft. Suddenly one of the beasts drops into the water. The water catches a spark of light from somewhere and dazzles you with a fugitive, livid, steely flash, as though of a naked knife blade. You turn away from the well with a cold shudder.

That is how it felt to look down into the street from one of the windows high up in the Telefónica.

At times the silence filled with dreaded sounds, that silence of a dead town, was ripped, and the shaft of the well came alive with piercing screams. Bundles of light swept through the street alongside the screeching sirens mounted on motorcycles, and the drone of bombers invaded the sky. The nightly slaughter began. The building quivered in its roots, the windows rattled, the electric lights waxed and waned. And then everything was choked and drowned in a pandemonium of hisses and explosions, of red, green, and blue glares, of twisting, gigantic shadows cast by crashing walls and disemboweled houses, of madly tolling fire bells, of whistles, of shouts, of cries. The broken glass showering down on the pavement tinkled musically, almost merrily.

[From Arturo Barea, *The Forging of a Rebel* (London: Davis-Poynter, 1972), 600–1.]

SIR HENRY POWNALL

8   The Collapse of the Franco-British-Belgian Armies in Belgium, May 1940

20 May

A pretty fair pig of a day. CIGS came as the bearer of a message from the *War Cabinet* that we should retire south-west towards Amiens. A scandalous (i.e. Winstonian) thing to do and in fact quite impossible to carry out—it would have involved a flank march across a gap which we know had some enemy mechanized parties in it, which would soon and certainly be reinforced by stronger forces. Luckily even CIGS was rapidly convinced of the folly of it, though how he could have allowed the Cabinet at a meeting at which he was present (Dill was not) to issue such an order not only puzzles me but also proves his futility. By the time we got to the office indeed we heard that Arras was being attacked by tanks, not a great number but an advanced guard. That convinced even him that Winston's flank march was impossible. I went with him and had a meeting with Billotte and Blanchard. They were in a proper dither, even Blanchard who is not *nerveux*. But the two of them and Alombert were all three *shouting* at one moment—Billotte shouted loudest, trembling, that he had no means to deal with tanks and that if his infantry were put into line they would not withstand attack. Tiny [Lord Gort, commander of BEF] was quite good in speaking to them firmly and getting them to take a pull and I had, too, a very straight talk with all three of them singly. C-in-C telephoned them (at Lens) to say he was putting in 50th and 5th Divisions to counter-attack southwards from the Scarpe tomorrow morning. We got the French to agree that they would co-operate also with two divisions (not so great an effort, as they have at least eight in the neighbourhood). This is our last reserve bar one brigade of 2nd Division and the Armoured Recce Brigade. We cannot do much *more* in the common cause. The visit did good in restoring badly shaken morale, it was badly needed. Weygand has just replaced Gamelin and gave Billotte a good telephone shake up when we were there—I'm glad to say he comes here tomorrow. On return we notified Swayne (for Georges), Billotte and Blanchard (through liaison officers) that in our view tomorrow's counter-attack had *got* to suceed—if it failed we could not continue to hold our present positions. This was meant partly as a kick but there is truth in it too. If considerable German army forces got behind our right rear making for Calais neither we nor the French *could* remain poked out here. In the evening strong enemy forces were reported as moving [to] Cambrai-Arras and Cambrai-Peronne, just what was to be expected. We have (I hope) turned our own bombers on. Bomber Command are to attack heavily tonight—we attack tomorrow and if it comes off it might well be the turning point. If it doesn't we may be *foutu*. During the afternoon I Corps were attacked and seem to have pushed every one back, largely with the bayonet. In the late evening more attacks against I and III Corps, also repulsed with the bayonet. All very good.

Nobody minds going down fighting but the long and many days of defence and recently the entire lack of higher direction and action, have been terribly wearing on the nerves of all of us. [. . .]

21 May

During the night 20/21 May reliable report received that a considerable mechanized column had reached the vicinity of Abbeville. We of course could have done nothing to prevent this or to put it right now. It's a hopeless position and too absurd because we haven't yet encountered the real German Army; this is only their (armoured) cavalry that is sending us reeling. The food situation is bad. We have about two and a half days with us. There is no communication from our bases down south and of course with Germans at Abbeville we needn't expect to get any from there. We can only pack in stuff via Boulogne and Calais if the Germans let us. But those places are pretty heavily bombed and mined and of limited capacity. Moreover the Germans will snatch them pretty soon. We are trying to scrape up a brigade and guns to send to Calais and have told the WO to send marines to both of them as quickly as possible.

Be it remembered also that we have behind us enormous quantities of pitiful refugees. They have encumbered our movements for many days. Now they are beginning to starve and will riot. What a situation!

Appendix to Diary (in longhand)

I spoke to [Major-General R. H.] Dewing about 11.30 a.m. 19 May, and explained to him in camouflaged language that the BEF might be forced to withdraw. The position on our right was very bad, if it deteriorated our right would be in the air and we could not stay where we were. We were therefore examining the possibility of a withdrawal in the direction of Dunkirk whence it might be possible to get some shipping to get some troops home. We were out of touch with Swayne and we felt that Georges should realize that the situation, as we knew it, was such that withdrawal might become inevitable if French operations further south, to close the gap, did not meet with success. The French next to us were in a pretty bad way, and as Dewing knew, further south still the situation was, we understood, very bad indeed. It was true that so far only small parties of Germans had passed through, but that was only a beginning unless the movement could be stopped.

I spoke to Dewing again at 13.30 on 19 May and told him that in addition to studying a withdrawal towards Dunkirk we were also examining a possible withdrawal towards Bruges and Ostend. I explained more than once that we were not going to carry out such a withdrawal unless it were forced on us by failure of the French operations to the south. If those failed the Germans would undoubtedly push through and we could do nothing to stop it. Dewing suggested a withdrawal to Boulogne but I explained to him that that was quite hopeless; the Germans would not only reach Boulogne before us but also hit us on the march.

I told him that we were in good heart, we definitely were not going to withdraw at present, but only if the necessity were forced upon us by the failure of the French to fill the gap. We were only trying to keep him in touch with what we were examining here so that he should be kept *au courant*. If the French operations were successful well and good, no withdrawal might be necessary. [. . .]

I also informed him that [Air Vice Marshal C.H.B.] Blount's actions towards thinning out some of the Air Component [which he commanded], with a view to supporting the BEF from England, were taken with C-in-C's approval. That that was so was a measure of the seriousness of the situation as we saw it. We could but hope we were wrong.

[From Brian Bond (ed.), *Chief of Staff: The Diaries of Lieutenant-General Sir Henry Pownall*, i, *1933–1940*, (2 vols.; London: Leo Cooper, 1972), 323–4, 327–8.]

TOM HARRISSON

9 Living Through the Blitz, 1940

One seemingly essential piece of the adjustment was to experience a bomb closely, for yourself. In London this soon became easy, so indiscriminate grew the scatter. This personal adventure was most readily achieved, however, in your garden shelter or home where it was individual in a way more difficult inside a communal shelter of some kind, with many sharing in the incident.

Associated with direct experience was the general atmosphere of excitement, adventure, a form of 'heroism' by escape, which we already noticed momentarily in the first bombs of August. Sharing in such drama was, by the standards of everyday living then, a terrific experience in its own right. The effect was, in more cases than not, to ease the burden of previous anxiety or present fear. As we had put in a report to Home Intelligence before the blitz got really under way:

In the immediate area of a severe raid, there is a period of shock and mental blankness. Usually, rapid readjustment follows, and most people are outwardly back to normal by the next day, though still getting special liberation by recounting their own experiences with intense excitement, in purely personal terms. Many get a great deal of pleasure from having been in the middle, it makes them feel braver.

Once the blitz came, bombs all about, Londoners almost invariably (we found) erred on the side of thinking the heard bomb was nearer than it really was. 'We're in the front line! Me own home—it's in the Front Line', declared a grizzled, elderly Cockney, staring at a wrecked house (not his own). People came from far away, at first, to look at the nearest damage. Sightseers from more than half a mile:

'We thought it was just out the back, you know. I could have sworn it fell absolutely in the back garden here. My, when I heard that whistling I thought it had Number 60 on it!' [laughs]
'When the explosion went off everybody [in his house] thought it was right here.'
'When I heard that awful whistling, when it began, I went all sort of numb. This is it, I thought; this is what it feels like when it gets you, all sort of numb. It seemed to be coming right at us, dead straight, right at this house . . . I couldn't credit it this morning when they told me it had fallen on the Grange [Cinema, half a mile away]. I just couldn't credit it.'

Edward Glover, Director of the London Clinic of Psychoanalysis, claimed in a broadcast at about this time that this feeling of the bomb 'coming right at me' was peculiar to 'over-anxious superstitious people who imagine that every bomb is aimed personally at them'. There is no factual support for this Harley Street view. People of all sorts and temperaments, of all degrees of 'courage' and 'cowardice', were liable to describe their first experience in these terms. [. . .]

[L]isten to five men taken *talking* at random in another part of London (Mill Hill) after the first severe raid there, towards the end of September, as reported next day by a resident observer who recorded a general attitude of 'excitement', while ARP and AFS personnel on the bomb scene reported, 'the householders—and the children in particular—thoroughly enjoyed the show':

'It was an awful night, I expect you heard about it; it was in the news. I was up half the night with incendiaries—the ARP couldn't cope, and we all turned out to help . . . we got a packet our way . . . I thought I'd feel like death this morning—but I don't. I feel marvellous—on top of the world.'

'We were coming home [from an ARP training class] last night, and about a quarter of a mile ahead a green flame sprang up, and we knew they were incendiaries! We were as pleased as punch!'

'I found a bomb—an incendiary—outside my house which hadn't gone off, so I rushed indoors and found a shovel to cover the bomb with earth. It was a brand-new shovel; and I was just putting down the earth . . . and it suddenly blew off! It burnt the hair off my hands; and broke my shovel in two! Did I swear at blasted Jerry then!—My new shovel!—I'd been enjoying it until that happened!' [Older clerk, talking eagerly, with much laughter and gesticulation].

'I helped to put out three. When I got in, my old woman pushed a heap of chips in front of me and said, "Eat those!" I never enjoyed anything so much in all my life.'

'I wouldn't mind having an evening like it say once a week. Ordinarily, there's no excitement, nothing to do or anything.'

The last phrase touches on a vital point. In those days, before TV, foreign air travel, packaged sunshine holidays and open sexual permissiveness, a great many British found life vaguely dull; more so surely than today, when the same feeling nevertheless remains quite near at least the urban surface?

The blitz introduced high drama. However subjective and confused, a clear pattern emerges, again and again, as far as large sections of the civilian population were concerned, at this stage Londoners especially. The London trajectory was greatly simplified in so far as the metropolis was constantly bombed, so that the people lived for weeks on end under continuous warning—whereas in the provinces, this was seldom to be the case, the experience was much more erratic (and could be bafflingly so), making steady 'learning' of adjustment routines markedly less easy for most people who 'stayed put'.

Without, then, being dogmatic, it seems reasonable to distinguish for London, five phases of *major* adjustment after direct bomb experience, each varyingly applicable under different conditions.

(1) (*First minutes*) Some shock: stupefaction: minor impairment of judgement. 'Normal' motivations such as fear, concern for others, anxiety, in abeyance. Physical pain is commonly not felt, and injuries can go unnoticed. Repetitive talking, giving of inappropriate orders, etc. (especially for male family heads, becoming stereotype masculine leaders).

(2) (*next 1 or 2 hours*) First-stage recovery; return of sense of reality and 'appropriate' emotions. Concern for others, and for extent of damage, etc. Injuries felt—pain, bleeding, losses begin to be noticed.

(3) (*succeeding hours*) Uncontrollable flood of communication, by word, gesture, laughter. Anecdotes, personal experiences; loud claims and counter-claims as to who has had the 'worst' experience. Excited speculations as to extent and nearness of damage. Repetitiveness in both vocabulary and subject-matter is characteristic—a person will repeat his story over and over again, in almost the

same words, often to the same listeners. Excitement at this stage is intense, almost at times manic.

(4) *(throughout about 48 hours after first-stage recovery)* From the babel of communication, individuals tend to emerge with a sense of intense pride, of enhanced personal worth. This sense of ego-enhancement may last hours, days, or years. A corresponding uprush of pride is also evident on a neighbourhood level— engendering great resentment when radio or press under-play the incident (this was stronger in smaller provincial centres).

(5) *(after about 48+ hours)* Return to 'normal'. The individual reacting with resourcefulness, annoyance etc. to the ensuing material discomforts—absence of water, heat, cooked food, etc. Concern for others and for damage sustained is back to near normal. But a basic 'term' is past, raids seldom hold further equivalent anxiety.

This is an ideal trajectory towards long-term adaptation. No one person followed it exactly like that.

[From Tom Harrisson, *Living Through the Blitz* (London: Collins, 1976), 76–7, 84–6.]

DONALD MACINTYRE

10   The Destruction of two U-Boats, March 1941

In the next hour, five ships were torpedoed. I was near to despair and I racked my brains to find some way to stop the holocaust. While the convoy stayed in impeccable formation, we escorts raced about in the exasperating business of searching in vain for the almost invisible enemy. Our one hope was to sight a U-boat's tell-tale white wake, give chase to force her to dive, and so give the asdics a chance to bring our depth-charges into action. Everything had to be subordinated to that end and so, with binoculars firmly wedged on a steady bearing, I put *Walker* into a gently curving course, thereby putting every point of the compass under a penetrating probe. It worked.

As her bows swung, a thin line of white water came into the lens of my glasses, a thin line which could only be the wake of a ship. There were none of ours in that direction; it had to be a U-boat! I shouted orders increasing speed to 30 knots and altered course towards the target. Suddenly, the U-boat spotted us and in a cloud of spray he crash-dived. A swirl of phosphorescent water still lingered as we passed over the spot and sent a pattern of ten depth-charges crashing down. We could hardly have missed; it had been so quick we must have dropped them smack on top of him. Then the depth charges exploded with great cracking explosions and giant water spouts rose to masthead height astern of us. Two and a half minutes later another explosion followed and an orange flash spread momentarily across the surface. We had every reason to hope that this was our first 'kill'. [. . .]

However, no U-boat was officially recorded as destroyed without tangible evidence and I continued the asdic search until such time as wreckage should come to the surface.

It was just as well. For half an hour later we gained contact with a certain U-boat. Our prey had not been 'killed'; he was, in fact, sneaking back towards the convoy still bent on attack.

Recalling *Vanoc* to assist in the hunt, we set about our target with a series of carefully aimed patterns of depth-charges.

Taking it in turns to run in to the attack, pattern after pattern of depth-charges went down as we tried to get one to within the lethal range of about twenty feet of our target. But he was a wily opponent and, dodging and twisting in the depths, he managed to escape destruction though heavily damaged.

Soon the waters became so disturbed by the repeated explosions, each one of which sent back an echo to the asdic's sound beam, that we could no longer distinguish our target from the other echoes and a lull in the fight was forced upon us.

I had for some time past noticed in the distance the bobbing lights from the lifeboats of one of our sunken ships, but with an enemy to engage there was nothing for it but to harden my heart and hope that the time might come later when I could rescue the crews. This lull seemed a good opportunity and perhaps if we left the area temporarily the U-boat commander might think he had shaken us off and be tempted into some indiscretion. So, the *Vanoc* steaming round us in protection, we stopped and picked up the master and thirty-seven of the crew of the SS *J. B. White*. [. . .] Yeoman of Signals Gerrard said, 'She's signalling to us, sir, but I can't read it as her light is flickering so badly.' I realised that *Vanoc* must be going ahead at her full speed and being, like *Walker*, an old veteran, her bridge would be shaking and rattling as her 30,000 h.p. drove her forward through the Atlantic swell.

Rupert Bray, on the bridge beside me, said, 'She must have sighted the U-boat.' Even as he spoke, *Vanoc* came on the air with his radio telephone, with the laconic signal: 'Have rammed and sunk U-boat.'

What a blissful moment that was for us, the successful culmination of a long and arduous fight. Something in the way of revenge for our losses in the convoy had been achieved.

There was grim joy on board *Walker*, and not least amongst the merchant seamen from the *J. B. White* who felt they had a personal score to settle. But for the moment our part was confined to circling *Vanoc* in protection, while she picked up the few survivors from the U-boat and examined herself for damage. We were glad of this breathing space as, with all the depth-charges carried on the upper deck expended, the depth-charge party led by Leading-Seaman Prout were struggling to hoist up more of these awkward heavy loads from the magazine, with the ship rolling in the Atlantic swell, and often with water swirling round their waists. They were not a moment too soon, for, as we circled *Vanoc*, I was electrified to hear the asdic operator A. B. Backhouse excitedly reporting 'Contact, Contact'. But I could hardly credit it, for not only was it unbelievable that in all the wide wastes of the Atlantic a second U-boat should turn up just where another had gone to the bottom, but I knew that there were sure to be areas of disturbed water persisting in the vicinity from our own and *Vanoc's* wakes. The echo was not very clear and I expressed my doubts to John Langton, but Backhouse was not to be disheartened. 'Contact definitely submarine,' he reported, and as I listened to the ping the echo sharpened and there could be no further doubt. With a warning to the men aft to get any charges ready that they had managed to hoist into the throwers and rails, we ran into the attack. It was a great test for John Langton for, with the maddening habit of the beautiful instruments of precision provided for us, they all elected to break down at the crucial moment. But much patient drill against just such an emergency now brought its reward. Timing his attack by the most primitive methods, Langton gave the order to fire. A pattern of six depth-charges—all that could be got ready in time—went down. As they exploded, *Walker* ran on to get sea-room to turn for further attacks, but as we turned, came the thrilling signal from *Vanoc*—'U-boat surfaced astern of me.'

A searchlight beam stabbed into the night from *Vanoc*, illuminating the submarine *U99* which lay stopped. The guns' crews in both ships sprang into action and the blinding flashes from the 4-inch guns and tracers from the smaller weapons made a great display, though I fear their accuracy was not remarkable. Destroyer night gunnery in such a mêlée is apt to be pretty wild and, in those days when flashless cordite was not issued to us, each salvo left one temporarily blinded. In *Walker* confusion soon reigned around the guns for the enthusiasm of our guests from *J. B. White* knew no bounds. Joining up with the ammunition supply parties, shells came up at such a phenomenal rate that the decks were piled high with them till the guns' crews were hardly able to work their guns. But fortunately we were able very soon to cease fire as a signal lamp flashing from the U-boat, 'We are sunking' (*sic*), made it clear that the action was over. Keeping end on to the U-boat in case he still had some fight left, we prepared to lower a boat in case there was a chance of a capture, but even as we did so the crew of the U-boat abandoned ship and she plunged to the bottom.

[From Donald Macintyre, *U-Boat Killer* (London: Weidenfeld & Nicolson, 1956), 35–8.]

11   **Defeat in the Battle of Alamein, November 1942**

The 3rd November will remain a memorable day in history. For not only did it become finally clear on that day that the fortunes of war had deserted us, but from that day on the Panzer Army's freedom of decision was continually curtailed by the interference of higher authority in its conduct of operations.

Already in the morning I had an uncomfortable feeling that in spite of our unequivocal situation reports, our higher command had not drawn the proper conclusions from the conditions we were facing, and I therefore decided to send my ADC, Lieutenant Berndt, to report direct to the Fuehrer. Berndt was to leave the Fuehrer's HQ in no doubt about our situation and was to indicate that the African theatre of war was probably already lost. He was to demand the fullest freedom of action for the Panzer Army. I wanted at all costs to avoid playing into the hands of the British in their efforts to surround and destroy us. I intended to fight delaying actions in as many intermediate positions as possible, forcing the enemy to bring up his artillery each time, and to avoid any decisive battle until either we had grown strong enough for it or the bulk of the African Army had been carried across to Europe, with only a small part left in Africa to cover the retreat.

At nine in the morning I drove east along the coast road as far as Forward HQ. Large numbers of vehicles, mainly Italian, were jammed up on the road, but surprisingly there were no British fighter-bombers about. At about 10.00 hours General von Thoma and Colonel Bayerlein reported that the British were lying in a semicircle in front of the Afrika Korps, which still possessed 30 serviceable tanks. The British were making only probing and local attacks and appeared to be reorganising and supplying their formations. The moment seemed propitious, and I gave orders for part of the Italian formations to march off. Despite our frequent reminders, the vehicles promised by Barbassetti had still not arrived, and so the Italians had to march. Dense columns of vehicles were already streaming westwards. The Italian infantry marched off and soon the road was full of traffic. But the British soon spotted our move and attacked the coast road with about 200 fighter-bombers. Their bomber squadrons were also extremely active that day. The Afrika Korps alone was attacked no less than eleven times during the morning by strong formations of bombers.

At about midday I returned to my command post, only just escaping, by some frantic driving, a carpet of bombs laid by 18 British aircraft. At 13.30 hours an order arrived from the Fuehrer. It read in roughly the following words:

To Field Marshal Rommel

In the situation in which you find yourself there can be no other thought but to stand fast and throw every gun and every man into the battle. The utmost efforts are being made to help you. Your enemy, despite his superiority, must also be at the end of his strength. It would not be the first time in history that a strong will has triumphed over the bigger battalions. As to your troops, you can show them no other road than that to victory or death.

Adolf Hitler

This order demanded the impossible. Even the most devoted soldier can be killed by a bomb. In spite of our unvarnished situation reports, it was apparently still not realised at the Fuehrer's HQ how matters really stood in Africa. Arms, petrol and aircraft could have helped us, but not orders. We were completely stunned, and for the first time during the African campaign I did not know what to do. A kind of apathy took hold of us as we issued orders for all existing positions to be held on instructions from the highest authority. I forced myself to this action, as I had always demanded unconditional obedience from others and, consequently, wished to apply the same principle to myself. Had I known what was to come I should have acted differently, because from that time on, we had continually to circumvent orders from the Fuehrer or Duce in order to save the army from destruction. But this first instance of interference by higher authority in the tactical conduct of the African war came as a considerable shock.

Movements in progress to the west were stopped and everything possible was done to strengthen our fighting power. To the Fuehrer we reported that any further stand in the positions which the Panzer Army was then holding would mean the inevitable loss of the army, and thus of the whole of North Africa.

The order had a powerful effect on the troops. At the Fuehrer's command they were ready to sacrifice themselves to the last man. An overwhelming bitterness welled up in us when we saw the superlative spirit of the army, in which every man, from the highest to the lowest, knew that even the greatest effort could no longer change the course of the battle.

Not until the afternoon did the British follow up the X Italian Corps' withdrawal in the southern sector, having spent the morning pouring artillery fire into the abandoned positions. Attacks on the corps' northern flank were beaten off. This corps suffered particularly badly from the activities of enemy armoured cars behind our front. A considerable number of these vehicles had broken through our line and were harassing our supply traffic, rendering the supply of X Corps' troops, even with the barest minimum of water and rations, almost an impossibility. Finally, we had to use Italian armoured cars to protect our supply convoys.

The Bologna Division was already on the march to the west and Italian staff officers had great trouble in getting it back to the front, for its march columns were almost impossible to locate.

3 Nov. 1942

DEAREST LU,

The battle still rages with unspent fury. I can no longer, or scarcely any longer, believe in its successful outcome. Berndt flies to the Fuehrer to-day to report.

Enclosed 25,000 lire that I've saved.

What will become of us is in God's hands . . .

PS—Have Appel exchange the lire. Currency regulations!

In the evening I sent Lieutenant Berndt off to the Fuehrer's HQ. He was to report that if the Fuehrer's order were upheld, the final destruction of the German-Italian Army would be a matter of days only, and was to add that we had already suffered immense harm because of it. Later that night Berndt informed me from Mersa Matruh that hundreds of low-flying aircraft had attacked the densely crowded road, packed with two lines of traffic, continuously from nightfall at about 17.00 hours until his arrival in Mersa Matruh at 21.00 hours. The road was blocked at many points by burning vehicles and vast traffic jams had developed. In many cases drivers and men had abandoned their vehicles and fled westwards on foot. Abandoned tanks and vehicles stood at many points on the road.

The night of the 3rd November also passed without any particular move from the British. This was all so much lost time for us, for we could meanwhile have got the whole of our force back to Fuka—in all probability with only small casualties. I had not dared hope that the British commander would give us such a chance. And now it was passing unused.

On the morning of the 4th November, the Afrika Korps under General von Thoma, adjoining the 90th Light Division under General von Sponeck, held a thin semicircular line on either side of Tell el Mampsra, extending to a point some 10 miles south of the railway line, where it linked up with the Italian Armoured Corps, consisting of the Ariete and the remnants of the Littorio and Trieste. The south was held by the Italian Trento Division, Parachute Brigade Ramcke, and X Italian Corps.

After about an hour's artillery preparation, the British opened their attack at about 8 a.m. By throwing in all their strength, the Afrika Korps—which General von Thoma commanded in the front line—and the 90th Light Division succeeded in beating off enemy attacks supported by about 200 tanks, which went on till midday. The German Panzer Corps had only 20 serviceable tanks left. [. . .]

Field Marshal Kesselring arrived at my HQ during the morning. As I imagined that the Fuehrer had based his decision on optimistic situation reports sent back by the Luftwaffe, some angry words passed between us.

Kesselring thought that the Fuehrer had learnt from his experience in the East that, in circumstances like these, the front must be held at all costs. I said to him very clearly: 'So far I've always taken it for granted that the Fuehrer left the command of the army to me. This crazy order has come like a bombshell. He can't just blindly apply experience he's gained in Russia to the war in Africa. He really should have left the decision here to me.'

In actual fact, the Fuehrer's order had been based on other, quite different grounds—as was to become increasingly clear as time went on. Paradoxical though it may sound, it was the custom at the Fuehrer's HQ to subordinate military interests to those of propaganda. They were simply unable to bring themselves to say to the German people and the world at large that Alamein had been lost, and believed they could avert its fate by a 'Victory or Death' order. Until this moment we in Africa had always had complete freedom of action. Now that was over.

[From Captain B. H. Liddell Hart (ed.), *The Rommel Papers* (London: Collins, 1963), 320–4.]

12   The End of the Warsaw Ghetto, January 1943

The battle of Warsaw Ghetto lasted for forty-two days and nights, beginning on the first Seder Night, April 19, 1943 and ending a week before Shevuoth. On that first night all of the forty thousand Jews still left in the ghetto after the wholesale deportations and massacres, went out to fight with weapons in their hands. [. . .]

The next morning the Germans opened the great battle. The ghetto was surrounded on all sides by tanks and cannon which subjected it to enormous fire. The Germans were determined to bombard the ghetto until it surrendered. In this, however, they failed. The German tanks and cannon were showered by bullets and bombs from the houses and streets of the ghetto. The special suicide squad of the Jews broke through the lines and wrought ruin among the enemy. Disguised in German uniforms they crawled under the German tanks and blew them up with hand grenades, losing their own lives in the fire which killed the Germans. Such was the havoc wrought by this method that the Germans were careful not to place groups of cannon behind tanks. Thus passed the day of the desperate battle. The Germans realized that they would not be able to vanquish the ghetto without heavy sacrifice. Hundreds of German soldiers lost their lives and splinters of German tanks and guns were mingled with the debris of ruined houses at the gates of the ghetto.

The German command then issued an order to have the whole ghetto blown up by incendiary bombs. A night of inferno then descended on the ghetto. All night incendiary bombs rained on it and fires broke out in many places. Houses came crashing down and among their ruins were heard the cries of wounded men, women and children. Many brave fighters perished among those ruins.

In the morning the ghetto stood in a sea of flames. The survivors, numbering some 30,000, began reorganizing for defense. The houses on the outskirts were vacated and the arms taken to the centre of the ghetto. Also the food which could still be saved was taken away. Special squads of the fighters fortified themselves again in the remaining buildings. When the enemy again attacked in the morning, he was confronted by stiff and desperate resistance at every step, near every building. The battle lasted all day long, and the Germans had to fight for hours before capturing a single house, even if it was but a ruin. In the evening the Germans managed to penetrate deeper into the ghetto and to capture a few of the taller buildings.

After the Night of Inferno and the ensuing battles on the following morning the leaders of the ghetto saw that the end was near unless new methods of warfare could be devised. They tried to reach an understanding with the Polish Underground and suggested that the non-Jewish population of the city rise against the Germans thus forcing the Germans to fight on both sides. But the Poles replied that the time had not yet come for a general uprising on their part. Under these circumstances the fighters of the ghetto abandoned their defense tactics for acts of terror and revenge. Groups of fighters went out of the ghetto, attacking and killing German soldiers. The Jewish heroes fought the Germans until they themselves were killed. Others fled to the woods and joined the Polish guerrillas. Many perished on the road, fighting German soldiers. Many others surrendered to the Germans, having hand grenades hidden in their clothes with which they later killed their guards, losing their own lives in the explosions.

After a few more days of fighting the Germans realized that they would have to contest every house in the ghetto. Every building now became an even more fortified stronghold. Whenever Germans appeared in front of a house they were fired on from the windows, from the garrets, from the roof, until they managed to blow up the house, and its heroic defenders perished in its ruins. In the last house were gathered all those who had survived and were still carrying on the fight. During the last few days the situation was horrible. There was hardly any food left and water could not be brought in because it was impossible to go out on the street. The Nazis committed terrible atrocities, bringing captured Jews and hanging them on the posts of the ghetto and otherwise exceeding their own record for brutality in all the years of their occupation.

On the forty-second day of the uprising there was only one four-story building left in the center of the ghetto over which the blue-and-white flag waved. For eight hours a battle raged over that house and by midnight the Germans captured it. Every floor, every step was hotly contested. When all defenders at the gates fell, the Germans entered the building, encountering the fierce resistance of those on the ground floor. When the first floor was taken, the second floor was contested just as desperately, and so on from floor to floor. The blue-and-white banner held by a young *halutz* was carried by the survivors from floor to floor. Late at night it fluttered from the top story where a desperate struggle was still going on.

When the shooting was over a crash was heard. The young *halutz* hurled himself down wrapped in the blue-and-white flag which he had guarded for forty-two days and nights. The flag was red with the blood of the martyr, the last fighter of the ghetto, who ended his life in this heroic manner.

The next morning the Germans 'triumphantly' announced that the ghetto of Warsaw no longer existed. Thousands of German soldiers paid for that 'victory' with their lives. The heroes of the ghetto fought and died like saintly martyrs.

[From *The Extermination of 500,000 Jews in the Warsaw Ghetto* (New York: The American Council of Warsaw Jews and American Friends of Polish Jews, 1944).

MILES TRIPP

13 Bombing Duisburg, October 1944

The tiny masked light in the bomb-aimer's compartment had to be switched off before take-off but until that time I made myself at home. I felt more secure here than anywhere else in the aircraft. There wasn't sufficient space in which to sit and so I lay, and my couch was the escape hatch. To my left was the bombsight computer box which was connected by two drives to the sighting head which was about eighteen inches away from my nose. The front turret was directly in front of, and above, the sighting head and it contained two Browning .303 machine-guns. To my right, and within reach of my hand, was the pre-selector box on which the order for releasing the bombs could be set and whether they were to fall singly or in salvo. Packed into the remainder of the compartment, and filling all the spare room, were sheaves of 'window'—thin metallized strips of paper which, when fed into the slipstream of hundreds of bombers blurred enemy ground radar screens. It was the bomb-aimer's task to push 'window' through a narrow chute near his right thigh.

While Dig warmed up the engines and tested the magnetos I loaded the front guns and then went aft to stand behind him and Ray for take-off.

It was a dark night and although we had been without sleep for twenty hours nobody felt tired. For me, this was the real thing, a night operation, and excitement at this new experience was stronger than fear for its outcome. The drive to experiment, and the hungry curiosity for adult experience which makes childhood seem in retrospect like a long famine, had not been sated. I didn't realize that vicarious excitement would eventually decline, and that a corresponding line of anxiety would rise, and that at some future point the two would meet on the same level and remain equal for a short while until the line of excitement dipped still further and the anxiety rose more steeply.

Over the English Channel I fused the bombs and put the Brownings on 'Fire'.

J-Jig ploughed through the night and we were encouraged by Les's report that according to his calculations we were making excellent progress and there was not the slightest danger of late arrival. The morning's experience would certainly not be repeated. When next he spoke it was to say that we were so well up on time that we were likely to arrive at the target before the Pathfinders. We were, in fact, leading all the might of a thousand-bomber raid. Eventually, with some anguish, he said, 'We're only two minutes away.'

I peered out at the darkness all around. At this point it was difficult to judge which was more harrowing—to be a long way behind the bomber stream or well ahead of it. I was wondering whether Dig would circle Duisburg and wait for the others to catch up when the night seemed to burst into flower and a rain of red and green blooms fell in front of us.

Les had navigated us to the target dead on time.

Immediately the coloured blooms were sprayed with the deadly sparkle of unleashed flak. It was a spectacle of startling beauty. I dropped our bombs on a cluster of red flares and Dig wheeled the aircraft on to the course for home.

Harry, who had long been silent, said, 'It's not nice to see a guy going down in flames.'

The return journey was routed over the North Sea and before we reached the English coast I climbed into the front turret to unload the guns. I thought they were on 'Safe', and the ammunition belt detached, when I pressed the triggers to clear the bullets in the spouts, but a stream of tracer began snaking ahead and my guns were chattering. At once I released the triggers but Dig thought I had opened fire on an enemy fighter and there was some consternation until I explained what had occurred. 'Bloody good job you didn't shoot down a Lancaster,' he said feelingly.

We landed exactly five hours and twenty minutes after take-off and by the time we had been interrogated, and had breakfast, we were ready for bed.

[From Miles Tripp, *The Eighth Passenger: A Flight of Recollection and Discovery: A Documentary Account of a World War Two Bomber Crew* (London: Macmillan, 1985), 26–8.]

TATSUICHIRO AKIZUKI

14 **A Doctor at Nagasaki, August 1945**

It was eleven o'clock. Father Ishikawa, who was Korean, aged about thirty-six and the hospital chaplain, was listening in the hospital chapel to the confessions of those Catholics who had gone to him to confess, one after the other, before the great festival, on 15 August, of the Ascension of the Virgin Mary, which was only a week away. Brother Joseph Iwanaga was toiling outside the hospital with some farm workers, digging another air-raid shelter in the shrubbery in the centre of the hospital yard. Mr Noguchi had just begun to repair the apparatus used to lift water from the well. Other members of staff were busy providing a late breakfast. Some were filling big bowls with miso soup; others were carrying them through the corridors or up the stairs. The hospital was a hive of activity after the all-clear.

'Well, we'll soon be getting our breakfast,' I said to Miss Murai. 'The patients must be hungry.'

So was I, but before we had our breakfast we would have to finish treating all the out-patients.

I stuck the pneumo-thorax needle into the side of the chest of the patient lying on the bed. It was just after 11 a.m.

I heard a low droning sound, like that of distant aeroplane engines.

'What's that?' I said. 'The all-clear has gone, hasn't it?'

At the same time the sound of the plane's engines, growing louder and louder, seemed to swoop down over the hospital.

I shouted: 'It's an enemy plane! Look out—take cover!'

As I said so, I pulled the needle out of the patient and threw myself beside the bed.

There was a blinding white flash of light, and the next moment—*Bang! Crack!* A huge impact like a gigantic blow smote down upon our bodies, our heads and our hospital. I lay flat—I didn't know whether or not of my own volition. Then down came piles of debris, slamming into my back.

The hospital has been hit, I thought. I grew dizzy, and my ears sang.

Some minutes or so must have passed before I staggered to my feet and looked around. The air was heavy with yellow smoke; white flakes of powder drifted about; it was strangely dark.

Thank God, I thought—I'm not hurt! But what about the patients?

As it became brighter, little by little our situation grew clearer. Miss Murai, who had been assisting me with the pneumo-thorax, struggled to her feet beside me. She didn't seem to have been seriously injured, though she was completely covered with white dust. 'Hey, cheer up!' I said. 'We're not hurt, thank God!'

I helped her to her feet. Another nurse, who was also in the consulting room, and the patient, managed to stand up. The man, his face smeared white like a clown and streaked with blood, lurched towards the door, holding his bloody head with his hands and moaning.

I said to myself over and over again: Our hospital has suffered a direct hit—We've been bombed! Because the hospital stood on a hill and had walls of red brick, it must, I thought, have attracted the attention of enemy planes. I felt deeply and personally responsible for what had happened.

The pervading dingy yellow silence of the room now resounded with faint cries—'Help!' The surface of the walls and ceiling had peeled away. What I had thought to be clouds of dust or smoke was whirling brick-dust and plaster. Neither the pneumo-thorax apparatus nor the microscope on my desk were anywhere to be seen. I felt as if I were dreaming.

I encouraged Miss Murai, saying: 'Come on, we haven't been hurt at all, by the grace of God. We must rescue the in-patients.' But privately I thought it must be all over with them—the second and third floors must have disintegrated, I thought.

We went to the door of the consulting room which faced the main stairway, and there were the in-patients coming down the steps, crying: 'Help me, doctor! Oh, help me, sir.' The stairs and the corridor were heaped with timbers, plaster, debris from the ceiling. It made walking difficult. The patients staggered down towards us, crying: 'I'm hurt! Help me!' Strangely, none seemed to have been seriously injured, only slightly wounded, with fresh blood dripping from their faces and hands.

If the bomb had actually hit the hospital, I thought, they would have been far more badly injured.

'What's happened to the second and third floors?' I cried. But all they answered was—'Help me! Help!'

One of them said: 'Mr Yamaguchi has been buried under the debris. Help him.'

No one knew what had happened. A huge force had been released above our heads. What it was, nobody knew. Had it been several tons of bombs, or the suicidal destruction of a plane carrying a heavy bomb-load?

Dazed, I retreated into the consulting room, in which the only upright object on the rubbish-strewn floor was my desk. I went and sat on it and looked out of the window at the yard and the outside world. There was not a single pane of glass in the window, not even a frame—all had been completely blown away. Out in the yard dun-coloured smoke or dust cleared little by little. I saw figures running. Then, looking to the south-west, I was stunned. The sky was as dark as pitch, covered with dense clouds of smoke; under that blackness, over the earth, hung a yellow-brown fog. Gradually the veiled ground became visible, and the view beyond rooted me to the spot with horror.

All the buildings I could see were on fire: large ones and small ones and those with straw-thatched roofs. Further off along the valley, Urakami Church, the largest Catholic church in the east, was ablaze. The technical school, a large two-storeyed wooden building, was on fire, as were many houses and the distant ordnance factory. Electricity poles were wrapped in flame like so many pieces of kindling. Trees on the near-by hills were smoking, as were the leaves of sweet potatoes in the fields. To say that everything burned is not enough. It seemed as if the earth itself emitted fire and smoke, flames that writhed up and erupted from underground. The sky was dark, the ground was scarlet, and in between hung clouds of yellowish smoke. Three kinds of colour—black, yellow and scarlet— loomed ominously over the people, who ran about like so many ants seeking to escape. What had happened? Urakami Hospital had not been bombed—I understood that much. But that ocean of fire, that sky of smoke! It seemed like the end of the world.

[From Tatsuichiro Akizuki, *Nagasaki 1945*, trans. Keiichi Nagata, ed. with introd. by Gordon Honeycombe (London: Quartet Books, 1981), 24–7.]

MAX HASTINGS

15 China Enters the Korean War, November 1950

China's initial force in Korea was organised as XIII Army Group, and comprised four armies, each of three 10,000-man infantry divisions, a regiment of cavalry, and five regiments of artillery. They crossed the Yalu bridges by night. Their first objective was to establish a wide enough bridgehead on the south bank to give themselves room to deploy. Had they permitted the United Nations to close up to the Yalu border along its length, they would have been confronted by the intolerable initial task of conducting an opposed river crossing before they could join battle. The 42nd Army came first, to block the road running north-west from the Chosin reservoir. The 38th Army was to deploy across the road north from Huichon. The 40th Army advanced from Sinuiju towards Pukchin. The 50th and 66th Armies followed.

It was an extraordinary achievement of modern warfare: between 12 and 25 October, the intelligence staffs of MacArthur's armies failed to discern the slightest evidence of the movement of 130,000 soldiers and porters. A combination of superb fieldcraft and camouflage by the Chinese, with their lack of use of any of the conventional means of detecting modern military movement—wireless traffic, mechanised activity, supply dumps—blinded the UN High Command to what was taking place on its front. Above all, perhaps, the generals were not looking for anything of this sort. They had persuaded themselves that the war was all but over. Their senses were deadened to a fresh consideration. [. . .]

It is sometimes forgotten that after twenty years of war, many Chinese soldiers were men of exceptional military experience. 'My first memories as a child were of the Japanese burning and destroying,' said Li Hebei, a twenty-two-year-old infantry platoon commander who crossed the Yalu with the 587th Regiment on 25 October. Li had served first with local guerrillas, armed only with a home-made rifle, then graduated to the PLA and a captured Japanese weapon when a unit passed through his devastated village when he was sixteen. Like thousands of politically aware young Chinese, he called the PLA 'the big university', for it was in its ranks that he learned to read and write. Between 1943 and 1947, he saw his family just once. He learned to march . . . forever. Mile upon mile he and his unit could walk or even trot, in their quilted cotton uniforms and tennis shoes, up mountain tracks hauling all that they possessed in the world: personal weapon, grenade, eighty rounds, spare foot rags, sewing kit, chopsticks, and perhaps a week's rations—tea, rice, a little sugar, perhaps a tin of fish or meat. Thirty-five years later, Hebei grinned at the memory: 'We had a saying—Red Army's two legs better than Kuomintang's four wheels. Life was very hard, but the atmosphere was very good, because we were full of hope.' A Chinese soldier required just eight to ten pounds of supply a day, against sixty for his UN counterpart. Thus, to sustain fifty divisions in combat, Peking needed to move only 2,500 tons of supplies a day south across the Yalu. This compared with 600 tons for a single US Army division, 700 tons for 1st Marine Division. Each of the tens of thousands of porters supporting the Chinese drive into Korea could carry 80–100 pounds on his shoulder pole or A-frame. Thus did the impossible become possible.

Yu Xiu was one of the men who stormed the 8th Cavalry's positions on 1 November, exulting to discover the success of their techniques of hard-hitting night assault. Yu was a twenty-nine-year-old from Chungsu province, brought up in the French sector of Shanghai, who joined the 4th Field Army when his father was killed by a Japanese bomb in 1937. A deputy political commissar of his regiment, he said that the overwhelming lesson the PLA learned from its first brushes with the Americans was of the need for speed. 'In the Liberation War, one might take days to surround a Kuomintang division, then slowly close the circle around it. With the Americans, if we took more than a few hours, they would bring up reinforcements, aircraft, artillery.'

Li Hua was twenty-three, from Shandung province, a veteran of 8th Route Army since he was sixteen, a peasant's son who had been trained at one of the PLA's officer schools. On the train south to the Yalu in October, he and his comrades were told nothing of their destination, 'but everybody guessed: we were going to support the Koreans against their invaders. We felt pretty confident, because we had just beaten the Kuomintang, with all their support from the Americans. We expected to do the same to Syngman Rhee's people. We weren't very wrong. They were a pushover compared with the Japanese.' They walked across the Yalu bridge by night in their long files, then fifty miles onwards to their initial contact near the Chosin reservoir. Li, the propaganda officer of his company, examined his unit's first American prisoner at much the same time, and with much the same curiosity, as Eighth Army were studying its captives from the PLA: 'This young American, he fell on his knees and begged for mercy. We felt sorry for him. He obviously didn't want to fight.'

Americans who found North Korea an alien land might have reflected that it was almost equally so to the Chinese. The men of the PLA found the Korean peasants at first cold and unfriendly, the weather and the mountains unyielding and vicious. They were guided across country only by a few old Japanese maps—one to a regiment. Yet this initial wave of PLA veterans, in the months before massive casualties caused their replacement by less promising material, possessed some notable advantages over the Americans. For all their lack of equipment and sophistication, these Chinese soldiers were among the hardiest in the world. Many had known no other life but that of war since their teens. Most were genuinely enthused by the spirit of revolution, the sense of participation in a new China that seemed to offer brighter promise than the old land of tyrannical landlordism and official corruption. In Korea, in the months to come, the PLA would suffer its own difficulties with shaken morale and growing disillusionment in its ranks, matching those of its enemies. But in the winter of 1950, the spur of early success outweighed the impact of high casualties in Peng's divisions.

[From Max Hastings, *The Korean War* (London: Macmillan, 1985), 160–3.]

16   President Kennedy and the Cuban Crisis, October 1962

[This is the transcript of an Executive Committee meeting held on 27 October 1962. The speakers are JFK: President John F. Kennedy; Nitze: Paul H. Nitze, Assistant Secretary of Defense; Ball: George W. Ball, Undersecretary of State; Bundy: McGeorge Bundy, Special Assistant to the President; Rusk: Dean Rusk, Secretary of State; RFK: Robert F. Kennedy, Attorney General; Speaker?: Speaker unknown or identity uncertain; McNamara: Robert S. McNamara, Secretary of Defense; Thompson: Llewellyn Thompson, Special Advisor for Soviet Affairs; Sorensen: Theodore C. Sorensen, Presidential Counsel. The tape begins with a discussion of plans to interdict the Soviet ship *Grozny* and proposals for surveillance missions. This discussion is interrupted as the President reads a news story coming over the wire.]

JFK [*reading*]: 'Premier Khrushchev told President Kennedy yesterday he would withdraw offensive missiles from Cuba if the United States withdrew its rockets from Turkey.' [. . .]

JFK: I ought to have—In case this *is* an accurate statement, where are we with our conversations with the Turks about the withdrawal of these—

NITZE: [US Ambassador to Turkey Raymond] Hare says this is absolutely anathema, and as a matter of prestige and politics. George is ready with a report from [US Ambassador to NATO Thomas] Finletter.

BALL: Yeah, we have a report from Finletter, and we've also got a report from Rome on the Italians which indicates that would be relatively easy. Turkey creates more of a problem. We would have to work it out with the Turks on the basis of putting a Polaris in the waters, and even that might not be enough according to the judgment that we've had on the spot. We've got a—we've got one paper on it already, and we're having more work done right now. It is a complicated problem, because these were put in under a NATO decision, and (words unclear).

NITZE: The NATO requirement involves the whole question as to whether we are going to denuclearize NATO, and I would suggest that what you do is to say that we're prepared only to discuss *Cuba* at this time. After the Cuban thing is settled we can thereafter be prepared to discuss anything—

JFK: —I don't think we can—if this is an accurate—and this is the whole deal—we just have to wait—I don't think we can take the position—

BUNDY: —It's very odd, Mr President, if he's changed his terms from a long letter to you and an urgent appeal from the counselor [Aleksandr Fomin] only last night, set in a purely Cuban context, it seems to me we're well within our—there's nothing wrong with our posture in sticking to that line.

JFK: But let's wait and let's assume that this is an accurate report of what he's now proposing this morning—there may have been changes over there—

BUNDY: He—uh—I still think he's in a difficult position to change it overnight, having sent you a personal communication—

JFK: —Well now let's say he has changed it. This is his latest position.

BUNDY: I would answer back saying I would prefer to deal with your—with your interesting proposals of last night.

JFK: Well now that's just what we ought to be thinking about. We're going to be in an insupportable position on this matter if this becomes his proposal. In the first place, we last year tried to get the missiles out of there because they're not militarily useful, number one. Number two, it's going to—to any man at the United Nations or any other rational man it will look like a very fair trade.

NITZE: I don't think so. I don't think—I think you would get support from the United Nations on the proposition, 'Deal with this Cuban thing'. We'll talk about other things later, but I think everybody else is worried that they'll be included in this great big trade, and it goes beyond Cuba—[. . .]

JFK: [*reading*] 'A special message appeared to call for negotiations and both nations, Cuba and Turkey, should give their consent to the United Nations to visit their territories. Khrushchev said the Security Council of the Soviet Union was solemnly pledged not to use its territory as a bridgehead for an attack on Turkey, called for a similar pledge from the United States not to let its territory be used as a bridgehead for an attack on Cuba—' Now we've known this was coming for a week—uh—we can't—it's going to be hung up here now [*words unclear*].

[*Mixed voices*]

JFK: How much negotiation have we had with the Turks?

RUSK: We haven't talked with the Turks. The Turks have talked with us—the Turks have talked with us in—uh—NATO.

JFK: Well, have we gone to the Turkish government before this came out this week? I've talked about it now for a week. Have we had any conversation in Turkey, with the Turks?

RUSK: We've asked Finletter and Hare to give us their judgments on it. We've not actually talked to the Turks.

BALL: We did it on a basis where if we talked to the Turks, I mean this would be an extremely unsettling business.

JFK: Well *this* is unsettling *now*, George, because he's got us in a pretty good spot here, because most people will regard this as not an unreasonable proposal, I'll just tell you that. In fact, in many ways—

BUNDY: But what most people, Mr President?

JFK: I think you're going to find it very difficult to explain why we are going to take hostile military action in Cuba, against these sites—what we've been thinking about—the thing that he's saying is, if you'll get yours out of Turkey, we'll get ours out of Cuba. I think we've got a very tough one here. [. . .]

JFK: Well, the negotiations. The point is—the point is that we're not in a position today to make the trade. That's number one. And we won't be—maybe—maybe in three or four days, I don't know, we have to wait and see what the Turks say. We don't want to be—we don't want the Soviet Union or the United Nations to be able to say that the United States rejected it. So I think we're better off to stick on the question; freeze, and then we'll discuss it—

BUNDY: Well there are two [*words unclear*] different audiences here, Mr President, there really are, and I think that if we sound as if we wanted to make this trade, to our NATO people and to all the people who are tied to us by alliance, we are in real trouble. I think that—we'll all join in doing this if it's the decision, but I think we should tell you that that's the universal assessment of everyone in the government that's connected with these alliance problems.

JFK: Well now what reports did you get from Chip [Charles] Bohlen, saying that?

BUNDY: That the knockdown in this White House statement this morning was well received. Finletter's report is in. Hare's long telegram is in. They all make the same proposition, that if we appear to be trading our—the defense of Turkey for the threat to Cuba we—we will—we just have to face a radical decline in the—

JFK: Yes, but I should say that also, as the situation is moving, Mac, if we don't for the next twenty-four or forty-eight hours, this trade has appeal. Now if we reject it out of hand and then have to take military action against Cuba, then we also face a decline. Now the only thing we've got for which I would think we'd be able to hold general support would be—well let's try to word it so that we don't harm NATO—but the thing that I think everybody would agree to—while these matters, which are complicated, are discussed, there should be a cessation of work. Then I think we can hold general support for that. If they don't agree to that, the Soviet Union, then we retain the initiative— . . .

JFK: I don't think the alternative's been explained to them. You see, they just think it's a continuation of the quarantine. They don't have any notion that we're about to *do* something. That's got to be on them. You see that hasn't been explained to NATO. I'm not going to get into *that* [. . .] before the strike. If it's necessary to strike tomorrow, there ought to be a NATO meeting tomorrow morning. [. . .]

SPEAKER?: Take them out.

JFK: I think that—uh—the real problem is what we do with the Turks first.

SPEAKER?: Yeah.

JFK: If we follow Secretary McNamara, what we're going to do is say to the Turks—which they're bound to think is—uh—under Soviet pressure, we want to get your missiles out of there.

MCNAMARA: Well what I'd say—what I'd say to the Turks: 'Look here, we're going to have to invade Cuba. You're in mortal danger. We want to reduce your danger while at the same time maintaining your defense. We propose that you defuse those missiles tonight. We're putting Polaris submarines along your coast. We'll cover the same targets that your Jupiter missiles did, and we'll announce this to the world before we invade Cuba and thereby would reduce the pressure on the Soviet Union to attack you, Turkey, as a response to our invasion of Cuba.' Now this is what I would say to the Turks.

RFK: Now, then they say—uh—what if the Soviet Union attacks us anyway. Will you use the missiles on the nuclear submarines?

MCNAMARA: Then, I think, before we attack Cuba I think we've got to decide how we'll respond to Soviet military pressure on NATO, and I'm not prepared to answer the question. [. . .]

THOMPSON: Mr President, if we go on the basis of a trade which I gather is—somewhat in your mind, we end up, it seems to me, with the Soviets still in Cuba with planes and technicians and so on even though the missiles are out, and that would surely be unacceptable and put you in a worse position—

JFK: Yeah, but our technicians and planes and guarantees would still exist for Turkey. I'm just thinking about what—what we're going to have to do in a day or so, which is [excised] sorties and [excised] days, and possibly an invasion, all because we wouldn't take missiles out of Turkey, and we all know how quickly everybody's courage goes when the blood starts to flow, and that's what's going to happen in NATO, when they—we start these things, and they grab Berlin, and everybody's going to say, Well that was a pretty good proposition. Let's not kid ourselves that we've got—that's the difficulty. Today it sounds great to reject it, but it's not going to, after we do something. [. . .]

JFK: Now the question really if two or three—two questions—first, whether we go immediately to the Turks and see if we can work out some—see if they're receptive to the kind of deal which the secretary talked about. If they're not receptive then we ought to go to the general NATO meeting because the NATO meeting may put enough pressure on them (*pause*). I just tell you I think we're better off to get those missiles out of Turkey and out of Cuba, because I think the way of getting them out of Turkey and out of Cuba is going to be very grave (*words unclear*), and very bloody, one place or another. [. . .]

SORENSEN: I wonder, Mr President, inasmuch as your statement this morning does give some answer to the public statement of the Soviets, whether we can't defer this for twenty-four or forty-eight hours while we try the private letter route in answer to his private letter of last night. There's always a chance that he'll accept that (*words unclear*). We meanwhile would have broken up NATO over something that never would have come to NATO. [. . .]

JFK: It seems to me what we ought to—to be reasonable. We're not going to get these weapons out of Cuba, probably, anyway. But I mean—by negotiation—we're going to have to take our weapons out of Turkey. I don't think there's any doubt he's not going to (*word unclear*) now that he made that public, Tommy, he's not going to take them out of Cuba if we—

THOMPSON: I don't agree, Mr President, I think there's still a chance that we can get this line going.

JFK: He'll back down?

THOMPSON: Well, because he's already got this other proposal which he put forward—

JFK: Now this other public one, it seems to me, has become their public position, isn't it?

THOMPSON: This is, maybe, just pressure on us, I mean, to accept the other, I mean so far—

[Mixed voices]

THOMPSON: The important thing for Khrushchev, it seems to me, is to be able to say, I saved Cuba, I stopped an invasion—and he can get away with this, if he wants to, and he's had a go at this Turkey thing, and that we'll discuss later. And then, and that discussion will probably take—

JFK: All right, what about at the end of this, we use this letter and say, 'will be a grave risk to peace. I urge—urge you to join us in a rapid settlement of the Cuban crisis as your letter [*word unclear*] suggests, and [*words unclear*]. The first ingredient, let me emphasize, for any solution is a cessation of the uh—work and the possibility [*word unclear*] under reasonable standards'—I mean, I want to just come back to that. Otherwise time uh—slips away on us.

[Pause. Words unclear and mixed voices.]

SORENSEN: In other words, Mr President, your position is that once he meets this condition of the—uh—halting of the work and the inoperability [*sic*], you're then prepared to go ahead on either the specific Cuban track or what we call the general détente track.

JFK: Yeah, now it all comes down—I think it's a substantive question, because it really depends on whether we believe that we can get a deal on just the Cuban—or whether we have to agree to his position of tying. Tommy doesn't think we do. I think that having made it public how can he take these missiles out of Cuba—if we just do nothing about Turkey. [. . .]

BUNDY: I think that Bobby's notion of a concrete acceptance on our part of how we read last night's telegram is very important.

TAYLOR: Mr Kennedy—

JFK: In other words, you want to—you have to say we accept your proposal.

RFK: [*Words unclear*] accept it and then say you—I just the last paragraph of the other letter and however you phrase it.

R: Mr President, the chiefs [the Joint Chiefs of Staff] have been in session during the afternoon on—really the same basis as we have over here. This if the recommendation they give is as follows: that the big strike OP Plan 3–12—be executed no later than Monday morning the 29th unless there is irrefutable evidence in the meantime that offensive weapons are being dismantled and rendered inoperable; that the execution of the Strike Plan be part of the execution of 3–16, the Invasion Plan, [*excised*] days later.

(Pause)

RFK: That was a surprise.

(*Laughter, mixed voices*)

[From audio tapes of the Executive Committee meeting, 27 Oct. 1962, John F. Kennedy Library, transcribed by McGeorge Bundy, Sept. 1987.]

DAVIDSON LOEHR

17   The Fresh Kill, Vietnam 1967

I served in Vietnam from July 1966 to August 1967 as an army lieutenant. I had graduated from Artillery Officer Candidate School nine months earlier, and had been sent over to be a forward observer (FO) with the First Infantry Division.

I didn't want to go. I was afraid. I had read in the paper a week before leaving that the life expectancy of FOs with the First Division was thirty-three days. I couldn't read a military map to save my life, and it threatened to become more than just a figure of speech. Also, the job of hiding quietly in the middle of nowhere for ten hours a day looking for Viet Cong or NVA troops to call in artillery fire on was a damned boring prospect.

For at least these reasons, I contrived a 'Catch-22' scheme to beat the game. And thanks to the nerve that can come from fear, I did beat the game, and in spades. Instead of becoming a forward observer, I became the Vietnam Entertainment Officer. They gave me a secretary and an air-conditioned office in Saigon, and my job consisted of meeting movie stars and professional entertainers at the airport, taking them out to dinner on an expense account, and keeping their refrigerator stocked with beer and soft drinks. After work, I stopped in at a steam bath on the way home for steam bath, massage, and sex; or, less often, spent the night with Thom, my favorite barmaid.

The celebrities I worked with included Martha Raye, Roy Rogers, and Dale Evans . . . Nancy Sinatra, Frank Sinatra, Jr., Arthur Godfrey, John Gavin, and Jennifer Jones (who danced divinely). At Christmas, I had a fourth-row seat for the Bob Hope show, three rows behind General Westmoreland. I would be running into him several more times during the coming year.

If the name of the game was survival, I had won.

And yet something wasn't right. What, deep down, was wrong? Why didn't I feel better about beating the game? Or *was* survival the name of the game?

Then one day a friend called, a man from my class at Officer Candidate School. Jim (I'll call him) said he was in town for the day, and I offered to take him out to dinner with one of the shows in town. Jim was mostly quiet, but Jim was almost always quiet. He just shook his head and flipped me the bird as we ate our fifty-dollar dinners at one of Saigon's best French restaurants.

A couple of weeks later, I went up with one of the shows to visit the First Division and to see my best friend Lou, who was a fire direction officer there. Lou asked if I had heard about Jim. I said I had seen him in Saigon a couple of weeks ago, and Lou said, 'Oh, then you know.'

Jim was in Saigon, it turned out, because he had just been released from the Third Field Hospital. The infantry company to which Jim was assigned had been hit by an early morning human wave assault, which means that about 600 Viet Cong rushed the camp, planning to lose hundreds of men, but to overrun the camp with those who could get through. It was like an infantry kamikaze mission. Jim's company commander, an infantry captain, was wounded in the shoulder and became hysterical, cringing in a corner and leaving his company without a leader. Jim was the only other officer present. He took command of the company, manned three radio networks, called in artillery fire, called the platoons to organize defenses, ordered point-blank artillery fire from their own guns when the attack neared, and shouted commands to organize the hand-to-hand fighting that ensued within the company perimeters.

When it was over Jim had a deep knife wound, hundreds of Viet Cong lay dead, no Americans were killed. He received a Purple Heart and a Silver Star, the third highest award for valor, for altruism under fire.

And something within me awoke.

Ten years later, in the movie *The Deer Hunter* Robert DeNiro says to a frightened young man, 'You have to take a shot. You don't have to get hit, but you have to take a shot.' A famous passage from a letter of Henry IV contains a similar insight: 'Hang yourself, brave Crillon; we fought at Arques, and you were not there.' And in the jargon of religion, we speak of a *kairos*, of that moment when the time is right and the time is ripe, when a decision must be made, a decision which will be a watershed for the rest of one's life. That's what awoke within me. It may not make any logical sense, but it has an existential force that cannot be denied or diluted. I knew that if I returned from that country without having experienced war, that in a deep and important way I would not be able to live with myself.

So I negotiated for a transfer to the field. Not to be a forward observer; I still couldn't read a map. I was not the stuff of which heroes are made, and I wanted a broader view of the war. I wanted to see and be in more aspects of it. So I negotiated a transfer to the field as a press officer and combat photographer for an armored cavalry regiment in Xuan Loc, about thirty-five kilometers east-north-east of Saigon, in the middle of dense woods and rubber trees. That was January 10, 1967, and I spent my remaining seven months in that job. I photographed the war, attended briefings from General

Westmoreland and other major unit commanders, dealt briefly with Mike Wallace and Morley Safer at CBS, and tagged along with *LIFE* magazine photographer, Co Rentmeester after convincing him to do a feature story on our regiment.

A week after arriving in the field, we got a call to go to a nearby hamlet. The Viet Cong had had a recruiting drive the night before. They assembled the people in the center of the hamlet, where the head of the hamlet refused to help them. So they took his two daughters, aged about six and eight, raped them, then slit their throats, and threw their bodies into the well to pollute the drinking water. Our interpreter from the South Vietnamese Army, Captain Trang, was with us, and he became violently ill. 'My two daughters,' he said, 'are the same ages, they are the same ages as my two girls, my girls are like that, they are like my little girls . . . ' He kept repeating it, over and over.

I never got to know Captain Trang very well, though we ate lunch together most of the time we were both in base camp. But half of what I ever knew about him I learned that morning.

The next story is about the first operation I went on, and it requires some background explanation. The armored unit I was attached to had three squadrons of about 2,000 men each. The first was commanded by a lieutenant colonel who was nicknamed 'Tiger'. He was a superb commander, and his men loved him. He volunteered them to be the lead element in every joint operation, and they were proud of being 'the Tiger's guys'. In their six months in the country, I don't think they had had a single man killed, though they had been involved in four or five major operations near Cambodia.

The second squadron remained a stranger to me until ten days before coming home, because Tiger's guys were always where the action was, and I needed action photos and stories to sell our little unit to the major news services. The third squadron was commanded by a man whose name I don't remember; he appeared to be a poor commander whose men followed his lead as Tiger's had followed his. The morale was so low in the third squadron that they couldn't be trusted to go out and fight, so they were left home to guard the base camp on every operation. In six months they had never seen a Viet Cong, never been in war. But they had had eight men killed while staying at home in base camp, in barracks fights, homosexual incidents, thefts, and all the other indicators of poor morale in a military unit.

Three days before a major operation we were to go with an infantry division, we were in a routine staff meeting when General Westmoreland walked in unannounced. General Westmoreland, it seemed, always came unannounced.

Unless you were in that man's presence over there, you just can't know the awesome look he had, the power of intimidation that he had, the unsettling ability he had to make everyone feel intensely uneasy at once. If he walked in here right now, I would probably salute him and still get that uneasy feeling we had all that day.

He stood at the side of the tent for awhile, then walked to the front to interrupt the meeting. He looked straight at the colonel without expression: 'You have a morale problem in your third squadron, colonel,' he said. 'What do you intend to do about it?'

The colonel stammered. The colonel always stammered when Westmoreland was near.

'Do you know how many men have been killed because of the poor morale in your third squadron?'

The colonel did not.

'Eight,' said the general. 'Eight of your men, eight of *my* men, have died without purpose. What are you going to do about the morale problem?' The colonel stammered again. 'This once,' said Westmoreland, 'I'll solve your leadership problem, colonel. The third squadron will be the lead element in the operation in three days. They need a fresh kill.'

Among the things I'll never forget is the matter-of-fact way that General Westmoreland said that, the feel of the atmosphere in the tent after he said it, the silence in the officers' tent after the meeting, and the tension three days later as I went with the third squadron on their and my first operation, in search of the fresh kill.

We rode for two full days in the one-hundred-twenty to one-hundred-thirty degree temperatures without ever seeing a Viet Cong, and our young driver began showing signs of tension. Principally, he kept driving off the road to attack small trees with the vehicle, rolling up them until they bent over to the ground, then hooting like a hillbilly. Then he hit a four-inch tree that was too big to bend. When it snapped back at us, we were covered with inch-long fire ants. They bit everything they landed on, and by the time we had sprayed DDT down each other's backs and finally killed them, we were all burning from the bites and the DDT.

It was about then, I think, that we saw a large bunker by the road. Since a whole column of armored vehicles had just driven by it, there was little chance that anyone was inside. Nevertheless, it was the first real prop of war we had seen up close, so the column stopped and three of us got out to inspect: two men with guns and me with my camera. The bunker was empty, and the two other men said they should check the area out. I stood on the bunker to wait for them.

They spread out in a V and had walked about ten feet when both of them turned and opened fire on a clump of grass about fifteen feet directly in front of me.

They got their fresh kill. Two North Vietnamese officers lay dead. One held a rocket launcher, the other lay with a Russian AK-47 rifle. The two American soldiers began taking souvenirs—sandals and so on—and asked me if I wanted one. I wondered what the men were doing when they were killed. One, they said, was aiming his rocket launcher at our vehicle; the other was aiming his rifle at my head, and both were pulling the triggers when they were shot. The rifle was off safety; we snapped back the bolt, and a bullet popped out of the chamber. I have that bullet in a drawer, and it still has an eerie power, a reminder of the significance of perhaps a hundredth of a second and the fact that mere chance lets me stand here reminiscing rather than a North Vietnamese captain.

But I was not prepared for what happened next.

The word of the fresh kill was radioed through the column, and war whoops resounded. The two men with me put the bodies on the front carrier of our ACAV and drove through the column like deer hunters. Everyone wanted to see them, to take pictures, to pose by the trophies.

And their *eyes*—the eyes of the American soldiers were positively on fire as they swarmed around this irrefutable proof that they were, in fact, in the war; that they had, in fact, taken their shot. In that instant I understood Joseph Conrad's short story 'The Heart of Darkness', and later understood why Francis Ford Coppola might base his movie *Apocalypse Now* on that story rather than directly on Vietnam.

The morale in the third squadron skyrocketed; they partied well into the night and ran on euphoria the next day. At last, something to write home about, at last they were off the bench and in the game, at last they were a part of this thing called the Vietnam War.

General Westmoreland had been right.

[From Davidson Loehr, 'To Care Without Judging', *The University of Chicago Magazine* (Spring 1985), 28–33]

PABLO CARBALLO

18 **Attacking the *Sir Galahad*, June 1982**

I became flight leader. I had never had that responsibility before but now, suddenly and by chance, I found myself in charge not only of one flight but of *two*. Before he left, the Captain told me: 'Attack at one minute intervals, three aircraft ahead and two behind . . . Take them to glory!' A very simple request, wasn't it? I felt a chill run up my spine but then I felt calmer, because the men who were following me were perfectly qualified for that kind of operation and the success of the mission depended on my command.

The succession of checkpoints forced me to concentrate on the flight. Over Cabo Belgrano [the southern tip of West Falkland] we went through a rainy area for a few seconds. Then we crossed over the southern part of

Falkland Sound. The sea was full of gulls floating calmly. We passed another checkpoint at Aquila Island [Speedwell Island] and then met a second area of rain, but we flew on heading straight towards Fitzroy. It poured with rain again for thirty seconds; during that time you can cover a distance of around eight kilometres. I was about to return, because I was afraid that the rain would cover all the islands, but fortunately we managed to see a clearance behind the curtain of water, and this encouraged me to continue with the planned course. As we got nearer to the target I ordered the flight to accelerate to 900 kph and stay right down on the sea.

Forty seconds before the target we saw a Sea Lynx helicopter, so I hid behind a hill to avoid being detected. Twenty seconds later we found a Sea King on the ground; we performed the same manœuvure and then reached Fitzroy Bay. There was nothing to be seen! I decided to fly on for another thirty seconds, but after that we turned right to start the return flight. Down on the ground we could see many British soldiers, who began shooting at us. A missile crossed behind our flight line from right to left at an angle of about 30 degrees. Just as we were completing the turn, 'Diablo' shouted: 'There are the ships!' Two grey silhouettes could be seen near the coast. I straightened up and banked to the left. Here we go again!

I released my bombs, which scored direct hits on the *Sir Galahad*. Number Two's bombs went long but luckily they hit a vehicle, overturned it and then they exploded. Ensign Carmona also hit the target. The section coming behind us saw that the ship had been hit so they attacked the *Sir Tristram*; 'Chango' and 'Diablo' did not waste their bombs. There was a long pipe on the deck where many life-jackets were tidily placed. Little men—little when seen from the distance—ran towards them, took one each and, one after the other, jumped into the cold sea.

I escaped by hugging the water. I checked to see if we were all there. We were. We looked at each other's damage; the 'Chango' and the 'Diablo' had been hit but not seriously. The enemy had been greatly hurt that day, and I had carried out what my flight leader had asked me to do: 'Take them to glory.'

[From Pablo Carballo, *Dios y los Halcones*. Translation used by Martin Middlebrook in *The Fight for the Malvinas* (London: Viking, 1989), 212–14. The description is by First Lieutenant Cachón.]

MARTIN MIDDLEBROOK

19 On the *Sir Galahad*

When the bombs went off, it was just like the scoring of a goal at a football match; everyone went 'WOOOH'—a surprise shout. I was knocked over by a large blast of hot air which propelled me about twelve feet through some panelling which was also smashed down by the blast, and I finished up lying on top of some stairs—ship's panelling and fitting all around me—knee-deep in places.

I stood up and there was a bloke in front of me who was injured in the back, bits of fitting stuck into his back. Two blokes were helping him out. I started to make my way out of the door on to the deck. I was in a queue of six people on my side when someone shouted 'Stand still!' It was a daft thing to say; there was no panic. A few seconds later, someone else said, 'No. Let's go; the smoke's bloody killing us.' It was thick, acrid, multi-coloured, very pungent, of the electrical sort and it had bits in it like the big bits of soot which float off when an acetylene torch burns. I decided to go back and started making my way down the stairs. Half-way down I found this bloke; he was sliding slowly down, head first—bump, bump, bump. He had obviously been knocked over by the blast. He wasn't badly hurt, just bashed about by the blast. I picked him up by the webbing straps on his back and just dragged him down the last few steps on his knees. He stood up then, brushed himself off, and we both made our way out of the door on to the middle deck. There were people moving about there—mainly in-jured men and others looking after them. One of them had a head wound and it must have been bad because blood was soaking through the dressing which another man was putting on him. But it was mainly blokes with severe burns. You couldn't tell which unit they came from; we had all lost our berets by that time.

[From Martin Middlebrook, *Operation Corporate: The Falklands War, 1982* (London: Viking, 1985), 307–8. The description is by Lance-Corporal Bill Skinner.]

ED CODY
20 Covering Grenada

The United States press covers wars in which the United States is not directly involved on the ground. The Middle East is an example of this. The axiom of how to cover a war like that and the conflicts you get into are very simple. You go, you look, you report on what you saw, and your difficulties are in obtaining access so that you can see. We can perhaps leave that aside because the more immediate problem before us is a war in which the United States military is directly involved on the ground. The methods, of course, are basically the same. You try to find out what you can by seeing it and then report back on what you saw.

But here we come against this conflict between the military's needs and the press' needs [. . .] The military's job is to win whatever battle it has been assigned to wage, and we reporters definitely do get in the way. It's hard to fault the military commander for trying to remove what he sees—and probably rightly—as impediments or at least distractions. This was what occurred in Grenada. [. . .]

[W]hat happened at Grenada was not a failure of the United States military or its political leadership to include the press in the operation, to take the press along. What happened was something beyond that. Let's be specific. It was not that the Navy did not take reporters on its ships to be present for whatever could be seen from the ships, or that the Air Force refused to allow reporters to hitch rides on the C-130's that were creating a virtual air bridge between Barbados and Grenada. That wasn't the problem. A large part of the problem was that there was an active attempt to prevent the press from getting to Grenada. The US Navy actually sent patrols around the island of Grenada to prevent reporters who had chartered boats from arriving on the island. The man who was directly in charge on the spot, Admiral Metcalf, actually said in public that he would shoot at those boats. Some Navy planes dropped buoys in front of boats that had been chartered, frightened the owners of the boats who, of course, depended on those boats for their livelihood, and prevented them from arriving in Grenada. We who were involved in this wondered why Admiral Metcalf wasn't busier doing something else in the middle of an operation that was supposed to last a few hours and instead lasted a few days. The whole thing illustrates why there are some new dimensions involved in this.

The first is that over the last decade or so, there is a new rule or axiom in covering wars, and that is that you cover both sides. That's something that hadn't been present before, or at least hadn't been present to a very great degree at all. It used to be that in World War I, World War II, Korea, Vietnam, that you covered the US Army in whatever war it was involved in. That's not the case anymore. Maybe the watershed was Beirut, where we were expected from the very beginning of 1975 to cover both sides or all sides, because of course there were more than two. But whatever the origin of it, it is now taken as a matter of course, that if a conflict arises, whether the United States is involved or not, that the networks and the newspapers will make an attempt to cover both sides. [. . .]

The second change is that the means of correspondents have increased enormously. Means is a euphemism for money. It is now just absolute standard practice for networks (and we in the newspapers have followed along behind) to charter an airplane, to charter a helicopter, to charter a boat, whatever is necessary; we can afford it now. We couldn't do that before. This is something quite different. To refer back to the Grenada example, I am absolutely convinced that if there had not been the active preventive measures taken, the American networks and the American newspapers would have had a regular hydrofoil or fast boat or something to service a shuttle operating between Grenada and either Trinidad or Barbados within hours of the invasion, shuttling film and copy back and forth had it not been prevented from happening by Admiral Metcalf [. . .]

[From Ed Cody, 'Covering Grenada', in William Schneider (ed.), *The Military and the Media* (Claremont, Calif.: The Keck Center for International Studies, July 1984), 23–5.]

ARTYOM BOROVIK

21 A Soviet Soldier Defects, Afghanistan, 1983

Movchan lit a cigarette and placed his hands on the table, interlacing his fingers. He continued with his story:

'In Afghanistan I served at Ghazni—the fall and winter of eighty-two, the winter and spring of eighty-three. In the beginning of the summer I left. Before I defected I served in a motorized infantry unit. Life in the unit was fairly calm, unless we were involved in operations, when everything was different. I have nothing bad to say about our army, but the things that went on outside the regiment were terrible. We didn't see any friendly Afghans anywhere—only enemies. Even the Afghan army was unfriendly. Only one village in the whole area had a more or less tolerant attitude toward our presence. When the propagandists would go out to solicit support for Soviet rule, so to speak, they would take along a company of men and tanks. They used to say that the situation was better in 1981. I really couldn't say.

'I served as a sergeant, but not in combat subunits. A regiment generally would send one battalion and one reconnaissance company to fight. But I was never in any of them. I served for six months and then took off. I deserted early in the morning, just before dawn. I was lucky. [. . .]

'The urge to defect came toward the end of my tour of duty. At first I had some doubts about whether we were in the right; then I was overcome with a feeling of despair. Everyone around us was an enemy. I remember an intense feeling of anger toward the rebels because so many of our guys were getting killed.

'I wanted revenge.

'Then I began to doubt the goals and methods of international aid. I had a difficult time deciding what I really believed. I just knew what I had to say during the political instruction meeting: that we were fighting "American aggression" and "Pakis". Why had we mined all the approaches to the regiment? I asked myself. Why were we aiming our machine guns at every Afghan? Why were we killing the people we came here to help?

'Whenever a peasant was blown up by a mine, no one took him to the medical unit. Everyone just stood around, enjoying the sight of his death. "This is an enemy," the officer said. "Let him suffer."

'It's grim. I didn't listen to my father. I deserted at dawn.

'That's my life. And now it's America. Another life. A movie. Yes, a movie.

'On the morning that I'd decided to desert, I stared at a field for a long time. Everything was still—very still. I just stood there and looked. The muscles of my legs tensed up involuntarily. I froze. Then I glanced at the rising sun and ran. When I looked back, the regiment was far, far away, on the other side of the field. Some of the Afghans who were working in the field helped me hide. I saw the helicopters approach. They saw me running and understood everything.

'After two days had passed we left the *kishlak* and went into the mountains. After walking for a long time we finally reached the rebels' camp. The rebels looked at me with curiosity but not hostility. They were armed only with ancient augers that went back to the time of the British invasion. In 1983 they had no other weapons. Can you imagine using flint augers against tanks, helicopters, and bombers? This is the truth. As it turned out, I was in Sayaf's group. They treated me well. At first I didn't understand a word, but later on a man who spoke decent Russian arrived; he'd studied in the USSR, served as an officer in the Afghan army, and then deserted.'

[From Artyom Borovik, *The Hidden War: A Russian Journalist's Account of the Soviet War in Afghanistan* (London: Faber, 1991), 174–6.]

22 The Start of Desert Storm, January 1991

At a secret staging area 700 miles west of Dhahran, just as the first wave of ten F-117A pilots was heading for Iraq, a flight of eight Apache AH-64 helicopters and four MH-53J Pave Low helicopters lifted off from a darkened tarmac. They were also headed north toward Iraq. Flying just thirty feet above the ground, Lieutenant Thomas Drew, a twenty-seven-year-old pilot from the 101st Airborne based at Fort Campbell, Kentucky, was embarking on the first combat mission of his life. Drew had been training for such a mission since September, but he had not been told where the target would be or how important it would be.

The information had been withheld from Drew and his colleagues for as long as possible. Finally, just days before, they had been told that they were to strike early-warning radar systems in southwestern Iraq. The original plan called for three separate teams—red, white, and blue teams of three Apaches and two Pave Lows each. Initially, they had been assigned to strike three radar sites. At the 10 p.m. briefing on January 16, however, Drew and his colleagues were handed a revised plan. One target had been dropped.

The radar facility had become inactive, intelligence officials said. So two Apaches of the blue team were assigned to the other teams, making two teams of four Apaches each. In memory of the D-Day invasion of the French coast in the Second World War, they were given the name Task Force Normandy.

The two early-warning radar systems left as targets were about thirty-five miles apart. One was located just seven miles inside Iraq; the other was fourteen miles across the Iraqi border from the Saudi desert village of Ar Ar. The two facilities provided defensive coverage of the southwestern Iraqi border and protection for Iraqi air bases and fixed launchers for Scud missiles there.

At 12.56 a.m. on January 17, the helicopters took off. The Pave Low helicopters were outfitted with global-positioning systems that could help the Apache pilots navigate in the desert in the dark. The Pave Lows were also equipped with sophisticated terrain-following radar and on-board computerized mapping systems that would enable the Apache pilots to locate their targets in even the worst weather.

Fifteen miles from the Iraqi border, Drew and the other Apache crews flew over what looked like a small Bedouin camp. Seconds later, there were surface-to-air missiles rising toward them. The missiles narrowly missed. One of the Pave Lows flying with Drew's team of Apaches shot at the Bedouins with a 7.62-mm machine gun. That was odd, Drew thought, being fired at from inside Saudi Arabia. There was no time to delay, however, so they flew on.

At 1.45 a.m., an hour and fifteen minutes before H-Hour marked the start of the air war, Lieutenant Drew and his small fleet of attack helicopters crossed the border into Iraqi airspace. Drew was the commander of the white team; he sat in the front seat of his Apache and controlled the weapons systems. Behind him sat his pilot, Chief Warrant Officer 2 Tim Zarnowski. Ten miles inside Iraq, Task Force Normandy was attacked again, this time by machine-gun fire. The helicopter pilots ignored it. They had a far more important objective. It was Drew's job to coordinate all aspects of the mission. The most important element of all, Drew had been told over and over again, was what the Air Force called 'time on target'. The Apache pilots had been instructed to destroy the two radar sites at precisely 2.38 a.m. No sooner, no later.

Soon after crossing into Iraqi air space, Drew and Zarnowski saw a dozen tiny white dots on their Forward Looking Infrared Radar scopes. Their range-finder told them the dots were twelve kilometers away. Five kilometers from their target site, the outlines of the radar facility became clear. Drew could see a line of squat buildings, trailers, and radar antennas. The layout, he knew, was characteristic of the Soviet-designed radar systems. They were supported by Soviet-made anti-aircraft artillery.

Just under five kilometers from the radar site, Drew got his team of four Apaches on line. Each weapons officer centered his cross hairs on the ghostly white shape of his target. Drew's first target was a trailer. His wingman would first hit a radar antenna. The two other Apaches would hit different antennas, control buildings, and the facility's communications vans. When ten seconds remained to launch time, Drew radioed to his team: 'Party in ten.' Five seconds passed and a pilot said, 'Here's one for you, Saddam.' Five seconds after that, Drew called, 'Get some.' Less than a second later, a swarm of missiles was screaming across the desert toward their targets.

At that same moment thirty-five miles away, the red team of Task Force Normandy was lined up on approach to the second radar site. Locking onto their targets with their Image Auto Gate Trackers, electronic rectangles on their scopes designed to find and hold targets by identifying their heat sources, the four Apache pilots of the red team released their missiles. The looping trajectories were visible for just seconds in the helicopters' thermal scopes before the targets exploded. The tiny figures of Iraqi soldiers could be seen on the Apaches' scopes, running. One of the Iraqis ran from a building that had just been attacked, apparently to warn soldiers in another building. At the very instant he opened the door to the second building, the structure exploded into flames.

Back at his target site, Lieutenant Drew ordered the white team to switch tactics. 'Okay,' he called over the radio, 'let's do rockets.' Their 2.75-inch rockets contained thousands of little fléchettes, or darts, to take out supply trucks and wiring systems. Then the Apaches mopped up with their 30-mm automatic cannons.

In a matter of minutes, Task Force Normandy had thoroughly destroyed the two targets. 'Okay,' an Apache pilot radioed Lieutenant Drew, 'I cannot see any more targets in my area.' On the red team nearby, another Apache pilot signaled a successful mission. 'Okay,' he radioed, 'we can get us out of here.' The world would think of the first bombs dropped on Baghdad as the beginning of the Gulf War. General Schwarzkopf and his staff saw the attack by Task Force Normandy as the real beginning of the war.

[From US News and World Report, *Triumph Without Victory: The Unreported History of the Persian Gulf War* (New York: Times Books, 1992), 219–21.]

VANESSA VASIC JANEKOVIC
....

23   **Ethnic Cleansing in Bosnia, June 1992**

Most of those detained in the Omarska camp came from Bosanska Krajina, a region of about 30,000 inhabitants in northwestern Bosnia, spread along the UN-controlled Croatian border. The small town of Kozarac is at its centre.

In all plans for territorial division, the region was supposed to be Serbian. Sometimes four municipalities in the far northwest were excepted. Two Muslim municipalities in the heart of the Krajina, Prijedor and Sanski Most, are especially important because they are inconvenient for both sides. They are practically surrounded by the Serbian area, cutting the local Muslims off from Muslim-held Bosnia, but their ethnic makeup obviously complicates the plan for a clearly defined Greater Serbia. So the Serbs came to a simple solution: displacement. The improvised mass murder that evolved was only a logical extension of the game.

In mid-June, a month after the bombardment of Sarajevo began, the people of Kozarac, in the Prijedor region, watched Serb forces drag weapons onto the surrounding hills. The first shots in the town were fired on June 22, a Sunday. On that day, a very small and poorly organised group of the Bosnian Territorial Defence attacked a tank that was in the convoy of military vehicles at the entrance to Kozarac. The shelling from the hills started immediately, and continued for three days.

The inhabitants of Kozarac decided to negotiate. They were promised that nothing would happen to them if they surrendered, and most of them did. But they didn't know about the buses that were already assembled and waiting for them on the outskirts of the town. The women and children were taken to Trnopolje, to the railway station, and loaded onto cattle wagons, which had also been waiting. The trains headed for Banja Luka, and stayed there for three days. The sinister wagons drew the attention of some of the more observant journalists, but no press were allowed access. Finally the prisoners were sent to Travnik and Doboj; most of them have ended up in Croatia and Slovenia.

The men had a quicker journey. Most of those who surrendered, Muslims of course, and some Croats, were immediately bused to the camps, arriving on the afternoon of their surrender.

Omarska, situated on the southeastern edge of Kozarac, was not inhabited until a mine was opened about 15 years ago. It has a Serbian majority, and was the launch point for most of the attacks on Kozarac. The camp was set up in the complex of buildings that used to house the mine's administrative offices, garages and surgery. The compound was secured by a surrounding mine field and two lines of guards. There were few escape attempts, and only one who tried to escape survived, although he was recaptured. (He is now in Britain.)

The camp was run in three shifts, by a commander and about 35 guards. Every day at 8 a.m., 10 police inspectors of the 'Serbian Republic Bosanska Krajina of B-H' would come to interrogate the prisoners, leaving the camp about 5 pm to return to Prijedor. The inspectors had a list of about 8,000 names from the JNA registers of people trained to fight, who in the old system would have been called to serve in the Bosnian Territorial Defence if necessary.

In the camp itself, the prisoners were roughly divided into three groups: the wealthy, intellectuals and priests (hodjas) were in one; those accused of fighting were in the second; and 'ordinary' civilians in the third. The estimated number of detainees was between 2,500 and 3,000, and during the 10 weeks of the camp's existence the number stayed more or less the same because new people were brought daily, village by village, replacing those who were killed. Only 1,400 survivors were found when the camp was finally closed on August 8. There was a sort of hierarchy of punishment meted out, depending on the group one was in, but it eventually got out of control, and guards had free reign. But the killings were not only the result of the guards' brutality. They were also part of a campaign of executing those inspectors deemed 'guilty' of participating in the Territorial Defence.

[From Vanessa Vasic Janekovic, 'Beyond the Detention Camps', *War Report*, Bulletin of the Institute for War and Peace Reporting (Oct. 1992), 12.]

Section B

The Causes of War

EFRAIM KARSH

Although war is probably the most brutalizing of human experiences, it has been an inseparable part of the evolution of mankind. How can this apparent contradiction be explained? Is there something fundamentally flawed in human nature to make it so belligerent? Or is war an inevitable outcome of the social and political institutions in which individuals and states operate?

To biologists, fighting is a natural part of animal behaviour, *Homo sapiens* included. As shown by Raymond Aron in 26, just as animals respond aggressively to fear, pain, or infringement on their space, so does human bellicosity stem from such crude stimuli as insecurity, greed, envy, selfishness, or stupidity. Some species may be more aggressive than others, and some may not be aggressive at all; yet, even the most peaceable animals will fight when attacked or threatened.

This linkage between animal and human behaviour has been extended to the geopolitical sphere. Building on Charles Darwin's theory of evolution, German geopolitician Friedrich Ratzel viewed the state as a living organism that, like all organisms, grows, matures, decays, and dies. As in Darwin's human jungle where only the fittest survive, Ratzel's state is engaged in a constant struggle for survival. In this struggle the stronger state tends to expand at the expense of its weaker neighbours; this, in turn, allows it to preserve its vigour and to prolong its life cycle. Once a state loses its expansionist impulse, it goes into a rapid decline, which, in many cases, ends in its eventual demise.

Enunciated at the turn of the twentieth century, Ratzel's ideas were further elaborated by a younger generation of German geopoliticians, most notably Karl Haushofer. Haushofer elevated the ideal of expansionism to a categorical imperative. In his view, since the state's very existence depended on the possession of an adequate living space (or *Lebensraum* in German), 'the preservation and protection of that space must determine all its policies. If the space has grown too small, it has to be expanded.' These expansionist geopolitical notions, summarized by Saul Cohen in 27, eventually penetrated the thinking and praxis of Adolf Hitler, with disastrous consequences for the entire world.

Historians and political philosophers are normally more cautious in making inferences about the human realm from animal behaviour, yet many of them view war as a reflection of human imperfection. Disputing Clausewitz's classical dictum that 'war is the continuation of political activity by other means', military historian Martin Van Creveld argues that 'war, far from being merely a means, has very often been considered an end'. He concedes that war is not 'biologically predetermined', but argues that it has nevertheless been 'a highly attractive activity for which no other can provide an adequate substitute' (28).

To a predominant school of thought, known as *political realism*, war is an inevitable outcome of human insecurity and the desperate quest for power it generates. In realist thinking, most saliently represented by American historian Hans Morgenthau, the world is a violent, hostile environment, in which the will to self-preservation rules. In such a setting, one must remain constantly on the alert, making others cower so that they do not attack, always ready to kill before being killed.

The only way to alleviate this bleak human condition is to establish a 'common power' that will keep mankind in awe. Yet, while history shows that the existence of 'common power' within a political community often reduces intra-communal violence, it casts a serious doubt about the feasibility of establishing such power among nations. Unlike individuals, who are willing to subordinate their personal interest to the 'common good', nations do not recognize a higher authority than their own. Consequently, international relations are characterized by an anarchic state of 'war of all against all', not in the sense of constant fighting, but, rather, in the ever-present tendency to do so.

The realist perception of war as an unavoidable corollary of human nature, something that could be partly modified by political institutions but not eradicated altogether, has been challenged by a rival school of thought, that of *political idealism*. At its extreme, idealist thinking maintains that peace, not war, constitutes the natural human condition. This is because there exists a 'harmony of interests' among human beings, wherein the interest of the individual (and by extension, the nation) and that of the community (or the community of nations) fully coincide. Hence, just as the individual promotes the general good by pursuing his own interest, and vice versa, so national interest is best served by promoting the universal goals of peace and prosperity.

More moderate idealists concur with their realist counterparts that war is endemic to human nature; however, they believe that this 'chronic disease' can be fully cured through the appropriate political institutions. Immanuel Kant maintained that eternal peace could be established provided all states were to become true republics, and then join together in an international federation of independent states.[1] Kant was fully aware that

---

[1] Immanuel Kant, *Eternal Peace and Other International Essays* (Boston: The World Peace Foundation, 1914).

domestic restructuring was a necessary but not a sufficient condition for the attainment of perpetual peace. Even if all the states in the world were to be converted into republicanism, there would still be a risk of the odd war breaking out for reasons beyond the control of individual states, such as accidental friction by contiguous powers.

The ideas that 'bad states' wage wars while 'good states' coexist in peace and harmony, and that universal organizations can decisively curb war, if not eliminate it altogether, gained political currency during most of the twentieth century. Given the numerous universal ideologies vying for supremacy, from liberalism, to Fascism, to Communism, to religious fundamentalism, the rival great powers have been increasingly disposed to portray themselves as champions of peace, and their opponents as warmongers. At the same time, establishing the League of Nations, and later the United Nations, those powers indicated a certain willingness to tone down the 'bad-state-good-state' recriminations in favour of a concerted effort to regularize international relations and reduce the occurrence of war.

In justifying his decision to take the United States into the First World War, merely a year after praising the merits of neutrality, President Woodrow Wilson described the move as implementation of a moral obligation to help the forces of light, the democratic states, in their Manichaean struggle against the forces of darkness, the authoritarian states. Some six decades later, another American President, Ronald Reagan, blamed the 'Second Cold War' on the 'evil empire', as he labelled the Soviet Union. When Communist regimes in Eastern Europe crumbled in a rapid succession during the momentous events of 1989 there was even talk of the End of History as the struggle between Liberal-Democracy and Communism was irreversibly decided in favour of the former, and Western liberalism triumphed as the universal ideology. War, as the world had known for quite a long time, would never be the same again. Michael Doyle's Kantian analysis supporting the proposition that democratic states do not fight each other (34) was much cited.

Not surprisingly, things looked differently on the other side of the Atlantic. To Marxist-Leninists, including those occupying the Kremlin between 1917 and 1991, the distinction between peaceful and aggressive states is immaterial. Rather, the nation-state as a socio-political institution is the root of all evil, the cause of war. As argued by Vladimir Lenin (32) war is nothing but an oppressive tool allowing the ruling classes to keep the oppressed classes in awe. Once Socialism triumphs, the state will wither away, and with it the phenomenon of war. Until then, war is a necessary, indeed a legitimate instrument to spread the socialist message throughout the world. There is nothing immoral in war as such: what determines its moral value is the cause for which it is fought. Wars waged by the oppressed classes against their oppressors are legitimate and just, wars fought to perpetuate reactionary and oppressive institutions are immoral. Nor do Third World societies share the Western definition of 'good' and 'bad'. While American intervention in Vietnam was officially justified by the need to contain Communist expansionism, it was viewed by many in the Third World as an offspring of America's own imperialist designs. When George Bush led an international coalition to war against Iraq under the banner of defending the New World Order, he was accused of cynically manipulating world public opinion to disguise his real agenda: ensuring the uninterrupted flow of cheap oil to the West.

While each of these criticisms has some validity, the truth is that war in the twentieth century has had less to do with the promotion of 'good' and the eradication of 'evil' than with the pursuit of specific self-serving interests. Wars have stemmed from such varied reasons as ambition, greed, or insecurity, and have been waged for such objectives as power seeking, territorial aggrandizement, ethnic and national rivalries, or religious schisms. It requires a real stretch of imagination to perceive America's consistent support for Third World dictators over the past half a century in terms of promotion of liberal ideals. Nor is it at all clear how Soviet backing of Third World regimes, at a time when these very regimes were suppressing their own Communist parties, could contribute to the spread of socialist values worldwide. Nor can Third World volatility be solely attributed to the colonial legacy, as many underlying causes of war and conflict in that part of the world predated European colonialism and have outlived its demise.

Debunking the popular image of warlike and peaceable animals, biologist Konrad Lorenz has pointed out that wolves possess the inhibition of pity, tending to spare their own kind, while doves are normally merciless to the vanquished. In his view, this dichotomy holds supreme significance for the future of the human race:

The day will come when two warring factions will have the possibility of exterminating each other completely. The day may come when all humanity will thus be divided into two opposing camps. Will we then behave like the doves or like the wolves? The answer to this question will settle humanity's fate.[2]

While Lorenz's fear of a possible nuclear armageddon appears to have been rendered largely anachronistic by the end of the Cold War and the emergence of the New World Order, his general observation regarding the human nature remains valid. As starkly demonstrated by the bitter internecine wars in the former Yogoslav and Soviet republics, war is far from being eliminated as a social and political phenomenon; rather, it is likely to continue to bedevil mankind for the foreseeable future.

[2] Konrad Lorenz, *King Solomon's Ring*, as cited in Raymond Aron, *Peace and War: A Theory of International Relations* (Malabasi, Fla.: Krieger, 1981), 356.

24 **Definitions of War**

In the broadest sense war is a *violent contact* of *distinct* but *similar* entities. In this sense a collision of stars, a fight between a lion and a tiger, a battle between two primitive tribes, and hostilities between two modern nations would all be war. This broad definition has been elaborated for professional purposes by lawyers, diplomats, and soldiers and for scientific discussion by sociologists and psychologists.

International lawyers and diplomats have usually followed Grotius' conception of war as 'the condition of those contending by force as such', though they have often excluded from the conception duels between individuals and insurrections, aggressions, or other conditions of violent contention between juridical unequals. Furthermore, they have insisted that 'force' refers to military, naval, or air force, that is, to 'armed force', thus excluding from the definition contentions involving only moral, legal, or economic force. Grotius criticized Cicero's definition of war as simply 'a contending by force' because, he said, war was 'not a contest but a condition'. Modern dictionaries, however, have followed Cicero, and sociologists have accepted the same popular conception with the qualification that violent contention cannot be called war unless it involves actual conflict and constitutes a socially recognized form or custom within the society where it occurs. From the sociological point of view war is, therefore, a socially recognized form of intergroup conflict involving violence.

Legal and sociological definitions suggest that 'states of war' are separated by exact points of time from 'states of peace' which precede and follow them. International lawyers have attempted to elaborate precise criteria for determining the moment at which a war begins and ends, but they have not been entirely successful, and, furthermore, they have been obliged to acknowledge the occurrence of interventions, aggressions, reprisals, defensive expeditions, sanctions, armed neutralities, insurrections, rebellions, mob violence, piracy, and banditry as lying somewhere between war and peace as those terms are popularly understood. The recognition of such situations casts doubt upon the reality of a sharp distinction between war and peace and suggests the utility of searching for a variable of which war and peace are extreme conditions. Such a variable might be found in the external forms or the internal substance of international relations.

Philosophically minded military writers have sought the first, emphasizing the degree in which military methods are employed. Thus, Clausewitz defined war as 'an act of violence intended to compel our opponents to fulfill our will', and elsewhere he emphasized the continuity of violence with other political methods. 'War', he wrote, 'is nothing but a continuation of political intercourse, with a mixture of other means.'

Psychologists, ignoring the form, have found the substance of war in the degree of hostile attitude in the relation of states. Thus, Hobbes compared the oscillations of war and peace to the weather: 'As the nature of foul weather lieth not in a shower or two of rain, but in an inclination thereto of many days together; so the nature of war consisteth not in actual fighting, but in the known disposition thereto during all the time there is no assurance to the contrary.' As the weather may manifest many degrees of fairness or foulness, so the relations of any pair of states may be cordial, friendly, correct, strained, ruptured, hostile, or any shade between.

We may thus conceive of the relations of every pair of states as continually varying and occasionally passing below a certain threshold, in which case they may be described by the term 'war', whether or not other states recognize the situation as juridically a 'state of war' and whether or not the precise form of conflict which sociologists designate 'war' has developed. Subjectively there might be war, although objectively there might not be.

Whatever point of view is selected, war appears to be a species of a wider genus. War is only one of many abnormal legal situations. It is but one of numerous conflict procedures. It is only an extreme case of group attitudes. It is only a very large-scale resort to violence. A study of each of these broader categories when applied to the specific characteristics of war— abnormal states of law between equals, conflict between social groups, hostile attitudes of great intensity, and intentional violence through use of armed force—may throw light upon the phenomenon of war, although war itself does not exist except when hostility and violence contemporaneously pass beyond a certain threshold producing a new situation which law and opinion recognize as war.

Combining the four points of view, war is seen to be a state of law and a form of conflict involving a high degree of legal equality, of hostility, and of violence in the relations of organized human groups, or, more simply, the legal condition which equally permits two or more hostile groups to carry on a conflict by armed force.

It is to be observed that this definition implies sufficient social solidarity throughout the community of nations of which both belligerents and neutrals are members to permit general recognition of the behaviors and standards appropriate to the situation of war. Although war manifests the weakness of the community of nations, it also manifests the existence of that community.

[From Quincy Wright, *A Study of War*, abridged by Louise Leonard Wright (Chicago and London: University of Chicago Press, 1966), 5–7.]

25   Man, the State, and War

Can man in society best be understood by studying man or by studying society? The most satisfactory reply would seem to be given by striking the word 'or' and answering 'both'. But where one begins his explanation of events makes a difference. The Reverend Thomas Malthus once wrote that, 'though human institutions appear to be the obvious and obtrusive causes of much mischief to mankind; yet, in reality, they are light and superficial, they are mere feathers that float on the surface, in comparison with those deeper seated causes of impurity that corrupt the springs, and render turbid the whole stream of human life.' Rousseau looked at the same world, the same range of events, but found the locus of major causes in a different ambit.

Following Rousseau's lead in turn raises questions. As men live in states, so states exist in a world of states. If we now confine our attention to the question of why wars occur, shall we emphasize the role of the state, with its social and economic content as well as its political form, or shall we concentrate primarily on what is sometimes called the society of states? Again one may say strike the word 'or' and worry about both, but many have emphasized either the first or the second, which helps to explain the discrepant conclusions reached. Those who emphasize the first in a sense run parallel to Milton. He explains the ills of the world by the evil in man; they explain the great ill of war by the evil qualities of some or of all states. The statement is then often reversed: If bad states make wars, good states would live at peace with one another. With varying degrees of justification this view can be attributed to Plato and Kant, to nineteenth-century liberals and revisionist socialists. They agree on the principle involved, though they differ in their descriptions of good states as well as on the problem of bringing about their existence.

Where Marxists throw the liberals' picture of the world into partial eclipse, others blot it out entirely. Rousseau himself finds the major causes of war neither in men nor in states but in the state system itself. Of men in a state of nature, he had pointed out that one man cannot begin to behave decently unless he has some assurance that others will not be able to ruin him. This thought Rousseau develops and applies to states existing in a condition of anarchy in his fragmentary essay on 'The State of War' and in his commentaries on the works of the Abbé de Saint-Pierre. Though a state may want to remain at peace, it may have to consider undertaking a preventive war; for if it does not strike when the moment is favorable it may be struck later when the advantage has shifted to the other side. This view forms the analytic basis for many balance-of-power approaches to international relations and for the world-federalist program as well. Implicit in Thucydides and Alexander Hamilton, made explicit by Machiavelli, Hobbes, and Rousseau, it is at once a generalized explanation of states' behavior and a critical *point d'appui* against those who look to the internal structure of states to explain their external behavior. While some believe that peace will follow from the improvement of states, others assert that what the state will be like depends on its relation to others. The latter thesis Leopold Ranke derived from, or applied to, the history of the states of modern Europe. It has been used to explain the internal ordering of other states as well.

Statesmen, as well as philosophers and historians, have attempted to account for the behavior of states in peace and in war. Woodrow Wilson, in the draft of a note written in November of 1916, remarked that the causes of the war then being fought were obscure, that neutral nations did not know why it had begun and, if drawn in, would not know for what ends they would be fighting. But often to act we must convince ourselves that we do know the answers to such questions. Wilson, to his own satisfaction, soon did. He appears in history as one of the many who, drawing a sharp distinction between peaceful and aggressive states, have assigned to democracies all the attributes of the first, to authoritarian states all the attributes of the second. To an extent that varies with the author considered, the incidence of war is then thought to depend upon the type of national government. Thus Cobden in a speech at Leeds in December of 1849:

Where do we look for the black gathering cloud of war? Where do we see it rising? Why, from the despotism of the north, where one man wields the destinies of 40,000,000 of serfs. If we want to know where is the second danger of war and disturbance, it is in that province of Russia—that miserable and degraded country, Austria—next in the stage of despotism and barbarism, and there you see again the greatest danger of war; but in proportion as you find the population governing themselves—as in England, in France, or in America—there you will find that war is not the disposition of the people, and that if Government desire it, the people would put a check upon it.

The constant interest of the people is in peace; no government controlled by the people will fight unless set upon. But only a few years later, England, though not set upon, did fight against Russia; and Cobden lost his seat in 1857 as a result of his opposition to the war. The experience is shattering, but not fatal to the belief; for it relives in the words of Wilson, for example, and again in those of the late Senator Robert Taft. In the manner of Cobden but in the year 1951, Taft writes: 'History shows that when the people have the opportunity to speak they as a rule decide for peace if possible. It shows that arbitrary rulers are more inclined to favor war than are the people at any time.' Is it true, one wonders, that there is a uniquely peaceful form of the state? If it were true, how much would it matter? Would it enable some states to know which other states they could trust? Should the states that are already good seek ways of making other states better, and thus make it possible for all men to enjoy the pleasures of peace? Wilson believed it morally imperative to aid in the political regeneration of others; Cobden thought it not even justifiable. Agreeing on where the causes are to be found, they differ in their policy conclusions.

But what of those who incline to a different estimate of major causes? 'Now people,' President Dwight Eisenhower has said, 'don't want conflict—people in general. It is only, I think, mistaken leaders that grow too belligerent and believe that people really want to fight.' Though apparently not all people want peace badly enough, for, on a different occasion, he had this to say: 'If the mothers in every land could teach their children to understand the homes and hopes of children in every other land—in America, in Europe, in the Near East, in Asia—the cause of peace in the world would indeed be nobly served.' Here the President seems to agree with Milton on where cause is to be found, but without Milton's pessimism—or realism, depending on one's preconceptions. Aggressive tendencies may be inherent, but is their misdirection inevitable? War begins in the minds and emotions of men, as all acts do: but can minds and emotions be changed? And, if one agrees that they can be, how much and how fast can whose minds and feelings be changed? And, if other factors are relevant as well, how much difference would the changes make? The answers to these questions and to those of the preceding paragraph are not obvious, but they are important. How can they best be sought?

Some would suggest taking possible answers as hypotheses to be investigated and tested empirically. This is difficult. Most English liberals at the time of the First World War argued, as did Wilson, that the militarist and authoritarian character of the German state prompted Germany to seek the war that soon spread to most of the world. At the same time some liberals, most notably G. Lowes Dickinson, argued that no single state could be held guilty. Only by understanding the international system, or lack of system, by which the leaders of states were often forced to act with slight regard for conventional morality, could one understand and justly assess the processes by which the war was produced. Dickinson was blasted by liberals and socialists alike for reversing the dominant inside-out explanation. Acceptance or rejection of explanatory theses in matters such as this most often depends on the skill of the pleaders and the mood of the audience. These are obviously not fit criteria, yet it would be foolish to argue that simply by taking a more intensive look at the data a compelling case could be built for one or the other explanatory theory. Staring at the same set of data, the parties to the debate came to sharply different conclusions, for the images they entertained led them to select and interpret the data in different ways. In order to make sense of the liberals' hypothesis we need somehow to acquire an idea of the interrelation of many possibly relevant factors, and these interrelations are not given in the data we study. We establish or, rather, assert them ourselves. To say 'establish' would be dangerous; for, whether or not we label them as such, we cannot escape from philosophic assumptions. The idea we entertain becomes a filter through which we pass our data. If the data are selected carefully, they will pass like milk through cheesecloth. The recalcitrance of the data may cause us to change one filter for another, to modify or scrap the theory we hold—or it may produce ever more ingenious selection and interpretation of data, as has happened with many Marxists trying to salvage the thesis that with the development of capitalism the masses become increasingly impoverished.

If empirical investigations vary in incidence and in result with the ideas the empiricists entertain, it is worth asking ourselves if the ideas themselves can be subjected to scrutiny. Obviously they can be. The study of politics is distinguished from other social studies by concentration upon the institutions and processes of government. This focuses the political scientists' concern without constituting a self-denying ordinance against the use of materials and techniques of other social scientists. On the latter point there is no difficulty for the student of international relations; there is considerable difficulty on the former, for international relations are characterized by the absence of truly governmental institutions, which in turn gives a radically different twist to the relevant processes. Yet there is a large and important sense in which traditional political philosophy, concentrating as it does upon domestic politics, is relevant for the student of international relations. Peace, it is often said, is the problem of the twentieth century. It is also one of the continuing concerns of political philosophers. In times of relative quiescence the question men put is likely to be: What good is life without justice and freedom? Better to die than live a slave. In times of domestic troubles, of hunger and civil war, of pressing insecurity, however, many will ask: Of what use is freedom without a power sufficient to establish and maintain conditions of security? That life takes priority over justice and freedom is taken to be a self-evident truth by St Augustine and Luther, by Machiavelli, Bodin, and Hobbes. If the alternative to tyranny is chaos and if chaos means a war of all against all, then the willingness to endure tyranny becomes understandable. In the absence of order there can be no enjoyment of liberty. The problem of identifying and achieving the conditions of peace, a problem that plagues man and bedevils the student of international relations, has, especially in periods of crisis, bedeviled political philosophers as well.

R. G. Collingwood once suggested that the best way to understand the writings of philosophers is to seek out the questions they were attempting to answer. It is here suggested that the best way to examine the problems of international political theory is to pose a central question and identify the answers that can be given to it. One may seek in political philosophy answers to the question: Where are the major causes of war to be found? The answers are bewildering in their variety and in their contradictory qualities. To make this variety manageable, the answers can be ordered under the following three headings: within man, within the structure of the separate states, within the state system. The basis of this ordering, as well as its relevance in the world of affairs, is suggested in the preceding pages. These three estimates of cause will subsequently be referred to as images of international relations, numbered in the order given, with each image defined according to where one locates the nexus of important causes.

Previous comments indicate that the views comprised by any one image may in some senses be as contradictory as are the different images *inter se*. The argument that war is inevitable because men are irrevocably bad, and the argument that wars can be ended because men can be changed, are contradictory; but since in each of them individuals are taken to be the locus of cause, both are included in the first image. Similarly, acceptance of a third-image analysis may lead to the false optimism of the world federalists or to the often falsely defined pessimism of a *Realpolitik* position. Since in all respects but one there may be variety of opinion within images and since prescription is related to goal as well as to analysis, there is no one prescription for each image. There are, however, in relation to each image-goal pairing, logical and illogical prescriptions.

One can say that a prescription is wrong if he can show that following it does not bring about the predicted result. But can one ever show that a prescription was actually followed? One often hears statements like this: 'The League of Nations didn't fail; it was never tried.' And such statements are irrefutable. But even if empirical disproof were possible, the problem of proving a prescription valid would remain to be solved. A patient who in one period of illness tries ten different medications may wonder just which pill produced the cure. The apportioning of credit is often more difficult than the assigning of blame. If a historical study were to show that in country A increases in national prosperity always followed increases in tariffs, to some observers this might seem to prove that high tariffs are a cause of prosperity; to others, that both of these factors are dependent on a third; and to still others, nothing at all. The empirical approach, though necessary, is not sufficient. The correlation of events means nothing, or at least should not be taken to mean anything, apart from the analysis that accompanies it.

If there is no empirical solution to the problem of prescription verification, what solution is there? Prescription is logically impossible apart from analysis. Every prescription for greater peace in the world is then related to one of our three images of international relations, or to some combination of them. An understanding of the analytical terms of each of the images will open up two additional possibilities for accepting or rejecting prescriptions. (1) A prescription based on a faulty analysis would be unlikely to produce the desired consequences. The assumption that to improve men in a prescribed way will serve to promote peace rests on the further assumption that in some form the first image of international relations is valid. The latter assumption should be examined before the former is made. (2) A prescription would be unacceptable if it were not logically related to its analysis. One who suffers from infected tonsils profits little from a skilfully performed appendectomy. If violence among states is caused by the evilness of man, to aim at the internal reform of states will not do much good. And if violence among states is the product of international anarchy, to aim at the conversion of individuals can accomplish little. One man's prognosis confounds the other man's prescription. If the validity of the images themselves can be ascertained, the critical relating of prescription to image becomes a check on the validity of prescriptions. There is, however, an additional complicating factor. Some combination of our three images, rather than any one of them, may be required for an accurate understanding of international relations. We may not be in a situation where one can consider just the patient's tonsils or his appendix. Both may be infected but removing either may kill the patient. In other words, understanding the likely consequences of any one cause may depend on understanding its relation to other causes. The possible interrelation of causes makes the problem of estimating the merit of various prescriptions more difficult still.

What are the criteria of merit? Suppose we consider again the person who argues that 'bad' states produce war, that 'good' states would live peacefully together, that therefore we must bring states into accord with a prescribed pattern. To estimate the merit of such a series of propositions requires asking the following questions: (1) Can the final proposition be implemented, and if so, how? (2) Is there a logical relation between prescription and image? In other words, does the prescription attack the assigned causes? (3) Is the image adequate, or has the analyst simply seized upon the most spectacular cause or the one he thinks most susceptible to manipulation and ignored other causes of equal or greater importance? (4) How will attempts to fill the prescription affect other goals? This last question is necessary since peace is not the only goal of even the most peacefully inclined men or states. One may, for example, believe that world government and perpetual peace are synonymous, but one may also be convinced that a world state would be a world tyranny and therefore prefer a system of nation-states with a perpetual danger of war to a world state with a promise of perpetual peace.

[From Kenneth Waltz, *Man, the State and War: A Theoretical Analysis* (New York: Columbia University Press, 1960), 5–15.]

26 **Biological and Psychological Roots**

Biologists call *aggressiveness* the propensity of an animal to attack another, of the same species or of a different species. Most animals, but not all, fight within each species. Some are not aggressive—that is, do not take the initiative of attack, but defend themselves when attacked.

According to biologists, fighting, in the animal kingdom, cannot be regarded as either accidental or abnormal. Aggression is a constant and apparently a useful part of the daily behavior of many animals and becomes destructive and harmful only under exceptional circumstances.

Vertebrates of all classes—fish, amphibians, reptiles, birds, mammals—fight. The primates, among which are included the human race, are very unequally combative from the 'gibbons in which both sexes fight so vigorously that they can exist only in small family groups to the howling monkeys whose fighting never grows beyond vocalization in either sex.'[1] The human race is situated on the upper part of the aggressiveness scale among the primates. Man, as an animal, is relatively combative—in other words, a slight stimulus is enough to release aggression.

The primary stimuli of aggression, in the animal kingdom, are many, and some of them suggest conflicts among human beings. An animal that is made to suffer reacts aggressively; the mouse whose tail is pinched by the experimenter tries to bite him. Many animals, fish and birds fight for the defense of their space, which one is tempted to call a territory. The European sticklebacks fight savagely near their nests, but not elsewhere. Hence they rarely indulge in death struggles unless their nests are near each other. At equal distance from their respective nests, the sticklebacks do not attack, but threaten each other. The outcome of the struggle depends on the distance between the respective nests. The fish closest to its nest is victorious and its adversary flees toward its own place of residence. Similarly, certain mammals live in peace as long as each group does not leave what it appears to regard as 'its territory'; on the other hand, an individual belonging to another group is attacked and repulsed if it crosses the line of separation. Food and females are the other frequent stimuli of animal aggressiveness, although the diversity is extreme from one species to the other.

Combativeness or the propensity to aggression varies, within the same species, with sex, age, and often with individuals. Within a species the females are generally less inclined to aggression than the males, but certain females in the upper range of the female aggression scale may be above certain males at the lower range of the masculine aggression scale. Each

[1] J. P. Scott, *Aggression* (Chicago, 1958), 6.

human individual is endowed by heredity with a certain amount of aggressiveness. We know today that this amount can be increased or diminished
by chemical substances. Doctors report that they are now or will be capable
of making any man into a lion or a lamb, temporarily or permanently.
Whether animal or human, combativity has a strictly biological root.

Combative behavior is modified by the experience of the individual, is
learned and is forgotten. Biologists have experimented on mice and shown
conditioned reflexes of combat, flight and passivity, in response to one
stimulus or another. The learning of combative behavior conforms to the
general principles of learning which the Pavlovian school has demonstrated
for other kinds of behavior. J. P. Scott insists on a particular characteristic
of combative behavior: it disappears slowly. A long time is needed to inhibit
the aggressive reaction (as a result of the physiological and emotional
phenomena that accompany aggressiveness).

One of the methods of training mice for struggle is particularly striking.
An animal that for several days has been allowed apparent victories over
adversaries introduced earlier into its cage and then withdrawn . . . will
fling itself upon the first rival that resists it. Generally a victor, it becomes
still more combative. By easy successes an animal is made capable of
fighting, and made into a fierce combatant. A contrary habit either of
fleeing battle or of submitting to the stronger without fighting is created
among individual mice who have received punishment.

Whether spontaneous or the result of learning, combative behavior, to
the human observer, often seems adaptive. Whether the bird drives away
the 'alien' that approaches its nest, or dogs or baboons fight over a female,
aggression tends to remove the cause of the possible danger, to insure
something valuable to the victor. Further, animal struggle often leads to a
kind of order as war leads to peace.

When two hens meet for the first time, they generally fight; one wins and
the other loses. The next time they fight again but the loser gives up more
rapidly. After some time, a habit is formed for one of them to threaten
combat and for the other to run away. The first is called dominant and the
other subordinate. And this hierarchy of force, confirmed by the experience
of struggle, is stable, durable, pacified. Experimenters have the greatest
difficulty reversing the hierarchy—for example, inciting a dominated
mouse to resume the struggle.

Pacification by hierarchy, as a result of the outcome of the struggle, is the
contrary of spontaneous pacification among animals raised together, or
even among the adults and young living with them. But this primitive
socialization also creates, in the animal kingdom, differentiation among
family members and aliens, among members of the group and others. The
pacification of intra-social relations is often accompanied by the hostility of
relations between groups or among individuals of distinct groups.

Among the higher vertebrates, groups or packs often manifest aggressiveness with regard to alien individuals. Thus the wolf differentiates between the members of its own pack and others. More rarely, it is among
groups or packs that the aggressiveness is released. In the human race, on
the other hand, manifestations of aggressiveness are inseparable from collective life. Even when it is a question of one individual against another,
aggressiveness is in many ways influenced by the social context. Aggressiveness of the group toward one of its members, toward an outsider, or
toward another group as such—these three phenomena are normally to be
found in any society. A group of young boys has its internal hierarchy and
sometimes its scapegoat. It offers a united front to the isolated individuals
who do not submit to discipline, and sometimes explodes into hostility
against a rival group.

The advent of a truly social existence is not the only factor responsible
for the new dimensions assumed by the phenomenon of aggressiveness:
frustration and non-adaptation resulting from the aggressive reaction constitute the major phenomenon in human relations. Now frustration is a
psychic experience; our consciousness reveals it to us. Every human individual experiences frustration from his earliest years. He suffers from being
deprived of food, affection, and rarely has the means of adapting himself by
aggression to this situation of which he feels himself the victim. He is
wounded by the behavior of others, and he cannot cure his wound by
fighting against his aggressor, whether the latter is deliberate or not. He
does not manifest his aggressiveness externally, but far from being 'at
peace' internally, he is quite agitated with repressed fury, with contained
hostility.

Psychoanalysts have analyzed the mechanisms by which psychic disturbances are produced by such frustrations. Biologists or psychologists with
objective leanings have sought the equivalent, in the animal kingdom or by
experimental learning, of the frustration-aggression mechanism. Pavlov's
disciples have produced, as we know, what might be called neurotic behavior: when two stimuli (a circle and an ellipse), one of which releases a
positive reflex and the other a negative reflex, tend to approach each other,
there comes a moment when the dog, incapable of distinguishing between
the two signals, behaves aggressively, howls and tries to bite. Unable to run
away or to adapt himself, he attacks his collar, anything at all. Other
experiments of the same type, the connecting of two contradictory reflexes, have yielded the same result, namely, 'artificial' neurosis and aggressive, non-adaptive behavior.

There is no contradiction, in fact, between the psychological interpretation of aggression in terms of learning and conditioned reflexes and the
Freudian interpretation in terms of frustration. Nonetheless, the facts do
not support the assertion that aggression, in the animal kingdom, always

has frustration for its cause (easy victories reinforce the tendency to combativeness) or that frustrations are always expressed by aggression. Certain animals fight less when they are deprived of food. Personally, however, I would not wholeheartedly subscribe to the formula according to which *'frustration leads to aggression only in a situation in which the individual has the habit of being aggressive,'*[1] but it does seem true to me that the frustrated individual is somehow irritable. The threshold of aggressive reaction is lower for him than it would be for another individual.

This, however, is not the essential point. Biologists, from an external viewpoint, can define frustration as the incapacity to make a response that is adapted to the situation. Frustration is first of all, for each of us, the experience of privation, of a goal desired and not obtained, of an oppression suffered. The brother who deprives the newborn baby of a share of his mother's attention provokes the baby's aggression. This aggression will generally be incapable of expressing itself in an 'adapted' manner. Often, it will express itself in no manner at all, or will be transferred, by identification, to some innocent person, or will be repressed in the unconscious. If non-adaptation is common to the reaction of the mouse that can neither fight nor run away, and to that of the child deprived of a share of his mother's love, what matters to us is not the identity or the similarity of the mechanism, but that men, from their earliest years, live in such a way that they inevitably come into conflict with each other, so to speak attack each other, and invent countless means, verbal and imaginary, to express their hostile sentiments without physical fighting.

A combative animal among the primates, man, according to the psychologists, is moved by impulses—sexuality, the desire for possession, the will to supremacy—which put him in competition with his kind and, almost inevitably, in conflict with some among them. Of course, he does not feel the need for combat as he feels the need for food or sexual satisfaction. The chain of causality which leads to emotions or acts of aggressiveness can always be traced back to an external phenomenon. There is no physiological evidence of a spontaneous impulse to fighting, the origin of which is in the body itself. The human animal happy enough to live in an environment offering no occasion, no motive for fighting, would suffer no damage, either physiological or nervous.

But, without even suggesting the death instinct Freud speaks of, ambivalence of feelings and rivalry among individuals for coveted goals are phenomena of experience, constants which reveal an *element of conflict* in most if not all interpersonal relations. Man does not fight his kind by instinct, but he is, at every moment, the victim and the executioner of his fellow man. Physical aggression and the will to destroy are not the only

---

[1] *Ibid.* 35 (Scott's italics).

response to frustration, but they are one of the possible responses and perhaps the spontaneous one. In this sense the philosophers were not mistaken to consider that man is *by nature* dangerous to man.

[From Raymond Aron, *Peace and War: A Theory of International Relations* (Malabari, Fla.: Krieger, 1981), 340–4.]

SAUL B. COHEN

27 Geopolitics

It fell to the German geographer Friedrich Ratzel to make the first systematic studies of political areas. Ratzel was not the first to recognize that differences in the physical and cultural environment contributed directly to the political division of the earth. He was, however, the first to treat space and location systematically in his comparative studies of states, and it is for this reason that Friedrich Ratzel is regarded as the founder of modern political geography. [. . .]

Perhaps the most significant contribution of Ratzel to our ideas of the geographical setting lay in correlating continental areas with political power. Ratzel felt that man's need for large space, and the ability to utilize it effectively, would be the political dictum of twentieth-century international politics. In this he was most deeply influenced (as Guyot had been) by his studies of the United States—the first modern state to evolve within a 'great space' framework. Relegating Europe, eventually, to a minor role in world politics, Ratzel felt that history would be dominated by larger states occupying continental areas, like North America, Asiatic Russia, Australia, and South America. In this continental approach there was, and still remains, the frequent contradiction between the advantages of large space and the disadvantages of location. This approach also is weakened when it fails to account for the qualitative and quantitative differences of man-resource ratios within comparable continental areas.

It remained for Halford Mackinder to combine great space and location in a view of the geographical setting that attributed pre-eminence to one continental portion of the world. Mackinder's geographic writings and lectures over the span of the first half of the twentieth century are best known for their influence upon German geopolitics and for the strategic counter-doctrines they inspired. [. . .]

Mackinder's theory, first propounded in 1904, was that the inner area of Eurasia is the pivot region of world politics. He warned that rule of the heart of the world's greatest landmass could become the basis for world domination. Mackinder felt that it was entirely possible for the land power that gained control of the pivot area (be it Russia, Germany, or even China) to outflank the maritime world. Eleven years later, James Fairgrieve was to point out even more forcefully that China was in an excellent position to dominate Inner Eurasia.

It can be seen that the pivot area, as defined in 1904, was that part of eastern Europe and northern Asia characterized by polar or interior drainage.[1]

What many critics have failed to note, as they have elaborated on Mackinder's theories, is that his views of the world kept changing. As a geographer, Mackinder was more aware than most of his critics that man's use of the physical environment constantly changes, and that even the environment itself changes, albeit at an almost indiscernible pace.

Mackinder's 1919 map demonstrates his changing views of the world. The Heartland, as defined in 1919, was revised to include the Tibetan and Mongolian upland courses of the great rivers of India and China. Also, while not labeled Heartland, Eastern and Central Europe were introduced as a strategic addition to the Heartland, and for all practical purposes are considered Heartland. Mackinder's new boundary took into account advances in land transportation, population increases, and industrialization. Because of these advances, he felt that the Baltic and Black Sea land areas had become strategically part of the Heartland. These areas essentially lie within the Eurasian Lowland Plain and within the winter snowline. The term *Heartland*, incidentally, was not actually introduced by Mackinder, but by James Fairgrieve in his 1915 work, *Geography and World Power*.

It was in Mackinder's 1919 volume that he enjoined the statesmen of the West to remember this saying: 'Who rules East Europe commands the Heartland: Who rules the Heartland commands the World-Island: Who rules the World-Island commands the World.' Thus, the middle tier of German and Slavic states, from Estonia to Bulgaria, becomes, in Mackinder's opinion, the key to world domination—a key then as available to Germany as to Russia.

Seldom have one man's theories been so exposed to critical examination as have those of Mackinder over the past decades—after years of passive or uncritical acceptance. But when all is said and done, most Western strategists continue to view the world as initially described by Mackinder. American foreign policy of containment in the postwar era, with overseas alliances peripheral to the Eurasian landmass, was an attempt to head off Soviet-controlled Heartland's dominion over the World-Island. Containment of Mainland China by the United States has had, as its objective, the sealing off of the remainder of the East Asian maritime reaches of the World Island, given the major breach made by the introduction of Communism to East Asia.

[1] Halford J. Mackinder, 'The Geographical Pivot of History', *Geographical Journal*, 23 (1904), 422.

German Geopolitics

German geopolitics adopted the world *Geopolitik*, and much of its organismic-Hegelian philosophy, from the Swedish political scientist Rudolph Kjellén. For its views of the geographical setting, geopolitics seized upon diverse and occasionally contradictory concepts that had been sketched out by Ratzel and Mackinder. Led by Karl Haushofer, the geopoliticians preached conflict, strategy, and total war. They made household slogans of such words as *Lebensraum* (living space) and *Autarchy* (economic self-sufficiency) in a post-World War One Germany which ached for the restoration of the *Reich* to world power status.

Three geographical settings kept recurring in the literature of German geopolitics: (1) Ratzel's large states, (2) Mackinder's World-Island, and (3) north–south combinations of continents. Haushofer, harking back to Ratzel's laws on the spatial growth of states, saw large states as the wave of the future. Mastery of Germany over smaller states to the west and the east within Europe was regarded as 'inevitable', and the conflict needed to bring this about as completely justifiable, because continental mastery in Europe was the goal.

Haushofer saw in Mackinder's World-Island the spatial framework for German hegemony over the new World Order. The German geopoliticians had two objectives in World-Island: (1) dominance over Russia to achieve Eurasian mastery, and (2) destruction of British seapower to gain complete World-Island rule. Haushofer held that landpower possessed a fundamental advantage over seapower. He looked to a German-Russian alliance as the core of Eurasian union with a broader transcontinental bloc that was to include China and Japan. Indeed, during most of the 1920s and 1930s, Haushofer called for Japan to accommodate itself with China and the Soviet Union, just as he propagandized for German-Soviet friendship.

Ratzel's correlating of continental areas with world power status influenced the geopoliticians in two ways: (1) their Pan- European concepts, and (2) their pan-regional concepts in general. The geopoliticians spoke of Eastern Europe as lying within the 'European law of geopolitics'. By so doing they claimed an inherent continental unity for Europe, whose eastern boundary was defined as a line running from Lake Peipus to the lower course of the Dneister River. The USSR was considered Asian by Haushofer. Europe, including the Slavic lands of Eastern Europe, was to be unified under Germany as the prerequisite to achieving accommodation with the Russians over the fate of Eurasia.

Thus, Eastern Europe was to be the springboard for German ambitions in Eurasia. The German geopoliticians generally hoped to force the Russians into a voluntary agreement in the control of Eurasia. Military conquest of the Soviet Union was never wholeheartedly subscribed to by

Haushofer, who doubted that blitzkrieg methods would succeed in conquering the vast Russian space.

A different form of continental setting was proposed by the geopoliticians in their pan-regional concepts. Alternately suggesting three or four regions (Pan-America, Pan-Eurafrica, Pan-East Asia, and when matters suited them, Pan-Russia), the geopoliticians suggested that the world be organized along north–south double-continent lines. This was to provide for complementary products and peoples. Within continental boundaries, they argued, lay the vast, contiguous space and the self-sufficiency of economy that would enable world power equilibrium to be attained.

In theory, however, Haushofer could never reconcile this pan-regional subdivision with an Old World-New World geopolitical division, which he frequently proposed. For he felt that Pan-Eurafrica, Pan-Russia, and Pan-East Asia would have to combine to stand on a par with Pan-America. In this last geographical setting, the Old World-New World equilibrium, we find a contradiction to the Mackinder view, which had also been espoused by Haushofer. This latter view considered the Americas as separate continental islands, destined to remain satellites of the World-Island.

The inadequacies of the pan-regional concept have been pointed out by many. Pan-regions could only be achieved by war. They did not offer the world a strategic equilibrium, for the southern half of each pan-region is not sufficiently remote from the opposing northern core region to be free of its pressures, and will therefore remain in an exploited rather than complementary state, preventing internal harmony by inhibiting stability. South America is no closer to North America than it is to Africa or Europe; Africa is as close to the USSR as it is to Germany; and India is not much farther away from East Asia than it is from most of the USSR.

Nonetheless, it must be pointed out that since the Second World War there has been a closer drawing together of the world on north–south lines, at least for economic purposes. Europe's withdrawal from South and East Asia has stimulated much stronger European-African economic contacts. Japan has increased its economic involvement with many of the lands to its south, and Mainland China has made strong inroads in part of Southeast Asia. Most recently, renewed United States concern with Latin America has redirected the thinking of many of our people along north–south lines. Whether economic lines necessarily presume or justify strategic ties, as suggested by the pan-regionalists is, of course, an entirely different proposition.

That German geopoliticians expressed such contradictory views of the geographical setting can be understood. *Geopolitik* lacked scientific limits. It was a normative rather than an empirical study. As a nationalist-propagandist doctrine in the Germany of the 1930's, *Geopolitik* did not have to meet standards of objective criticism, and thus lacked the basic elements of scholarly self-discipline. Also, with the launching of the Nazi attack against the Soviet Union, the geopoliticians dared not publish opinions that ran counter to Hitler's strategy of the moment. In fact, Karl Haushofer was imprisoned in the Dachau concentration camp in 1944, and his son Albrecht, also a geopolitician, was executed for having become implicated in the army plot against Hitler of 1944.

[From Saul B. Cohen, Geography and Politics in a World Divided (New York: Oxford University Press, 1975), 39–48.]

MARTIN VAN CREVELD

28 Why Men Fight

[T]his volume does not argue that war is biologically predetermined—no more, say, than are religion, science, productive work, or art. However, it does argue that war, far from being merely a means, has very often been considered an end—a highly attractive activity for which no other can provide an adequate substitute. The reason why other activities do not provide a substitute is precisely because they are 'civilized'; in other words, bound by artificial rules. Compared to war, *der Ernstfall* as the Germans used to say, every one of the many other activities in which men play with their lives is merely a game, and a trivial one at that. Though war too is in one sense an artificial activity, it differs from all the rest in that it offers complete freedom, including paradoxically freedom from death. War alone presents man with the opportunity of employing all his faculties, putting everything at risk, and testing his ultimate worth against an opponent as strong as himself. It is the stakes that can make a game serious, even noble. While war's usefulness as a servant of power, interest, and profit may be questioned, the inherent fascination it has held for men at all times and places is a matter of historical fact. When all is said and done, the only way to account for this fascination is to regard war as the game with the highest stakes of all.

Thus, to explain the occurrence of war, there is no need to see it as having been programmed into human nature; on the other hand, there is no proof that this is not so. In recent decades numerous experiments, some of them bizarre, have been carried out to determine whether the brain has a center where aggression is concentrated. The results have been ambiguous, since electrical stimulation of one and the same region is apparently capable of eliciting different responses under different circumstances. Even if the existence of such a center is ultimately confirmed, however, the relationship between it and the social activity known as war is bound to be exceedingly complex. A 'fighting neural complex', 'war gland', or 'aggressive gene' almost certainly will never be discovered, nor need one be postulated. So far nobody has the foggiest idea which structures in the brain are responsible for such typically human qualities as our ability to appreciate the true, the beautiful, the good, and the sacred. Yet few people—least of all the scientists who perform the experiments—have suggested that, because of this, the quest for sanctity, goodness, beauty, and truth does not form part of human nature.

The premise that war can, and often does, prove absolutely fascinating is by no means gainsaid by the fact that not all people fight all of the time, and that some of them have managed to avoid doing so for considerable periods. Most people never visit a museum nor attend a concert in their lives; yet this is not to say that paintings and music are not wonderful things. In war, as in every other field, the thrill is often vicarious. The fact that, in football, for the thousands of persons who roar their approval from the stands or from in front of the TV there are so few actual players does not mean that the game is not enjoyable—quite the contrary. Throughout history, a very large fraction of all games, literature, history, and art created by man owed their existence to the fact that they either imitated war or provided substitutes for it. It is true that, at any one given time and place, most people neither participate in games nor enjoy art. Still, the majority cannot be denied at least the inherent capacity of doing so, for to deny it to them would be to deny it to ourselves also. Furthermore, had war been going on at all times and at all places it would inevitably have become boring. This may be the best explanation as to why every war must ultimately end.

Nor is this in any way contradicted by the existence of countries that have managed to avoid war for comparatively long periods. War not merely serves power, it *is* power; to recall the episode in Swift where the Lilliputians battled each other on Gulliver's outstretched handkerchief, for the small to fight in the presence of the strong is self-defeating and invites ridicule. This consideration may help explain how countries such as Denmark and the Netherlands, which used to wage war with the best, acquired their present pacifism—and also how they may yet abandon that pacifism in the future. The same applies to such bitter enemies as France and Germany, Hungary and Romania, Bulgaria and Yugoslavia, that not so long ago were constantly at each other's throats. Having been gathered under the aegis of much stronger powers, it was probably shame as much as any other factor that caused these countries to halt their squabbles after 1945. However, the world is round. Already today there are abundant signs that in eastern Europe and parts of the Soviet Union at any rate the story has not yet come to an end.

Even Swiss neutrality, that great shining example, is only as old as are trinitarian social structures, and the state that embodies them. The *Eidgenossenschaft* of the disparate Swiss cantons was formed in 1291 under the pressure of war, nor would there have been much point to swearing an *Eid* (oath) of mutual assistance if there had not been a common enemy to fight. For some three centuries after that the people of the mountains had a reputation for bellicosity second to none, so much so that as mercenaries they were the preferred choice of every ruler from the Pope down. The usual explanation for Swiss neutrality—the country's geographical position—cannot account for the change. Clearly in this case neutrality hinges on the existence of frontiers and states as well as the latter's ability to prevent people from crossing the borders. It being the essence of low-intensity conflict that it recognizes neither states nor frontiers, however, the inference is clear. Already there have been cases when French, West German, and Italian terrorists sought refuge on Swiss soil; nor, probably, are terrorist organizations altogether without connections in Switzerland. Should the countries by which the Swiss are surrounded succumb to extensive low-intensity conflict, no doubt the time will come when Swiss people too zestfully join the fray.

All this boils down to saying that, in order to explain the occurrence of war, it is not necessary to postulate the existence of any ulterior objectives other than war itself. This study has had much to say concerning the shifting goals for which war has been fought at different times and places, yet throughout these changes war itself has always been a given. No doubt future generations will resort to various lines of reasoning, some of them so novel as to be almost unimaginable today, in order to justify to themselves and to others the wars that they wage. Meanwhile war's own by no mean negligible attractions will remain intact. No attempt at understanding, planning, and conducting it is likely to succeed if it fails to take those attractions into account; nor will taking them into account do much good unless they are valued, cherished, even loved, for their own sake. Thus, conventional strategic wisdom must be turned upside down. There exists a sense in which war, more than any other human activity, can make sense only to the extent that it is experienced not as a means but as an end. However unpalatable the fact, the real reason why we have wars is that men like fighting, and women like those men who are prepared to fight on their behalf.

To repeat, the true essence of war consists not just of one group killing another but of its members' readiness to be killed in return if necessary. Consequently the only way to bring about perpetual peace would be to somehow eradicate man's willingness, even eagerness, to take risks of every kind up to, and including, death. Whether this eagerness is biologically programmed—whether, to believe with Freud, there exists in the mind of each of us a death wish—this work cannot presume to decide. Even if such a wish does exist, very likely it is neither localized at one particular spot in the brain nor unlinked with other drives. To judge by what psychotherapeutic drugs do to those subjected to them, probably it can be excised only by turning people into zombies: that is, by simultaneously destroying other qualities considered essential to humanity, such as playfulness, curiosity, inventiveness, creativity, even the sheer joy of living. What all these activities have in common is that they involve coping with the unknown. To the extent that coping with the unknown both results in a feeling of power and is a manifestation of it, they themselves may be considered pale imitations of war. In the words of Helmut von Moltke, eternal peace is a dream. Given the price that we would have to pay, perhaps it is not even a beautiful dream.

To say that war involves playing with death is not to equate it with suicide; as the story of Massada proves, suicide is not the beginning of war but its end. Short of tampering with the mind of man, probably the only way to eliminate war is to so increase the power of government as to render its outcome certain in advance. It is conceivable, though most unlikely, that a world-wide, repressive, totalitarian, big-brother type regime will one day attempt to achieve this goal. Probably such a regime could establish itself only in the aftermath of a major nuclear war in which one center of power would somehow manage to eradicate all the rest without itself being eradicated. Nuclear bombardment would have to be followed by extensive police operations conducted, presumably, in a radioactive environment. Once secure in power, the regime would have to rely on a pervasive police apparatus as well as sophisticated technical equipment capable of monitoring everybody all of the time. To prevent the humans in the loop from being outwitted, subverted, or simply negligent, the technology in question would have to be automated in respect to both operation and maintenance. A completely automated thought-reading machine—for nothing less would do—would have to be hooked up with the human brain and capable of influencing it by chemical or electrical means. Robots would have to control men, men themselves turned into robots. We find ourselves caught in a cross between Huxley's *Brave New World* and Orwell's *1984*. So monstrous is the vision as to make even war look like a blessing.

The third way in which the will to fight, and hence war, might conceivably be eliminated would be to have women participate in it, not as auxiliaries or surreptitiously, but as full-fledged, equal partners. This is not the place to expound on the often imaginary psychological differences between the sexes, nor on the respective importance of biological and social factors in governing those differences. Suffice it to repeat that, with the exception of their disparate roles in the physical acts of procreation, childbearing, and nursing, nothing has ever been more characteristic of the relationship between men and women than men's unwillingness to allow women to take part in war and combat. Throughout history men have resented having to perform a woman's role as an insult to their manhood, even to the point where it was sometimes inflicted as a punishment; had they been forced to fight at the side of, and against, women, then either the affair would have turned into mock war—a common amusement in many cultures—or else they would have put down their arms in disgust. However desirable such an outcome may be in the eyes of some, it belongs to the realm of phantasy. One suspects that, should they ever be faced with such a choice, men might very well give up women before they give up war.

These, of course, are speculations. Their practical significance lies in the fact that, but for its fighting spirit, no armed force is worth a fig. Over the last few decades, regular armed forces—including some of the largest and the best—have repeatedly failed in numerous low-intensity conflicts where they seemed to hold all the cards. This should have caused politicians, the military, and their academic advisers to take a profound new look at the nature of war in our time; however, by and large no such attempt at re-evaluation was made. Held captive by the accepted strategic framework, time and time again the losers explained away their defeat by citing mitigating factors. Often they invoked an alleged stab in the back, blaming the politicians who refused them a free hand or else the home public which did not give them the support to which they felt entitled. In other cases they thrust their head in the sand and argued that they were defeated in a political war, psychological war, propaganda war, guerrilla war, terrorist war, in short anything but war properly speaking.

As the twentieth century is drawing to its conclusion, it is becoming clearer every day that this line of reasoning will no longer do. If only we are prepared to look, we can see a revolution taking place under our very noses. Just as no Roman citizen was left unaffected by the barbarian invasions, so in vast parts of the world no man, woman, and child alive today will be spared the consequences of the newly-emerging forms of war. Even in the most stable societies, the least they can expect is to have their identity checked and their persons searched at every turn. The nature of the entities by which war is made, the conventions by which it is surrounded, and the ends for which it is fought may change. However, now as ever war itself is alive and well; with the result that, now as ever, such communities as refuse to look facts in the face and fight for their existence will, in all probability, cease to exist.

[From Martin Van Creveld, *The Transformation of War* (New York: The Free Press, 1991), 218–23.]

IBN KHALDUN

29 **Four Kinds of War**

[R]oyal authority is a noble and enjoyable position. It comprises all the good things of the world, the pleasures of the body, and the joys of the soul.

Therefore, there is, as a rule, great competition for it. It rarely is handed over (voluntarily), but it may be taken away. Thus, discord ensues. It leads to war and fighting, and to attempts to gain superiority. [. . .]

Wars and different kinds of fighting have always occurred in the world since God created it. The origin of war is the desire of certain human beings to take revenge on others. Each (party) is supported by the people sharing in its group feeling. When they have sufficiently excited each other for the purpose and the two parties confront each other, one seeking revenge and the other trying to defend itself, there is war. It is something natural among human beings. No nation and no race (generation) is free from it.

The reason for such revenge is as a rule either jealousy and envy, or hostility, or zeal in behalf of God and His religion, or zeal in behalf of royal authority and the effort to found a kingdom.

The first (kind of war) usually occurs between neighbouring tribes and competing families.

The second (kind)—war caused by hostility—is usually found among savage nations living in the desert, such as the Arabs, the Turks, the Turkomans, the Kurds, and similar peoples. They earn their sustenance with their lances and their livelihood by depriving other people of their possessions. They declare war against those who defend their property against them. They have no further desire for rank and royal authority. Their minds and eyes are set only upon depriving other people of their possessions.

The third is the (kind) the religious law calls 'the holy war'.

The fourth (kind), finally, is dynastic war against seceders and those who refuse obedience.

These are the four kinds of war. The first two are unjust and lawless, the other two are holy and just wars.

> [From Ibn Khaldun, *The Muqaddimah: An Introduction to History*, trans. from the Arabic by Franz Rosenthal, ed. and abridged by N. J. Daood (Princeton, NJ: Princeton University Press, 1967), 123, 223–4.]

MARTIN WIGHT

30 Wars of Gain, Fear, and Doctrine

If we ask about the cause of a particular war, the answer we normally find satisfying, and the answer the historian normally gives us, is in terms of a motive inspired by relationships of power. The classic example is Thucydides' judgement that the real reason for the Peloponnesian War (though the reason the least often given) was the fear aroused in Sparta by the growth of Athenian power. This sentence has earned criticism from a generation of classical historians, who have reproved Thucydides for neglecting the social and economic causes. Nevertheless it endures for the student of politics as the prototypic statement of how we usually express the causes of war. When all our research on the framework of necessity is complete, we find the origins of wars in the decisions of governments, and sometimes the passions of peoples, prompted by relationships of power.

There are many kinds of wars: aggressive wars and preventive, prestige wars and wars of security, idealistic wars and perhaps even just wars. But it is convenient to classify them under three chief motives: wars of gain, wars of fear, and wars of doctrine. This grouping corresponds to the causes of war suggested by Hobbes, who was himself adapting the motives of Athenian imperialism described by Thucydides. We must remember that every war has at least two belligerents, and every belligerent has complex motives; but a predominant motive is generally not beyond the power of historians to arrive at agreement about.

The motive of gain is seen most unmixed in the wars by which the European powers extended the frontiers of international society to enclose the whole world, and in the subsequent wars for dividing the spoils of this imperialist expansion—those wars with a transparently economic motive, like the Anglo-Dutch wars in the seventeenth century and the Anglo-French in the eighteenth, which Adam Smith ascribed to 'the impertinent jealousy of merchants and manufacturers'. If these colonial wars are put on one side, the motive of gain, of sheer aggrandizement, is less conspicuous in international politics than you may expect. The peoples of Asia and Africa might be right in supposing that Western society has kept its aggressive impulses for export. To counter such a view (and confining ourselves to the great powers) we could only cite the earlier wars of both Louis XIV and Frederick the Great, together with Hitler's war, which was so shocking to Europeans precisely because he adopted within Europe the most ruthless methods of colonial expansion and exploitation.

With wars of fear, on the other hand, the problem is rather one of exclusion. By fear we mean, not an unreasoning emotion, but a rational apprehension of future evil, and this is the prime motive of international politics. For all powers at all times are concerned primarily with their security, and most powers at most times find their security threatened. It is worth remembering that the motive of fear prompts preventive war as well as defensive war, and that in the majority of wars between great powers the aggressor's motive has been preventive. 'There is perhaps no factor', G. F. Hudson has said, 'which drives a state into war so inexorably as a steady loss of relative power. Sooner or later a desperate now-or-never mood overcomes the calculations of prudence, and the belief that a war may be won today, but cannot be won tomorrow, becomes the most convincing of all arguments for an appeal to the sword.' This is a luminous statement of the Thucydidean fear. It is also, like all political truths, prophetic. It describes the Japanese attitude towards the United States, and was written five years before Pearl Harbor.

War of doctrine means missionary or crusading war, war to assert principles and advance a cause. If qualitative change is more important than quantitative, the striking development in war in the past two hundred years is not its growing destructiveness, but the way it has increasingly become the instrument of doctrinal conviction. For since the end of the eighteenth century, international society has been in a condition of stasis. It is convenient to use this Greek word for strife within communities as distinct from strife between them, since the English equivalents (civil discord or class-war) are both too narrow and too flaccid. Stasis appears in the international community when, in several states, bodies of men acquire loyalties which attach them more to bodies of men in other states than to their own fellow-citizens. The consequence, said Burke, who is our supreme commentator on the matter, 'is to introduce other interests into all countries than those which arise from their locality and natural circumstances'. Or, to borrow Arthur Koestler's language, 'horizontal forces' shake and distort 'the vertical structure of competing national egotisms'. The word horizontal is useful since it allows us to avoid the ambiguities of the word 'international'. The members of international society have never all been national states, and nationalism itself has been one of the most disruptive international doctrines, an inter-state revolutionary movement. Besides Marx's International there have been Mazzini's and Hitler's. The climax of international stasis is when a horizontal doctrine acquires a territorial foothold. The doctrine then becomes an armed doctrine, and the state where it is enthroned becomes, for its adherents abroad, an examplar, an asylum, and perhaps a saviour.

International stasis changes both the motive and character of war. On the one hand, it approximates war to revolution; on the other, it blurs the distinction between war and peace. The classic example of the doctrinal motive is the French Revolutionary War, when France 'attacked Europe in order to regenerate it'. Probably a purer example was the Soviet invasion of Poland in 1920, when the Red Army crossed the Curzon Line westwards in an enthusiastic confidence of European revolution. Nor is it beyond question whether this motive stirred in Stalin's mind when the second Soviet invasion of Europe began in 1944. But every war in Europe since 1792 has had some doctrinal motive, asserting some horizontal right against some vertical legitimacy, offering some state as saviour and liberator of some group of foreigners. Of the Crimean War this is least true, but yet not wholly untrue. And the assimilation of war to revolution is seen in effects as well as motives. Since the American Declaration of Independence in 1776, every war between great powers, with three exceptions and those before 1860, has led to revolution on the losing side.

The distinction between war and peace is the foundation of civilized life, and its observance rests on common moral and political standards. The horizontal doctrine repudiates the old international morality and the old international law; in Burke's phrase, it makes 'a schism with the whole universe'. Camus has penetratingly observed how the adherents of the universal doctrine set out to build the universal city, and how, by the logic of history and of the doctrine itself, the universal city becomes transformed into an empire, an empire proclaiming: 'Beyond the confines of the empire there is no salvation'. Since 1918, more effort has been spent than ever before on delimiting the theoretical borderline between peace and war, and in defining those acts which transgress it; while in practice the border-line has become more smudged than at any time since the Wars of Religion. Today it requires a mental effort from us to regard as abnormal circumstances in which ships are sunk and aircraft shot down without warning, peaceable citizens are kidnapped and disappear, traitors flee from one side to the other bringing secrets and receiving moral acclaim, prisoners are tortured into apostasy, and diplomacy is replaced by propaganda.

This blending of war with revolution, this indistinctness of war from peace, gives a new social dimension to war, and produces a range of military activities which outstrip both international law and military science, the kind of irregular warfare whose heroes are Garibaldi and T. E. Lawrence and Marshal Tito, which played a large part in the Second World War and has been the prevalent warfare in the world since. Such revolutionary sub-war is characteristic of doctrinal conflict. We all know that Engels described insurrection as an art, and expounded its principles; it is less often remembered that Mazzini, the Gandhi of nineteenth-century liberalism, wrote a set of 'Rules for the Conduct of Guerrilla Bands'.

Revolution involves counter-revolution; doctrinal war encourages war of counter-doctrine. Is doctrinal warfare to be met by containment, whose aim is security and whose motive fear, or by liberation—liberation from the ascendancy of the doctrine—whose aim is counter-revolutionary? The question is not answered by an appeal to the principle of collective security, for this itself can be inspired by either motive. In Korea, collective security meant a coalition whose predominant motive was fear: eleven of the seventeen powers that sent contingents experienced the direct threat of Communism. The collective security we dreamed of in the 'thirties, the war against Mussolini, inspired and purified by the moral censure and punitive purpose of the fifty sanctionist states, would have been much more a war of principle, a doctrinal war, logically evoking stasis in Italy and entailing the overthrow of the aggressor regime. The same motive prompted General MacArthur's desire to chastise Red China. In the earlier

years of the cold war the West debated this issue of containment or liberation, of limited war or counter-revolutionary crusade, and decided clearly
in favour of containment. If we were to put it in terms of the ancient
doctrine which lays down that there can be no just war without a right
intention, we might say that it is the consensus of the West today that there
can be no right intention in going to war unless the motive is fear.

[From Martin Wight, *Power Politics*, ed. Hedley Bull and Carsten Holbraad
(Harmondsworth: Penguin, 1979), 138–42.]

ROBERT GILPIN

31 **Hegemonic war and international change**

The disequilibrium in the international system is due to increasing disjuncture
between the existing governance of the system and the redistribution of power
in the system. Although the hierarchy of prestige, the distribution of territory,
the rules of the system, and the international division of labor continue to favor
the traditional dominant power or powers, the power base on which the
governance of the system ultimately rests has eroded because of differential
growth and development among states. This disjuncture among the components of the international system creates challenges for the dominant states
and opportunities for the rising states in the system. [. . .]

Throughout history the primary means of resolving the disequilibrium
between the structure of the international system and the redistribution of
power has been war, more particularly, what we shall call a hegemonic war.
In the words of Raymond Aron, describing World War I, a hegemonic
war 'is characterized less by its immediate causes or its explicit purposes than
by its extent and the stakes involved. It affected all the political units inside one
system of relations between sovereign states. Let us call it, for want of a better
term, a war of hegemony, hegemony being, if not conscious motive, at any
rate the inevitable consequence of the victory of at least one of the states or
groups.'[1] Thus, a hegemonic war is the ultimate test of change in the relative
standings of the powers in the existing system.

Every international system that the world has known has been a consequence of the territorial, economic, and diplomatic realignments that have
followed such hegemonic struggles. The most important consequence of a
hegemonic war is that it changes the system in accordance with the new
international distribution of power; it brings about a reordering of the basic
components of the system. Victory and defeat reestablish an unambiguous
hierarchy of prestige congruent with the new distribution of power in the

[1] Aron, *Peace and War*, 359.

system. The war determines who will govern the international system and whose interests will be primarily served by the new international order. The war leads to a redistribution of territory among the states in the system, a new set of rules of the system, a revised international division of labor, etc. As a consequence of these changes, a relatively more stable international order and effective governance of the international system are created based on the new realities of the international distribution of power. In short, hegemonic wars have (unfortunately) been functional and integral parts of the evolution and dynamics of international systems.

It is not inevitable, of course, that a hegemonic struggle will give rise immediately to a new hegemonic power and a renovated international order. As has frequently occurred, the combatants may exhaust themselves, and the 'victorious' power may be unable to reorder the international system. The destruction of Rome by barbarian hordes led to the chaos of the Dark Ages. The Pax Britannica was not immediately replaced by the Pax Americana; there was a twenty year interregnum, what E. H. Carr called the 'twenty years' crisis'. Eventually, however, a new power or set of powers emerges to give governance to the international system.

[From Robert Gilpin, *War and Change in World Politics* (Cambridge: Cambridge University Press, 1983), 186, 197–8.]

VLADIMIR LENIN

32   Socialism and War

Socialists have always condemned wars between nations as barbarous and brutal. Our attitude towards war, however, is fundamentally different from that of the bourgeois pacifists (supporters and advocates of peace) and of the anarchists. We differ from the former in that we understand the inevitable connection between wars and the class struggle within a country; we understand that wars cannot be abolished unless classes are abolished and socialism is created; we also differ in that we regard civil wars, i.e. wars waged by an oppressed class against the oppressor class, by slaves against slaveholders, by serfs against landowners, and wage-workers against the bourgeoisie, as fully legitimate, progressive and necessary. We Marxists differ from both pacifists and anarchists in that we deem it necessary to study war historically (from the standpoint of Marx's dialectical materialism) and separately. There have been in the past numerous wars, which, despite all the horrors, atrocities, distress and suffering that inevitably accompany all wars, were progressive, i.e. benefited the development of mankind by helping to destroy most harmful and reactionary institutions (e.g. an autocracy or serfdom) and the most barbarous despotisms in

Europe (the Turkish and the Russian). That is why the features historically specific to the present war must come up for examination.

The Great French Revolution ushered in a new epoch in the history of mankind. From that time down to the Paris Commune, i.e. between 1789 and 1871, one type of war was of a bourgeois-progressive character, waged for national liberation. In other words, the overthrow of absolutism and feudalism, the undermining of these institutions, and the overthrow of alien oppression, formed the chief content and historical significance of such wars. These were therefore progressive wars; during *such* wars, all honest and revolutionary democrats, as well as all socialists, always wished success to that country (i.e., that bourgeoisie) which had helped to overthrow or undermine the most baneful foundations of feudalism, absolutism and the oppression of other nations. For example, the revolutionary wars waged by France contained an element of plunder and the conquest of foreign territory by the French, but this does not in the least alter the fundamental historical significance of those wars, which destroyed and shattered feudalism and absolutism in the whole of the old, serf-owning Europe. In the Franco-Prussian war, Germany plundered France but this does not alter the fundamental historical significance of that war, which liberated tens of millions of German people from feudal disunity and from the oppression of two despots, the Russian tsar and Napoleon III.

The period of 1789–1871 left behind it deep marks and revolutionary memories. There could be no development of the proletarian struggle for socialism prior to the overthrow of feudalism, absolutism and alien oppression. When, in speaking of the wars of *such* periods, socialists stressed the legitimacy of 'defensive' wars, they always had these aims in mind, namely revolution against medievalism and serfdom. By a 'defensive' war socialists have always understood a '*just*' war in this particular sense (Wilhelm Liebknecht once expressed himself precisely in this way). It is only in this sense that socialists have always regarded wars 'for the defence of the fatherland', or 'defensive' wars, as legitimate, progressive and just. For example, if tomorrow, Morocco were to declare war on France, or India on Britain, or Persia or China on Russia, and so on, these would be 'just', and 'defensive' wars, *irrespective* of who would be the first to attack; any socialist would wish the oppressed, dependent and unequal states victory over the oppressor, slaveholding and predatory 'Great' Powers. [. . .]

It is almost universally admitted that this war is an imperialist war. In most cases, however, this term is distorted, or applied to one side, or else a loophole is left for the assertion that this war may, after all, be bourgeois-progressive, and of significance to the national-liberation movement. Imperialism is the highest stage in the development of capitalism, reached only in the twentieth century. Capitalism now finds that the old national states, without whose formation it could not have overthrown feudalism, are too cramped for it. Capitalism has developed concentration to such a degree that entire branches of industry are controlled by syndicates, trusts and associations of capitalist multimillionaires and almost the entire globe has been divided up among the 'lords of capital' either in the form of colonies, or by entangling other countries in thousands of threads of financial exploitation. Free trade and competition have been superseded by a striving towards monopolies, the seizure of territory for the investment of capital and as sources of raw materials, and so on. From the liberator of nations, which it was in the struggle against feudalism, capitalism in its imperialist stage has turned into the greatest oppressor of nations. Formerly progressive, capitalism has become reactionary; it has developed the forces of production to such a degree that mankind is faced with the alternative of adopting socialism or of experiencing years and even decades of armed struggle between the 'Great' Powers for the artificial preservation of capitalism by means of colonies, monopolies, privileges and national oppression of every kind. . . .

Since 1876, most of the nations which were foremost fighters for freedom in 1789–1871, have, on the basis of a highly developed and 'over-mature' capitalism, become oppressors and enslavers of most of the population and the nations of the globe. From 1876 to 1914, six 'Great' Powers grabbed 25 million square kilometres, i.e. an area two and half times that of Europe! Six Powers have enslaved *523 million* people in the colonies. For every four inhabitants in the 'Great' Powers there are five in 'their' colonies. It is common knowledge that colonies are conquered with fire and sword, that the population of the colonies are brutally treated, and that they are exploited in a thousand ways (by exporting capital, through concessions, etc., cheating in the sale of goods, submission to the authorities of the 'ruling' nation, and so on and so forth). The Anglo-French bourgeoisie are deceiving the people when they say that they are waging a war for the freedom of nations and of Belgium; in fact they are waging a war for the purpose of retaining the colonies they have grabbed and robbed. The German imperialists would free Belgium, etc., at once if the British and French would agree to 'fairly' share their colonies with them. A feature of the situation is that in this war the fate of the colonies is being decided by a war on the Continent. From the standpoint of bourgeois justice and national freedom (or the right of nations to existence), Germany might be considered absolutely in the right as against Britain and France, for she has been 'done out' of colonies, her enemies are oppressing an immeasurably far larger number of nations than she is, and the Slavs that are being oppressed by her ally, Austria, undoubtedly enjoy far more freedom than those of tsarist Russia, that veritable 'prison of nations'. Germany, however, is fighting, not for the liberation of nations, but for their oppression. It is not the business of socialists to help the younger and stronger robber

(Germany) to plunder the older and overgorged robbers. Socialists must take advantage of the struggle between the robbers to overthrow all of them. To be able to do this, socialists must first of all tell the people the truth, namely, that this war is, in three respects, a war between slave-holders with the aim of consolidating slavery. This is a war, firstly, to increase the enslavement of the colonies by means of a 'more equitable' distribution and subsequent more concerted exploitation of them; second-ly, to increase the oppression of other nations within the 'Great' Powers, since *both* Austria *and* Russia (Russia in greater degree and with results far worse than Austria) maintain their rule only by such oppression, intensi-fying it by means of war; and thirdly, to increase and prolong wage slavery, since the proletariat is split up and suppressed, while the capitalists are the gainers, making fortunes out of the war, fanning national prejudices and intensifying reaction, which has raised its head in all countries, even in the freest and most republican. [. . .]

The Military Program of the Proletarian Revolution Their principal argument is that the disarmament demand is the clearest, most decisive, most consist-ent expression of the struggle against all militarism and against all war.

But in this principal argument lies the disarmament advocates' principal error. Socialists cannot, without ceasing to be socialists, be opposed to all war.

Firstly, socialists have never been, nor can they ever be, opposed to revolutionary wars. The bourgeoisie of the imperialist 'Great' Powers has become thoroughly reactionary, and the war *this* bourgeoisie is now wag-ing we regard as a reactionary, slave-owners' and criminal war. But what about a war *against* this bourgeoisie? [. . .]

To deny all possibility of national wars under imperialism is wrong in theory, obviously mistaken historically, and tantamount to European chau-vinism in practice: we who belong to nations that oppress hundreds of millions in Europe, Africa, Asia, etc., are invited to tell the oppressed peoples that it is 'impossible' for them to wage war against 'our' nations!

Secondly, civil war is just as much a war as any other. He who accepts the class struggle cannot fail to accept civil wars, which in every class society are the natural, and under certain conditions inevitable, continuation, develop-ment and intensification of the class struggle. That has been confirmed by every great revolution. To repudiate civil war, or to forget about it, is to fall into extreme opportunism and renounce the socialist revolution.

Thirdly, the victory of socialism in one country does not at one stroke eliminate all war in general. On the contrary, it presupposes wars. The development of capitalism proceeds extremely unevenly in different coun-tries. It cannot be otherwise under commodity production. From this it follows irrefutably that socialism cannot achieve victory simultaneously *in all* countries. It will achieve victory first in one or several countries, while the others will for some time remain bourgeois or pre-bourgeois. This is bound to create not only friction, but a direct attempt on the part of the bourgeoisie of other countries to crush the socialist state's victorious proletariat. In such cases a war on our part would be a legitimate and just war. It would be a war for socialism, for the liberation of other nations from the bourgeoisie. Engels was perfectly right when, in his letter to Kautsky of September 12, 1882, he clearly stated that it was possible for *already victorious* socialism to wage 'defensive wars'. What he had in mind was defence of the victorious proletariat against the bourgeoisie of other countries.

Only after we have overthrown, finally vanquished and expropriated the bourgeoisie of the whole world, and not merely of one country, will wars become impossible. And from a scientific point of view it would be utterly wrong—and utterly unrevolutionary—for us to evade or gloss over the most important thing: crushing the resistance of the bourgeoisie—the most difficult task, and one demanding the greatest amount of fighting, in the *transition* to socialism. The 'social' parsons and opportunists are always ready to build dreams of future peaceful socialism. But the very thing that distinguishes them from revolutionary Social-Democrats is that they refuse to think about and reflect on the fierce class struggle and class *wars* needed to achieve that beautiful future.

[From V. I. Lenin, *Collected Works*, xxi and xxiii (originally published in 1915 and 1916). Taken from Bernard Semmel, *Marxism and the Science of War* (New York: Oxford University Press, 1981), 164–71.]

SEYOM BROWN
....

33   Structural Factors

The 'Balance of Power'

Quotation marks appear around *balance of power* to indicate the special meaning given here to an otherwise ambiguous concept. As used here, this term refers to the relative capabilities countries have for coercing one another. Balances of power may be global or local, and their components will vary with different issues. [. . .] [M]ilitary components usually constitute the heaviest weights in a coercive balance. But the balance of power also includes nonmilitary pressures that countries in conflict can bring to bear on each other.

The components of a particular balance may be almost entirely economic, as in the balance of power between Japan and her oil suppliers in the Middle East. In such cases, the balance of power is virtually indistinguishable from the pattern of interdependence. [. . .]

When there are economic and political goods and privileges that the parties can provide or withold from each other in a given negotiation or conflict, these assets constitute the balance of power for the issue at hand, and altercations over the issue have a good chance of being resolved without the invocation of the military balance between the participants.

However, if the overall balance of power between the countries in an altercation is lopsided in favor of one of them when the nonmilitary weights are counted, but lopsided in favor of the other when the military balance is calculated, the militarily superior country will be tempted to invoke the military balance to compensate for its nonmilitary inferiority. Thus in bargaining over oil supply issues and the Arab-Israeli conflict, threats by the Arab oil producers to embargo oil shipments to the United States and some of its NATO partners typically produce counterthreats, often in the form of public speculation by Western military experts about appropriate action to secure the oil supplies.

Generally, countries engaged in a rich range of transactions across a number of issue areas can invoke many bargaining counters—opportunities to withhold or proffer items of value to each other, that is—without resorting to military threats. The converse also generally holds: countries not normally engaged in substantial nonviolent interaction with one another may jump quickly to the military balance as the only balance of power relevant when conflicts arise. [. . .]

The Pattern of Interdependence

Interdependent relationships clearly are not necessarily peaceful. The nature of the dependencies and the context of the overall relationships among the parties will determine whether interdependence is likely to produce conflict and violence or cooperation and peace. Indeed, the presence of crucial dependencies—in which one country is highly dependent on others for military security or for its basic economic well-being—can also provide opportunities for intolerable provocations that seem to be 'worth a war' to terminate. [. . .]

If a pattern of heavy cooperation between countries fails to produce what either or both had been led to expect would be the result, there may be greater bitterness and much less room for compromise than in disputes among countries whose interactions have concerned only secondary or peripheral interests. Where there are the highest incentives to cooperate, because vital interests are involved, noncooperation becomes all the more intolerable and the sanction of war looms, implicitly or explicitly, in the background.

Alliances

A prominent structural feature of international relations is the pattern of alliances. Usually formed against a common opponent or set of opponents, alliances typically involve mutual pledges of military help in case one or more of the members is attacked. An important determinant of who is likely to fight whom—when, where, and how—alliances themselves reflect balance-of-power needs and material dependency relationships. They also can reflect ideological or cultural affinities and enmities, sometimes even those that contradict material needs. On the basis of the historical record, whether alliances tend more often to cause or to deter wars remains an open question.

Sometimes alliances deter war by presenting a would-be aggressor with an adverse balance of power. But, on the other hand, when they increase the aggressor's power, they can make the outbreak of war likelier. Sometimes merely the formation of an alliance is regarded as a serious provocation by the country or countries it is targeted against—stimulating them to threaten one or another of the member countries to 'test' and possibly break the alliance by exposing the fact that the commitment of some members is not firm or credible.

The range of possible responses to alliances and our inability to specify the effect they generally have on the tendency of countries to resort to war does not mean that alliances play a trivial determinative role. The existence of an alliance always importantly shapes the calculations of potential war outcomes, costs, and risks. By affecting the amount of armed forces available, the existence, membership, and terms of any alliance help determine the deterrent or provocative effects of coercive threats, including the decision to go to war, and they contribute importantly to the dimensions of wars that are fought. [. . .]

On the eve of World War I, the crisis in the Balkans was mismanaged because of overcommitments by the great powers to their smaller allies. What policymakers thought they learned from the fiasco of 1914 was that alliances are pernicious and more often than not will cause unwanted wars. But partly because the policymakers disparaged and discouraged alliances during the interwar period, Hitler was able to roll over his weaker neighbors with ease until the cumulative and diplomatically irreversible effects on the balance of power made another world war virtually inevitable.

What, then, can be said in general about alliances as a determinant of war? Not any more than can be said, really, about the role of armaments and coercive diplomacy: Like weapons and threatening postures, alliances may either deter or provoke an opponent. The existence of an alliance does mean that if a war comes, it will probably involve more parties. This is what happened in World War I, as an alliance commitment from Germany brought an otherwise timid Austria to the brink of war under the mistaken assumption that her immediate opponents, Serbia and Russia, would be intimidated by the coalition they would face, as well as inhibited by the conflicting interests within their own coalition.

Polarization

The calculations of antagonists about the array of armed enemies they will face if they go to war are affected not only by formal alliances but also by the extent to which alliance members and other prospective parties to the action are bound to one another and for what reasons. If most of the international system is polarized into only two camps, and if the bonding between countries in each camp is known to be tight across a range of issues, almost any war within the system has the strong potential for becoming a world war.

In such a tightly polarized system, however, miscalculations of the balance of power because of false assumptions about which countries will fight on each side are less likely, and therefore war should be less likely, than in more loosely structured international systems. [. . .]

The first dimension is the number of dominant power centers, or poles of attractions: *two are called bipolarity*; a few, say three to ten, are referred to as *multipolarity*; and many, more than ten, perhaps even hundreds, are termed *polyarchy*.

The second dimension is the degree of coalescence of groupings of states, nongovernmental associations, political movements, and other entities around the polar centers. In a refined model, this could be plotted on a continuum; but for our purposes it is sufficient to establish two categories: *tight coalitions* and *loose coalitions*. [. . .]

The most dangerous international systems tend to be those characterized by either loose bipolarity or loose multipolarity. They are dangerous in two respects: the likelihood of war and the likelihood that war anywhere in the system will draw in the major powers. War is likelier because the ambiguity of mutual security commitments in the loose coalitions leads to opportunities for miscalculation and bluffing. These characteristics also provide temptations for great-power intervention in local conflicts and the need for smaller powers to invoke coalition ties, however loose, to deter their adversaries from ganging up.

These dangerous instabilities are present in the current loose and still largely bipolar configuration of international alignments and antagonisms. They are both the product of and exacerbated by a set of mutually reinforcing conditions: (1) each superpower can devastate the other in a nuclear war, no matter which one strikes first; (2) each superpower exhibits a substantial but not total inhibition from going to war against the other in defense of its allies or clients; (3) there is tremendous disparity between the military power of the United States or the Soviet Union, on the one hand, and the military power of any other country, on the other; and (4) national values and interests diverge greatly among the coalition partners within both the US-led and the Soviet-led coalitions.

These conditions of today's ambiguous pattern of polarization can create terrible temptations on the part of either superpower to use force against lesser powers—even against allies of the rival superpower—in confidence that the rival superpower will be inhibited from countermoves that carry a high risk of direct military engagement between them. Either the Soviet Union or the United States might well try such a power play, placing on its principal rival the choice of accepting the new status quo or attempting to reverse it at the risk of igniting World War III.

The most ominous prospect is that the move to establish such a fait accompli by one of the superpowers will be vigorously met by the other, embroiling them in a fateful nuclear confrontation from which neither can back off without great humiliation. [. . .] This seemingly insane scenario is even 'rational' within the structure of the loose bipolar system. And though humanity has been lucky that such a mutually suicidal superpower confrontation has not yet materialized, only a naïve optimism would rest content that this luck will continue to hold.

The safest international system presented in the model is tight multipolarity. In the multipolar configuration, the world is divided into a number of international subsystems, each a largely self-contained commercial and security community. Conflict is managed within these communities, with little likelihood of outside intervention in their affairs.

While in theory tight multipolarity should reduce the chances of a world war, this optimistic result is derived simply by defining the subsystems as self-contained. The optimism seems unrealistic, if only because of the progressive global interdependence of nations across all traditional regional lines, along with the increasing economic and strategic importance to all major countries of the 'commons' areas (the oceans, the biospheric environment, and outer space) where countries can get in one another's way. Why should new regional subsystems, any more than the regional empires of the past, be expected to be sufficiently content with what they have and refrain from balance-of-power games against each other?

Even the formation of such intended self-contained regional subsystems appears entirely theoretical, for there no longer are universally acceptable definitions of which peoples constitute what regions. Are not some countries in the 'Middle East', for example, part of Africa or Southwest Asia or Southeast Europe? Who is to decide disputes over such regional definitions, and by what criteria? In most continents, there is profound jealousy and suspicion that would-be regional hegemons, like Brazil, or Japan, would lord it over other members of a self-contained regional community. Moreover, if multipolar regional subsystems do temporarily emerge, the ever-present prospect of their disintegration will present outside powers with temptations to cultivate local clients and, in the event of actual disintegration, to intervene competitively.

War is least likely in the tight bipolar system, but is most difficult to contain. Tight bipolarity seemed the direction in which world society was moving during the first two decades after World War II, and many leaders and theorists in the United States and the Soviet Union looked favorably upon this configuration as one likely to reduce the prospect of war. This was because of the expectation that as the coalitions became internally more integrated, between them encompassing most of the countries of the world, two constraints would more strongly operate on them. First, members of each coalition would have little opportunity for significant international action not authorized by the entire coalition. Second, since an attack on any part of the rival coalition would be on the whole coalition, the attacker could not hope to control his risks by attacking a small or weak opponent under the assumption that the target country's allies would not want to become involved. The temptation to 'nibble' at or 'salami slice' the rival coalition that characterizes loosely polarized configurations would be minimized in the tightly polarized system.

The principal deficiency of tight global bipolarity is that it is an all-or-nothing deterrence system. If, despite the built-in inhibitions against war, a conflict between two tightly polarized coalitions should escalate to major open hostilities in some corner of the globe, the war—unless terminated at once—would almost certainly expand into a world war with few if any sanctuaries and with high prospects of rapid escalation to nuclear holocaust.

A world in the configuration of polyarchy (which may well be the way ours is evolving) would be more warprone than others, but more likely than others to keep wars localized. A polyarchical world society would feature many sources and patterns of rule, authority, and power, not all of them congruent with the nation-state basis of the existing international system. Such varied identities, loyalties, and associations—based on nationality, domicile, ethnicity, religion, economic role, social class, occupation, and ideology—would determine who is on whose side and who is likely to fight against whom or to attempt to make peace with other units in the polyarchy. Many groups would transcend the borders of particular nation-states, and institutions representing various identities and interests would often come into conflict over their respective jurisdictions and over which of them has the primary or ultimate authority in particular fields.

With so many crosscutting loyalties and associations, credible multinational alliances would be difficult to sustain. Every country would have to be prepared to fend for itself. War might therefore be less deterred than in the polarized systems, unless most countries developed their own nuclear arsenals or other mass-destruction capabilities—a distinct possibility; on the other hand, the thickening and spread of diverse interdependencies across national and ideological lines might inhibit the degree of nation-to-nation hostility that must be generated to fight large wars. In general, the prognosis would be for more wars than in the bipolar or multipolar models; but wars which did break out might be more easily isolated or dissipated locally before engulfing the whole system.

[From Seyom Brown, *The Causes and Prevention of War* (New York: St Martin's Press, 1987), 62–75.]

MICHAEL W. DOYLE

34 Liberal States and War

What difference do liberal principles and institutions make to the conduct of the foreign affairs of liberal states? A thicket of conflicting judgments suggests that the legacies of liberalism have not been clearly appreciated. For many citizens of liberal states, liberal principles and institutions have so fully absorbed domestic politics that their influence on foreign affairs tends to be either overlooked altogether or, when perceived, exaggerated. Liberalism becomes either unself-consciously patriotic or inherently 'peace-loving'. For many scholars and diplomats, the relations among independent states appear to differ so significantly from domestic politics that influences of liberal principles and domestic liberal institutions are denied or denigrated. They judge that international relations are governed by perceptions of national security and the balance of power; liberal principles and institutions, when they do intrude, confuse and disrupt the pursuit of balance-of-power politics.

Although liberalism is misinterpreted from both these points of view, a crucial aspect of the liberal legacy is captured by each. Liberalism is a distinct ideology and set of institutions that has shaped the perceptions of and capacities for foreign relations of political societies that range from social welfare or social democratic to laissez faire. It defines much of the content of the liberal patriot's nationalism. Liberalism does appear to disrupt the pursuit of balance-of-power politics. Thus its foreign relations cannot be adequately explained (or prescibed) by a sole reliance on the balance of power. But liberalism is not inherently 'peace-loving'; nor is it consistently restrained or peaceful in intent. Furthermore, liberal practice may reduce the probability that states will successfully exercise the consistent restraint and peaceful intentions that a world peace may well require in the nuclear age. Yet the peaceful intent and restraint that liberalism does manifest in limited aspects of its foreign affairs announces the possibility of a world peace this side of the grave or of world conquest. It has strengthened the prospects for a world peace established by the steady expansion of a separate peace among liberal societies. [. . .]

In foreign affairs liberalism has shown, as it has in the domestic realm, serious weaknesses. But unlike liberalism's domestic realm, its foreign affairs have experienced startling but less than fully appreciated successes. Together they shape an unrecognized dilemma, for both these successes and weaknesses in large part spring from the same cause: the international implications of liberal principles and institutions.

The basic postulate of liberal international theory holds that states have the right to be free from foreign intervention. Since morally autonomous citizens hold rights to liberty, the states that democratically represent them have the right to exercise political independence. Mutual respect for these rights then becomes the touchstone of international liberal theory. When states respect each other's rights, individuals are free to establish private international ties without state interference. Profitable exchanges between merchants and educational exchanges among scholars then create a web of mutual advantages and commitments that bolsters sentiments of public respect.

These conventions of mutual respect have formed a cooperative foundation for relations among liberal democracies of a remarkably effective kind. *Even though liberal states have become involved in numerous wars with nonliberal states, constitutionally secure liberal states have yet to engage in war with one another.* No one should argue that such wars are impossible; but preliminary evidence does appear to indicate that there exists a significant predisposition against warfare between liberal states. Indeed, threats of war also have been regarded as illegitimate. A liberal zone of peace, a pacific union, has been maintained and has expanded despite numerous particular conflicts of economic and strategic interest. [. . .]

Statistically, war between any two states (in any single year or other short period of time) is a low probability event. War between any two adjacent states, considered over a long period of time, may be somewhat more probable. The apparent absence of war among the more clearly liberal states, whether adjacent or not, for almost two hundred years thus has some significance. Politically more significant, perhaps, is that, when states are forced to decide, by the pressure of an impinging world war, on which side of a world contest they will fight, liberal states wind up all on the same side, despite the real complexity of the historical, economic and political factors that affect their foreign policies. And historically, we should recall that medieval and early modern Europe were the warring cockpits of states, wherein France and England and the Low Countries engaged in near constant strife. Then in the late eighteenth century there began to emerge liberal regimes. At first hesitant and confused, and later clear and confident as liberal regimes gained deeper domestic foundations and longer international experience, a pacific union of these liberal states became established. [. . .]

No one of these constitutional, international or cosmopolitan sources is alone sufficient, but together (and only where together) they plausibly connect the characteristics of liberal polities and economies with sustained liberal peace. Liberal states have not escaped from the Realists' 'security dilemma', the insecurity caused by anarchy in the world political system considered as a whole. But the effects of international anarchy have been tamed in the relations among states of a similarly liberal character. Alliances of purely mutual strategic interest among liberal and nonliberal states have been broken, economic ties between liberal and nonliberal states have proven fragile, but the political bond of liberal rights and interests have proven a remarkably firm foundation for mutual non-aggression. A separate peace exists among liberal states.

[From Michael W. Doyle, 'Kant, Liberal Legacies, and Foreign Affairs', *Philosophy and Public Affairs*, 12/3 (1983), 205–6, 213–20.

Section C

War and the Military Establishment

CHRISTOPHER DANDEKER

In the history of sociological enquiry three approaches to the study of war and the military establishment can be identified. Two of these, the liberal theory of industrial society and Marxism, have been the more influential, at least until recently. Both are rooted in the idea of history as 'progress', emphasizing that the development of modern industrial society will lead to the decline of war and the military establishment. In contrast, the third, 'realist' or 'neo-Machiavellian' perspective stresses that these institutions will not wither away but are part of the human condition.

Giddens (35) discusses the interplay between these three traditions in the history of modern social theory. The liberal theory of industrial society stems from Saint-Simon, Comte, Spencer, and Durkheim. Its key idea is that, in comparison with warfare, the combination of democracy and market capitalism provides a successful alternative method of gaining economic prosperity and security. This is because democratic values promote respect for the rule of law and provide the basis for an overall moral and political consensus amongst states that adhere to them. Consequently the means of resolving any remaining conflicts that might arise between democratic states are also provided. Furthermore the interdependencies between societies promoted by market capitalism establish ties between nations that make the economic benefits of peace far outweigh those of war.

Marxism, in contrast, emphasizes that capitalism is an exploitative system of class relations in which military power is an instrument of class domination. This is of significance not only within society, as in the use of military force in industrial and other domestic conflicts, but also in the interaction between societies, for example, in the competition between capitalist powers for foreign markets or their efforts to subjugate colonial populations. For Marxism, peace depends not on the extension of capitalism but on its abolition and the creation of a classless, world society based on a peaceful confederation of socialist nation-states.

In contrast with both these perspectives, writers drawing on the neo-Machiavellian approach, such as Hintze and Weber, argue that war is inherent in society. A variety of reasons for this have been suggested ranging from the eternal struggle between conflicting values, the competition for economic and other resources, and the fact that, in a world divided into different states and political communities, it is rational for each one to ensure that it has sufficient military means to preserve its own security interests.

Until recently, this tradition of sociological thought has been pushed to the margins of the discipline. However, there was a 'mini-renaissance' of the sociology of war and military power in the early 1980s and this involved a rediscovery of neo-Machiavellian social theory particularly by those on the left. This process was stimulated by political debates on defence in what turned out to be the closing stages of the Cold War and, more significantly, the intellectual exhaustion of Marxism and its inability to provide a coherent account of the nature of war and military power in the modern world.

As Giddens has argued, sociologists study 'societies'; yet few acknowledge that the sharply demarcated boundaries between one society and another and the interconnections amongst the different elements within them are quite recent. They are, in fact, achievements of the modern state; and war and military organization have been central to the development of the state system that still provides the basic organizing principle of human societies across the globe.

The development of modern armed forces formed the administrative backbone of the modern state as an organization exercising sovereignty over territory and as an actor in the international system (36). Through the technological, financial, and demographic resources released by the industrial and democratic revolutions, the modern state was able to build disciplined, bureaucratically organized, armed forces. This emergent relationship between military and civilian élites has provided the focal point for studies of civil–military relations in military history and political science. A key element in the political structure of modern liberal democracies is the idea of civilian supremacy and the 'apolitical' military. This theme is explored by Vagts who, while accepting that, formally, the military profession is excluded from political involvement, argues that it none the less forms an influential corporate group in all states (38).

In contrast with writers drawing on the perspectives of military history and political science, military sociologists have been more inclined to take a broader view of civil–military relations, preferring to analyse the links between armed forces and society as a whole rather than just the political interaction between élites. This is the context in which one should view the contributions of Morris Janowitz. He was a key figure in the development of military sociology after the Second World War and emphasized the importance of the historical perspective in the study of armed forces and society. The selection from his classic work *The Professional Soldier* is on five hypotheses that have provided much of the research agenda of military sociologists since the 1960s (37). The impact of modern technology and changing social values has stimulated debate on the extent to which the military in modern society is becoming less of a vocation or way of life, separate from society yet commanding strong legitimacy, and more like other jobs in civilian society.[1]

Moskos discusses the role of armed forces in what he calls a 'warless society' (41). He is not thinking of the emergence of a warless planet. Rather he envisages a world in which economic competition replaces military conflict or stand-off as the principal connection between the advanced industrial societies, while regional, ethnic, and other conflicts continue to plague the developing countries. Indeed, these conflicts might well draw in the advanced societies.

This post-cold-war context leads armed forces in the advanced societies to move to a new organizational format: one characterized by a smaller regular army with greater reliance on reserve forces. In addition, the military profession will be required to broaden its educational base in order to prepare the armed forces for a wider range of roles from high intensity war through lower intensity conflicts and various types of peace-keeping and humanitarian aid missions. At the same time, the relationships between armed forces and society will change with public opinion becoming less supportive and more sceptical of the armed forces. By implication their prestige and ability to defend the legitimacy of their budgets will also decline, but then all these arguments rest on the premiss that the risk of war amongst the industrial societies, including those in the post-Communist world, will continue to be low.

Stewart (44) provides a useful summary of research on group cohesion and combat. Such research raises the question of what differences can be identified in the armed forces of different societies and in different historical periods. For example, is the importance of leadership a constant factor or is it more important in modern democratic societies? Are the populations of modern society both within and outside the armed forces more sensitive to casualties than the 1914–18 generation? If so, is logistics, particularly on the medical side, more important in sustaining morale in today's more casualty sensitive era? An interesting issue raised by the sociology of combat and tackled by Elshtain (40), is whether the introduction of women to combat groups proves that armed forces sacrifice their strategic imperatives to social responsiveness at their peril?

[1] See C. Moskos, 'The Military: Institution or Occupation?', *Soldiers and Sociology*, S. L. A. *Marshal Chair* (United States Army Research Institute for the Behavioral and Social Sciences, 1988).

A. GIDDENS

35 **States and Military Power in Social Theory**

Opening any textbook of sociology, the reader will find there discussions of most modern institutions—the family, class, deviance, etc. But it is very unlikely that he or she will discover any discussion of military institutions, or of the impact of military violence and war upon modern society. Much of the same is true of more rarified treatises on social theory, which concentrate upon capitalism, industrialism and so on. Yet who, living in the twentieth century, could for a moment deny the massive impact which military power, preparation for war, and war itself, have had upon the social world?

To explain what on the face of things seem extraordinary lapses in sociological thought, we have to look back to the influence of nineteenth-century social thought upon theoretical thinking in the social sciences. I think it true to say that we live today in circumstances for which the traditional sources of social theory have left us quite unprepared, especially those forms of social theory associated broadly with liberalism and with socialism. We live in a world dominated by the nation-state form, in which a fragile equality in weaponry possessed by the two most powerful nation-states is the main brake upon global violence within the context of a novel international order. The world is quite different from that which most nineteenth-century thinkers anticipated; and the styles of thought that dominate the social sciences today tend to be heavily indebted to their nineteenth-century origins.

Let us consider [. . .] Durkheim and Marx to illustrate both how and why this has come to be so. Durkheim was in a general way affiliated to liberalism, and Marx's writings are at the core of the most flourishing forms of socialist theory. Yet neither thinker gives any detailed attention to the nation-state as a generic phenomenon and neither, in a systematic way, connects the nature of the modern state either with control of the means of violence or with territoriality. Durkheim's theory of social evolution, from which his account of the state is derived, in general allocates little import-ance to military power, in traditional or in modern societies. This was not true of all authors of the same period, as the writings of Herbert Spencer demonstrate. In respect of the interpretation of non-modern societies, Spencer was more representative, perhaps, of nineteenth-century lib-eralism than was Durkheim. Spencer attributes the origins and nature of agrarian states largely to warfare. But whereas pre-industrial societies are pre-eminently warlike, industrial society, according to Spencer, is inherent-ly pacific, depending upon peaceful co-operation rather than antagonism between human collectivities. With the expansion of industrial activities, 'in place of a uniform belief imperatively enforced, there come multiform beliefs voluntarily accepted . . . military conformity coercively maintained gives place to a varied nonconformity maintained by a willing union.'[1]

Durkheim may not have emphasized the importance of military power and war in non-modern cultures, but his analysis of the development of 'organic solidarity', in spite of the specific criticisms he offers of Spencer, has a similar orientation to Spencer's interpretation of industrialism. Organic solidarity refers to the interdependence in which individuals increasingly find themselves as a result of the expansion of the division of labour stimulated by the progress of modern industry. The modern state is a direct expression of this trend, because the co-ordination of complex economic ties demands a 'social intelligence' of a centralized type. In the biological analogy Durkheim sometimes favours, the complex but unified entity which is a modern society needs a differentiated 'brain' to oversee its co-ordination and further development. Durkheim is critical of concepts of the state associated with socialism—including that of Marx—which he saw as treating modern political organization as wholly concerned with economic transactions. For Durkheim, the state cannot be *aufgehoben* and is of particular significance as a moral organization. But far from leading him to analyse the state as a nation-state, and as bound up with military power and territoriality, the effect is to distance him almost entirely from these concerns. The spread of organic solidarity, with its accompanying moralization of the 'cult of the individual', is inevitably international, because the ties of interdependence involved depend solely upon the spread of modern industry. 'War', Durkheim asserts, 'except for some passing setbacks [!] . . . has become more and more intermittent and less common'. The traits of particular nations will not necessarily disappear in the grand sweep of social evolution, but will become elements of a peaceful order of humanity. 'The national will merges with the human ideal'; each state will have as its aim 'not to expand, or to lengthen its borders, but to set its own house in order and to make the widest appeal to its members for a moral life on an ever higher level'. By this means 'all discrepancy between national and human morals would be excluded'.[2]

Marx and Engels—especially Engels—did give some mind to military power and war. Engels wrote to Marx in 1858, 'I am now reading, among other things, Clausewitz's *On War*.' Those other things included the work of Jomini and von Bülow; Engels continued to maintain his interest in such matters throughout his life, writing articles on military topics under Marx's name in the *New York Daily Tribune* and a number of other surveys of

---

[1] T. Herbert Spencer, *The Evolution of Society*, ed. R. L. Corneiro (Chicago: Chicago University Press, 1967), 61.

[2] E. Durkheim, *Professional and Civic Morals* (London, Routledge & Kegan Paul, 1957), 53, 74.

'military science'. Marx also read Clausewitz and sporadically dipped into other sources suggested by Engels, but apart from one or two minor pieces wrote nothing on the nature of war. The notion of 'the nation' crops up often in Marx's writings, but rarely if ever in the context of his major theoretical discussions of modern capitalism. Sometimes he means by it a state, but characteristically he uses it to refer to the cultural attributes of national communities. The *Communist Manifesto* rejects the idea that socialists have the objective of abolishing 'nationalities', arguing that these are legitimate expressions of cultural identity. But the same document does envisage the dissolution of all significant divisive influences among humankind, as socialism comes to further processes already begun by the spread of capitalism. Through promoting the existence of a 'world market', the bourgeoisie give 'a cosmopolitan character to production and consumption in every country'. Marx and Engels continue: 'All old-established national industries have been destroyed or are daily being destroyed . . . national one-sidedness and narrow-mindedness become more and more impossible.'

Alert though Marx might have been to the significance of military power, like Engels his concern with it was above all in respect of revolutionary and counter-revolutionary violence. Warfare between nations would become increasingly less consequential than the struggle between classes. There seems no way to dispute the conclusion that Marx unaffectedly believed that what workers shared in common would eventually triumph over what divided them nationally. To hold that 'workers have no country' was obviously an expression of hope as much as a factual observation but, as a projection of immanent trends, it was perfectly in line with the main impetus of Marx's theory of capitalist development. For Marx, the modern world is far more riven with conflict than for Durkheim, because of the deeply founded class divisions that demand nothing short of revolutionary change for their resolution. Nonetheless, Marx's anticipated future commonwealth of nations in essence resembles that which Durkheim foresaw. As a student of Marx's writings on the nation and nationhood has commented:

An enlightened patriotism which recognised the bearing of international progress upon national welfare seemed to Marx compatible and even fairly synonymous with sound internationalism. The true patriot must further the advance of other nations if only to assure the progress of his own; the true internationalist must strive for the advance of particular countries as the sound basis of world progress . . . [Marx] was an internationalist, not only in the sense of advocating a system of cooperative world relations, but in the more specific sense of conceiving that system as the resultant or function of the friendly interaction of large nations which were organised harmoniously from within.[1]

---

[1] Solomon Bloom, *The World of Nations* (New York: Oxford University Press, 1941), 206–7.

This absence in liberal sociology and in Marx's writings—the lack of a systematic interpretation of the rise of the territorially bounded nation-state and its association with military power—can be traced to the legacy of Saint-Simon in political theory and to the influence of classical political economy. There is more than a hint in Marx, and an open embrace of the idea by Engels, of the Saint-Simonian doctrine that, in the emergent society to which social evolution is leading, the administration of human beings by others will give way to the administration of human beings over things. Durkheim was less preoccupied with this theme of Saint-Simon than by the notion, also in some part drawn from Saint-Simon, that the state in an industrialized order will have a moral role to play in relation to the societal community. That is to say, in contrast to Marx, he was more influenced by Saint-Simon's later writings than by his earlier ones. But in neither case does there result an understanding of the state in an industrialized society as inherently associated with control of the means of violence, in which the administrative order relates to defined territorial boundaries. The industrial state, in short, is not a nation-state, and the industrial order—whether intrinsically marked by class struggle or not—is portrayed as progressively overcoming the militaristic tendencies of pre-existing types of society. Both liberal and Marxist conceptions of the state are heavily influenced by their respective critiques of political economy. Whatever their differences, which are of course in some respects very profound, both schools of thought conceive of industrialism as essentially a pacific force, inevitably going beyond national communities, unifying the globe through interdependent economic exchange. Marx may have been a more radical critic of the 'de-humanizing' effects of the division of labour than was Durkheim but, for both, modern economic life stimulates interdependence and therefore—once class division has disappeared—social unity on a global scale.

Now it might seem plain that, if these traditions of thought are deficient in the manner indicated, the answer is to turn to 'right-liberal' or conservative thinkers, who have tended to be more preoccupied with the state as a warlike entity. Thus Otto Hintze, a member of the so-called 'Prussian school' of historians, shares a good deal in common, in some of his emphases at any rate, with Max Weber. Hintze stresses the general association between the existence of states and the consolidation of military power, and sees such power both as involved with the development of capitalism/industrialism and as shaping their future course of development. He is strongly critical of Marxist assumptions: 'It is one-sided, exaggerated and therefore false to consider class conflict the only driving force in history. Conflict between nations has been far more important.'[1] Hintze criticizes

[1] Felix Gilbert, *The Historical Essays of Otto Hintze* (New York: Oxford University Press, 1975), 183.

Schumpeter for trying to show, in quasi-Marxist vein, that capitalism and 'the nation' are antithetical. 'The rise and development of capitalism', according to Hintze, 'remain unintelligible without insight into how they were conditioned by the course of national formation.'[1] In many respects, he goes on to claim, the expansion of capitalism and the increasing power of the nation-state march in tandem. [. . .]

But in spite of the importance which, put alongside liberal and Marxist traditions, the views of Hintze, Weber, and others holding comparable positions have, I do not think one can simply turn to them, abandoning the others, in analysing the nature of the modern nation-state in relation to military power. Thus in Weber, who attempted in a certain sense to merge those two incompatibles, Marx and Nietzsche, we do not find a satisfactory treatment either of the nation-state or of its relation to the development of capitalism and industrialism. As has been mentioned, this is partly because Weber defines the state in such a way as to make it difficult to distinguish some of the specific characteristics of the nation-state. It is also, however, because Weber, like most theorists inclined towards the political right on these matters, tends to see violence and war as an inescapable part of the human condition. The 'Nietzschean element' is most strongly represented in Weber precisely in the conjunction between his overall concept of the state and his philosophical stance about the irrationality of 'ultimate values'. Beyond 'ultimate values' there lies only force, the clash of mutually irreconcilable cultures, defended and protected by states that necessarily operate in a 'house of power'. I do not believe this view to be philosophically defensible, and it deflects attention from the ways in which the relations between nation-states in the modern world differ from those of earlier states. If the liberal and Marxist standpoints are notably deficient in certain respects, they do nonetheless draw our attention to the fact that capitalist-industrialism injects a whole set of novel dynamics into social change.

The above discussion concentrates upon the forerunners of modern sociology and we might ask the question, Have not each of the three general traditions of thought made considerable progress since then? Naturally they have done so in many respects, but I think it undemanding to demonstrate that their failings still remain. Marxist thought in the twentieth century has certainly not ignored the phenomena of war, force and violence. How could it be otherwise in a period which might not have seen the realization of Marx's projections for the revolutionary transformation of the industrialized countries, but has been otherwise the true 'century of revolutions'? Virtually everyone sympathetic to Marxism in current times accepts that Marx failed to develop anything more than the rudiments of a

[1] Ibid.

theory of the modern state. The result over the last two decades or so has been a spate of Marxist writing designed to help rectify this omission, some of which is very instructive indeed. But virtually all of it is preoccupied either with the role of the state in economic life, or with the state as the focus of 'internal' oppression. Where it is analysed theoretically at all, the nation-state still tends to appear in these discussions as reducible to economic relations of one kind or another. An example of the fatuous consequences to which this can lead is the division of the 'world system' into 'core', 'semi-periphery' and 'periphery', where the second of these categories includes the state socialist societies of Eastern Europe. The Soviet Union may be less developed than the Western countries economically, but in terms of its deployment of military power it is absurd to include it in the 'semi-periphery'.

Liberal authors have written extensively about the nation-state, although often in relation only to the 'state-building' efforts of the Third World. Unlike the majority of Marxists, some such writers have devoted considerable effort to grasping the nature of the nation-state. Examples are the works of T. H. Marshall and Reinhard Bendix. Each has written on the nation-state, and on nationalism, but in their thinking these occupy a strictly subordinate place to what Marshall terms 'citizenship' or 'citizenship rights'. Bendix's recent and most major work is, as he says, concerned with 'power and the mandate to rule', and with 'the use of force as an attribute of authority'.[1] But its overwhelming emphasis is upon how arbitrary power is overturned by the rise of government through popular delegation. 'Authority in the name of the people' has come to replace 'the authority of Kings'. No one, surely, would wish to deny the importance of such a phenomenon. Bendix has, moreover, played a leading part in attacking evolutionary theories of social change, stressing the diversity of routes which different states have taken towards modernization. However, like others in this tradition of thought, he has fought shy of attempting to analyse how industrial organization has become bracketed to military power, and how each of these in turn is connected with the character of the modern nation-state. The state appears as 'political community' within which citizenship rights may be realized, not as the bearer of military power within a world of other nation-states. Bendix frequently cites Hintze as well as Max Weber. But some of their distinctive emphases, particularly the 'Nietzschean strain' in Weber, barely appear in Bendix's work at all.

Nietzsche has, however, become influential again in present-day social thought, particularly in the works of those critical of liberal and Marxist perspectives. Thus the 'new philosophers' in France, who started out on the left, in abandoning Marx have moved to Nietzsche. In turning their

[1] Reinhard Bendix, *Kings or People* (Berkeley, Calif.: University of California Press, 1978), 16.

backs on Marxism, and discovering the absence in Marx not only of an elaborated account of the state, but of a generic theory of power (as distinct from class power), the new philosophers have made the state and power the fundamental components of social life.

We must break with the metaphysics of property, foundation and infrastructure . . . For the problem does not lie there; it is infinitely more radical: power does not appropriate the world, it continually *engenders* it in all its dimensions. It does not *expropriate* men and their homes, it *places them under house arrest*, deepens and fortifies the corners where they take part. Far from malignantly tearing the thread of their social fabric, power is what weaves the cloth of every reality . . . If the reality of capital, as we know, provokes despair, it is useless to place our dreams and hopes in another reality.[1]

This style of thought, with its rhetorical flourishes, sacrifices most of the insights it has achieved by a monolithic emphasis upon the ubiquity of power. Power is everywhere, so its particular manifestations are uninteresting. All states are pyramids of power; there is no point in differentiating between them in terms of their specific qualities or characteristics. In such writing, the nature of the state is approached only obliquely, never directly, and far from helping to identify the characteristics of nation-states, this approach hopelessly befuddles them.

[From A. Giddens, *The Nation-State and Violence* (London: Polity Press, 1985), 22–30.]

C. DANDEKER

36 The Bureaucratization of Force

The industrial and democratic revolutions changed military organization in three ways: first there was a revolution in the means of destruction; second there was an increase in the mobility of force; and third there occurred a bureaucratization of command, control and communications systems; producing an increase in the surveillance capacity of armed forces. As before, the cases of military and naval power can be considered separately.

The industrial revolution increased dramatically the capacity of the means of destruction in terms of firepower. Between 1840 and 1900, factory production in metal working and steel industries was applied to armaments. The infantryman's smooth bore, muzzle loading, musket was replaced by the breech loading and relatively rapid firing rifle. This enabled him to fire with greater accuracy and range, and allowed him to lie down when loading. Concealment was increased further after 1870 with advances in explosives, particularly smokeless charges. According to Strachan, be-

[1] Bernhard-Henri Lévy, *Barbarisms with a Human Face* (New York: Harper, 1977):

tween 1840 and 1900, the range and rate of infantry rifles had increased tenfold. Military organizations generally placed emphasis on the mass firing of rifles by infantry in the context of the full use of cover and entrenchments. The primacy of infantry (with cavalry as important auxiliary forces), was itself challenged by the ever-increasing destructive power of artillery.

The increased significance of artillery was an outgrowth of the most developed metal working industries and, as always, military competition between states provided a powerful stimulus to innovation. Modern artillery and the invention of the machine gun meant that there was a relative shift to the power of the defence on the battlefield, although this was not fully recognized until the first world war.

In addition to advances in firepower, the armies of states increased in size dramatically during the same period. This was due to a combination of political and economic factors. [. . .] [T]he French revolution had provided the political condition for national mass armies. In much of Europe, particularly in France, Prussia and Austria, the restoration of the ancien regime in 1815 involved the revival of long-serving professional forces. The ruling classes feared the political consequences of arming the people. This situation remained largely intact for 40 years. Meanwhile, industrialization and the consequent rapid rise in population growth provided the material basis for an expansion in the size of armies, although the political cost of such a move was formidable.

The Prussian solution to squaring this apparent circle involved a process of 'militarization' rather than 'civilianization'. The people were armed, thus increasing their participation in the state, yet autocratic political structures were retained, including the power of the officers' corps within the highest agencies of decision-making. Short service recruits were conscripted to an army manned by a professional core of officers and NCOs. Conscripts served three years: long enough to be inculcated with the values of discipline and obedience to the autocratic state. They then passed into the reserves and territorial formations, under the supervision of the army and not local civilian notables. Throughout Prussian military organization, the idea of a 'peoples' army' was subordinated to that of an army manned by the people. [. . .] '[F]undamental democratization'—the participation of all the population in the state—is quite compatible with autocratic political structures. This pattern of organization was widespread on the continent though Britain, for example, did not adopt a mass conscript army throughout the nineteenth century.

The emergence of this 'European' system of militarized conscription enabled industrial states to view their military potential in terms of national population size. The realization of this military equation depended on states acquiring a detailed knowledge of the size and distribution of national populations. Thus the extension of conscription (as well as taxation) was linked closely with the spread of national census systems in the nineteenth century. As a result of these changes, 'in 1870, the North German confederation deployed against France exactly twice the number of men Napoleon had led into Russia—1,200,000. By 1914, the German figures had again doubled, to 3,400,000 with comparable increases among her neighbours.'[1]

Yet this system could not operate without important technical and organizational innovations. Crucial here were the railways, the electric telegraph and bureaucratic staff organizations that regulated the large-scale movements of populations associated with modern mass armies. With these developments, a powerful bureaucratized war machine emerged.

In the nineteenth century, the railway and electric telegraph were the new means of transport and communication on land. They became elements of an integrated communications network. In conjunction with the extension of education and literacy in the second half of the century, these conditions unified national populations across time-space in dramatic fashion. States like Prussia, France, and later Russia, lost no time in realizing the military potential of this developing infrastructure.

The impact of railways was dramatic: they provided a network of communication which was far in advance of what was possible with the roads of the period. In addition, the 'pulling-power' of steam locomotion facilitated the speedier and more reliable transportation of heavier weights of both goods and people. In England, railway building occurred after the initial process of industrialization, and rail networks were not planned centrally by the state. However, the continental railways constituted the very basis of industrialization. In addition, the military organizations there were more politically influential than their English counterpart. They were quick to realize the military potential of railways in respect of war and in controlling internal disorder. In Prussia and elsewhere in continental Europe, they were able to determine the sitings of stations, routes and junctions on the basis of military and geopolitical considerations.

Railways caused a strategic revolution by increasing the size of armies and facilitating their movement and control. They increased the speed of war; military power came to be defined in terms of mobilization times, and there was a frantic search for means of reducing them in the second half of the nineteenth century.

In the 1840s and 1850s, Prussia and Austria used railways for moving troops. In 1859, 600,000 men and 129,000 horses transported from France to Italy in a sixth of the time it would have taken by horse. Railway communications were crucial to the Prussian defeat of Austria in 1866, and the defeat of France in 1871 can be attributed, in part, to mismanagement of the French railways. In the 1890s, the German Schlieffen plan for fighting

---

[1] Michael Howard, *War in European History* (Oxford: Oxford University Press, 1976), 99–100.

a war on two fronts against France and Russia depended on the efficient use of railways. France was to be attacked first, as Russia, with its lower level of industrialization and railway development, had a slower mobilization speed than France. One of the reasons why the plan failed in 1914 was that, by then, Russia had developed a far more effective railway network and industrial organization, much to the consternation of German war planners. As a result, more troops had to be taken from the west to mask Russia while France was attacked.

Railways provided the technological means of realizing the equation between military power and size of the adult male population. With a rail network, the state could mobilize its resources, transport them to depots to join their professional cadres and equipment. From there, they could be transported to the war fronts. With the railway, a whole society could be mobilized for war, its armies replenished with manpower and material resources. The division between military organization and society characteristic of the eighteenth century was broken; the bureaucratic military machine extended into society itself.

The impact of railways on the mobility of armies should not be exaggerated. Strategic advances were not always matched at the tactical level. Forces could in principle be deployed by rail and could be re-supplied. However, in the field away from the railheads, armies relied upon horses and feet for the movement of men and supplies, unless recourse could be had to captured rail networks. Indeed, until the process of motorization initiated by the internal combustion engine in the twentieth century, the size and destructive powers of armies quite outgrew their means of mobility. As a result, in the comparatively limited space of western Europe (when compared with the eastern front) armies were to grind to a halt in a bloody war of attrition in 1914. For all the reliance on railways in the Schlieffen plan of 1914, the timetable for the conquest of France rested on calculations of *marching* times. In addition, railways posed problems of their own. Synchronizing the arrival of men and their equipment was an immensely complicated administrative problem. The flow of men and materials to and from the front could be interrupted by shortages of double track lines or queues in either direction.

Bearing these qualifications in mind, railways did permit the creation of a much larger military machine. Its strategic movements could be determined centrally and in detail. It could also be connected with the resources of an industrial economy. The operation of this war machine depended on the development of new means of command and control. These were the electric telegraph and bureaucratic staff organizations epitomized by the German general staff.

The war machine made possible by the railways could not have operated without the surveillance network that was provided by the electric telegraph.

It emerged in the 1840s and was soon applied to military and civilian use, usually being established alongside the rail networks. Although it was a fixed land line system, it was particularly useful for co-ordinating movements of men and materials through the rail system and in connecting HQ with units in the field. As Pearton has argued, the Crimean War, 'was the first in which the commander was directed from home by means of the telegraph'.[1]

However, as with the railway, the telegraph provided limited means of control to the central authorities. It was used primarily for the communication of military information rather than commands, mainly because the system suffered from problems of reliability. In addition, its security could be breached by wire tapping. For these reasons, the German army realized that considerable initiative would have to remain with commanders in the field. Communication between units in the field was not easy, and this remained the case until the invention of wireless telegraphy in the early twentieth century.

The movement of troops and supplies to their predetermined positions of deployment, the allocation of routes of advance, targets and timetables, generated a huge volume of administrative tasks. New bureaucratic staffs were established to plan the movement of trains and troops, to write instructions, communicate them through the system, and monitor the system's performance. [. . .] [T]echnical imperatives—the volume and complexity of administrative tasks—forced railway companies and other large business enterprises to create similar planning staffs independently of any military exigencies. However, here I want to discuss staff organizations in terms of their contribution to the operation of an industrial war machine dependent on railways. Modern military staffs are 'central military organs assisting the supreme military authority of the state . . . in determining and implementing the higher directives which are to govern military activity'.[2]

A distinction can be drawn between staffs concerned with planning war, and thus with the operational *use* of military organization, and those which are concerned with the administration or maintenance of the instruments of war: recruitment and personnel, supply of materials, etc. These are no less important activities, and are performed within the parameters of planning directives established by the war or 'capital' staffs. This distinction between capital or planning staffs and administrative staffs is important. [. . .] [A] similar distinction can be identified in the organization structures of the larger business enterprises in the late nineteenth and early twentieth centuries. [. . .]

---

[1] M. Pearton, *The Knowledgeable State: War, Diplomacy and Technology since 1830* (London: Hutchinson, 1982), 58.

[2] D. D. Irvine, 'The Origins of Capital Staffs', *Journal of Modern History*, 10/2 (1938), 162.

The novelty of the war staffs lay not in their activities as such, but rather in their performance in a complex and differentiated administrative structure: the 'brain' of military organizations became collectivized. There were two related reasons for the development of these staffs: first, as a result of the democratization and industrialization of war, the volume and complexity of administrative tasks expanded beyond the capacities of personalized forms of administration. Second, at the same time there were those in the military who were aware that in order to realize the full potential of the new technologies of war (particularly to increase the speed of mobilizations and deployments) systematic and collective planning would offer distinct military advantages to any state which advanced in this direction. The spread of the staff system in Europe and beyond, for instance to the USA and Japan, was because of the military advantages it offered in a competitive world of nation-states.

The roots of the modern staff system lay in the late eighteenth century, when the French army had established a staff that gathered information and prepared plans for a war against England. Despite its technical achievements, the French staff organization was stunted by the effects of Napoleon's personalized command system. It was Prussia that was crucial in the development of modern military staffs. While their foundations were laid between 1780 and 1830, these organizations were developed into formidable bureaucratic instruments of war in the period 1840–80.

[From C. Dandeker, *Surveillance, Power and Modernity* (London: Polity Press, 1990), 82–8.]

M. JANOWITZ

37 The Military Professional

Five working hypotheses supply the point of departure for an analysis of the military profession over the last fifty years, for to speak of the modern military in the United States is to speak of the last half century. These working hypotheses were designed, in particular, for an understanding of the changes that have occurred in the political behavior of the American military. [. . .]

1. *Changing Organizational Authority*. There has been a change in the basis of authority and discipline in the military establishment, a shift from authoritarian domination to greater reliance on manipulation, persuasion, and group consensus. The organizational revolution which pervades contemporary society, and which implies management by means of persuasion, explanation and expertise, is also to be found in the military.

It is common to point out that military organization is rigidly stratified and authoritarian because of the necessities of command and the possibilities of war. The management of war is a serious and deadly business. It is therefore asserted that effective military command permits little tolerance for informal administration. Moreover, because military routines tend to become highly standardized, it is assumed that promotion is in good measure linked to compliance with existing procedures. These characteristics are found in civilian bureaucracies, but supposedly not to the same extent and rigidity. Once an individual has entered the military establishment, he has embarked on a career within a single comprehensive institution. Short of withdrawal, he thereby loses the 'freedom of action' that is associated with occupational change in civilian life.

The hypothesis concerning the shift in organizational authority, however, is designed to elucidate the realities of military command, since these realities condition the political behavior of the military elite. It is true that a large segment of the military establishment resembles a civilian bureaucracy insofar as it deals with the problems of research, development, and logistics. Yet, this hypothesis should apply even in areas of the military establishment which are primarily concerned with combat or the maintenance of combat readiness. In fact, the central concern of commanders is no longer the enforcement of rigid discipline, but rather the maintenance of high levels of initiative and morale.

It is in this crucial respect that the military establishment has undergone a slow and continuing change. The technical character of modern warfare requires highly skilled and highly motivated soldiers. In any complex military team an important element of power resides in each member who must make a technical contribution to the success of the undertaking. Therefore, the more mechanized the military formation, the greater the reliance on the team concept of organization.

What dilemmas does this shift in authority pose for an organization with traditions of authoritarian discipline and conservative outlook? If the organizing principle of authority is domination—the issuing of direct commands without giving the reason why—the image of the professional officer is that of the disciplinarian. What are the consequences for the political perspectives of traditional military leaders, if they must operate under this new type of organizational authority?

2. *Narrowing Skill Differential Between Military and Civilian Elites.* The new tasks of the military require that the professional officer develop more and more of the skills and orientations common to civilian administrators and civilian leaders. The narrowing difference in skill between military and civilian society is an outgrowth of the increasing concentration of technical specialists in the military. The men who perform such technical tasks have direct civilian equivalents: engineers, machine maintenance specialists, health service experts, logistic and personnel technicians. In fact, the concentration of personnel with 'purely' military occupational specialties has fallen

from 93.2 per cent in the Civil War to 28.8 per cent in the post-Korean Army, and to even lower percentages in the Navy and Air Force.

More relevant to the social and political behavior of the military élite is the required transformation in the skills of the military commander. This hypothesis implies that in order to accomplish his duties, the military commander must become more interested and more skilled in techniques of organization, in the management of morale and negotiation. This is forced on him by the requirements of maintaining initiative in combat units, as well as the necessity of coordinating the ever-increasing number of technical specialists.

Furthermore, the military commander must develop more political orientation, in order to explain the goals of military activities to his staff and subordinates. He must develop a capacity for public relations, in order to explain and relate his organization to other military organizations, to civilian leadership, and to the public. This is not to imply that such skills are found among all top military professionals. Specific types of career lines seem to condition these broad managerial orientations, but the concentration of such skills at the top echelon of the military hierarchy is great, and seems to be growing. As a result, along with a narrowing skill differential between military and civilian elites, transferability of skills from the military establishment to civilian organization has increased.

3. *Shift in Officer Recruitment.* The military elite has been undergoing a basic social transformation since the turn of the century. These elites have been shifting their recruitment from a narrow, relatively high, social status base to a broader base, more representative of the population as a whole.

This broadening of the base of recruitment reflects the growth of the military establishment and the demand for larger numbers of trained specialists. In Western Europe, as skill became the basis of recruitment and advancement, the aristocratic monopoly over the officer corps was diminished. In the United States an equivalent process can be demonstrated, although historically, social lines have been more fluid. The air force, with its increased demand for technical skill and great expansion over a very short period of time, has offered the greatest opportunity for rapid advancement.

The question can be raised as to whether the broadening social base of recruitment of military leaders is necessarily accompanied by 'democratization' of outlook and behavior. One aspect of 'democratization' of outlook and behavior implies an increased willingness to be accountable to civilian authority. On the basis of European experiences, particularly in pre-Nazi Germany, there is reason to believe that 'democratization' of entrance into the military profession can carry with it potential tendencies to weaken the 'democratization' of outlook and behavior.

Are the newer strata in the American military establishment less influenced by the traditions of democratic political control? As the officer corps becomes more socially representative and more heterogeneous, has it become more difficult to maintain organizational effectiveness, and at the same time enforce civilian political control? And, finally, what does representative social recruitment imply for the prestige of the military? Historically, the officer's social prestige was regulated by his family origin and by an ethos which prized heroism and service to the state. What society at large thought of him was of little importance, as long as his immediate circle recognized his calling. This was particularly true of the British officer corps with its aristocratic and landed-gentry background and its respectable middle-class service families.

But, as the military profession grows larger and socially more heterogeneous, as it becomes more of a career, does not pressure develop for prestige recognition by the public at large? Every professional soldier, like every businessman or government official, represents his establishment and must work to enhance the prestige of his profession. In turn, a military figure can become a device for enhancing a civilian enterprise. Do not such trends force the military to become more obtrusive and place a strain on traditional patterns of civilian-military relations?

4. *Significance of Career Patterns.* Prescribed careers performed with high competence lead to entrance into the professional elite, the highest point in the military hierarchy at which technical and routinized functions are performed. By contrast, entrance into the smaller group—the elite nucleus— where innovating perspectives, discretionary responsibility, and political skills are required, is assigned to persons with unconventional and adaptive careers.

This hypothesis is probably applicable to all organizations, for top leadership, especially in a crisis, is seldom reserved for those who take no risks. But among the military the belief in a prescribed career is particularly strong. An unconventional career, within limits, can imply a predisposition toward innovation, or, at least, criticism of the operation of the military establishment at any given moment. It implies that the officer has undergone experiences which have enabled him to acquire new perspectives, new skills, and a broader outlook than is afforded by a routine career. Unconventional or unusual careers, however, must be developed within the framework of existing institutions, since officers who express too openly their desire to innovate or to criticize are not likely to survive.

All types of elites must be skilled in managing interpersonal relations, in making strategic decisions, and in political negotiations, rather than in the performance of technical tasks. Yet, they enter these leadership roles through prescribed careers which emphasize technical tasks. If this is a correct hypothesis, then the study of career development in the armed forces should throw some light on the process by which a minority of military leaders departed from their prescribed careers to become concerned with broader military issues, and with the social and political consequences of violence in international relations.

5. *Trends in Political Indoctrination.* The growth of the military establishment into a vast managerial enterprise with increased political responsibilities has produced a strain on traditional military self-images and concepts of honor. The officer is less and less prepared to think of himself as merely a military technician. As a result, the profession, especially within its strategic leadership, has developed a more explicit political ethos. Politics, in this sense, has two meanings; one internal, the other external. On the internal level politics involves the activities of the military establishment in influencing legislative and administrative decisions regarding national security policies and affairs. On the external level politics encompasses the consequences of military actions on the international balance of power and the behavior of foreign states. The two aspects of military 'politics' are, of course, intertwined.

Since the outbreak of World War II, career experiences and military indoctrination at all levels have resulted in much broader perspectives—social and political—than had been the tradition. Yet, what the consequences are likely to be for civil-military relations in a democratic society is very much an open question. It may well be that these experiences have had the effect of making the military profession more critical of, and more negative toward, civilian political leadership.

[From M. Janowitz, *The Professional Soldier: A Social and Political Portrait* (New York: The Free Press, 1971), 7–12.]

A. VAGTS

38   The Military and Politics

It is a common assumption in the civilian world, as well as a pretense on the part of the military, that 'soldiers are so little politicians generally'. If only party and parliamentary politics are in review, or those formal political deliberations from which most states have excluded their active soldiers, a nonpolitical character for the soldier is somewhat credible. Even without an express prohibition it would appear doubtful whether officers as a type have the ability, the suppleness, the temperament, or the time for a continuous application to politics. The absence of such gifts, tastes, and opportunities, of which the military man has himself been aware, has sharpened his criticisms of the civilian politicians and officials, such as the British major general's outburst: 'Politicians make us soldiers sick, soldiers being perchance too straight and honest for them.' The rather simple-minded Haig, so little a politician that he could hardly have consorted much with that fraternity, wrote home from the Boer War that he wished 'to disband the politicians for ten years. We would all be the better without them.' When the peace was concluded with the Boers, it seemed to him to be so civilian in character that he condemned the politicians for their clemency, though, in point of fact, Kitchener was largely responsible for this mildness while the civilian, Milner, had opposed it.

Officers' judgments on parties and party politicians have run true to form since the time of Marlborough. Accomplished politician and diplomat though he was, Marlborough had his troubles with the Whigs, who supported his wars, but with whom he did not sympathize politically; and he had difficulties with the Tories, to whom he inclined, but who supported the navy rather than his establishment. As he told his wife, this experience made him no party man. His impartiality, he said, 'is not designed to get favour, or to deceive anybody, for I am very little concerned what any party thinks of me; I know them so well that if my quiet depended upon either of them I should be most miserable, as I find happiness is not to be had in this world, which I did flatter myself might have been enjoyed in a retired life. I will endeavour to leave a good name behind me in countries that have hardly any blessing but that of not knowing the detested names of Whig and Tory.'

Nevertheless, though debarred from formal association with parties, the army in every country forms to some extent a class or 'estate' with positive professional interests and corresponding views on state and society. Group interests and personal interests force every army to be 'in politics' in the larger sense. This the War Minister of Japan, and head of the most political army on the eve of the Second World War, confessed: 'It is impossible for soldiers, who are part of the nation, to be entirely unconcerned about politics.' But he insisted or promised that 'their views must be expressed only through the War Minister. My assistants have connections with other departments of the government for purposes of investigation and study, and it is necessary, from the broader viewpoint of national defense, that they express opinions. Junior officers must make inquiries, but only the War Minister translates the results into action.' The Minister carefully refrained from mentioning other military politics than the interdepartmental.

As in other professions, a large proportion, perhaps even a majority, of officers may be unpolitical as so-called experts or specialists, fully absorbed by their specific tasks, are inclined to be. But in fact, while waiting for action during intervals in their true business, war, they have more leisure than most experts in which to apply thought and wish to political activity. And since the early days in the history of modern military expansion they have had in fact an élite at work in politics—an informal group representation, that 'terrible organization' of professional interests which Carnot learned to fear.

This élite has not been an open organization, since that was forbidden by concepts of duty and expediency; but groups, cliques, camarillas, schools within armies, have taken it upon themselves to voice, represent, and realize military interests, through politics, without having any mandate conferred upon them by the majority of officers, save, perhaps, the assumption that most of the men agreed with them. Such cliques have established and maintained contacts, usually well screened, with the civilian political groups holding or striving for power. Thus the jealous Gates, in the trying times of Valley Forge, gathered a cabal of officers around himself with the intention of removing Washington from command, and the ring-leaders found some members of the Congress ready to listen to them. In monarchies, such camarillas have almost always understood how to get hold of the monarch himself, as they did in Russia or Prussia. Where the monarch is not so readily managed, he may be threatened and even treated with violence, as he was in Serbia in 1903.

In such extreme cases officer politics takes the form of conspiracy, either against governments at home or abroad. Serbian officers, including the chief of the information department of the General Staff, who had himself founded the nationalistic secret society, 'Unity or Death', helped to prepare the murderers of Sarajevo. It was the same department in France which persecuted Dreyfus. Revolutionary and other unsettled conditions have turned generals into traitors to the country they were serving, as in the cases of Charles Lee, Benedict Arnold, Pichegru, or Lafayette. More regularly, officer politics pursues minor objects, such as improvements of pay and living conditions, the winning of favors, and transfers. As Clemenceau's closest military adviser, General Mordacq, described the opposition of officers to the attempts to rejuvenate the French officer body during and after the war: 'Always haunted by that spirit of camaraderie which, in the army, has done us so much harm, certain high functionaries hesitated to apply the red-hot iron where it was needed.'

The very barriers in the way of officer politics have provoked a great deal of anonymous activity on the part of officers, such as the writing and publishing of brochures and articles. These may be penned with the consent of the officer's superiors, as were the reactionary pamphlets of Roon's friend, Lieutenant Colonel von Griesheim, the 'Berlin Cavaignac', who in 1848 extolled the superior qualities of the Russian army in order to frighten the Frankfurt parliament. Again, in *Only Soldiers Help Against Democrats*, published in 1848, he exalted the old Prussianism. Sometimes, however, anonymity has been used to cover opinions which the governing hierarchy did not want to have discussed.

The natural tendency of armies is not only toward a self-government brooking no outside influences, but also toward the extension of their power beyond their own circles. Bismarck, who knew them so well, observed that many officers considered all things outside the army 'as alien enemies'. In an age which has highly cherished democratic self-govern-ment, the army organization has often sought praise as being democratic itself. The Prussian army, for instance, liked to point to such of its features as the election of officer aspirants by the whole officer corps. Even the Russian officer corps of 1914 was said not to be 'really a distinct class. Men of humble origin were to be found even among the generals occupying high positions. . . . The corps was fundamentally very democratic' in spite of some regulations 'which had been drawn up under strong German influences'. Yet in reality such egalitarian rudiments in officer relationships were due to feudal hangovers rather than to democratic influences.

[From A. Vagts, *A History of Militarism, Civilian and Military*, revised edn. (New York: The Free Press, 1959), 294–6.]

PHILIPPE MANIGART

39 Mass Armed Forces in Decline

Since the early 1950s, most Western industrialized countries have been undergoing a profound alteration in the organizational structure of their armed forces. This mutation was similar in scale to those that occurred during the 14th and 15th centuries with the decline of the feudal model of military organization and during the 19th century with the advent of mass armed forces. The model of the decline of the mass armed forces is an attempt to explain, in the most parsimonious way, this complex multina-tional historical process. The model specifies that, in response to important technological and sociopolitical changes that took place outside the milit-ary establishments (the exogenous variables in the model), Western military organizations had to adapt their structures, their missions and their goals (the dependent variables), in order to survive.

Van Doorn singles out three meanings of the word mass. The first is the most evident but also the least important. It refers to size: mass armed forces were large-scale military organizations. The second dimension refers to the degree of societal mobilization necessary for the system's mainten-ance: mass armies rested on large-scale military participation. Finally, the third, and most important, dimension refers to the degree of organizational homogeneity: mass armies were relatively simple organizations, without much social differentiation.

The organizational format of the mass armed forces was that of an army organized around a small core of professional soldiers (cadres), which used conscription to recruit its manpower. The functions occupied by these soldiers were not much differentiated and purely military in nature (i.e.

they were combat functions). Consequently, if military institutions were relatively homogeneous organizations, they were also very different from civilian society.

In fact, with the decline of the mass armed forces one observes a transformation similar to the one that has affected complex civilian organizations in the industrialized world, i.e. the transition from labor- to capital-intensive organizations. A model based on universal conscription in peacetime and national mobilization in wartime was displaced by a new form of organization that Janowitz called force-in-being, i.e. 'a smaller, fully professional, and more fully alerted and self-contained military force'.

The ideal type (in the Weberian sense) of the force-in-being is a structurally and functionally differentiated organization that uses very sophisticated technologies. As technology, to a large extent, replaces labor, it follows that these military organizations are smaller than mass armies and that ground forces (and particularly the infantry) cease to be the dominant element. Personnel is mostly composed of specialists. Indeed, in a force-in-being, the number of unspecialized tasks is reduced to a minimum. They have either been automatized or transferred to civilian personnel. Strictly military functions, i.e. combat functions, have become a minority and have been supplanted by technical, logistical and administrative functions. It follows that such organizations have skill structures more similar to those of civilian organizations than was the case with mass armies.

In theory, the ideal form of the force-in-being should be the all-volunteer force (AVF). Indeed, the AVF appears to be the logical outcome of the process of social differentiation at work in our societies, i.e. of the division of labor in the Durkheimian sense. Such a process is characterized by a tendency to transfer to specialists a series of tasks formerly assumed by the whole society. In this perspective, the professionalization of the military would merely be one example among many of the professionalization process.

However, if the AVF constitutes the ideal type of the force-in-being, economic and political constraints can work against such an outcome. In other words, if the decline of the mass armed forces can lead to an AVF, the AVF is not its predetermined outcome. Thus, one should not equate, as some authors have done mistakenly, the decline of the mass army with the end of the draft. Let us not forget, for instance (and it is a very important factor to the extent that, proportionally speaking, defense expenditures tend to decrease as a result of sociocultural trends associated with the decline of the mass armed forces), that an AVF costs very much, especially if one wants to recruit quality manpower. This is why, in several countries, one has adopted—or one considers to adopt—intermediate military systems that, while based on a certain amount of military participation by the citizens, would be compatible with the force-in-being format. It would indeed be misleading to believe that there exist no more unspecialized functions in a force-in-being. One of the systems that best answers the technological (need for specialists), economic (cost), and political constraints (maintenance of a certain form of conscription) appears to be the two-tier system. A two-tier system is a system in which volunteers and conscripts coexist but, unlike the mixed system, are functionally differentiated. The advantages of a two-tier system are that, on the one hand, it would allow the professional military to receive more sophisticated weapons and, on the other hand, the presence of conscripts would allow an army of a sufficient size to exist, and would lessen the fears engendered by an entirely professional system.

Operationally, the model of the decline of the mass armed forces predicts that there should be

(1) a substantial decline in total personnel and less manpower fluctuation between peacetime and wartime;

(2) a decline in the military participation ratio, a reduction in the significance of conscription as the primary source of recruitment, and a decrease in the size and role of the reserve forces;

(3) a growing complexity as regards the division of labor, as indicated by a shift from a pyramidal rank structure to a diamond-shaped one, and an increase in technical, logistical and administrative functions.

[From Philippe Manigart, 'The Decline of the Mass Armed Forces in Belgium 1900–1985', *Forum International*, 9 (1990), 40–4.]

JEAN ELSHTAIN

40   Feminism's War with War

Over the past year, in one poll after another, women have staked out a clear position—against Reaganomics, against nuclear arms—and gradually men have drifted over to share those beliefs. . . . For whatever reasons—because of our culture, because of our history or because of motherhood—nonviolent convictions are more pervasive among women.

ELLEN GOODMAN, *Washington Post*, 22 May 1982

It seems to me that one of the risks of the much-heralded peace gap is that women may rest on their moral superiority. It is easy, after all, to stake the high ground—peace—when you aren't slogging through the daily mud of foreign policy. . . . Women have had a certain luxury in being the outsiders. It's the luxury of not being directly involved, not being responsible.

ELLEN GOODMAN, *Washington Post*, 1 November 1983

The subtle shift over a year's span in the position of a liberal feminist, the syndicated columnist Ellen Goodman, helps illustrate a deep feminist dilemma. From its inception, feminism has not quite known whether to fight men or to join them; whether to lament sex differences and deny their importance or to acknowledge and even valorize such differences; whether to condemn all wars outright or to extol women's contributions to war efforts. At times, feminists have done all of these things, with scant regard for consistency. Feminism moves along a number of planes: as the action of women in and on the world; as abstract theories and utopian evocations; and as a story of self-conscious feminists breaking down extant barriers to take their place in previously all-male institutions—for example, the military. To be sure, the vast majority of women in the armed forces of the United States, at present, do not identify themselves as feminist; but because their identities and actions have been given a feminist gloss and representation, it seems appropriate to take up military women under this general rubric. The story of feminism and male/female identifications is, as I have previously suggested, a tumult of ongoing encounters with a long, grand genealogy—from the prototypical maternal figure, the Madonna, to the exemplary woman warrior, Joan. As discourse, feminism is not just a series of explicit endorsements but a cluster of implicit presumptions guiding rhetorical choices and controlling dominant tropes and metaphors.

The reflections to follow are being written at a time of flux when several ways to occupy the category *woman* present themselves, though only a few get the stamp of approval from one variety of feminism or another: 'right to fight' feminists, who are endorsed by integrationist feminism incarnated by the National Organization for Women; revolutionary women in Third World countries, approved by most mainstream feminists and feminist anti-militarist groups save for absolute pacifists; the woman peace activist, sanctified by a plethora of old (Women's International League for Peace and Freedom) and new ('Greenham Common', as a generic for all-women peace encampments and direct action) efforts. At the anti-war end of the pole, pressure is put on military women to decamp; at the liberal-egalitarian end, urgent compulsions are reversed as women who overidentify (on this reading) their femaleness with peacefulness find this identification challenged or at least fretted about as simply another way to reinforce old stereotypes. All forms of feminism put pressure on 'sleeping with soldiers', on the age-old union of Eros with Mars that makes of men in uniform attractive targets for libidinal fixation.

A polyphonic chorus of female voices whose disparate melodies are discernible sounds now in the land. Among the many voices are latter-day Antigones ('Hell, no, I won't let *him* go'); traditional women ('I don't want to be unprotected and men are equipped to do the protection'); the home-front bellicist ('Go, man, go and die for our country'); the civicly incapacitated

('I don't rightly know'); women warriors ('I'm prepared to fight, I'd like to kick a little ass'); and women peacemakers ('Peace is a woman's way'). Each of these voices can be construed as the tip of a pyramid descending on either side to congeal into recognizable social identities that sometimes manifest themselves as movements: a feminist revolution to end all wars (the penultimate earthly triumph of the victims); a socialist revolution to end all wars (the earthly triumph of total justice); a psychological revolution (the 'hearts and minds' approach), with men being reconstructed along pacific lines; or, more modestly, a feminist *movement*, short of revolution, to gain female parity of power/force with men. Then, of course, there are women fighting changes, seeking, instead, a resurrection of traditional identities and a restoration of old complementarities. At the moment, feminists are not only at war with war but with one another, as well as being locked in combat with women not self-identified as feminist.

[From Jean Elshtain, *Women and War* (Brighton: Harvester Press, 1987), 231–3.]

CHARLES C. MOSKOS

41 Armed Forces in a Warless Society

The very old idea that aversion to war was a sign of decadence was reversed by the founders of modern social thought. Immanuel Kant, Adam Smith, Auguste Comte, Herbert Spencer, Karl Marx, among many others, held in common (about the only thing such a diverse group did hold in common) the notion that industrial societies were evolving toward greater pacification, even toward a warless world. Events of the century that followed belied the prognostications of these founders, but the contemporary period again sees a revival of the notion of a future without war.

No serious observer, of course, sees the imminent end of large-scale violence. The prevailing discussion of the termination of the Cold War, a denuclearized Europe, greatly reduced conventional armies, is not so naive as to mean the literal end of war. The future will not be absent of regional conflicts, internal wars within countries, ethnic strife, and major power interventions in spheres of influence. But events rapidly developing in Europe and between the two superpowers augur that some meaningful, even momentous, not illusionary change is occurring.

The absence of wars between parliamentary bourgeois democracies has long been noted. What is new is that wars between developed countries, socialist or capitalist, now also may be moving into the realm of improbability. The operating assumption is that we are witnessing the dawning of an era in which war—at least between superpowers and major European powers—is no longer the principal, much less inevitable, mode of conflict resolution. We also note the marked reluctance of the American (and apparently the Soviet) public to become engaged in protracted uncertain wars in secondary parts of the world. I call this new era, for shorthand purposes, a warless society.

How will the central institution that developed during the period of modern warfare—the armed forces—be affected by and, more importantly, affect these developments? Our procedure here is to posit a warless society and then seek to understand the probable structure and function of armed forces under warless conditions. From this perspective, armed forces are both an independent and dependent variable in the emerging warless society.

At first glance, the salience of the armed forces in arms control and disarmament would hardly seem to be a debatable point. An examination of armed forces would be seen to be entering an arena already crowded with thousands of books and almost as many entrenched assumptions. Yet, surprisingly, a systematic and comparative examination of the sociology of armed forces in arms control has not been attempted previously.

Even at this late date in the new era of good feelings, the role of arms forces in disarmament often falls between theoretical schools, both of which understate the institutional role of the military. One tends to emphasise trends in strategic doctrine, weapons technology, and 'correlations of forces'. The other looks to underlying sources of conflict with a corresponding stress on peace theory and practise. Either way, the military's active and reactive role on arms control is typically given short shrift.

Any typology does an injustice to reality. But our concern is to grasp the whole, to place the salient fact, and to have a framework to appraise the emergent armed forces. Although the typology draws heavily from the experience in Europe and the North Atlantic countries since World War II, the essential difference between armed forces in the three types of societies are phrased in terms suitable for broader cross-national research. These differences are summarised in the table next page.

The master hypothesis is that as modern states move from war readiness to war deterrence to warless societies the sociology of the military changes accordingly. The paradigm presented herein is a starting guide to systematise research findings.

Such a typology and its correlative variables ought not, however, be applied mechanically to the armed forces examined. A prime consideration is to see how the overarching scheme fits, or must be reworked, when applied to military systems differentially shaped by a country's unique civil-military history and geopolitical position.

We argue that war probabilities shape relationships between armed forces and society. We propose a threefold typology of armed forces and society: war readiness, war deterrence, and warless. The contrast between these types of societies is easy to overdraw, but the social analyst must use

Table: *Armed Forces and Society*

Armed Forces Variable	Type of Society		
	War Readiness	War Deterrence	Warless
Formal Organization	mass army	professional military	cadre and reserve force
Major Item in Personnel Budget	aggregate personnel costs	per capita personnel costs	reserve infrastructure
Major Item in Weapons Budget	low-technology weapons	high-technology weapons	low- and high-techn. wpn.
Membership Identification	institutional	occupational	civic
Organizational Tension	service roles	budget fights	mission substitution
Conscientious Objection	limited or prohibited	permitted on routine basis	subsumed in alternative civilian sv.
Recruitment	representative of male youth (military only)	stratified per labor market (military only)	represent. of young adults (military + civil)
Dominant Type of Military Professional	combat leader	managerial technician	soldier-scholar
Public Attitude Toward Military	supportive	apathetic	skeptical
Military Attitude Toward Disarmament	hostile	skeptical	apathetic

pure types to advance conceptual understanding. War readiness societies are characterised by most NATO and Warsaw Pact countries in the 1950s through 1960s: large standing forces, typically conscripted, with a high manoeuvre tempo. War deterrence societies are more typical of American, Canadian, and British forces of the 1970s and 1980s, though parallels are readily found in all NATO countries (with similar trends seemingly occurring in the Soviet Union): force size shrinks as emphasis shifts from a mass army to a well-paid professional and technical force.

Warless societies may be what the armed forces of West Europe and North Atlantic are moving toward (to some extent exemplified by Sweden, Switzerland, and Canada), with even the United States moving somewhat in the same direction: a transition from a large force in being to a small cadre backed by reserve forces.

Perhaps the most easily observed markers that distinguish armed forces and society are budgetary figures. Military budgets as a percent of gross national product are high in both war readiness and war deterrence societies. The expectation is that the military budgets will shrink under warless conditions, yet we note that the military expenditures presently continue as major outlays in such warless societies as Sweden and Switzerland (though not Canada).

What does change, however, is how the military spends its money. In war readiness societies, military spending mainly goes to the personnel costs associated with a large force structure and to large numbers of (relatively) low-technology weapons. In war deterrence societies, because of higher per capita salaries, personnel costs remain constant even though force size declines; likewise individual weapon systems become increasingly expensive because of higher technology. In warless societies, the bulk of the military budget consists of personnel training costs and the maintenance of a reserve infrastructure. The sophistication of weapons in a warless society, we hypothesise, will be a mix of low and high technology.

Internal organisational formats and tensions change. The military social structure of war readiness is heavily institutional with sharp divergences from civilian structures, while that of war deterrence becomes more occupational with greater civilian convergences. War readiness usually sees the primary intra-military conflict revolving around definitions of the roles of land, air and sea forces. In the mode of war deterrence, budget fights more than service roles characterise conflict within ministries of defence. In the warless society, military membership is defined mainly as a civic obligation, transcending the institutional and occupational dichotomy, including non-military forms of civic obligation and performance. Whether or not the military should substitute other goals for its warfighting mission becomes a major topic of discussion and controversy.

Major changes in civil-military relations occur as well, though these are not subject to easy quantification. Conscientious objection in the mass army is either prohibited (as was true of Mediterranean Europe and the Warsaw Pact until the 1980s), or limited to traditional peace churches (as in the United States and Northern Europe through the 1960s). With the advent of the professional and technical military, however, conscientious objection becomes a recognised and widespread right, often subsuming itself into alternative forms of broad national service. These trends are clearly evident in North Europe and are now appearing in Mediterranean countries of NATO and even in the socialist countries of East Europe. In warless societies, we hypothesise, military and civilian service will attain some sort of functional equivalence.

The conscription system that goes along with war readiness results in a military broadly representative of male youth, at least in theory. A recruitment system attuned to market conditions accompanies the professional army, which in turn leads to a military social composition mirroring the basic stratification system of the larger society: a well paid professional force coexists with lower ranks receiving working-class wages. In the warless society, the active-duty force shrinks dramatically to a (well paid) cadre who train (modestly compensated) long-term reservists. A militia and territorial defence system evolves. In warless societies, moreover, civilian service (including large numbers of women) becomes a common alternative to military service.

Probably the most documented finding in military sociology is how the dominant type of military professional shifts—from the combat leader in times of war readiness to the managerial technician in the military of war deterrence. We hypothesise, perhaps somewhat unexpectedly, that the dominant professional type in the warless society will be the soldier-scholar, reminiscent of the career officer in the period between the two world wars in Western nations. We can also expect, however, a residue of the warrior spirit to continue into the officer corps of the indefinite future.

The public evaluation of the armed forces varies. When military readiness is paramount, public support of the military tends to be high. In times of war deterrence and the shift to a market recruiting system, the public tends to adopt a more apathetic attitude toward the armed services. In a warless society, we suggest, not surprisingly, that public attitudes will become skeptical toward the armed services per se. We also speculate, however, that there may develop support for a more general form of civic service, to include the performance of civilian as well as militia tasks.

We can now turn to the military's attitude toward any disarmament in the emerging warless society. During eras of war readiness, most military professionals are opposed to any such notions and display a strong hostility toward peace activists. In times of war deterrence—the present era, more or less, a generally skeptical attitude persists, but the feasibility of arms control is not entirely dismissed. Although we can only conjecture as to the warless society, we propose that military professionals will adapt an apathetic viewpoint toward disarmament proposals, viewing such trends as inevitable in the dawning era.

The warless society thesis seeks to identify an overarching trend. Concretely, of course, war readiness and war deterrence features will persist into the warless society era. But the conception of a continuum highlights the ever-changing interface between the armed forces and society. This also alerts us to emergent trends within the military organisation. Over the years, incremental developments amount to deep changes. A shift in the rationale of the armed forces toward the warless model implies profound organisational consequences for armed forces.

As military organisations face goal displacement in warless societies, what new goals might appear, if any, become central in analysis. One can speculate on such new roles, but certain examples come readily to mind:

multinational peacekeeping in world trouble spots, space and arctic exploration, anti-drug trafficking, immigration control, education and job training for deprived youth, disaster relief, to name a few. We hypothesise that what precise new functions will develop will reflect the national singularities of the military, but that the warless society does mean that some kind of goal displacement will take place. Also attention must be paid to the political and social consequences of demobilised military personnel, a topic hitherto rarely considered in discussions of the shift from a war to a peace society.

We repeat that our purpose here is not to appraise the likelihood of a warless society, but to ascertain the probable role of armed forces in that eventuality. In a manner of speaking, however, the trends we have described are not really predictions. Rather they are partial observations. Much of what we have discussed has already happened—albeit only in bits and pieces or only in countries at the margins of the Cold War. The full impacts of the warless society are yet to come.

[From Charles C. Moskos, 'Armed Forces in a Warless Society', *Forum International*, 13 (1992), 3–10.]

BRIAN HOLDEN REID AND JOHN WHITE

42   Desertion in the American Civil War

The American Civil War has frequently been judged by historians as 'the first of the modern wars', partly because it heralded the mass involvement of the two world wars of this century. An aspect of this development which has excited less interest is the high degree of desertion from both the Southern and Northern armies, which would suggest that the causes fought for engaged the loyalties of fewer Americans than the nationalistic fervour which pervaded the conflict might suggest. Compilations from Union reports show that, on 1 February 1865, absentees totalled 338,536 as against 630,924 present for duty. Approximate figures for the Confederacy indicate 194,494 officers and men were absent, while only 160,198 were at their posts. The basic problem in assessing Civil War desertion is how to resolve the apparent contradiction between this remarkably high level of absenteeism and the patriotic zeal displayed by both sides. This article explores the causes of desertion in the Union and Confederate armies and the nature of the soldiers' grievances, assesses the response of the military authorities and considers the effects of desertion on the conduct of the war.

The actual meaning of the term 'desertion' was broadly similar for both Union and Confederate armies. By deserting, a Confederate soldier, like his Federal counterpart, violated the oath which he had sworn on enlistment to the Confederate States and its officers according to the 'Rules and Articles of War'. A deserter was a soldier who left the army with no intention of returning. The difficulty in discerning motives—except in cases of overt cowardice in the face of the enemy—made it difficult to distinguish between desertion and straggling. The *motive* and not the act determined what constituted desertion. The majority of those who deserted made for their homes and it was generally supposed that such absentees would return to their regiments at a later date. Soldiers before courts martial would frequently plead guilty to absence without leave, not desertion, and produce evidence of their intention to return, statements of reliable character, accounts of extenuating circumstances prevailing at home, or affidavits of voluntary return to the army. These were accepted by both Federal and Confederate courts as proof of intention not to desert, especially if the difficulties experienced in obtaining furloughs were taken into account. But the euphemism 'absent without leave' did not alter the hard fact that absenteeism occurred on a great scale. Generals Bragg and Lee declared that absence during a whole campaign was proof of the intention to desert. This view was not adopted by the courts. It was left to the discretion of regimental and company officers to determine the point when absenteeism became desertion. They were reluctant to take the decision themselves, especially in the South, aware that conditions at home, occupation of territory by the enemy, or sickness prevented the return of some absentees.

The term desertion was also applied popularly not only to 'absence without leave' but also to 'straggling', 'skulking' (the avoidance of military service by fraud, such as securing forged parole papers, furloughs or exemptions, collusion with medical boards, or the bribing of junior officers in pretending disability) and 'loafing', as indicated by the large numbers of officers that hung about their hotels in Washington. W. R. Barksdale wrote from a camp near Harper's Ferry in June 1861: 'It reminds me of Jake and his chills to see some of these fellows drooping about here trying to look sick.' In sum, desertion was an act for which no precise definition existed in the opposing armies during the Civil War. Also because desertion was distinguished from absence without leave only by intention, it gave the deserter the benefit of the doubt and reduced the risks of an act which in a European army would have been fraught with hazard.

The disciplinary structure of the Union and Confederate armies clearly has a great bearing on this problem. Chronologically, desertion followed the same pattern in the North and in the South: the rate was lowest in 1861 and highest in 1865. The United States army in 1861 was a small frontier police force, 13,000 strong. It was a professional army which combined harsh discipline with little *esprit de corps*. Army life was dull and many soldiers took solace in drink; morale was low and up to one-third of the total enrolments deserted annually. If caught deserters were severely punished: some deserters were humiliated by being exhibited in front of their companies wearing dresses. The War of 1812 and the Mexican War had not greatly affected the mass of the population. Americans could identify with military sacrifice and admire courage under fire without personal involvement in the cost and suffering. The outbreak of the Civil War had provoked a great wave of martial enthusiasm. With a vastly increased in-take of recruits, the pre-1861 system of discipline broke down: professional standards of discipline could no longer be enforced. [. . .]

Perhaps the true significance of desertion from both armies lies in its measure of unpreparedness to meet the challenges and suffering of a war in the industrial age. The indecisiveness of the early campaigns of the American Civil War, by comparison with the lavish promises of glory that had prevailed after Fort Sumter, provoked a widespread cynicism among American soldiers about the value of their respective causes proclaimed in so many speeches. For these men, whenever there was a clash of values, personal considerations outweighed loyalty to the flag, or at least to the *colours of their regiment*. The regimental structure compelled little feeling of group loyalty; which would not necessarily be the case in European armies, with harsher discipline, greater control and regimentation of the men and greater readiness to put men before a firing squad.

Desertion is a natural outgrowth of any conflict and is a reflection of certain political and social mores. American society in the nineteenth century was very decentralized. Localism, states' rights and a marked aversion to central authority—and the trappings of military authority in particular— resulted in a very high level of desertion. In the Southern case, the problem is complicated by the degree of support enjoyed by the Confederacy. Kenneth M. Stampp has advanced a persuasive argument that many Southerners had doubts about the ultimate validity of the Southern cause, and that some contemplated defeat if not with enthusiasm, at least with equanimity. General D.H. Hill complained in 1863:

There is a powerful faction in the State [North Carolina] poisoning public sentiment and looking to a reconstruction. The soldiers are induced by these traitors to believe that this is an unjust war on the part of the South and that their state soldiers and citizens have been slighted and wronged by the Confederate States Government.

Taken as a whole, the South did not evince the kind of passionate commitment, or identity with a distinct nationalistic cause, which would have gone some way to compensate for its numerical inferiority. It is not necessary to accept wholeheartedly David Donald's verdict that the South 'Died of Democracy' to suggest that the Confederacy should have altered the informal character of its military discipline as this promoted desertion.

It did not necessarily follow that a direct relationship existed between the patriotism displayed by soldiers of both sides and desertion, because patriotic feeling was not linked to any conception of deference or obedience to a central authority—especially if that authority was military. There was some connection between the degree of patriotism felt by recruits and their response to the duration and intensity of the conflict. McClellan observed in 1862 that 'More than once have battles, nearly lost by veterans, been restored by the intrepid obstinacy of new soldiers'. But this kind of enthusiasm became rarer as the war continued and the novelty of battle wore off. A high proportion of foreign-born recruits deserted because they felt little devotion either to their communities (and thus regiments) or to the United or Confederate States; up to 39 per cent of foreign-born recruits deserted in some companies. The other factor that qualified patriotic feeling was the bounty system. This was most widespread in the North but other aspects of the system, such as substitution, also had a bearing in the South. Northern states vied with one another to offer the highest bounties. The system was inefficient and costly: bounty expenditure of $750,000,000 equalled the total cost of Union army pay throughout the war. New York, which paid the highest bounties (one district offering on average $407.74 per volunteer) experienced the highest percentage of deserters: 89.06 per thousand compared with the average national rate of 62.51 per thousand.

The commandant of the Annapolis parole camp observed in 1863 of some Union deserters recently exchanged for Confederates that, 'If the men in my camp were a sample of our army, we would have nothing but a mob of stragglers and cowards'. This kind of sweeping statement indulged in by contemporaries conceals the complexity of motive and the ineffectiveness of sanctions. Desertion in both the Union and Confederate armies reflects upon attitudes towards authority in the United States in a conflict whose intensity and duration was unexpected. It also reflects upon the American military tradition. Before 1861 it did not embrace mass involvement. After 1865 the idea of a nation in arms—the Grand Army of the Republic—became more acceptable. The United States army in 1917–18—the next great conflict requiring mass involvement—did not face the scale of disciplinary problems encountered during the Civil War. Observers hoped immediately after 1865 that a taste of military discipline would iron out an unfortunate penchant for individualism and looked for the 'establishment of an orderly spirit and a settled regard for law'. These hopes were in vain over the short term but they did contribute towards making the rigours of military discipline rather more acceptable to the next generation of Americans called to the colours in a war of mass involvement.

[From Brian Holden Reid and John White, ' "A Mob of Stragglers and Cowards": Desertion from the Union and Confederate Armies, 1861–65', *Journal of Strategic Studies*, 8/1 (1985), 64–5, 74–5.]

EDWARD SHILS AND MORRIS JANOWITZ

43 **Undermining German Morale**

At the beginning of the second world war, many publicists and specialists in propaganda attributed almost supreme importance to psychological warfare operations. The legendary successes of Allied propaganda against the German Army at the end of the first world war and the tremendous expansion of the advertising and mass communications industries in the ensuing two decades had convinced many people that human behavior could be extensively manipulated by mass communications. They tended furthermore to stress that military morale was to a great extent a function of the belief in the rightness of the 'larger' cause which was at issue in the war; good soldiers were therefore those who clearly understood the political and moral implications of what was at stake. They explained the striking successes of the German Army in the early phases of the war by the 'ideological possession' of the German soldiers, and they accordingly thought that propaganda attacking doctrinal conceptions would be defeating this army.

Studies of the German Army's morale and fighting effectiveness made during the last three years of the war throw considerable doubt on these hypotheses. The solidarity of the German Army was discovered by these studies—which left much to be desired from the standpoint of scientific rigor—to be based only very indirectly and very partially on political convictions or broader ethical beliefs. Where conditions were such as to allow primary group life to function smoothly, and where the primary group developed a high degree of cohesion, morale was high and resistance effective or at least very determined, regardless in the main of the political attitudes of the soldiers. The conditions of primary group life were related to spatial proximity, the capacity for intimate communication, the provision of paternal protectiveness by NCO's and junior officers, and the gratification of certain personality needs, e.g., manliness, by the military organization and its activities. The larger structure of the army served to maintain morale through the provision of the framework in which potentially individuating physical threats were kept at a minimum—through the organization of supplies and through adequate strategic dispositions.

The behavior of the German Army demonstrated that the focus of attention and concern beyond one's immediate face-to-face social circles might be slight indeed and still not interfere with the achievement of a high degree of military effectiveness. It also showed that attempts to modify behavior by means of symbols referring to events or values outside the focus of attention and concern would be given an indifferent response by the vast majority of the German soldiers. This was almost equally true under conditions of primary group integrity and under conditions of extreme primary group disintegration. In the former, primary needs were met adequately through the gratifications provided by the other members of the group; in the latter, the individual had regressed to a narcissistic state in which symbols referring to the outer world were irrelevant to his first concern—'saving his own skin'.

At moments of primary group disintegration, a particular kind of propaganda less hortatory or analytical, but addressing the intensified desire to survive, and describing the precise procedures by which physical survival could be achieved, was likely to facilitate further disintegration. Furthermore, in some cases aspects of the environment towards which the soldier might hitherto have been emotionally indifferent were defined for him by prolonged exposure to propaganda under conditions of disintegration. Some of these wider aspects, e.g., particular strategic considerations, then tended to be taken into account in his motivation and he was more likely to implement his defeatist mood by surrender than he would have been without exposure to propaganda.

It seems necessary, therefore, to reconsider the potentialities of propaganda in the context of all the other variables which influence behavior. The erroneous views concerning the omnipotence of propaganda must be given up and their place must be taken by much more differentiated views as to the possibilities of certain kinds of propaganda under different sets of conditions.

It must be recognized that on the moral plane most men are members of the larger society by virtue of identifications which are mediated through the human beings with whom they are in personal relationships. Many are bound into the larger society only by primary group identifications. Only a small proportion possessing special training or rather particular kinds of personalities are capable of giving a preponderant share of their attention and concern to the symbols of the larger world. The conditions under which these different groups will respond to propaganda will differ, as will also the type of propaganda to which they will respond.

[From Edward Shils and Morris Janowitz, 'Cohesion and Disintegration in the Wehrmacht in World War II', *Public Opinion Quarterly*, 12 (summer 1948).]

N. KINZER STEWART

44 Military Cohesion

Four brave men who do not know each other will not dare to attack a lion. Four less brave, but knowing each other well, sure of their reliability and consequently of mutual aid, will attack resolutely.

ARDANT DU PICQ

Military historians, sociologists, and psychologists have long meditated on the issue of why men stand and fight or break and run. The task of military leaders has always been to meld young men into unified troops who would bravely face an enemy's sword, crossbow, or cannon after withstanding trials of forced marches, hunger, thirst, cold, vermin, loneliness, and disillusionment. Military commanders have long sought reasons why men will fight. Is it one or a combination of: charismatic leadership, superb tactics, adequate logistics, superior firepower, patriotism, or that ephemeral quality of esprit? The answer is some of the above, or all of the above, but always and most important that will-o'-the-wisp known as esprit, or morale, or will. This concept is hardly new. After a long and arduous campaign, Greek military leader Xenophon (434–355 BC) wrote: 'You know I am sure that not numbers or strength bring victory in war; but whichever army goes into battle stronger in soul, their enemies generally cannot withstand them.'

Commanders prior to and since Xenophon have pondered the problem of turning young boys into fighting men. In time of dire crisis, young children, old men, and even women have been pressed into service, but most armies have consisted of adolescent males. Civilians have been dragooned into armies by press gangs. Soldiers have fought fortified by drugs or alcohol. They have rushed to their deaths inspired by belief in Holy Crusades or desire for nirvana. Officers holding swords and lances have prodded men sick with fear into firefights. Without exception, all famed military leaders—Xenophon, Sun Tzu, Caesar, Genghis Khan, Charlemagne, Napoleon, Wellington, Washington, Lee, MacArthur, Montgomery, Mao—agree that men united for a cause, trusting in each other, and confident in their leaders will be an effective and victorious army. This unity or sense of belonging manifests itself in the elegant phrase 'esprit de corps' or a simple word like 'buddy'. British historians have emphasized the raison d'être of a fighting force to be the regimental spirit or the sense of belonging. This chapter presents some of the pertinent literature concerning the 'human dimension of combat'. Strategic planners usually focus on order of battle and quantifiable items such as numbers and types of weapons or level of technology, while ignoring those difficult to measure sociopsychological variables such as leadership style, organizational climate, level of personnel turbulence, cohesion, and morale. The broadbrush overview that follows shows that there is indeed a large body of scientific research dealing with these complex and ephemeral issues. [. . .]

With the advent of World War II, social psychologists worked assiduously to determine what were the elements that made men fight, fight well, or break down completely. Stouffer et al.'s work is still a landmark and forms an important part of the basis for military psychology and sociology. Stouffer and his colleagues found that a majority of men in combat admitted to fear; were not overly concerned with issues of patriotism; did not hate unduly the enemy; prayed when they were frightened; and believed in a code of masculinity. Loyalty to the group or unit was paramount to high-performing units, which were defined as units with low rates of nonbattle casualties. These units were those in which the men developed bonds of loyalty to the group; had favorable attitudes toward the officers; trusted in the medical care they would receive in battle; and had pride in the unit's accomplishments.

But fear was ever present. Officers and enlisted men in the Mediterranean said that combat became more frightening the more they saw of it. Eighty-three percent of Stouffer's sample of 1,766 combat veterans in Italy in 1944 reported that they had seen a man overcome by fear. Those who observed that extreme manifestation of fear or 'crack-up' reported that they too were upset and concerned. This focus on overcoming fear is a direct outcome of the emphasis placed on the diagnosis of shell shock of World War I vintage and the growth of psychiatry and psychology in the 1920–40 period.

Continuing in the same intellectual tradition, the founders of military sociology, Edgar Shils and Morris Janowitz, interviewed German prisoners of war to determine why some Wehrmacht soldiers fought against insurmountable odds and why other units and individuals surrendered or ran away. They concluded that the following factors contributed to cohesive groups—those that stood and fought: small-group ties, physical proximity to other groups, devotion to Hitler, fear of retribution against one's family, belief in National Socialism, paternal protectiveness of senior NCOs and junior officers, and disbelief in enemy propaganda. Those German soldiers who surrendered did so because their primary-group ties had been broken. Some of these soldiers were isolated in bunkers or cellars with no ties to the larger group, and lacked food, warm clothing, and supplies. Other soldiers were Poles or Slavs with no ties to the German fatherland. Of the German nationals, some knew that their families' town had already been overrun by Allied or Soviet troops and there was no sense of having to defend their homeland for the sake of their families. Thus, these frightened, lonely, cold, and hungry troops surrendered singly or in groups or waited, huddled in their sleeping bags or hidden in bunkers, to be captured. During World War II, commanders realized that a frightened soldier who was not bonded to the group often would not fire his weapon. If you fired your weapon, it meant that the enemy knew where you were and would fire his weapon at you.

Roger Little's insightful work on infantry platoons in combat and in garrison during the Korean War further underscored combat leaders' observations of men not firing their weapons. The title of Little's essay (written with Morris Janowitz), 'Buddy Relations and Combat Performance', provides the essence of his results. Men were closely bonded together as buddies during combat. These bonded relationships meant that men would fight together as a unit and thus live to another day. Basic survival meant they all had to band together, work as a team, and protect each other. One person who failed the group meant the group might not survive and individual men would never see Iowa or Indiana again. Little also had some salient comments on the relationship between officers and soldiers. In garrison, officers were removed from the men and were more concerned with the ceremonial aspect of army life. However, in combat, the officers lived with their men, shared their discomfort and fears. Status differences became blurred in combat to such an extent that officers allied themselves with their men and tended to ignore higher-echelon requests. When officers endured the same dreadful conditions as their men, rank tended to disappear and survival, not saluting, became the norm. Officers bonded to their men and not to the rear echelon headquarters types. Like the Israeli Army today, with its constant demands for battle readiness and need to move out immediately, Little's officers and men paid scant attention to rigid demands of class, rank, or unearned status—respect was earned in combat.

Over and over, research in military psychology and sociology in the United States and other Allied nations reaffirms the interrelationship of small-group ties, loyalty, bonding, esprit, and combat performance. Yet the majority of US Army planners continue to emphasize training, tactics, firepower, and weapons systems and, if not ignore, at least downplay the issue of the sociopsychological effect of cohesion on high performance in battle. Fortunately, not all military analysts or members of the armed services ignore the human factors in battle.

One theorist who is a noticeable exception to the emphasis on machines and weapons, Col. W. D. Henderson, has written two very interesting books on the issue of cohesion and battlefield performance. His 1979 book, *Why the Vietcong Fought*, analyzes the reasons the Vietcong won in Vietnam against a US force with greater concentrated firepower and air and naval support. For every one US or Allied casualty the United States forces inflicted five casualties against the Vietnamese enemy. In spite of these staggering losses: 'One army endured, and the other did not . . . the North Vietnamese Army endured, maintained its cohesion, and remained on the battlefield when all others had retired.' Henderson's work refines the trailblazing participant observation research of Charles Moskos.

Moskos lived, marched, ate C rations with, and interviewed enlisted men during the Vietnam War. Following in the footsteps of Shils and Janowitz and Little, Moskos well understood that cohesion is a key element in the soldier's survival, since an individual has to be part of the group in order to increase his chances of survival. Moskos quickly realized that the one-year Vietnam tour, which was thought to be the best manpower situation, was in reality a disaster from the point of view of developing cohesive units who are combat-effective even though the individual combat soldier had high morale. Men were rotated in and out of units as single replacements. A lieutenant might have three weeks' experience, his sergeant two months', and the men varying degrees of experience ranging from a few weeks to eleven months. Thus, the group had little primary-group cohesion or loyalty and, even more important, had disparate amounts of actual combat experience. As men were rotated in and out of the system as so many pieces on a chessboard or as interoperable replacement parts in the Lean Green Machine, friendships were transient at best. Groups were more often than not single units of individuals who counted months, then days, then hours until their rotation date.

Army psychiatrist Peter Bourne was also sure that the one-year tour was a decisive factor in a lack of group cohesiveness, which, in turn, led to increased rates of psychiatric casualties. Twenty years prior to Bourne, Stouffer had already made a clear relationship between a replacement's integration to the group and the new soldier's subsequent combat performance. Each new replacement fresh from a training base in the United States had to make two adjustments upon arrival in a unit. First he had to learn the individual whims and foibles of his new comrades, and second and often simultaneously he had to adjust quickly to the terror of combat.

Research has repeatedly shown that there is a strong relationship between cohesion, soldiers' level of morale, and combat efficiency. Stouffer provided the basis for this understanding of the link between cohesion and combat efficiency in the study of infantrymen and bomber crews in World War II. What keeps men in battle are ties of friendship, affection, good humor, machismo, sense of honor, or sportsmanlike behavior. Whatever those ties may be, they bind and entangle a man's psyche in such a way that he will not run away, will not curl up in his foxhole and cry, and will not climb into his sleeping bag and feign sleep in the middle of an artillery barrage. Stoically, with feigned insouciance, or cynically with gallows humor, he endures and goes forward. He stays in the swirl and din of combat because to run away would be worse than death itself. He would know himself as a coward—and worst of all his comrades would know that awful truth as well.

Henderson defines military cohesion as follows:

Cohesion exists in a unit when the primary day-to-day goals of the individual soldiers, of the small group with which he identifies, and of unit leaders are congruent—with each giving his primary loyalty to the group so that it trains and fights as a unit with all members willing to risk death to achieve a common objective.

Herein lies the crux of military cohesion. Disparate men from varied socioeconomic backgrounds, of different ethnic origins and levels of education are expected to become not just a collection of individuals but a unit in which an individual will sacrifice his life and die in order to preserve the group. Because of well-developed ties of friendship or camaraderie, men will fight individually as part of a unit to defend the group as a unit, its honor, or its combat efficiency. We are not referring to job efficiency, or meeting production quotas, or increasing the point total of a football team, but death and dying for the good of the group. That's the essence of military cohesion. Because combat is a nasty, brutish place to be.

Military memoirs, Hollywood movies, television series, and countless novels have attempted to paint the reality of combat. But still there is the adage, 'You had to be there to know what it is like.' Combat is hunger, privation, diarrhea, trench foot, trench mouth, flatulence, leeches, mosquitoes, rain, burning sun, and wet rain forest. A soldier's life even in training exercises is not pleasant and not a Hollywood movie. In battle, young men who have never seen a wounded animal watch their friends place their hands over their intestines and try to stave off death for a few moments. Amid the frantic thunder of artillery barrages, they hear teammates cry out for their mothers. No, combat is not a pleasant place at all. The one saving grace or the only thread of sanity in that insane world is the presence of your buddies and the knowledge that somehow because you trust your comrades in arms and know your lieutenant you won't get killed. Somehow you will get out of this situation. Friendship ties men to each other; during a firefight, with imminent death a possibility, men fight and kill so that each one may live.

[From N. Kinzer Stewart, *Mates and Muchachos: Unit Cohesion in the Falklands/Malvinas War* (London: Brassey's, 1991), 11–18.]

Section D

The Ethics of War

BARRIE PASKINS

There are few easy answers in the ethics of war and many different kinds of perspective need to be taken into account. Wilfred Owen's expression of the pity of war is a necessary challenge to every attempt at glamorizing war, while Herbert Read's 'To a Conscript of 1940' reminds us that pity is not enough (45). After 1918, the war literature of which Owen's 'Dulce et Decorum est' is a moving example seemed to many people in some countries to identify war itself as the supreme evil, but events soon enforced a sharp distinction between the pacifists who reject all war and those, 'peace-oriented non-pacifists [who] have considered warfare a conceivable if distasteful possibility' (46; 47).

Hans Morgenthau is a self-styled realist. Note two vital features of his celebrated account of international politics as 'interest defined in terms of power' (48). First, he shifts our perspective, inviting us to look from the viewpoint of the state and the enlightened decision-maker rather than the anguished individual. He wants us to remember that whatever our private attitudes to war, we are also citizens of a state which, he thinks, tends to behave in ways which are characteristic of all states. Second, Morgenthau is not 'a-moral', as some writers seem to think that realists are bound to be by definition. He is 'aware of the moral significance of political action' but 'refuses to identify the moral aspirations of a particular nation with the moral laws that govern the universe'. Is his state-centred realism too calm, too remote, to measure up to the urgencies of Owen and Read?

An approach sometimes considered as a compromise between peace and war is the use of *sanctions*, whose usefulness was invoked in discussions of the war to evict Iraq from Kuwait. Many pacificists say that Iraq's aggression could not be allowed to go unchallenged but that sanctions were not given enough time before the air and land assault known as 'Desert Storm'. In such a context, 'sanctions' is ambiguous. One thing it might mean is 'non-lethal signalling of political will'. Of this, there was a great deal before 'Desert Storm'. The sale of Iraqi oil was stopped. Months of intense diplomatic activity included the good offices of friendly states such as the USSR and France. Personal initiatives by private citizens as eminent as Willy Brandt were rewarded with no more than a handful of hostage releases. During this time, a mighty coalition force was gathering, whose need to be used when ready was politically unmistakable. As a last resort, the UN Secretary-General visited Baghdad but was deliberately humiliated. It is hard to imagine a more comprehensive process of political signalling.

If 'sanctions' did not mean such signalling, its other obvious meaning was the imposition of a siege or a blockade, the subject of extract 50 from Michael Walzer's *Just and Unjust Wars*, probably the best one-volume introduction to the ethics of war. As Walzer makes painfully clear, if 'sanctions' do involve a siege or a blockade, then this is no easy option but on the contrary a form of warfare as terrible as it is ancient. Indeed, we now need to darken Walzer's picture still further. He says 'in the direness of a siege, people have a right to be refugees'. The experience in Bosnia in 1992 has taught us that 'the right to be refugees' can be an effective instrument of war. The extract from the history of the Gulf War by Lawrence Freedman and Efraim Karsh demonstrates the extent to which a strategy of patient pressure can allow an aggressor to consolidate his gains (49).

Ethical reflection in our time inevitably turns to the Nuremberg Trial, to date the supreme attempt to bring legal categories to bear on the atrocities of war. As they strove to do justice in 'the last act of the war and the first act of the peace', the Allies found themselves insisting not on Morgenthau's 'interest defined in terms of power' but on the elemental rule of law, that each individual is responsible for his or her own actions. Three of the accused were acquitted and all of those executed were convicted of war crimes or crimes against humanity (genocide). The achievements and imperfections of the Nuremberg Trial are the subject of several excellent books, notably those by John and Ann Tusa and Airey Neave.[1] In *Victors' Justice*, Richard Minear argues persuasively that the Tokyo Trial of Japanese war criminals was a less satisfactory proceeding, to which the label 'victors' justice' more readily belongs.[2]

Many other trials followed those at Nuremberg and Tokyo. One of the most discussed, that of Adolf Eichmann, who was captured in Argentina and tried in Israel, was studied by the philosopher Hannah Arendt in a controversial book. Extract 51 is from the final pages, which end with the words of her celebrated subtitle, the 'banality of evil'. Eichmann's grotesque banality brings into sharp relief one kind of doubt about the very idea of ethics of war which we find it difficult to avoid. Faced with such a person, in some ways so ordinary, and with such deeds, and with the difficulty of doing justice to the perpetrator of such actions, we wonder what words or feelings are appropriate. With the poets Wilfred Owen and Herbert Read we know where we stand, but what is one to make of

[1] Anne Tusa and John Tusa, *The Nuremberg Trial* (London: Macmillan, 1983); Airey Neave, *Nuremberg* (London: Hodder & Stoughton, 1978).

[2] Richard H. Minear, *Victors' Justice* (Princeton, NJ: Princeton University Press, 1971).

Eichmann? The Nuremberg Trial insisted on individual responsibility but the laws of war are based upon *realpolitik*. What are we to say of such laws applied to such a man as Eichmann?

If grave moral dangers beset us, what guidance can be found about our positive duties? As an example, my essay (52) investigates the little-discussed vacuum in which defence scientists operate. Since Nuremberg, a relatively well-defined framework of laws has emerged to instruct soldiers in their duty, but war is not made only by soldiers. Should the kind of framework I sketch be developed for all the types of occupation most centrally involved in war, or is this idea as 'meaningless' as a legal ban on nuclear weapons would be? If we are to be realists with Morgenthau, is any framework of duties possible which can preserve us from sinking into the abyss of Eichmann? The final essay by Paul Warnke considers the question of the punishment of war crimes alleged to have been committed by American personnel during the American intervention in Vietnam (55). Once again the fundamental question arises: is *law* adequate to articulate the ethics of war? Does responsibility lie with the state to such an extent that it makes little sense to prosecute lowly personnel such as Lieutenant Calley? Or is individual responsibility so clear-cut and self-evident that the individual can realistically be held responsible? There are few easy answers in the ethics of war.

45 **Two Poems**

Dulce Et Decorum Est

Bent double, like old beggars under sacks,
Knock-kneed, coughing like hags, we cursed through sludge,
Till on the haunting flares we turned our backs
And towards our distant rest began to trudge.
Men marched asleep. Many had lost their boots
But limped on, blood-shod. All went lame; all blind;
Drunk with fatigue; deaf even to the hoots
Of tired, outstripped Five-Nines that dropped behind.

Gas! GAS! Quick, boys!—An ecstasy of fumbling,
Fitting the clumsy helmets just in time;
But someone still was yelling out and stumbling
And flound'ring like a man in fire or lime . . .
Dim, through the misty panes and thick green light,
As under a green sea, I saw him drowning.

In all my dreams, before my helpless sight,
He plunges at me, guttering, choking, drowning.

If in some smothering dreams you too could pace
Behind the wagon that we flung him in,
And watch the white eyes writhing in his face,
His hanging face, like a devil's sick of sin;
If you could hear, at every jolt, the blood
Come gargling from the froth-corrupted lungs,
Obscene as cancer, bitter as the cud
Of vile, incurable sores on innocent tongues,—
My friend, you would not tell with such high zest
To children ardent for some desperate glory,
The old Lie: Dulce et decorum est
Pro patria mori.

(Wilfred Owen)

To a Conscript of 1940

*Qui n'a pas une fois désespéré de l'honneur,
Ne sera jamais un héros.—George Bernanos.*

A soldier passed me in the freshly-fallen snow,
    His footsteps muffled, his face unearthly grey;
And my heart gave a sudden leap
    As I gazed on a ghost of five-and-twenty years ago.

I shouted Halt! and my voice had the old accustomed ring
    And he obeyed it as it was obeyed
In the shrouded days when I too was one
    Of an army of young men marching

Into the unknown. He turned towards me and I said:
    'I am one of those who went before you
Five-and-twenty years ago: one of the many who never returned,
    Of the many who returned and yet were dead.

We went where you are going, into the rain and the mud;
    We fought as you will fight
With death and darkness and despair;
    We gave what you will give—our brains and our blood.

We think we gave in vain. The world was not renewed.
    There was hope in the homestead and anger in the streets
But the old world was restored and we returned
    To the dreary field and workshop, and the immemorial feud

Of rich and poor. Our victory was our defeat.
    Power was retained where power had been misused
And youth was left to sweep away
    The ashes that the fire had strewn beneath our feet.

But one thing we learned: there is no glory in the deed
    Until the soldier wears a badge of tarnished braid;
There are heroes who have heard the rally and have seen
    The glitter of a garland round their head.

Theirs is the hollow victory. They are deceived.
    But you, my brother and my ghost, if you can go
Knowing that there is no reward, no certain use
    In all your sacrifice, then honour is reprieved.

To fight without hope is to fight with grace,
    The self reconstructed, the false heart repaired.'

Then I turned with a smile, and he answered my salute
  As he stood against the fretted hedge, which was like white lace.

(Herbert Read)

[From Wilfred Owen, *Collected Poems* (London: Chatto & Windus, 1963), 55; Herbert
Read in Oscar Williams (ed.), *A Little Treasury of Modern Poetry* (London: Routledge,
1948), 223–5.]

JOHN YODER

46 **The Pacifism of Absolute Principle**

If there be then such a thing as 'absolute principles', whether we think we find these expressed in the text of the Ten Commandments or in some other form, it is very likely that the sanctity of human life will be one of them. Such a position can be held in puritanical and legalistic ways, but it need not be. It can be quite at home within a sectarian understanding of the place of the church in the world, but it need not be limited to that context. It can be the expression of naive assumptions about how God gave the Ten Commandments to Israel, but need not be. This position has found its most categorical expression in recent years on the part of the Austrian Roman Catholic theologian Johannes Ude. The command 'Thou shalt not kill' is according to Ude an absolute, admitting of no exceptions. It is on a quite different level of authority from the various other political practices and prescriptions in the Old Testament which still left a place for violence.

The *axiom* underlying this stance is that man is not capable of auto-salvation; that he must be guided through meaningful general directives received by revelation and bearing authority over him. 'Revelation' is the religious label; non-theistic moral man will lean in a similar way on similarly structured generalizations which he accepts as coming to him from 'reason' or 'human dignity' or 'the experience of the race'.

It is not a significant shortcoming of this position that it can easily be caricatured by the naive who apply it legalistically, in a self-righteous or self-deceiving way, or by the libertines who reject it because they are unaware of their own irrational commitments to authorities outside themselves. Such weak spots are found in every system; their presence is more a fruit of varying levels of sophistication than of differing ethical postures. They are unavoidable if an ethical posture is to be taken by a whole community, by simple and busy people.

The more serious weaknesses are on the logical level. Even the most categorical command is still communicated in human language and carried by human documents. Whether the documents be the human mind or the Old Testament, the meaning of a verbal command is not unequivocal. The giving and receiving of communication, even if it be in the name of God, is subject to shadings of meaning which the habit of thinking of a limited number of absolute principles fails to respect. This is well exemplified by the very case of the Ten Commandments, where the strictest translation would probably read not, 'Thou shalt not kill' but rather 'Thou shalt commit no murder'.

The second difficulty of this approach is the problem of 'collision' when more absolutes than one are calling for allegiance in the same situation. Situations can easily be imagined, or documented from history, in which it is evidently necessary to choose between not lying and not taking life or between not taking one life and not defending another. The concept of absolute principle does not suffice here.

Still another shortcoming is the negative form which such absolutes almost inevitably must take. Very easily the effort to respect such prescriptions becomes transformed into a search for moral purity for its own sake, rather than an expression of love of the neighbor. It is possible to be very scrupulous about not taking life, and yet lack insight into the positive obligations which flow from a genuine respect for that same life.

Nevertheless, in the serious ethical decision-making process the language of absolute obligation, whatever its practical and philosophical shortcomings, is still the clearest language we have. The burden of proof still lies with those who claim that it is possible to have a community of moral discourse without certain shared understandings which function somehow like 'principles'. When speaking to the individual's decision-making in a given context, the situation-ethicists have much that is wholesome to say about flexibility, about the importance of loving motivation, and about the uniqueness of each choice. But they say this to persons who have already acquired somewhere a set of understandings about what constitutes the neighbor's welfare, with which they can then afford to be flexible. They have not demonstrated how ethical decision can be the subject of *community* concern—in justifying or condemning choices, in nurturing the immature, in adjudicating conflicts between the differing demands of different loves, in aiding the individual to keep watch on his own hasty and unworthy loves for the sake of his longer-range and worthier love of neighbor—without recourse to principle.

After all, any case that can be made *for* war also appeals to principles claiming to stand above the individual, and they are generally less flexible, less humane, and less moral than those appealed to against it. In the concrete conflict situation, it is over against other absolutes, equally blunt and oversimplified, that this one is to be weighed. Courage, comradeship, freedom, a particular preferred form of government, the direction of history, or the integrity of territory are all, when they become reasons for killing, just as 'absolute' in their demands, and far less human or humane in the attitude they express. They are still more degrading than the pacifist absolutes when applied in legalistic, self-justifying, ways by the naive and those who are not equipped (as the situationist is) for the luxury of situationally anguished existential choices. These pagan absolutes function with the same logical weaknesses as those of the Ten Commandments but are far less worthy of such respect. They are more rigid not only psychologically (who can argue with 'better dead than red'?) but also institutionally; the provision for killing is self-authenticating and self-governing. The military establishment has to be code-bound in a way that the church may, but need not be.

'Thou shalt not kill' is, as an absolute, still immeasurably more human, more personalistic, more genuinely responsible than the competitive absolute, 'Thou shalt not let Uncle Sam down' or 'Thou shalt fight for freedom' or 'Never give up the ship'. As in the age of Abraham or Moses the blanket prohibition of killing freed the Hebrews from the scourge of infant sacrifice, so today such a person-centered absolute prohibition may well help free us from other idolatries.

[From John Yoder, *Nevertheless: A Meditation on the Varieties and Shortcomings of Religious Pacifism* (Scottdale, Pa.: Herald Press, 1971), 27–31.]

MARTIN CEADEL

47 Pacific-ism

[T]he pacific-ism/pacifism distinction is etymologically artificial: 'pacific-ism' is really the correct form of the word now almost invariably contracted to 'pacifism'. Yet it is not wholly contrived, since when originally coined (soon after 1900), the word 'pacificism' connoted exactly what pacific-ism is here defined as meaning. As its meaning narrowed to absolute rejection of all war (which it more or less had done by the mid-1930s), so the original and correct form of the word dropped out of common usage. Since the 1930s, in consequence, there has been no word to describe non-pacifist peace sentiment. As early as July 1936, for example, the British prime minister, Stanley Baldwin, experienced this lack when telling a deputation of Conservative backbenchers of the 'very strong, I do not know about pacifist but pacific feeling in the country after the war' (which had, he claimed, hindered rearmament). So, for all its inelegance, pacific-ism is here pressed into service again.

How old a theory is it? Plans for the abolition of war are presumably almost as old as war itself, as F. H. Hinsley has pointed out; and modern plans are often simply re-inventions of the wheel. Yet pacific-ism cannot be said properly to have existed before two related developments took place. The first was a gradual and partial stabilization of the international system so that the bellicist view that war is inevitable did not seem so indisputably true. The second was the emergence of a domestic political process in some states, so that there was some prospect of mobilizing support for peace plans.

The late eighteenth century thus saw the origins of pacific-ism, and the mid-nineteenth its taking root. It was in the period from the 1730s to the 1760s that peace plans [. . .] began to take on a more modern form. And, with both French *philosophes* and British political economists stressing the harmony of interests between states during the eighteenth century, it can be said that by its end, to quote Michael Howard, 'a complete liberal theory of international relations, of war and peace, had thus already developed'. The Napoleonic Wars led during 1815–16 in the United States and Britain to the formation of the first peace societies (as distinct from pacifist religious sects) and also brought into being a recognizably modern international system. In these years, moreover, the combined impacts of the American, French and industrial revolutions were inaugurating modern politics within many states.

Pacific-ism thus presupposes a considerable measure of optimism regarding the prospects of domestic and international progress. [. . .] [I]ts utopian fringe—believers in the immediate feasibility of world government, for example—require a very large measure indeed. But its mainstream needs this to be offset with a moderate dose of pessimism, since excessive optimism harms it in two ways. First, if the domestic and international outlook is too rosy then war will not be feared, and the abolition of war will not be a salient issue. Second, if those who even so become interested in this issue are too optimistic about the chances of success, they may opt for more extreme approaches such as pacifism of the optimistic variety or, in powerful states, crusading. On balance, therefore, pacific-ism flourishes where there is the right blend of optimism and pessimism.

[From Martin Ceadel, *Thinking about Peace and War* (Oxford: Oxford University Press, 1987), 102–3.]

HANS MORGENTHAU

48 Six Principles of Political Realism

1. Political realism believes that politics, like society in general, is governed by objective laws that have their roots in human nature. In order to improve society it is first necessary to understand the laws by which society lives. The operation of these laws being impervious to our preferences, men will challenge them only at the risk of failure.

Realism, believing as it does in the objectivity of the laws of politics, must also believe in the possibility of developing a rational theory that reflects, however imperfectly and one-sidedly, these objective laws. It believes also, then, in the possibility of distinguishing in politics between truth and opinion—between what is true objectively and rationally, supported by evidence and illuminated by reason, and what is only a subjective judgment, divorced from the facts as they are and informed by prejudice and wishful thinking.

Human nature, in which the laws of politics have their roots, has not changed since the classical philosophies of China, India, and Greece endeavored to discover these laws. Hence, novelty is not necessarily a virtue in political theory, nor is old age a defect. The fact that a theory of politics, if there be such a theory, has never been heard of before tends to create a presumption against, rather than in favor of, its soundness. Conversely, the fact that a theory of politics was developed hundreds or even thousands of years ago—as was the theory of the balance of power—does not create a presumption that it must be outmoded and obsolete. A theory of politics must be subjected to the dual test of reason and experience. To dismiss such a theory because it had its flowering in centuries past is to present not a rational argument but a modernistic prejudice that takes for granted the superiority of the present over the past. To dispose of the revival of such a theory as a 'fashion' or 'fad' is tantamount to assuming that in matters political we can have opinions but no truths.

For realism, theory consists in ascertaining facts and giving them meaning through reason. It assumes that the character of a foreign policy can be ascertained only through the examination of the political acts performed and of the foreseeable consequences of these acts. Thus we can find out what statesmen have actually done, and from the foreseeable consequences of their acts we can surmise what their objectives might have been.

Yet examination of the facts is not enough. To give meaning to the factual raw material of foreign policy, we must approach political reality with a kind of rational outline, a map that suggests to us the possible meanings of foreign policy. In other words, we put ourselves in the position of a statesman who must meet a certain problem of foreign policy under certain circumstances, and we ask ourselves what the rational alternatives are from which a statesman may choose who must meet this problem under these circumstances (presuming always that he acts in a rational manner), and which of these rational alternatives this particular statesman, acting under these circumstances, is likely to choose. It is the testing of this rational hypothesis against the actual facts and their consequences that gives meaning to the facts of international politics and makes a theory of politics possible.

2. The main signpost that helps political realism to find its way through the landscape of international politics is the concept of interest defined in terms of power. This concept provides the link between reason trying to

understand international politics and the facts to be understood. It sets politics as an autonomous sphere of action and understanding apart from other spheres, such as economics (understood in terms of interest defined as wealth), ethics, aesthetics, or religion. Without such a concept a theory of politics, international or domestic, would be altogether impossible, for without it we could not distinguish between political and nonpolitical facts, nor could we bring at least a measure of systematic order to the political sphere.

We assume that statesmen think and act in terms of interest defined as power, and the evidence of history bears that assumption out. That assumption allows us to retrace and anticipate, as it were, the steps a statesman—past, present, or future—has taken or will take on the political scene. We look over his shoulder when he writes his dispatches; we listen in on his conversation with other statesmen; we read and anticipate his very thoughts. Thinking in terms of interest defined as power, we think as he does, and as disinterested observers we understand his thoughts and actions perhaps better than he, the actor on the political scene, does himself.

The concept of interest defined as power imposes intellectual discipline upon the observer, infuses rational order into the subject matter of politics, and thus makes the theoretical understanding of politics possible. On the side of the actor, it provides for rational discipline in action and creates that astounding continuity in foreign policy which makes American, British, or Russian foreign policy appear as an intelligible, rational continuum, by and large consistent within itself, regardless of the different motives, preferences, and intellectual and moral qualities of successive statesmen. A realist theory of international politics, then, will guard against two popular fallacies: the concern with motives and the concern with ideological preferences.

To search for the clue to foreign policy exclusively in the motives of statesmen is both futile and deceptive. It is futile because motives are the most illusive of psychological data, distorted as they are, frequently beyond recognition, by the interests and emotions of actor and observer alike. Do we really know what our own motives are? And what do we know of the motives of others?

Yet even if we had access to the real motives of statesmen, that knowledge would help us little in understanding foreign policies, and might well lead us astray. It is true that the knowledge of the statesman's motives may give us one among many clues as to what the direction of his foreign policy might be. It cannot give us, however, the one clue by which to predict his foreign policies. History shows no exact and necessary correlation between the quality of motives and the quality of foreign policy. This is true in both moral and political terms.

We cannot conclude from the good intentions of a statesman that his foreign policies will be either morally praiseworthy or politically successful.

Judging his motives, we can say that he will not intentionally pursue policies that are morally wrong, but we can say nothing about the probability of their success. If we want to know the moral and political qualities of his actions, we must know them, not his motives. How often have statesmen been motivated by the desire to improve the world, and ended by making it worse? And how often have they sought one goal, and ended by achieving something they neither expected nor desired?

Neville Chamberlain's politics of appeasement were, as far as we can judge, inspired by good motives; he was probably less motivated by considerations of personal power than were many other British prime ministers, and he sought to preserve peace and to assure the happiness of all concerned. Yet his policies helped to make the Second World War inevitable, and to bring untold miseries to millions of men. Sir Winston Churchill's motives, on the other hand, were much less universal in scope and much more narrowly directed toward personal and national power, yet the foreign policies that sprang from these inferior motives were certainly superior in moral and political quality to those pursued by his predecessor. Judged by his motives, Robespierre was one of the most virtuous men who ever lived. Yet it was the utopian radicalism of that very virtue that made him kill those less virtuous than himself, brought him to the scaffold, and destroyed the revolution of which he was a leader.

Good motives give assurance against deliberately bad policies; they do not guarantee the moral goodness and political success of the policies they inspire. What is important to know, if one wants to understand foreign policy, is not primarily the motives of a statesman, but his intellectual ability to comprehend the essentials of foreign policy, as well as his political ability to translate what he has comprehended into successful political action. It follows that while ethics in the abstract judges the moral qualities of motives, political theory must judge the political qualities of intellect, will, and action.

A realist theory of international politics will also avoid the other popular fallacy of equating the foreign policies of a statesman with his philosophic or political sympathies, and of deducing the former from the latter. Statesmen, especially under contemporary conditions, may well make a habit of presenting their foreign policies in terms of their philosophic and political sympathies in order to gain popular support for them. Yet they will distinguish with Lincoln between their *official* duty', which is to think and act in terms of the national interest, and their *personal* wish', which is to see their own moral values and political principles realized throughout the world. Political realism does not require, nor does it condone, indifference to political ideals and moral principles, but it requires indeed a sharp distinction between the desirable and the possible—between what is desirable everywhere and at all times and what is possible under the concrete circumstances of time and place.

It stands to reason that not all foreign policies have always followed so rational, objective, and unemotional a course. The contingent elements of personality, prejudice, and subjective preference, and of all the weaknesses of intellect and will which flesh is heir to, are bound to deflect foreign politics from their rational course. Especially where foreign policy is conducted under the conditions of democratic control, the need to marshal popular emotions to the support of foreign policy cannot fail to impair the rationality of foreign policy itself. Yet a theory of foreign policy which aims at rationality must for the time being, as it were, abstract from these irrational elements and seek to paint a picture of foreign policy which presents the rational essence to be found in experience, without the contingent deviations from rationality which are also found in experience.

Deviations from rationality which are not the result of the personal whim or the personal psychopathology of the policy maker may appear contingent only from the vantage point of rationality, but may themselves be elements in a coherent system of irrationality. The conduct of the Indochina War by the United States suggests that possibility. It is a question worth looking into whether modern psychology and psychiatry have provided us with the conceptual tools which would enable us to construct, as it were, a counter-theory of irrational politics, a kind of pathology of international politics.

The experience of the Indochina War suggests five factors such a theory might encompass: the imposition upon the empirical world of a simplistic and *a priori* picture of the world derived from folklore and ideological assumption, that is, the replacement of experience with superstition; the refusal to correct this picture of the world in the light of experience; the persistence in a foreign policy derived from the misperception of reality and the use of intelligence for the purpose not of adapting policy to reality but of reinterpreting reality to fit policy; the egotism of the policy makers widening the gap between perception and policy, on the one hand, and reality, on the other; finally, the urge to close the gap at least subjectively by action, and kind of action, that creates the illusion of mastery over a recalcitrant reality. According to the *Wall Street Journal* of April 3, 1970, 'the desire to "do something" pervades top levels of Government and may overpower other "common sense" advice that insists the US ability to shape events is negligible. The yen for action could lead to bold policy as therapy.'

The difference between international politics as it actually is and a rational theory derived from it is like the difference between a photograph and a painted portrait. The photograph shows everything that can be seen by the naked eye; the painted portrait does not show everything that can be seen by the naked eye, but it shows, or at least seeks to show, one thing that the naked eye cannot see: the human essence of the person portrayed.

Political realism contains not only a theoretical but also a normative element. It knows that political reality is replete with contingencies and systemic irrationalities and points to the typical influences they exert upon foreign policy. Yet it shares with all social theory the need, for the sake of theoretical understanding, to stress the rational elements of political reality; for it is these rational elements that make reality intelligible for theory. Political realism presents the theoretical construct of a rational foreign policy which experience can never completely achieve.

At the same time political realism considers a rational foreign policy to be good foreign policy; for only a rational foreign policy minimizes risks and maximizes benefits and, hence, complies both with the moral precept of prudence and the political requirement of success. Political realism wants the photographic picture of the political world to resemble as much as possible its painted portrait. Aware of the inevitable gap between good—that is, rational—foreign policy and foreign policy as it actually is, political realism maintains not only that theory must focus upon the rational elements of political reality, but also that foreign policy ought to be rational in view of its own moral and practical purposes.

Hence, it is no argument against the theory here presented that actual foreign policy does not or cannot live up to it. That argument misunderstands the intention of this book, which is to present not an indiscriminate description of political reality, but a rational theory of international politics. Far from being invalidated by the fact that, for instance, a perfect balance of power policy will scarcely be found in reality, it assumes that reality, being deficient in this respect, must be understood and evaluated as an approximation to an ideal system of balance of power.

3. Realism assumes that its key concept of interest defined as power is an objective category which is universally valid, but it does not endow that concept with a meaning that is fixed once and for all. The idea of interest is indeed of the essence of politics and is unaffected by the circumstances of time and place. Thucydides' statement, born of the experiences of ancient Greece, that 'identity of interests is the surest of bonds whether between states or individuals' was taken up in the nineteenth century by Lord Salisbury's remark that 'the only bond of union that endures' among nations is 'the absence of all clashing interests'. [. . .]

Yet the kind of interest determining political action in a particular period of history depends upon the political and cultural context within which foreign policy is formulated. The goals that might be pursued by nations in their foreign policy can run the whole gamut of objectives any nation has ever pursued or might possibly pursue.

The same observations apply to the concept of power. Its content and the manner of its use are determined by the political and cultural environment. Power may comprise anything that establishes and maintains the control of man over man. Thus power covers all social relationships which serve that end, from physical violence to the most subtle psychological ties by which one mind controls another. Power covers the domination of man by man, both when it is disciplined by moral ends and controlled by constitutional safeguards, as in Western democracies, and when it is that untamed and barbaric force which finds its laws in nothing but its own strength and its sole justification in its aggrandizement.

Political realism does not assume that the contemporary conditions under which foreign policy operates, with their extreme instability and the ever present threat of large-scale violence, cannot be changed. The balance of power, for instance, is indeed a perennial element of all pluralistic societies, as the authors of *The Federalist* papers well knew; yet it is capable of operating, as it does in the United States, under the conditions of relative stability and peaceful conflict. If the factors that have given rise to these conditions can be duplicated on the international scene, similar conditions of stability and peace will then prevail there, as they have over long stretches of history among certain nations.

What is true of the general character of international relations is also true of the nation state as the ultimate point of reference of contemporary foreign policy. While the realist indeed believes that interest is the perenial standard by which political action must be judged and directed, the contemporary connection between interest and the nation state is a product of history, and is therefore bound to disappear in the course of history. Nothing in the realist position militates against the assumption that the present division of the political world into nation states will be replaced by larger units of a quite different character, more in keeping with the technical potentialities and the moral requirements of the contemporary world.

The realist parts company with other schools of thought before the all-important question of how the contemporary world is to be transformed. The realist is persuaded that this transformation can be achieved only through the workmanlike manipulation of the perennial forces that have shaped the past as they will the future. The realist cannot be persuaded that we can bring about that transformation by confronting a political reality that has its own laws with an abstract ideal that refuses to take those laws into account.

4. Political realism is aware of the moral significance of political action. It is also aware of the ineluctable tension between the moral command and the requirements of successful political action. And it is unwilling to gloss over and obliterate that tension and thus to obfuscate both the moral and the political issue by making it appear as though the stark facts of politics were morally more satisfying than they actually are, and the moral law less exacting than it actually is.

Realism maintains that universal moral principles cannot be applied to the actions of states in their abstract universal formulation, but that they must be filtered through the concrete circumstances of time and place. The individual may say for himself: '*Fiat justitia, pereat mundus* (Let justice be done, even if the world perish)', but the state has no right to say so in the name of those who are in its care. Both individual and state must judge political action by universal moral principles, such as that of liberty. Yet while the individual has a moral right to sacrifice himself in defense of such a moral principle, the state has no right to let its moral disapprobation of the infringement of liberty get in the way of successful political action, itself inspired by the moral principle of national survival. There can be no political morality without prudence; that is, without consideration of the political consequences of seemingly moral action. Realism, then, considers prudence—the weighing of the consequences of alternative political actions—to be the supreme virtue in politics. Ethics in the abstract judges action by its conformity with the moral law; political ethics judges action by its political consequences. Classical and medieval philosophy knew this, and so did Lincoln when he said:

I do the very best I know how, the very best I can, and I mean to keep doing so until the end. If the end brings me out all right, what is said against me won't amount to anything. If the end brings me out wrong, ten angels swearing I was right would make no difference.

5. Political realism refuses to identify the moral aspirations of a particular nation with the moral laws that govern the universe. As it distinguishes between truth and opinion, so it distinguishes between truth and idolatry. All nations are tempted—and few have been able to resist the temptation for long—to clothe their own particular aspirations and actions in the moral purposes of the universe. To know that nations are subject to the moral law is one thing, while to pretend to know with certainty what is good and evil in the relations among nations is quite another. There is a world of difference between the belief that all nations stand under the judgment of God, inscrutable to the human mind, and the blasphemous conviction that God is always on one's side and that what one wills oneself cannot fail to be willed by God also.

The lighthearted equation between a particular nationalism and the counsels of Providence is morally indefensible, for it is that very sin of pride against which the Greek tragedians and the Biblical prophets have warned rulers and ruled. That equation is also politically pernicious, for it is liable to engender the distortion in judgment which, in the blindness of crusading frenzy, destroys nations and civilizations—in the name of moral principle, ideal, or God himself.

On the other hand, it is exactly the concept of interest defined in terms of power that saves us from both that moral excess and that political folly.

For if we look at all nations, our own included, as political entities pursuing their respective interests defined in terms of power, we are able to do justice to all of them. And we are able to do justice to all of them in a dual sense: We are able to judge other nations as we judge our own and, having judged them in this fashion, we are then capable of pursuing policies that respect the interests of other nations, while protecting and promoting those of our own. Moderation in policy cannot fail to reflect the moderation of moral judgment.

6. The difference, then, between political realism and other schools of thought is real, and it is profound. However much the theory of political realism may have been misunderstood and misinterpreted, there is no gainsaying its distinctive intellectual and moral attitude to matters political.

Intellectually, the political realist maintains the autonomy of the political sphere, as the economist, the lawyer, the moralist maintain theirs. He thinks in terms of interest defined as power, as the economist thinks in terms of interest defined as wealth; the lawyer, of the conformity of action with legal rules; the moralist, of the conformity of action with moral principles. The economist asks: 'How does this policy affect the wealth of society, or a segment of it?' The lawyer asks: 'Is this policy in accord with the rules of law?' The moralist asks: 'Is this policy in accord with moral principles?' And the political realist asks: 'How does this policy affect the power of the nation?' (Or of the federal government, of Congress, of the party, of agriculture, as the case may be.)

The political realist is not unaware of the existence and relevance of standards of thought other than political ones. As political realist, he cannot but subordinate these other standards to those of politics. And he parts company with other schools when they impose standards of thought appropriate to other spheres upon the political sphere. It is here that political realism takes issue with the 'legalistic-moralistic approach' to international politics. That this issue is not, as has been contended, a mere figment of the imagination, but goes to the very core of the controversy, can be shown from many historical examples.

[From Hans Morgenthau, *Politics Among Nations*, 5th edn. (New York: Alfred Knopf, 1973), 4–12.]

LAWRENCE FREEDMAN AND EFRAIM KARSH

49   Why Bush Went to War

There seems little doubt that [President George] Bush was influenced most of all by the need to uphold the principle of non-aggression and the analogy with the failure of appeasement in the 1930s. This remained a seminal experience for Bush's generation (and for that matter Margaret Thatcher's and François Mitterrand's). The President himself tended to describe the crisis in these terms. When he spoke to Congressmen the day he took his decision on doubling forces, he reported that he had been reading Martin Gilbert's lengthy history of the Second World War.

The rule that the stronger should not devour their weaker neighbours, and that borders between states should not be changed through armed force, was why Iraq was so clearly isolated in the United Nations. It was part of Saddam's case that Kuwait had been an artificial entity and, in consequence, that its boundary with Iraq was illogical and lacked historical justification. This contention was in itself dubious, but even if valid to act upon it would produce an awkward precedent, for around the world there are numerous comparable disputes.

Only the most diehard supporters of Saddam argued in favour of one state being allowed to take over another by force. Even Cuba and Yemen voted in the Security Council against the annexation of Kuwait. So there was little doubt that an important principle of international relations was at stake. As it was affirmed in a series of United Nations resolutions, this was also of some significance to those who have criticized Western policy in the past for its neglect of the UN. Resisting aggression provided the classic basis for a 'just war'.

Nonetheless, there were a number of arguments used to question the firm application of the principle in this case. One was that the Kuwaiti regime lacked legitimacy and had brought the crisis upon itself through its provocative behaviour during the first half of 1990. Examination of the al-Sabah regime made it clear that this was no paragon of democracy, and that the Kuwaitis themselves had shown greed and insensitivity in the past. In this they were not unusual in the Middle East. It was also pointed out that a number of the Arab members of the coalition scored badly on human rights. However, it had never been claimed by the Bush Administration that democracy was at stake in the Gulf, and in fact the Kuwaiti regime in many ways had been comparatively mild and generous when compared with some of its neighbours. Nor was a principle very impressive if there was only going to be a response when the victims were nice, inoffensive souls. As the philosopher Michael Walzer observed, 'aggression is always an attack on the status quo'. Resisting it does not endorse the status quo—all that is required is that 'it be changed by other means and by different people'.

Another dubious precept was that rules which cannot be enforced completely should not be enforced at all. However, the accusation that opposition to aggression tended to be extremely selective was damaging, especially in the Middle East. The response to Saddam's aggression was 'unprecedented', thundered Noam Chomsky, only 'because he stepped on the wrong toes'. A number of examples of double standards could be cited, including Syria's involvement in Lebanon, the 1974 Turkish partition of Cyprus and, from outside the region, the Indian takeover of Goa and the Indonesian of East Timor. Another two examples revolved around the failure to act against Iraq's attack on Iran in 1980, compounded by the courting of Saddam since the early 1980s, and Israel's occupation of Arab territories since 1967. Israel, complained one critic, had been violating the UN Charter 'every month and every day and every week'.

[. . .] [T]he comparison with Israel was particularly sensitive in the Middle East, but not so much in the United States where there was sympathy for Israel's security predicament. The comparison at any rate was not exact. The case of the Iraqi invasion of Iran in 1980 was different in that it was used to suggest that Iraqi misbehaviour was condemned only when it suited the West to do so. Unlike the invasion of Kuwait, there were mitigating circumstances in 1980. Revolutionary Iran was generally considered to be a dangerous state and was attempting to subvert the regime in Iraq. Nonetheless, the muted objections to what was still overt aggression, and the general attempt by Western countries to ingratiate themselves with Baghdad in the search for large contracts, did not provide an impressive backdrop to a principled stand in 1990. Yet, as in the 1930s, past appeasement provided no grounds against taking on a dictator when the nature of his regime became impossible to ignore—it only made the task more difficult. The West was paying for past over-indulgence of Saddam Hussein, but that in itself was no reason to continue the practice.

The final type of qualification to the principle of non-aggression was that it was being applied in the Kuwait case only as a cover for less elevated motives. Even if justified, this charge would not invalidate the principle. Virtuous acts do not cease to be so even when prompted by non-virtuous purposes. Slogans such as that used by the anti-war protest movement in the United States of 'no blood for oil' neatly side-stepped the whole question of aggression. A number of hawks, as well as doves, also felt more comfortable with the hard realism implied by an economic rationale. They judged it entirely proper to contemplate war for the sake of energy supplies. They agreed with the doves only that the simple principle of opposing aggression served as an inadequate justification and an unconvincing explanation.

Oil was obviously an extremely relevant factor in the crisis. If it were not for oil, Kuwait would not have been invaded in the first place, nor would the Americans have moved so resolutely to defend Saudi Arabia. Given America's dependence on foreign oil, it was not a complete caricature to suggest that troops were sent initially to the desert 'to retain control of oil in the hands of a pro-American Saudi Arabia, so prices will remain low', although it is doubtful that many of those involved in the decision considered their own motives to be primarily economic.

How important oil was in influencing the decision to liberate Kuwait was less clear. The Iraqis were happy to stress their readiness to sell oil to the United States. They were price hawks, but if they were not controlling Saudi reserves then their ability to push the price up would be limited. Moreover, the prospect of war amid the oilfields had made markets jittery, and many warned that the oil price would reach historic highs in the event of a war which, for example, could see serious damage inflicted on the Saudi oilfields. Nonetheless, the importance of secure oil supplies was stressed by the Administration and its supporters, although they also oscillated with regard to the importance it deserved. Thus one week (16 October) Bush insisted that there was no concern about oil, only aggression, while the next (22 October) he warned how 'our jobs, our way of life, our own freedom, would all suffer if control of the world's great oil reserves fell into the hands of that one man, Saddam Hussein'. [. . .]

[I]n an address to Congress on 12 September, he added an extra objective—a 'new world order'—to American policy in the Gulf. This was 'a unique and extraordinary moment'. Though 'grave', the crisis offered 'a rare opportunity to move toward an historic period of co-operation'.

If the exuberant language was taken at face value Bush was promising an impossibly complete transformation in international politics. It was easy to point out that much of the old political game would go on as before. To get the necessary votes in the United Nations and hold together the anti-Iraq coalition, it was imperative to help sustain Gorbachev in power even as the bases of communist rule crumbled beneath him, to forget the Chinese massacre in Tiananmen Square and to find common cause with Asad of Syria.

Americans might feel that they had reason to wonder whether theirs was the only country actually interested in this new world order. As evidence of growing domestic problems mounted, the lack of effort of other richer nations, such as Japan and Germany, was used to suggest that the United States was being taken for a ride. This charge was eased by the Administration's efforts to draw as many nations as possible into the coalition, obliging those who were unwilling to send forces at least to contribute funds. [. . .] The idea that the United States had been reduced to providing mercenaries for feudal Gulf rulers, reinforced by the 'tin-cup exercise', could be presented as being degrading rather than the pursuit of a noble idea of world order.

William Pfaff warned of the characteristic American errors of 'moralization of the war and demonization of the enemy', being unwilling 'to accept conflicts on their own terms', so that each is 'held to be of vast significance, and any failure or compromise is said to threaten disaster in series'. By putting the future of the world at stake in this particular instance, Bush could be criticized for setting himself impossible standards. This criticism grew in force with each additional requirement for the 'new world'. For example, if 'just treatment for all peoples' was to be a central value, then this would require an unprecedented degree of intervention in the internal affairs of other states which could give the impression of an attempt to refashion the world according to Western values.

However, this was not Bush's intention. Indeed, his political instincts warned him against getting too involved in Third World disputes. The Panama experience, in which the drug-trafficking and corruption he had sought to eradicate through the intervention and seizure of General Manuel Noriega had soon resurfaced, warned against any attempt to impose change on very different societies. The new world order was less a charter for universal human rights than a belief that traditional rights of states could now be protected if the world's great powers could both show respect themselves and demand it from others.

Understanding Bush's concept helps make sense of his approach to the 'Saddam problem'. Just as had been the case before the crisis broke, he showed little interest in the effect of Saddam's regime on the Iraqi people. He would have been prepared to continue to turn a blind eye to the internal repression and the persecution of the Kurds if Saddam had been prepared to play a more responsible role in regional affairs. There was no attempt to cultivate an alternative Iraqi leadership or show support for Kurdish aspirations. Bush and his advisers could see problems flowing from a close association with the Kurds because of the implications of Kurdish autonomy for Turkey, or with the Shi'ite community because the Saudis still felt more comfortable with the minority Sunni élite, and there was also no desire to encourage the sort of Islamic fundamentalism that had caused so much grief in Iran.

The problem with Saddam was that he was aggressive. Bush showed himself to be enormously moved by the reports of Iraqi atrocities within Kuwait because this illustrated precisely why aggression was so terrible and had to be opposed. On 21 September he was shown intelligence material demonstrating the extent to which Iraq was systematically plundering and dismantling Kuwait. A week later the President and his advisers met the Emir of Kuwait in the Oval Office, in a meeting intended to demonstrate that there could be no compromise over the position of the al-Sabah regime in Kuwait. It seems, however, to have had a more significant impact. The Emir described, in 'quiet, almost under-stated terms', how Kuwait was being steadily dismantled and depopulated, through murder and forced emigration. He told of Kuwait being raped, of people being pulled from their homes, tortured and killed.

The effect was quite emotional. For Bush and his officials this came as a timely reminder that at stake was more than just 'abstractions and principles' but also the fate of thousands of people. When Bush discussed the visit with Mrs Thatcher, the Prime Minister's adviser noted that he had 'rarely seen a man so moved to suppressed fury and disgust by what he had heard, and I think it became a very important part of his overall approach to resolving this problem'. According to Scowcroft, it reinforced rather than created a tendency in the President's thinking by bringing home Kuwait's fate in personal terms. It emphasized that the process could reach a point where Kuwait could not be put back together again. There was thereafter an increased sense of a time limit: the longer the liberation took the less would be left of Kuwait. [. . .]

This moral framework also helps explain Bush's regular comparisons between Saddam and Hitler, which began in August. At one point he even suggested that Saddam was the worse of the two. Yet Bush was unwilling to solve the 'Saddam problem' in the way that the 'Hitler problem' had been solved in 1945, because he did not want to get involved in the restructuring of the Iraqi state. It was also clear that any attempt to 'get Saddam' in person would impose extra demands on any military operation. Far greater force would be required, as it would be necessary to take Baghdad. The Iraqi leader had spent most of the 1980s fighting a war against an enemy which was quite explicitly pursuing his elimination, and it was evident that if stakes were raised too high then any concessions became impossible, for it would mean the end of Saddam's personal rule. So although Bush's rhetoric created the strong impression that Saddam was his target, at no point did he ever suggest that this was a formal objective. It was more that the descriptions of Saddam encouraged the view that this *should* be the objective or that, despite disclaimers, it actually was.

[From Lawrence Freedman and Efraim Karsh, *The Gulf Conflict, 1990–91: Diplomacy and War in the New World Order* (London: Faber, 1993), 212–19.]

MICHAEL WALZER

50 Sieges

Siege is the oldest form of total war. Its long history suggests that neither technological advance nor democratic revolution are the crucial factors pushing warfare beyond the combatant population. Civilians have been attacked along with soldiers, or in order to get at soldiers, as often in ancient as in modern times. Such attacks are likely whenever an army seeks what might be called civilian shelter and fights from behind the battlements or from within the buildings of a city, or whenever the inhabitants of a threatened city seek the most immediate form of military protection and agree to be garrisoned. Then, locked into the narrow circle of the walls, civilians and soldiers are exposed to the same risks. Proximity and scarcity make them equally vulnerable. Or perhaps not equally so: in this kind of war, once combat begins, noncombatants are more likely to be killed. The soldiers fight from protected positions, and the civilians, who don't fight at all, are quickly made over (in a phrase I have taken from the military literature) into 'useless mouths'. Fed last, and only with the army's surplus, they die first. More civilians died in the siege of Leningrad than in the modernist infernos of Hamburg, Dresden, Tokyo, Hiroshima, and Nagasaki, taken together. They probably died more painfully, too, even if in old fashioned ways. [. . .]

A city can indeed be defended against the will of its citizens—by an army, beaten in the field, that retreats within its walls; by an alien garrison, serving the strategic interests of a distant commander; by militant, politically powerful minorities of one or another sort. If they were competent casuists, the leaders of any of these groups might reason in the following way: 'We know that civilians will die as a result of our decision to fight here rather than somewhere else. But we will not do the killing, and the deaths will not in any way benefit us. They are not our purpose, nor a part of our purpose, nor a means to our purpose. By collecting and rationing food, we will do all we can to save civilian lives. Those who die are not our responsibility.' Clearly, such leaders cannot be condemned under the principle of double effect. But they can be condemned nevertheless—so long as the inhabitants of the city decline to be defended. There are many examples of this sort of thing in medieval history: burghers eager to surrender, aristocratic warriors committed (not to the burghers) to continue the fight. In such cases, the warriors surely bear some responsibility for burgher deaths. They are agents of coercion within the city, as the besieging army is without, and the civilians are trapped between the two. But such cases are rare today, as they were in classical times. Political integration and civic discipline make for cities whose inhabitants expect to be defended and are prepared, morally if not always materially, to endure the burdens of a siege. Consent clears the defenders, and only consent can do so.

What of the attackers? I assume that they offer surrender on terms; that is simply the collective equivalent of quarter and should always be available. But surrender is refused. There are then two military options. First, the strongholds of the city can be bombarded and the walls stormed. No doubt, civilians will die, but for these deaths the attacking soldiers can rightly say that they are not to blame. Though they do the killing, these deaths are, in an important sense, not their 'doing'. The attackers are cleared by the refusal of surrender, which is an acceptance of the risks of war (or, moral responsibility is shifted onto the defending army, which has made surrender impossible). But this argument applies only to those deaths that are in fact incidental to legitimate military operations. The refusal of surrender does not turn the civilians into direct objects of attack. They have not thereby joined the war, though some of them may subsequently be mobilized for warlike activities within the city. They are simply in their 'proper and permanent abode', and their status as citizens of a besieged city is no different from their status as citizens of a country at war. If they can be killed, who cannot be? But then it would appear that the second military option is ruled out: the city cannot be surrounded, cut off, its people systematically starved. [. . .]

The legal norm is the *status quo*. The commander of the besieging army is not conceived to be, and does not think himself to be, responsible for those people who have always lived in the city—who are there, so to speak, naturally—nor for those who are there voluntarily, who sought the protection of city walls, driven only by the general fear of war. He is in the clear with regard to these people, however horribly they die, however much to his purpose it is that they die horribly, because he did not force them into their death place. He did not push them through the gates of the city before he locked them in. This is, I suppose, an understandable way of drawing the line, but it does not seem to me the right way. The hard question is whether the line can be drawn differently without ruling out sieges altogether. In the long history of siege warfare, this question has a specific form: should civilians be allowed to leave the city, saving themselves from starvation and relieving pressure on the collective food supply, after it has been invested? More generally, isn't locking them into the besieged city morally the same as driving them in? And if it is, shouldn't they be let out, so that those that remain, to fight and starve, can really be said to have chosen to remain?

[From Michael Walzer, *Just and Unjust Wars* (Harmondsworth: Penguin, 1980), 160–5.]

HANNAH ARENDT

51   The Trial of Adolf Eichmann

Eichmann [. . .] had steadfastly insisted that he was guilty only of 'aiding and abetting' in the commission of the crimes with which he was charged, that he himself had never committed an overt act. The judgment, to one's great relief, in a way recognized that the prosecution had not succeeded in proving him wrong on this point. For it was an important point; it touched upon the very essence of this crime, which was no ordinary crime, and the very nature of this criminal, who was no common criminal; by implication, it also took cognizance of the weird fact that in the death camps it was usually the inmates and the victims who had actually wielded 'the fatal instrument with [their] own hands'. What the judgment had to say on this point was more than correct, it was the truth: 'Expressing his activities in terms of Section 23 of our Criminal Code Ordinance, we should say that they were mainly those of a person soliciting by giving counsel or advice to others and of one who enabled or aided others in [the criminal] act.' But 'in such an enormous and complicated crime as the one we are now considering, wherein many people participated, on various levels and in various modes of activity—the planners, the organizers, and those executing the deeds, according to their various ranks—there is not much point in using the ordinary concepts of counseling and soliciting to commit a crime. For these crimes were committed en masse, not only in regard to the number of victims, but also in regard to the numbers of those who perpetrated the crime, and the extent to which any one of the many criminals was close to or remote from the actual killer of the victim means nothing, as far as the measure of his responsibility is concerned. On the contrary, in general *the degree of responsibility increases as we draw further away from the man who uses the fatal instrument with his own hands* [my italics].' [. . .]

The death sentence had been expected, and there was hardly anyone to quarrel with it; but things were altogether different when it was learned that the Israelis had carried it out. The protests were short-lived, but they were widespread and they were voiced by people of influence and prestige. The most common argument was that Eichmann's deeds defied the possibility of human punishment, that it was pointless to impose the death sentence for crimes of such magnitude—which, of course, was true, in a sense, except that it could not conceivably mean that he who had murdered millions should for this very reason escape punishment. On a considerably lower level, the death sentence was called 'unimaginative', and very imaginative alternatives were proposed forthwith—Eichmann 'should have spent the rest of his life at hard labor in the arid stretches of the Negev, helping with his sweat to reclaim the Jewish homeland', a punishment he would probably not have survived for more than a single day, to say nothing of the fact that in Israel the desert of the south is hardly looked upon as a penal colony; or, in Madison Avenue style, Israel should have reached 'divine heights', rising above 'the understandable, legal, political, and even human considerations', by calling together 'all those who took part in the capture, trial, and sentencing to a public ceremony, with Eichmann there in shackles, and with television cameras and radio to decorate them as the heroes of the century'.

Martin Buber called the execution a 'mistake of historical dimensions', as it might 'serve to expiate the guilt felt by many young persons in Germany'—an argument that oddly echoed Eichmann's own ideas on the matter, though Buber hardly knew that he had wanted to hang himself in public in order to lift the burden of guilt from the shoulders of German youngsters. (It is strange that Buber, a man not only of eminence but of very great intelligence, should not see how spurious these much publicized guilt feelings necessarily are. It is quite gratifying to feel guilty if you haven't done anything wrong: how noble! Whereas it is rather hard and certainly depressing to admit guilt and to repent. The youth of Germany is surrounded, on all sides and in all walks of life, by men in positions of authority and in public office who are very guilty indeed but who *feel* nothing of the sort. The normal reaction to this state of affairs should be indignation, but indignation would be quite risky—not a danger to life and limb but definitely a handicap in a career. Those young German men and women who every once in a while—on the occasion of all the *Diary of Anne Frank* hubbub and of the Eichmann trial—treat us to hysterical outbreaks of guilt feelings are not staggering under the burden of the past, their fathers' guilt; rather, they are trying to escape from the pressure of very present and actual problems into a cheap sentimentality.) Professor Buber went on to say that he felt 'no pity at all' for Eichmann, because he could feel pity 'only for those whose actions I understand in my heart', and he stressed what he had said many years ago in Germany—that he had 'only in a formal sense a common humanity with those who took part' in the acts of the Third Reich. This lofty attitude was, of course, more of a luxury than those who had to try Eichmann could afford, since the law presupposes precisely that we have a common humanity with those whom we accuse and judge and condemn. As far as I know, Buber was the only philosopher to go on public record on the subject of Eichmann's execution (shortly before the trial started, Karl Jaspers had given a radio interview in Basel, later published in *Der Monat*, in which he argued the case for an international tribunal); it was disappointing to find him dodging, on the highest possible level, the very problem Eichmann and his deeds had posed.

Least of all was heard from those who were against the death penalty on principle, unconditionally; their arguments would have remained valid, since they would not have needed to specify them for this particular case. They seem to have felt—rightly, I think—that this was not a very promising case on which to fight.

Adolf Eichmann went to the gallows with great dignity. He had asked for a bottle of red wine and had drunk half of it. He refused the help of the Protestant minister, the Reverend William Hull, who offered to read the Bible with him: he had only two more hours to live, and therefore no 'time to waste'. He walked the fifty yards from his cell to the execution chamber calm and erect, with his hands bound behind him. When the guards tied his ankles and knees, he asked them to loosen the bonds so that he could stand straight. 'I don't need that', he said when the black hood was offered him. He was in complete command of himself, nay, he was more: he was completely himself. Nothing could have demonstrated this more convincingly than the grotesque silliness of his last words. He began by stating emphatically that he was a *Gottgläubiger*, to express in common Nazi fashion that he was no Christian and did not believe in life after death. He then proceeded: 'After a short while, gentlemen, *we shall all meet again.* Such is the fate of all men. Long live Germany, long live Argentina, long live Austria. *I shall not forget them.*' In the face of death, he had found the cliché used in funeral oratory. Under the gallows, his memory played him the last trick; he was 'elated' and he forgot that this was his own funeral.

It was as though in those last minutes he was summing up the lessons that this long course in human wickedness had taught us—the lesson of the fearsome, word-and-thought-defying *banality of evil.*

> [From Hannah Arendt, *Eichmann in Jerusalem: A Report on the Banality of Evil* (London: Fabes, 1963), 224–5, 228–31. The trial of Adolf Eichmann began in Israel in April 1961. He was executed a year later.]

BARRIE PASKINS

52 The Responsibilities of Defence Scientists

It is on reflection astounding that the law is more demanding of soldiers than of scientists. In the great cycle from research and development through deployment to combat use, the soldier occupies a peculiarly difficult position, subject as he is to the rigours of military discipline, the emphasis upon obedience and loyalty in the military ethos and not least the urgent dangers of combat. The defence scientist is not liable to be shot at in battle. He works far from the field of combat in an environment in which there is or should be room if anywhere for sustained deliberation about the legitimacy of actions that may have military significance. If the soldier is required only to disobey manifestly illegal orders, some higher expectation seems in order with respect to the scientist in view of his greater freedom of manoeuvre. But this is not what we find. Instead, the law imposes no specific obligation upon the defence scientist corresponding to that laid down for the soldier. Here, surely, is a loophole which needs to be closed if the law is to continue to develop towards clear articulation of the international duties of the individual.

Does it matter whether the soldier has, or the scientist lacks, clear duties laid down for him relative to the law of war? What is it about this law that is worth the effort given the absence of an international law enforcement agency and the widespread disillusion with the way in which the UN has discharged its Charter obligations to provide a new context for international relations? Two functions of law need to be distinguished if we are to answer these questions. First, the law of war like domestic criminal law has the usual function of regulating conduct and providing for the punishment of offenders. All armies have military codes of law. These codes are evidence of what the law of war is at a given time and normally incorporate explicit international law as it evolves. Armies have this law not out of nebulous internationalist sentiment but because an army without law would lack discipline and amount to no more than a lethally dangerous armed mob. Not the least important reason for proceeding with prosecutions for massacres, however invidiously selective such prosecutions may be in leaving the high command untouched, has been in order for the rule of law in the affected army to be (re-)asserted. The controversial prosecutions of Lieutenant Calley and Major Medina for the My Lai massacre illustrate this.

A second function of the law of war is to provide a framework for the examination of foreign and military policy. [. . .]

The scientist needs to know both some of the fine-print complexities of the law and also something of its broad history, purposes, dilemmas and relation to technology. Clear-cut rules of action of the sort a soldier requires to control combat are less important for the defence scientist than the informed conviction that there are questions to be asked about the lawfulness of his work, answers to which are to be sought within relatively definite limits and fairly well defined areas of legitimate controversy. This is the knowledge appropriate to his position. With it, he should be able to contribute towards making the law applicable to the early stages of the research–development–deployment–use cycle. [. . .]

The obligation of a soldier consequent upon his instruction in the law of war is that he disobey manifestly illegal orders. The obligation that should devolve upon the defence scientist cannot be pinned down so precisely. One is worried about the scientist because the growing research and development efforts of which he is a part are peculiarly difficult to control even given the will. Suppose the title of his research project is published: this is utterly uninformative to the innumerate citizen such as myself and almost equally unilluminating, I am told, even for the scientifically literate worker in a closely kindred field. Furthermore, very many scientists are innocents about strategy and proceed in almost entire ignorance of the basic characteristics of the strategic ideas by which the societies in which they live conduct military affairs. As things stand now, external regulation of 'the military-industrial complex' is simply unfeasible even given the political will: any watchdog would have insuperable technical difficulties invigilating defence-related work, and a grave political problem of balancing defence secrecy and the need to be at a distance from the state. As for self-regulation by the scientists, so long as the scientist's responsibilities are seen exclusively in terms of the private conscience and social responsibility views there seems to be no way in which the scientists, who occupy many different points on the moral and political spectra, can make common cause to move towards self-regulation. This is the problem from which to determine the responsibilities of the defence scientist who has been educated in the law of war. It is of course imperative for him to use his freedom of enquiry to ensure that his work is not contributing to definite breaching of the law of war (for example, by contributing the development of illegal weapons). Equally if not more important is that he accept a modicum of responsibility to contribute to extending the capacity of the law of war to regulate all aspects of the weapons cycle and not solely the intrinsically difficult stage of the cycle at which soldiers in danger have the new weapons in their hands. To formulate the defence scientist's responsibility in this way is to recognise the enormous discretion that lies with him. Our dependence on him in this regard, however, is not a weakness in my argument but a stark fact. What I am attempting to do is not to curtail this freedom of his by some external fiat but to draw attention to that body of thought which may enable him to exercise his freedom in the knowledge that he has it and that it brings with it a responsibility which forms part of the international duties of the individual.

The law's demands upon the soldier are backed by stern sanctions. He may be imprisoned or executed for war crimes. The professional demands upon a doctor are also backed by sanctions which, together with the law, carry serious implications for the individual (e.g. the implications of being struck off). What sanctions if any should be part of the defence scientist's duties? The sanction I would propose is a modest one: that the individual be answerable to his professional body for the discharge in good faith of his obligation to avoid work on projects which are prohibited by the law of war and to join in extending that law to regulate the entire weapons cycle. This may rarely or never mean a penalty such as striking off but one would be mistaken if one supposed that accountability without such sanctions is toothless: many will be concerned to be good professionals for the sake of professionalism; some of those, not least the ambitious, who lack such high standards, will nevertheless have an anxiety about reputation which will give professional expectations a hold over them. Above all, perhaps, the body of argument which professional seriousness about this matter would inevitably call forth would surely make *recherché* work more available to and regulable by a wider public.

I am, then, suggesting the following division of responsibility:

for the UN, to prod states towards encouraging initiatives by professional bodies;
for states, to strengthen (not least by supportive legislation) such moves as may be forthcoming from professional bodies to incorporate education in the law of war among the requirements for professional competence of members who are likely to engage in scientific activity with military significance;

for professional bodies, to find educators capable of developing in the scientist serious practical reflectiveness about the relation between the detailed provisions of the law of war, the purposes of that law and the legality and morality of his own work;

for the individual scientist, to make reasonably extensive enquiries to ensure that a project does not threaten to contribute towards breach of the law of war, and to join in extending that law's power to regulate and contain the destructive potential of military affairs.

[From Barrie Paskins, 'Prohibitions, Restraints and Scientists', in Nicholas Sims (ed.), *Explorations in Ethics and International Relations* (London: Croom Helm, 1981), 74–80.]

W. V. O'BRIEN

53 Just-War Doctrine and Revolutionary War

It is clear that revolutions do not usually break out unless there is a situation so bad as to invite revolution. The question is, Who has the right to speak for the revolution, to initiate or terminate the revolution, to determine the strategies and tactics of revolutionary war? In practice, the answer seems to be purely pragmatic. Whoever can mount revolutionary activity on a significant and sustained basis has competent authority and claims the right to speak for the people and their revolution.

[. . .] [R]evolutionary power tends to derive primarily from the ability to subvert, tear down, or destroy the incumbent regime and/or existing social system. There is little question of legitimacy involved. The effective practice of revolutionary warfare, often in the form of extensive terrorism, may have little relation to the desires of the people or to their grievances.

On the counterinsurgent side, competent authority to conduct counter-revolutionary war is presumed to reside with the incumbent regime, subject to whatever constitutional limitations exist. The issue of competent authority is raised at the point where revolutionary resistance is so successful and/or regime counterinsurgency measures are so unsuccessful that the regime appears to lack both the political/military base and the legal-moral legitimacy to warrant its continuation of a counterinsurgency war. This is also a point of controversy regarding its competence to invite external assistance.

This is a more difficult standard of competent authority than that applied to the revolutionaries. The regime must govern adequately as well as fight, whereas the revolutionary forces need only disrupt governmental functions and fight a revolutionary war sufficiently sustained and effective to wear down the regime and the patience of the population.

I do not have a satisfactory solution for this problem. For the moment it appears that the best approach is roughly that of the 1977 Geneva Protocol

II. Following that approach, one would judge revolutionary competent authority (belligerent status under international law) mainly on the basis of indications of military success plus such political success (for example, control of areas of the country) as might be manifested. Meanwhile, I would recognize the regime's competent authority to wage counterinsurgency war unless the regime was so clearly tyrannical and lacking in popular support or acceptance as to forfeit its rights (for example, Idi Amin's regime in Uganda, admittedly an extreme case).

I am not at all sure how much order can be brought to this difficult subject. Perhaps, after much more intense analysis, we would still be limited to the working proposition that as long as a belligerent in a revolutionary/counterinsurgency war could maintain a continuing, significant war effort, it should be considered as having competent authority to authorize and order belligerent operations. [. . .]

The present international-law approach to revolutionary war is essentially one of self-determination by a Darwinian process of armed conflict. Whatever side prevails is legitimate, is the 'self' that has been 'determined'. The great concern is to exclude foreign intervention in this Darwinian trial by ordeal. What moral and political theory exists at present regarding the right of revolution and its limits, if any, is all on the side of Marxist revolutionaries. There seems to be no substantial discussion of the right of revolution in Marxist societies against Marxist governments. This abdication of the field of revolutionary theory by non-Marxist theorists should be remedied. It is ridiculous that the right of revolution, even for Christians, should be conceived of mainly in Marxist terms when the spirit of resistance to communist tyranny is alive in Afghanistan and Poland and struggling to stay alive in many other communist countries. The need for a modern just-war/just-revolution doctrine is great. [. . .]

[I]t may well be the case that success in revolutionary wars requires means that are clearly indiscriminate and whose proportionality is only legitimized by appeals to distant utopian goals. On the counterinsurgent side, both morality and prudence require greater discrimination and respect for proportionality defined in a more modest and traditional sense than that invoked by the rebels.

Much more serious study would be required before strategies and tactics could be suggested for revolutionaries that would conform to the just-war standards of proportion and discrimination. This is a work that needs to be done. There is more expert opinion on enlightened self-interest options for counterinsurgents [. . .] These options need to be pursued notwithstanding the provocations of the revolutionaries and their enjoyment of what amounts to a double standard of conduct in revolutionary/counterinsurgency warfare.

[From W. V. O'Brien, *War: The Conduct of Just and Limited War* (New York: Praeger, 1981), 333–9.]

J. E. HARE AND CAREY B. JOYNT

54 Intervention

Intervention has been defined by a leading authority as 'forcible inter-ference, short of declaring war, by one or more powers in the affairs of another power'. That is to say intervention involves the notion of 'coercion short of war'. It always involves the use or threat of force, whether in the internal or external affairs of another state. It may be invited or not and it may involve a desire to change or to preserve the existing distribution of power. In short, the term 'intervention' covers a vast array of very differ-ent sorts of political action and no simple moral principle can cover them all. [. . .]

The moral analyst gets very little help from international law. This is partly because intervention involves a conflict of two basic principles—the right of self-defence and the right of self-government. All nations recognize that intervention is 'unlawful' but they do not agree 'on what is this intervention that is unlawful'. This disagreement began to take its modern form following the end of the Napoleonic wars when Austria and France intervened in 1821 and 1823 in Italy and Spain, respectively, to prevent revolution in these states, when the United States proclaimed the Monroe Doctrine to preserve the independence of the rebellious Spanish colonies and when the great powers intervened on various occasions to protect, on grounds of humanity, the inhabitants of the Ottoman empire. Disagree-ments were even sharper when political change was involved, for example in a rebellion or civil war, and it was controversial at what stage support for one side or the other was 'justified'. Whether consent of an existing govern-ment does or does not excuse intervention is still a matter of dispute, with the positions depending upon whether or not the government in question is held to represent the free choice of the people. In despair, one authority concludes that the only clear line is to hold to the view that Article 2(4) of the United Nations Charter prohibits cases of 'direct, overt aggression capable of objective and persuasive proof'.

The legal result is to leave the problem in a kind of limbo. If agreed-upon legal norms existed, great moral weight could be attached to their mainten-ance or violation; but where, as here, this is not the case, moral analysis is left to appraise the issues involved with precious little support from the legal writers.

[. . .] [S]ome general considerations can be advanced. In the first place *not* to intervene may have as serious consequences as actually to intervene. The case of the civil war in Spain is an example, where the Western powers refused to act and thereby aided the victory of the rebels under Franco. This case exemplifies the famous comment of Talleyrand that 'non-intervention is a term of political metaphysics signifying almost the same thing as intervention'. It could also be argued that in the case of intervention against a great power which is already involved in a country the burden of moral proof lies on the intervening state, since great powers are clearly likely to resist intervention by force. While this criterion by itself would not *justify* the successive US interventions in Central America, it would render them less objectionable simply because less risky. It is also true that collective intervention by the great powers poses fewer dangers to the general peace than unilateral intervention. Such collective undertakings assume agreement on rules of behaviour which would in effect be a return to the concert system of the nineteenth century. A pattern of this sort could emerge over time and would be an immense improvement over present great power behaviour which relies on unilateral action and sometimes accepts the risks of competitive intervention through the use of proxies. It should be pointed out, however, that the concert system systematically ignored demands for justice by the smaller powers. To the extent that these powers have gained in influence their demands will be harder to ignore.

Beyond this point the moral problems become more difficult and it is often hard to discover clear guidelines. The key general issue, however, revolves around one's view of the importance of the balance of power as a general force for order, stability and peace. If, as a matter of empirical fact, a stable balance tends to reduce the chances of war, then intervention to maintain such a state of affairs would have considerable moral merit; though this is not a point of view which would find much support in 'revolutionary' capitals. But even disregarding the balance, it is not true that revolutionary regimes always make conditions better for their people, or always make them worse, and each case of intervention therefore has to be judged on its own merits. If this is objected to by visceral anti-communists, it should be pointed out that it might well be desirable for the Western powers to intervene temporarily in order to prevent cases of gross injustice or to undercut those regimes, whether communist or not, which clearly present an active threat to the peace of the region. Thus intervention to bring down a barbaric regime like Amin's in Uganda was met with wide moral acceptance.

In general, a test which might survive moral scrutiny would be this: If intervention threatens to change permanently the existing territorial balance of power, it should be ruled out as too dangerous. For such radical shifts threaten to produce counter-action and hence pose considerable dangers of wider conflict. It is an empirical fact, borne out by many examples, that 'attempts to preserve the status quo, even if accompanied by measures of the utmost brutality, appear to be viewed with greater tolerance by the opposite camp than forcible efforts towards a change in the world balance'. This is a political fact with moral implications. The main point is that a balance of power is highly dynamic and that strong measures will be taken to prevent serious reductions in the power of one's own side and to counter increases in the power of the other. [. . .]

We could sum up by stating a theory reminiscent of the 'just' or justified war theory. [. . .] Unilateral and coercive intervention can be justified if it is (1) a response to intervention by one's opponents; (2) a defence of the integrity of the internal political process; (3) a means to re-establish the balance, not to destabilize it; (4) a venture with a reasonable chance of success; (5) a last resort, following humane and constructive efforts to deal with the fundamental problems; (6) an undertaking proportional in its means to the value of its end; (7) not a violation of basic moral principles such as the proscription on murder. As with the principles of just war theory, these principles should be regarded as overridable in unusual situations. But these situations must be unusual, and the principles should be very widely applicable.

[From J. E. Hare and Carey B. Joynt, *Ethics and International Affairs* (London: Macmillan, 1982), 151–3, 160.]

PAUL C. WARNKE

55 Vietnam and Nuremberg

War raises many questions for which law has no answers. From Saint Augustine to President Nixon, the waging of war has been rationalized as a road to peace. The standards developed for individual behavior have proven to be uneasy analogues in the international regime when resort is made to violence to achieve foreign-policy objectives. Time may show that the use of military force was unwarranted and its objectives unworthy. But history's assessment of national error, and the less remote assessment of the fitness of a nation's wartime leaders to retain or resume high office, must be reviewed as an issue apart from that of combatant conduct.

Books such as Gen. Telford Taylor's document the anomaly of seeking to distinguish degrees of dreadfulness in the context of this most dreadful of human phenomena. What the Vietnam tragedy should have made even clearer, however, is the distinction drawn at the Nuremberg and Tokyo trials between the crime of war and 'war crimes'. Instead, for some the Vietnam experience has seemed to blur the differences and to require suspension of individual responsibility for crimes in a war that they regard as intrinsically criminal.

The novelty of Nuremberg was the attempt to define and deter as criminal conduct the decisions of national leaders to wage aggressive war. In a world of autonomous national states, this can only be a crime reserved for losers. But the inability to get an objective ruling on the justice of a nation's war effort should not preclude a fair trial for those individuals who engage in, order, or condone acts of calculated cruelty.

Eradication of the crime against peace obviously would put an end to war crimes as well. Those who purposefully cause war are thus the master criminals—guilty, in the Nuremberg judgment's words, of 'the supreme international crime differing only from other war crimes in that it contains within itself the accumulated evil of the whole'. But the question of responsibility for bringing a war into being is highly resistant to legal resolution. Probably this responsibility can be assessed in the contemporary context only in a tribunal convened by the victor to try the vanquished.

In the case of Vietnam, the United States military participation has been both defended and attacked under the Nuremberg principles of crimes against peace. Opinions have differed on such fundamental issues as whether Vietnam is one or two countries, and thus on whether the United States was defending a small ally against foreign attack or meddling officiously, and illegally, in the internal affairs of another country.

In the past, common perception of the national interest has generally foreclosed domestic attacks on a nation's war effort. As General Taylor has pointed out, the Soviets could thus sit in solemn judgment on Germany's conduct of an aggressive war in which the Soviet Union was for a time its ally. The Vietnam War was perhaps unique, however, in that sizable numbers of Americans have questioned the legitimacy of our country's role.

But no conceivable outcome of the conflict in Vietnam could have made the legitimacy of that role a justiciable question. Military defeat was never in the cards. Thus it is still true that no American President has 'lost a war'. And, as I have already said, formal charges of crimes against peace are reserved for losers. In another, profounder sense, all the men who occupied the Presidency in the Vietnam War years have been losers from it. Their appreciation of the national interest, or the international interest, has been, at least in hindsight, demonstrably faulty. A heavy political penalty is appropriate and has, in part, already been paid.

But criminal responsibility for personal conduct that transgresses recognized standards is a different, and, I suggest, a far simpler question requiring no novel doctrine and no deep assessment of national motivation and morality.

In an article that appeared in April 1971, Hans Morgenthau asserted: 'It is the contrast between the judgment of condemnation handed down by the military court in the case of Lt.Calley and the judgment of acquittal issued by the court of public opinion every day in the case of our leaders and ourselves that deprives the Calley verdict of moral validity.' I believe that this confuses quite separate issues. The lack of a national consensus as to the justice of our cause in Vietnam has no bearing on Lieutenant Calley's guilt or innocence. Dr Morgenthau later maintained that Lieutenant Calley 'did what he was ordered to do and what many others did who were lucky enough to escape public attention'. To the extent that Lieutenant Calley's superiors may be shown in fact to have ordered what happened at My Lai, their equal responsibility as war criminals would be undeniable—though their complicity would not excuse those who executed an order obviously illegal under the rules of war. Those who sought to ignore or obscure what happened are guilty too—as accessories after the fact and as stimuli to similar atrocities.

But direct involvement in atrocities—whether as actor or director—involves none of the complexities of determining if a conflict should be deemed unwarranted aggression rather than the 'collective defense' authorized by article 51 of the United Nations Charter. On this latter issue, the judgment of history may be merciless. I question, however, whether contemporary concern can or should yield penal consequences.

War crimes must continue to be distinguished from crimes against peace. To do otherwise would turn the Nuremberg principles into a shield for those chargeable with the ultimate inhumanity to defenseless human beings. We can, I believe, accept the proposition that mean-minded men can do bad things in the best of wars. I might suggest also that good men in good faith may involve their country in a bad war. But history's assessment is not necessary to support the prosecution and conviction of those responsible for incidents of atrocity. That not all can be found and punished is a failing in the most meticulous attempt at application of criminal law, whether civilian or military.

A war's ultimate justice or injustice is basically irrelevant to the criminality of the actions of an individual combatant. Those who fought in Vietnam and abided by the rules of war should not be subject to prosecution under any construction of the Nuremberg principles. For example, Capt. Howard Levy's contention that war crimes were being committed by others in Vietnam gave him no automatic 'Nuremberg defense' for his refusal in this country to obey an intrinsically lawful order to train medical aides.

The ultimate legality of our participation in Vietnam is, as General Taylor has pointed out, not now 'susceptible to solution by judicial decree'. The resolution of this question, and the fate of those responsible for the American involvement, may—and should—be left for political action. But individual crimes in the Vietnam theater are proper grist for the judicial mill.

Some have argued that the entire idea of war crimes should be abandoned and any personal conduct excused. Their rationale is that war would then become so horrible as to revolt the conscience of the world and lead to its eradication. This is perhaps as misconceived as the argument that soldiers who kill under orders with no colorable military justification should be excused because their military and civilian leaders may be guiltier.

There are significant humanitarian purposes served by the international laws of war. As General Taylor has noted, the rules protecting prisoners of war have saved millions of lives in earlier conflicts. These rules were relied on for protection of United States military personnel held captive in North Vietnam. The scrapping of these restraints would lead directly to the death of countless innocents in current and future armed conflicts.

At the same time it is true, as General Taylor points out, that this has been 'a pretty bloody century and people do not seem to shock very easily'. This is, as he notes, distressingly confirmed in much of the reaction both to reports of My Lai and to the trial and conviction of an American officer who flatly admitted his role in the slaughter of unarmed civilians—men and women, children and the aged.

The Nuremberg concept of aggressive war as a crime susceptible of legal proof and judicial determination can be regarded as a noble experiment. It could even have some deterrent efficacy, if the combatants, whether they win or lose, could be persuaded to accept the jurisdiction of an international tribunal. Until that millennium, the risk of prosecution is but one small element in the greater risk of total military defeat. But win, lose, or draw, a civilized country with any claim to national morality can and must punish its citizens who violate basic norms of human behavior in contravention either of domestic laws or of the rules of war.

There are those who disagree about whether the personal guilt of combatants can be assessed in the Vietnam context. Not too strangely with respect to this strangest of wars, some of them support the righteousness of the United States cause and others believe the war to have been unjust and immoral. Those who were ardent hawks contend in substance that, because our cause was just, My Lai probably never happened and anyway they were Communists who had it coming. And former doves feel that it is unfair to punish individual soldiers who were caught up in a war that the doves deem itself a far graver crime.

The first argument does not deserve an answer. But as to the second, if the overall injustice of a nation's cause waives individual and personal responsibility on the part of members of its fighting forces, then Lidice, Oradea, and the systematic slaughter of Jewish populations in occupied countries cannot be construed as the acts of war criminals. And if any individual behavior is allowable for those compelled by superior authority to fight in a 'bad' cause, then perhaps the unfortunate General Yamashita had a better defense than lack of knowledge and inability to control the conduct of his forces in the Philippines in the closing days of World War II. But we hanged General Yamashita because, in the words of General MacArthur: 'The soldier, be he friend or foe, is charged with the protection of the weak and unarmed. It is the very essence and reason for his being.' General MacArthur added that when the soldier 'violates his sacred trust he not only profanes his entire cult but threatens the very fabric of international society'.

There are, of course, the cloudy cases in which arguments of military necessity lead to actions that in less compelling circumstances would earn the condemnation of the civilized world. The bombardment of Coventry and Cologne, of London and Hiroshima, were plainly bound to kill civilians. It is hard to stomach the argument that they were directed at the war-making potential of the other side and intended to bring the war to a close by crippling this potential. Likewise, no one can genuinely believe that in Vietnam air strikes were surgical or that the napalm used by United States military forces distinguished the armed foe from the peasant child. As General Taylor points out, '"necessity" is a matter of infinite circumstantial variation'. But there are, in any war, instances in which discrimination and decision are not difficult; in which casual and deliberate inhumanity can have no arguable effect in bringing further killing to a close. There are, in any war, individuals who allow that war to be an opportunity to satisfy their darkest urges. To excuse them because all wars are dreadful or because a particular one may not be justified by the national interest is, in my view, consonant neither with justice nor with its basic aim of providing and protecting an ordered society.

Perhaps in the grey area, popular wars win readier acceptance of marginal military justification for tactics that cause noncombatant casualties. But there is an area of conduct that is unrelievedly black, and no hand wringing or breast beating about the immorality of the particular conflict or the responsibility of those who brought it about can change this black to white. Some such offenses are sufficiently clear to have been spelled out in the Hague Regulations and Geneva Conventions. Among them is the declaration of article 4 of the annex to the Hague Convention No. IV of 1907, that enemy soldiers who have surrendered are not to be killed. The Geneva Civilians Convention similarly commands safety for enemy civilians. Thus the suggestions that events at My Lai may somehow be excusable because it was a 'combat village' and 'even the babies might have been booby trapped' are without possible merit. Even if those slaughtered in the huts and ditches of My Lai had previously been armed enemies resisting the attack on their hamlet, their summary execution would still be a clear violation of established international law.

It has been suggested that the tragic peasants of My Lai might not have been 'protected persons' within the terms of article 4 of the Geneva Civilians Convention, because they were not enemy civilians but instead 'nationals of a co-belligerent state'. An open season on 'friendlies' might remove legal doubts about some uses of American firepower in Laos,

Cambodia, and South Vietnam. It might also decrease enthusiasm for security commitments from the United States. But any such legalism may be countered by the further legalism that under the 1954 Geneva Accords, the seventeenth parallel 'should not in any way be interpreted as a political or territorial boundary'.

Perhaps a better answer is that, as General Taylor points out, '[t]he laws of war remain a body of what lawyers call "customary" laws—that is to say, laws that are not created by statutes and enacted by legislators, but develop from societal customs and practices.' The Hague Convention No. IV of 1907 stated that questions not covered should be resolved by 'the principles of the law of nations, as they result from usages established among civilized people, from the laws of humanity, and from the dictates of the public conscience'. Disputed questions of nationality thus cannot control the guilt of those in any way responsible for the massacre.

Some would argue that the responsibility for My Lai extends to any and all who brought about our presence in Vietnam. They contend that the application of massive American military force to put down a native insurgency would become inevitably a war against civilians and that My Lai thus, in the words of its main executioner, was not 'any big deal'. In antiguerrilla action, in which the people are Mao's sea within which the guerrillas swim and survive, the prospects of widespread civilian suffering are obviously far greater than in the classic clash of front-line forces. This fact should lead to serious reconsideration of the merits of a counterinsurgent policy. It should lead also to more vivid realization that a decision to wage war is a decision to sacrifice an indeterminate number of innocent lives. It should lead to a resolve that military force should be used only on the most compelling showing of imminent danger to our national security.

But from my own experience and from the firsthand reports of those whose word and judgment I trust, I regard My Lai as the exception and believe that hundreds of similar military actions were conducted in Vietnam without the wholesale slaughter of helpless humans.

The inability to bring national leaders to the bar of justice under principles that were novel at Nuremberg cannot excuse failure to prosecute those guilty of committing, ordering, or authorizing actions that the common conscience must recognize as criminal. Close cases may be found. A commander who established a free-fire zone may have done so without considering the ratio of armed enemy to farm families. A pilot may have dropped his bombs with inadequate concern for whether the target was an ammunition cache or a field hospital. An ill-advised war may have multiplied the circumstances in which voiceless noncombatants were sacrificed to poorly perceived aspirations for peace.

A conscientious desire to live by the international and humanitarian standards we espouse would lead to the trial even of the tougher issues. But neither the Nuremberg novelty of war as a crime in itself, nor the problems of proof in close cases, should lead us in clear cases to make bad law.

[From Peter D. Trooboff (ed.), 'Individual Responsibility in Warfare' *Law and Responsibility in Warfare* (Chapel Hill, NC: University of North Carolina Press, 1975), 187–93.

Section E

Strategy

BEATRICE HEUSER AND LAWRENCE FREEDMAN

In Europe, the eighteenth century was an age of mainly limited wars, in which expensive professional and mercenary armies were sent into battle by cautious princes, to be recalled as soon as defeat seemed imminent or the losses suffered outweighed the potential gains of a campaign limited not only in means but also in ends. This, at any rate, was the perception of the eighteenth century in the minds of contemporaries and of the following generation. Under Napoleon Bonaparte's generalship the well-ordered world of the *ancien régime* was shattered. He married the engagement of the entire population, the *levée en masse*, with the quest for total victory and the total defeat of the enemy. As a result he became the yardstick and focus of subsequent thinking about strategy. The Maxims he left behind, however, consist mainly of banal truisms about government (often contradictory) and of strategies—for conquest in love! It was left mainly to others to draw out lessons and principles from his campaigns. The two most important analysts of his warfare were Henri de Jomini, a Swiss who temporarily fought in Napoleon's army, and Carl von Clausewitz, who fought on the opposite side. Both correctly identified some of the guiding principles applied by Napoleon, as a glance at the excerpts of his Maxims printed here show (61), such as his emphasis on the deployment of troops, his use of the concentration of forces, of manœuvre, and of enveloping movements, and his exploitation of the offensive.

Jomini, like Clausewitz, recognized that the highest level of reflection about war was that of politics, and that strategy, 'grand tactics', tactics and everything else were dominated by politics. His definitions of strategy, 'grand tactics', and tactics have remained useful until this day (60). But he never went as far as Clausewitz in recognizing warfare as the function of politics and much of his analysis was apolitical. Like others who sought to reduce war to its essentials, Jomini was at the same time aware of reasons to doubt the value of such an exercise. Thus he could describe war as 'a great drama, in which a thousand physical and moral causes operate more or less powerfully, and which cannot be reduced to mathematical calculations', yet went on to assert the existence of 'a small number of fundamental principles of war, which could not be deviated from without danger, and the application of which, on the contrary, has been in almost all time crowned with success'.

By contrast, Clausewitz's intellectual curiosity (and his most interesting writing) focused on the strategic-political level of war, or even on its philosophical dimension. Where Jomini grew most enthusiastic in his discussion of inner and outer lines of operations, Clausewitz's principal intellectual contribution to strategic thinking was his reflection on the use of force in a wider context. Why had war been so limited in the eighteenth century? Why was it so much more all-encompassing in Napoleon's campaigns? Could it ever go back to a limited nature? What were the differences between the societies involved in the limited wars of the eighteenth century, and those involved in Napoleon's wars? What relationship was there between political aims and military means?

It was only late in his life that Clausewitz began to realize the full complexity of these issues. The wars that unfolded under Napoleon's leadership seemed to Clausewitz to be in their scale and horror almost perfect examples of ideal wars, of what war could be in its purest form of unmitigated violence and destruction. He was so impressed by the Napoleonic campaigns that in his reflections in *On War* he initially wrote only about this ideal or 'absolute' form of war, a war completely without restraints, and with unlimited war aims. As Napoleon's political aims in these wars were limitless, Napoleon's military aims had no limitations either, and accordingly, in his wars, violence had not been limited. In Clausewitz's first draft, and thus in his thinking on war during the longest part of his life, politics therefore played no part.

Thus, Clausewitz the Idealist postulated that in war, all is decided in battle, and indeed, there are decisive large battles which become central to victory. It was only in 1827, after twelve years of the post-Napoleonic era in which the Holy Alliance guarded the *status quo* in Europe, that Clausewitz suddenly realized that his analysis of war was too exclusively that of 'absolute war', and thus perhaps not applicable to all real wars. Why were some wars not like the Napoleonic 'absolute' war? The answer was that war was an instrument of politics, and war could only unfold itself to its ideal dimensions if politics did not place restraints upon it. Thus limited political aims resulted in the definition of limited war aims, and in restraints imposed upon the way in which these aims would be reached. He then began to rewrite his book but never completed the task (59).[1]

It was through Clausewitz's writings (and mainly through his unrevised first chapters) that the Napoleonic techniques of warfare lived on, and thus mainly in Prussia, not in France. General Helmuth von Moltke, or Moltke the Elder, Chief of Staff of the Prussian Army from 1857 to 1887, made this work of Clausewitz the Idealist his guiding principles. Moltke was the key

---

[1] See Azar Gat, *The Origins of Military Thought: From the Englightenment to Clausewitz* (Oxford: Oxford University Press, 1989).

practitioner who focused all German battle plans on the aim of the total destruction of the enemy's forces (62). While he was fashioning the Prussian military with iron discipline and tactical flexibility, the French were suffering a decline, which led to their shock defeat at the hands of the Prussians in 1870.

One response to the Prussian gains and the French decline is found in the writings of Charles Ardant du Picq, a French officer who concentrated largely on tactics, and stressed the importance of the morale and discipline of the soldiers, almost to the exclusion of shock and other physical factors (63). The reasons why the 'spirit of offensive' was adopted in French strategy are complex (see 75 in next section) but it contributed to the great slaughter of 1914–18. Much of the strategic writing that followed the First World War took as its point of departure the need to avoid a comparable experience. If war itself could not be avoided then its conduct must be more decisive and less costly. This was the essential philosophy behind Liddell Hart's 'indirect approach' (66). The innovations of the aircraft and the tank, which gradually imposed themselves during the course of the First World War, provided the natural starting-point for the innovators in strategic thinking.

Air power, it seemed, would dominate the warfare of the future, and to enthusiasts such as the Italian Giulio Douhet (65) it offered a means of avoiding the need for any surface combat at all, concentrating instead on the civilian population who, he assumed, would be unable to withstand air bombardment. Douhet was the most systematic, if not necessarily the most influential of the air-power theorists. By the Second World War air forces had developed in a variety of ways. The British had reason to be grateful in 1940 that they had built fighter aircraft for defence and had not taken the fatalistic view that the bomber would always get through. As the war progressed there were opportunities to assess the impact of mass air raids: there was little support for the view that the civilian morale would crumble and societies would cease to function. Some of the most successful uses of air power proved to be in the role of influencing combat on the land or on the sea.

The arrival of nuclear weapons just in time to conclude the war suggested that the logic of war had now worked itself through to the point where civil society had become hopelessly vulnerable. As the sources of conflict had not vanished totally, the hope had to be that awareness of the awful consequences of letting such a conflict get out of hand would act to deter all war. The most optimistic (69) saw this working to congeal all conflict so that the status quo would be sustained: even the most radical states would not dare accept the risks connected with the initiation of war. In the United States, where there was less confidence that the benign workings of deterrence could be taken for granted, a new set of strategists began to wrestle with the problem of how to use the fear of nuclear war as an instrument of policy even when it was evidently too dangerous to actually initiate nuclear war deliberately. The most creative of these new strategists was Thomas Schelling, who had trained in economics and who applied new methods, such as game theory, to the problem. In extract 58 he sets out his own distinctive approach to strategic analysis; in 70 this approach is applied in the notion of the 'threat that leaves something to chance'. Here Schelling, essentially drawing on ideas comparable to Clausewitz's on the processes by which a limited war might tend towards the absolute, shows how an opponent might be sufficiently impressed by the sense that matters were slipping out of control to look for a negotiated solution to a developing war.

In the hands of less gifted analysts this rather formal approach was used to combine detailed consideration of the properties of individual weapons systems with rather mechanistic political judgements. It was against this tendency that Michael Howard wrote his article on the forgotten dimensions of strategy (57), encouraging a wider grasp of the dynamics of war, and in the process providing a useful introduction to its study.

56 **The Logic of Strategy**

Si vis pacem, para bellum (If you want peace, prepare war) goes the Latin tag attributed to Roman wisdom, still much used today by speakers preaching the virtues of strong armament. Thus we are told that a prepared ability to fight dissuades attack that weakness could invite, thereby averting war. It is just as true that a prepared ability to fight can ensure peace in quite another way, by making war unnecessary as the weak are induced to give way to the strong without a fight; but that corollary would not be advertised nowadays, as it might have been before 1914. Worn down by overuse into a cliché, the Roman admonition has lost the power to arouse our thoughts, but it is precisely its banality that is significant: the phrase is of course paradoxical in presenting blatant contradiction as if it were a straightforwardly logical proposition—and that is scarcely what we would expect of a mere banality.

Why is the contradictory argument accepted so unresistingly, indeed dismissed as obvious? To be sure, there are some who disagree, and the entire new academic venture of 'peace studies' is dedicated to the proposition that peace should be studied as a phenomenon in itself and actively worked for in real life: *si vis pacem, para pacem*, its advocates might say. But even those who explicitly reject the paradoxical admonition do not denounce it as a self-evidently foolish contradiction that any breath of commonsense should sweep away. On the contrary, they see it as a piece of wrongheaded conventional wisdom, to which they oppose ideas that they themselves would describe as novel and unconventional.

And so the question remains: why is the blatant contradiction so easily accepted? Consider the absurdity of equivalent advice in any sphere of life but the strategic: if you want *A* strive for *B*, its opposite, as in 'if you want to lose weight, eat more; if you want to become rich, earn less'—surely we would reject all such. It is only in the realm of strategy, which encompasses *the conduct and consequences of human relations in the context of actual or possible armed conflict*, that we have learned to accept paradoxical propositions as valid.

Of this the most obvious example is the entire notion of nuclear 'deterrence', by now so thoroughly assimilated that to many it seems prosaic. To defend, we must stand ready to attack at all times. To derive their benefit, we must never use the nuclear weapons that we continue to build so assiduously. To be ready to attack is evidence of peaceful intent, but to prepare defenses is aggressive, or at least 'provocative'—such are the conventional views on the subject. Controversy on the safety of nuclear deterrence is periodically rekindled, and there is certainly much debate on every detailed aspect of nuclear-weapons policy. But the obvious paradoxes that form the very substance of nuclear deterrence are deemed unremarkable.

The large claim I advance here is that strategy does not merely entail this or that paradoxical proposition, contradictory and yet recognized as valid, but rather that *the entire realm of strategy is pervaded by a paradoxical logic of its own*, standing against the ordinary linear logic by which we live in all other spheres of life (except for warlike games, of course). In settings where conflict is merely incidental to purposes of production and consumption, of commerce and culture, of social relations and consensual governance, with strife and competition more or less bound by law and custom, a noncontradictory linear logic applies, whose essence is captured by what we think of as commonsense.

Within the sphere of strategy, on the other hand, where human relations are conditioned by armed conflict actual or possible, another and quite different logic is at work. It often violates ordinary linear logic *by inducing the coming together and even the reversal of opposites*, and it therefore, incidentally, tends to reward paradoxical conduct while confounding straightforwardly logical action, by yielding results ironical if not lethally self-damaging. [. . .]

In spite of obstacles, friction, and risk, the general theory here presented does offer some scope for practical application. It may not help soldiers and statesmen as explorers may be helped by a good topographic map, but it can serve them at least as jungle explorers are served by a guide to poisonous plants; negative advice can also be valuable.

First, once it is understood that the paradoxical logic conditions all that is conflictual, strategic practice can be freed from the systematically misleading influence of commonsense logic. For the conduct of foreign policy, this offers the prospect of an eventual liberation from the false discipline of consistency and coherence, to allow scope for concerted policies that are purposefully contradictory. Military leaders have always been able to pursue paradoxical tactics and operational methods (so much so that unconventional moves now coincide with commonsense notions of how war should be fought), but a new recognition of the pervasive reach of the logic can release them from the imposition of linear-logical thinking on peacetime military policy, with its harmful derivatives and misleading criteria of efficiency.

Second, once the dynamic consequences of the logic are understood, the exercise of restraint in pursuing success in war or peace, in the conduct of an offensive or in the building of weapons, will no longer depend on vague instincts of moderation but can instead be sustained by a compelling rationale as culminating points are approached. Mere awareness of the endless dynamics of the logic can serve as a warning against excess, to provide a stout wall of caution against the momentum of animal desires for unlimited success.

Third, once the structure of strategy is understood, with its distinct levels and dimensions, an entire class of errors can be exposed, resisted, or directly inhibited—those frequent errors that arise from decisions made at some level chosen arbitrarily with other levels ignored, and from the pursuit of success in one dimension alone in disharmony with the other.

But a discipline need not be of practical value to merit our attention: the study of strategy should be its own reward because it alone can explain the tantalizing continuities and baffling contradictions that pervade the human experience of conflict.

[From Edward Luttwak, *Strategy: The Logic of War and Peace* (Cambridge, Mass.: Harvard University Press, 1987), 3–5, 236.]

MICHAEL HOWARD

57 **The Dimensions of Strategy**

I

The term 'strategy' needs continual definition. For most people, Clausewitz's formulation 'the use of engagements for the object of the war', or, as Liddell Hart paraphrased it, 'the art of distributing and applying military means to fulfil the ends of policy', is clear enough. Strategy concerns the deployment and use of armed forces to attain a given political objective. Histories of strategy usually consist of case studies, from Alexander the Great to MacArthur, of the way in which this was done. Nevertheless, the experience of the past century has shown this approach to be inadequate to the point of triviality. In the West the concept of 'grand strategy' was introduced to cover those industrial, financial, demographic, and societal aspects of war that have become so salient in the twentieth century. In communist states all strategic thought has to be validated by the holistic doctrines of Marxism-Leninism. Without discarding such established concepts, I shall offer here a somewhat different and perhaps slightly simpler framework for analysis, based on a study of the way in which both strategic doctrine and warfare itself have developed over the past 200 years. [. . .]

II

Clausewitz's definition of strategy was deliberately and defiantly simplistic. It swept away virtually everything that had been written about war (which was a very great deal) over the previous 300 years. Earlier writers had concerned themselves almost exclusively with the enormous problems of raising, arming, equipping, moving, and maintaining armed forces in the field—an approach which Clausewitz dismissed as being as relevant to fighting as the skills of the sword-maker were to the art of fencing. None of this, he insisted, was significant for the actual conduct of war, and the inability of all previous writers to formulate an adequate theory had been due to their failure to distinguish between the *maintenance* of armed forces and their *use*.

By making this distinction between what I shall term the *logistical* and the *operational* dimensions in warfare, Clausewitz performed a major service to strategic thinking; but the conclusions he drew from that distinction were questionable and the consequences of those conclusions have been unfortunate. In the first place, even in his own day, the commanders he so much admired—Napoleon, Frederick the Great—could never have achieved their operational triumphs if they had not had a profound understanding of the whole range of military activities that Clausewitz excluded from consideration. In the second place, no campaign can be understood, and no valid conclusions drawn from it, unless its logistical problems are studied as thoroughly as the course of operations; and logistical factors have been ignored by ninety-nine military historians out of a hundred—an omission which has warped their judgments and made their conclusions in many cases wildly misleading.

Clausewitz's dogmatic assertion of priorities—his subordination of the logistical element in war to the operational—may have owed something to a prejudice common to all fighting soldiers in all eras. It certainly owed much to his reaction against the super-cautious 'scientific' generals whose operational ineptitude had led Prussia to defeat in 1806. But it cannot be denied that in the Napoleonic era it *was* operational skill rather than sound logistical planning that proved decisive in campaign after campaign. And since Napoleon's campaigns provided the basis for all strategic writings and thinking throughout the nineteenth century, 'strategy' became generally equated in the public mind with *operational* strategy.

But the inadequacy of this concept was made very clear, to those who studied it, by the course of the American Civil War. There the masters of operational strategy were to be found, not in the victorious armies of the North, but among the leaders of the South. Lee and Jackson handled their forces with a flexibility and an imaginativeness worthy of a Napoleon or a Frederick; nevertheless they lost. Their defeat was attributed by Liddell Hart, whose analyses seldom extended beyond the operational plane, primarily to operational factors, in particular, to the 'indirect approach' adopted by Sherman. But, fundamentally, the victory of the North was due not to the operational capabilities of its generals, but to its capacity to mobilize its superior industrial strength and manpower into armies which such leaders as Grant were able, thanks largely to road and river transport, to deploy in such strength that the operational skills of their adversaries were rendered almost irrelevant. Ultimately the latter were ground down in a conflict of attrition in which the *logistical* dimension of strategy proved more significant than the operational. What proved to be of the greatest importance was the capacity to bring the largest and best-equipped forces into the operational theatre and to maintain them there. It was an experience that has shaped the strategic doctrine of the US Armed Forces from that day to this.

But this capacity depended upon a third dimension of strategy, and one to which Clausewitz was the first major thinker to draw attention: the *social*, the attitude of the people upon whose commitment and readiness for self-denial this logistical power ultimately depended. Clausewitz had described war as 'a remarkable trinity', composed of its political objective, of its operational instruments, and of the popular passions, the social forces it expressed. It was the latter, he pointed out, that made the wars of the French Revolution so different in kind from those of Frederick the Great, and which would probably so distinguish any wars in the future. In this he was right.

With the end of the age of absolutism, limited wars of pure policy fought by dispassionate professionals became increasingly rare. Growing popular participation in government meant popular involvement in war, and so did the increasing size of the armed forces which nineteenth-century technology was making possible and therefore necessary. Management of, or compliance with, public opinion became an essential element in the conduct of war. Had the population of the North been as indifferent to the outcome of the Civil War as the leaders of the Confederacy had initially hoped, the operational victories of the South in the early years might have decisively tipped the scales. The logistical potential of the North would have been of negligible value without the determination to use it. But given equal resolution on both sides, the capacity of the North to mobilize superior forces ultimately became the decisive factor in the struggle. Again Clausewitz was proved right: *all other factors being equal*, numbers ultimately proved decisive.

III

In one respect, in particular, other factors were equal. The Civil War was fought with comparable if not identical weapons on both sides, as had been the revolutionary wars in Europe. The possibility of decisive *technological* superiority on one side or the other was so inconceivable that Clausewitz and his contemporaries had discounted it. But within a year of the conclusion of the American Civil War, just such a superiority made itself apparent in the realm of small arms, when the Prussian armies equipped with breech-loading rifles defeated Austrian armies which were not so equipped. Four years later, in 1870, the Prussians revealed an even more crushing superiority over their French adversaries thanks to their steel breech-loading artillery. This superiority was far from decisive: the Franco-Prussian War in particular was won, like the American Civil War, by superior logistical capability based on a firm popular commitment. But technology, as an independent and significant dimension, could no longer be left out of account.

In naval warfare, the crucial importance of technological parity had been apparent since the dawn of the age of steam, and in colonial warfare the technological element was to prove quite decisive. During the latter part of the nineteenth century, the superiority of European weapons turned what had previously been a marginal technological advantage over indigenous forces, often counterbalanced by numerical inferiority, into a crushing military ascendancy, which made it possible for European forces to establish a new imperial dominance throughout the world over cultures incapable of responding in kind. As Hilaire Belloc's Captain Blood succinctly put it: 'Whatever happens, we have got The Maxim gun, and they have not.' Military planners have been terrified of being caught without the contemporary equivalent of the Maxim gun from that day to this.

So by the beginning of this century, war was conducted in these four dimensions: the *operational*, the *logistical*, the *social*, and the *technological*. No successful strategy could be formulated that did not take account of them all, but under different circumstances, one or another of these dimensions might dominate. When, in 1914–15, the operational strategy of the Schlieffen Plan, for the one side, and of the Gallipoli campaign, for the other, failed to achieve the decisive results expected of them, then the logistical aspects of the war, and with them the social basis on which they depended, assumed even greater importance as the opposing armies tried to bleed each other to death. As in the American Civil War, victory was to go, not to the side with the most skilful generals and the most courageous troops, but to that which could mobilize the greatest mass of manpower and firepower and sustain it with the strongest popular support.

The inadequacy of mere numbers without social cohesion behind them was demonstrated by the collapse of the Russian Empire in 1917. But the vulnerability even of logistical and social power if the adversary could secure a decisive technological advantage was equally demonstrated by the success of the German submarine campaign in the spring of 1917, when the Allies came within measurable distance of defeat. The German Empire decided to gamble on a technological advantage to counter the logistical superiority which American participation gave to their enemies. But they lost.

IV

From the experiences of the First World War, different strategic thinkers derived different strategic lessons. In Western Europe, the most adventurous theorists considered that the technological dimension of war would predominate in the future. The protagonists of armoured warfare in particular believed that it might restore an operational decisiveness unknown since the days of Napoleon himself—the first two years of the Second World War were to prove them right. Skilfully led and well-trained armed forces operating against opponents who were both militarily and morally incapable of resisting them achieved spectacular results.

But another school of thinkers who placed their faith in technology fared less well. This school included those who believed that the development of air power would enable them to eliminate the operational dimension altogether and to strike directly at the roots of the enemy's *social* strength, at the will and capacity of the opposing society to carry on the war. Instead of wearing down the morale of the enemy civilians through the attrition of surface operations, air power, its protagonists believed, would be able to attack and pulverize it directly.

The events of the war were to disprove this theory. Technology was not yet sufficiently advanced to be able to eliminate the traditional requirements of operational and logistical strategy in this manner. Neither the morale of the British nor that of the German people was to be destroyed by air attack; indeed, such attack was found to demand an operational strategy of a new and complex kind in order to defeat the opposing air forces and to destroy their logistical support. But operational success in air warfare, aided by new technological developments, did eventually enable the Allied air forces to destroy the entire logistical framework that supported the German and Japanese war effort, and rendered the operational skills, in which the Germans excelled until the very end, as ineffective as those of Jackson and Lee.

Technology had not in fact transformed the nature of strategy. It of course remained of vital importance to keep abreast of one's adversary in all major aspects of military technology, but given that this was possible, the lessons of the Second World War seemed little different from those of the First. The social base had to be strong enough to resist the psychological impact of operational set-backs and to support the largest possible logistical build-up by land, sea and air. The forces thus raised had then to be used progressively to eliminate the operational options open to the enemy and ultimately to destroy his capacity to carry on the war.

V

The same conclusions, set out in somewhat more turgid prose, were reached by the strategic analysts of the Soviet Union—not least those who in the late 1940s and early 1950s were writing under the pen-name of J. V. Stalin. But Marxist military thinkers, without differing in essentials from their contemporaries in the West, naturally devoted greater attention to the social dimension of strategy—the structure and cohesiveness of the belligerent societies. For Soviet writers this involved, and still involves, little more than the imposition of a rigid stereotype on the societies they study.

Their picture of a world in which oppressed peoples are kept in a state of backward subjection by a small group of exploitative imperialist powers, themselves domestically vulnerable to the revolutionary aspirations of a desperate proletariat, bears little resemblance to the complex reality, whatever its incontestable value as a propagandistic myth. As a result their analysis is often hilariously inaccurate, and their strategic prescriptions either erroneous or banal.

But the West is in no position to criticize. The stereotypes which we have imposed, consciously or unconsciously, on the political structures that surround us, have in the past been no less misleading. The Cold War image of a world which would evolve peacefully, if gradually, toward an Anglo-Saxon style of democracy under Western tutelage if only the global Soviet-directed Marxist conspiracy could be eradicated was at least as naïve and ill-informed as that of the Russian dogmatists. It was the inadequacy of the sociopolitical analysis of the societies with which we were dealing that lay at the root of the failure of the Western powers to cope more effectively with the revolutionary and insurgency movements that characterized the post-war era, from China in the 1940s to Vietnam in the 1960s. For in these, more perhaps than in any previous conflicts, war really was the continuation of political activity with an admixture of other means; and that political activity was itself the result of a huge social upheaval throughout the former colonial world which had been given an irresistible impetus by the events of the Second World War. Of the four dimensions of strategy, the social was here incomparably the most significant; and it was the perception of this that gave the work of Mao Tse-tung and his followers its abiding historical importance.

Military thinkers in the West, extrapolating from their experience of warfare between industrial states, naturally tended to seek a solution to what was essentially a conflict on the social plane either by developing operational techniques of 'counter-insurgency' or in the technological advantages provided by such developments as helicopters, sensors, or 'smart' bombs. When these techniques failed to produce victory, military leaders, both French and American, complained, as had the German military leaders in 1918, that the war had been 'won' militarily but 'lost' politically—as if these dimensions were not totally interdependent.

In fact, these operational techniques and technological tools were now as ancillary to the main socio-political conflict as the tools of psychological warfare had been to the central operational and logistical struggle in the two World Wars. In those conflicts, fought between remarkably cohesive societies, the issue was decided by logistic attrition. Propaganda and subversion had played a marginal role, and such successes as they achieved were strictly geared to those of the armed forces themselves. Conversely, in the conflicts of decolonization which culminated in Vietnam, operational and technological factors were subordinate to the socio-political struggle. If that was not conducted with skill and based on a realistic analysis of the societal situation, no amount of operational expertise, logistical back-up or technical know-how could possibly help.

VI

If the social dimension of strategy has become dominant in one form of conflict since 1945, in another it has, if one is to believe the strategic analysts, vanished completely. Works about nuclear war and deterrence normally treat their topic as an activity taking place almost entirely in the technological dimension. From their writings not only the socio-political but the operational elements have quite disappeared. The technological capabilities of nuclear arsenals are treated as being decisive in themselves, involving a calculation of risk and outcome so complete and discrete that neither the political motivation for the conflict nor the social factors involved in its conduct—nor indeed the military activity of fighting—are taken into account at all. In their models, governments are treated as being as absolute in their capacity to take and implement decisions, and the reaction of their societies are taken as little into account as were those of the subjects of the princes who conducted warfare in Europe in the eighteenth century. Professor Anatole Rapoport, in a rather idiosyncratic introduction to a truncated edition of Clausewitz's *On War*, called these thinkers 'Neo-Clausewitzians'. It is not easy to see why. Every one of the three elements that Clausewitz defined as being intrinsic to war—political motivation, operational activity and social participation—are completely absent from their calculations. Drained of political, social and operational content, such works resemble rather the studies of the eighteenth-century theorists whom Clausewitz was writing to confute, and whose influence he considered, with good reason, to have been so disastrous for his own times.

[From Michael Howard, 'The Forgotten Dimensions of War', repr. in his *The Causes of War* (London: Temple Smith, 1983), 101–9.]

THOMAS SCHELLING

58 | **The Strategy of Conflict**

Among diverse theories of conflict—corresponding to the diverse meanings of the word 'conflict'—a main dividing line is between those that treat conflict as a pathological state and seek its causes and treatment, and those that take conflict for granted and study the behavior associated with it. Among the latter there is a further division between those that examine the participants in a conflict in all their complexity—with regard to both 'rational' and 'irrational' behavior, conscious and unconscious, and to motivations as well as to calculations—and those that focus on the more rational, conscious, artful kind of behavior. Crudely speaking, the latter treat conflict as a kind of contest, in which the participants are trying to 'win'. A study of conscious, intelligent, sophisticated conflict behavior—of successful behavior—is like a search for rules of 'correct' behavior in a contest-winning sense.

We can call this field of study the *strategy* of conflict. We can be interested in it for at least three reasons. We may be involved in a conflict ourselves; we all are, in fact, participants in international conflict, and we want to 'win' in some proper sense. We may wish to understand how participants actually do conduct themselves in conflict situations; an understanding of 'correct' play may give us a bench mark for the study of actual behavior. We may wish to control or influence the behavior of others in conflict, and we want, therefore, to know how the variables that are subject to our control can affect their behavior.

If we confine our study to the theory of strategy, we seriously restrict ourselves by the assumption of rational behavior—not just of intelligent behavior, but of behavior motivated by a conscious calculation of advantages, a calculation that in turn is based on an explicit and internally consistent value system. We thus limit the applicability of any results we reach. If our interest is the study of actual behavior, the results we reach under this constraint may prove to be either a good approximation of reality or a caricature. Any abstraction runs a risk of this sort, and we have to be prepared to use judgment with any results we reach.

The advantage of cultivating the area of 'strategy' for theoretical development is not that, of all possible approaches, it is the one that evidently stays closest to the truth, but that the assumption of rational behavior is a productive one. It gives a grip on the subject that is peculiarly conducive to the development of theory. It permits us to identify our own analytical processes with those of the hypothetical participants in a conflict; and by demanding certain kinds of consistency in the behavior of our hypothetical participants, we can examine alternative courses of behavior according to whether or not they meet those standards of consistency. The premise of 'rational behavior' is a potent one for the production of theory. Whether the resulting theory provides good or poor insight into actual behavior is, I repeat, a matter for subsequent judgment.

But, in taking conflict for granted, and working with an image of participants who try to 'win', a theory of strategy does not deny that there are common as well as conflicting interests among the participants. In fact, the richness of the subject arises from the fact that, in international affairs, there is mutual dependence as well as opposition. Pure conflict, in which the interests of two antagonists are completely opposed, is a special case; it would arise in a war of complete extermination, otherwise not even in war. For this reason, 'winning' in a conflict does not have a strictly competitive meaning; it is not winning relative to one's adversary. It means gaining relative to one's own value system; and this may be done by bargaining, by mutual accommodation, and by the avoidance of mutually damaging behavior. If war to the finish has become inevitable, there is nothing left but pure conflict; but if there is any possibility of avoiding a mutually damaging war, of conducting warfare in a way that minimizes damage, or of coercing an adversary by threatening war rather than waging it, the possibility of mutual accommodation is as important and dramatic as the element of conflict. Concepts like deterrence, limited war, and disarmament, as well as negotiation, are concerned with the common interest and mutual dependence that can exist between participants in a conflict.

Thus, strategy—in the sense in which I am using it here—is not concerned with the efficient *application* of force but with the *exploitation of potential force*. It is concerned not just with enemies who dislike each other but with partners who distrust or disagree with each other. It is concerned not just with the division of gains and losses between two claimants but with the possibility that particular outcomes are worse (better) for *both* claimants than certain other outcomes. In the terminology of game theory, most interesting international conflicts are not 'constant-sum games' but 'variable-sum games': the sum of the gains of the participants involved is not fixed so that more for one inexorably means less for the other. There is a common interest in reaching outcomes that are mutually advantageous.

To study the strategy of conflict is to take the view that most conflict situations are essentially *bargaining* situations. They are situations in which the ability of one participant to gain his ends is dependent to an important degree on the choices or decisions that the other participant will make. The bargaining may be explicit, as when one offers a concession; or it may be by tacit maneuver, as when one occupies or evacuates strategic territory. It may, as in the ordinary haggling of the market-place, take the *status quo* as its zero point and seek arrangements that yield positive gains to both sides; or it may involve threats of damage, including mutual damage, as in a strike, boycott, or price war, or in extortion.

Viewing conflict behavior as a bargaining process is useful in keeping us from becoming exclusively preoccupied either with the conflict or with the common interest. To characterize the maneuvers and actions of limited war as a bargaining process is to emphasize that, in addition to the divergence of interest over the variables in dispute, there is a powerful common interest in reaching an outcome that is not enormously destructive of values to both sides. A 'successful' employees' strike is not one that destroys the employer financially, it may even be one that never takes place. Something similar can be true of war. [. . .]

There are two points worth stressing. One is that, though 'strategy of conflict' sounds cold-blooded, the theory is not concerned with the efficient *application* of violence or anything of the sort; it is not essentially a theory of aggression or of resistance or of war. *Threats* of war, yes, or threats of anything else; but it is the employment of threats, or of threats and promises, or more generally of the conditioning of one's own behavior on the behavior of others, that the theory is about.

Second, such a theory is nondiscriminatory as between the conflict and the common interest, as between its applicability to potential enemies and its applicability to potential friends. The theory degenerates at one extreme if there is no scope for mutual accommodation, no common interest at all even in avoiding mutual disaster; it degenerates at the other extreme if there is no conflict at all and no problem in identifying and reaching common goals. But in the area between those two extremes the theory is noncommittal about the mixture of conflict and common interest; we can equally well call it the theory of precarious partnership or the theory of incomplete antagonism. [. . .]

Both of these points—the neutrality of the theory with respect to the degree of conflict involved, and the definition of 'strategy' as concerned with constraining an adversary through his expectation of the consequences of his actions—suggest that we might call our subject the *theory of interdependent decision*.

Threats and responses to threats, reprisals and counter-reprisals, limited war, arms races, brinkmanship, surprise attack, trusting and cheating can be viewed as either hot-headed or cool-headed activities. In suggesting that they can usefully be viewed, in the development of theory, as cool-headed activities, it is not asserted that they are in fact entirely cool-headed. Rather it is asserted that the assumption of rational behavior is a productive one in the generation of systematic theory. If behavior were actually cool-headed, valid and relevant theory would probably be easier to create than it actually is. If we view our results as a bench mark for further approximation to reality, not as fully adequate theory, we should manage to protect ourselves from the worst results of a biased theory.

[From Thomas Schelling, *The Strategy of Conflict* (New York: Oxford University Press, 1963), 3–6, 15–16.]

CARL VON CLAUSEWITZ

59 Key Concepts

War is nothing but a duel on a larger scale. Countless duels go to make up war, but a picture of it as a whole can be formed by imagining a pair of wrestlers. Each tries through physical force to compel the other to do his will; his *immediate* aim is to *throw* his opponent in order to make him incapable of further resistance.

War is thus an act of force to compel our enemy to do our will. [. . .]

When whole communities go to war—whole peoples, and especially *civilized* peoples—the reason always lies in some political situation, and the occasion is always due to some political object. War, therefore, is an act of policy. Were it a complete, untrammeled, absolute manifestation of violence (as the pure concept would require), war would of its own independent will usurp the place of policy the moment policy had brought it into being; it would then drive policy out of office and rule by the laws of its own nature, very much like a mine that can explode only in the manner or direction predetermined by the setting. This, in fact, is the view that has been taken of the matter whenever some discord between policy and the conduct of war has stimulated theoretical distinctions of this kind. But in reality things are different, and this view is thoroughly mistaken. In reality war, as has been shown, is not like that. Its violence is not of the kind that explodes in a single discharge, but is the effect of forces that do not always develop in exactly the same manner or to the same degree. At times they will expand sufficiently to overcome the resistance of inertia or friction; at others they are too weak to have any effect. War is a pulsation of violence, variable in strength and therefore variable in the speed with which it explodes and discharges its energy. War moves on its goal with varying speeds; but it always lasts long enough for influence to be exerted on the goal and for its own course to be changed in one way or another—long enough, in other words, to remain subject to the action of a superior intelligence. If we keep in mind that war springs from some political purpose, it is natural that the prime cause of its existence will remain the supreme consideration in conducting it. That, however, does not imply that the political aim is a tyrant. It must adapt itself to its chosen means, a process which can radically change it; yet the political aim remains the first consideration. Policy, then, will permeate all military operations, and, in so far as their violent nature will admit, it will have a continuous influence on them.

WAR IS MERELY THE CONTINUATION OF POLICY BY OTHER MEANS

It is clear, consequently, that war is not a mere act of policy but a true political instrument, a continuation of political activity by other means. What remains peculiar to war is simply the peculiar nature of its means. War in general, and the commander in any specific instance, is entitled to require that the trend and designs of policy shall not be inconsistent with these means. That, of course, is no small demand; but however much it may affect political aims in a given case, it will never do more than modify them. The political object is the goal, war is the means of reaching it, and means can never be considered in isolation from their purpose.

Friction

If one has never personally experienced war, one cannot understand in what the difficulties constantly mentioned really consist, nor why a commander should need any brilliance and exceptional ability. Everything looks simple; the knowledge required does not look remarkable, the strategic options are so obvious that by comparison the simplest problem of higher mathematics has an impressive scientific dignity. Once war has actually been seen the difficulties become clear; but it is still extremely hard to describe the unseen, all-pervading element that brings about this change of perspective.

Everything in war is very simple, but the simplest thing is difficult. The difficulties accumulate and end by producing a kind of friction that is inconceivable unless one has experienced war. Imagine a traveler who late in the day decides to cover two more stages before nightfall. Only four or five hours more, on a paved highway with relays of horses: it should be an easy trip. But at the next station he finds no fresh horses, or only poor ones; the country grows hilly, the road bad, night falls, and finally after many difficulties he is only too glad to reach a resting place with any kind of primitive accommodation. It is much the same in war. Countless minor incidents—the kind you can never really foresee—combine to lower the general level of performance, so that one always falls far short of the intended goal. Iron will-power can overcome this friction; it pulverizes every obstacle, but of course it wears down the machine as well. We shall often return to this point. The proud spirit's firm will dominates the art of war as an obelisk dominates the town square on which all roads converge.

Friction is the only concept that more or less corresponds to the factors that distinguish real war from war on paper. The military machine—the army and everything related to it—is basically very simple and therefore seems easy to manage. But we should bear in mind that none of its components is of one piece: each part is composed of individuals, every one of whom retains his potential of friction. In theory it sounds reasonable enough: a battalion commander's duty is to carry out his orders; discipline welds the battalion together, its commander must be a man of tested capacity, and so the great beam turns on its iron pivot with a minimum of friction. In fact, it is different, and every fault and exaggeration of the theory is instantly exposed in war. A battalion is made up of individuals, the least important of whom may chance to delay things or somehow make them go wrong. The dangers inseparable from war and the physical exertions war demands can aggravate the problem to such an extent that they must be ranked among its principal causes.

This tremendous friction, which cannot, as in mechanics, be reduced to a few points, is everywhere in contact with chance, and brings about effects that cannot be measured, just because they are largely due to chance. One, for example, is the weather. Fog can prevent the enemy from being seen in time, a gun from firing when it should, a report from reaching the commanding officer. Rain can prevent a battalion from arriving, make another late by keeping it not three but eight hours on the march, ruin a cavalry charge by bogging the horses down in mud, etc. [. . .]

1 THE CONCEPT OF DEFENSE

What is the concept of defense? The parrying of a blow. What is its characteristic feature? Awaiting the blow. It is this feature that turns any action into a defensive one; it is the only test by which defense can be distinguished from attack in war. Pure defense, however, would be completely contrary to the idea of war, since it would mean that only one side was waging it. Therefore, defense in war can only be relative, and the characteristic feature of waiting should be applied only to the basic concept, not to all of its components. A partial engagement is defensive if we await the advance, the charge of the enemy. A battle is defensive if we await the attack—await, that is, the appearance of the enemy in front of our lines and within range. A campaign is defensive if we wait for our theater of operations to be invaded. In each of these cases the characteristic of waiting and parrying is germane to the general idea without being in conflict with the concept of war; for we may find it advantageous to await the charge against our bayonets and the attack on our position and theater of operations. But if we are really waging war, we must return the enemy's blows; and these offensive acts in a defensive war come under the heading of 'defense'—in other words, our offensive takes place within our own positions or theater of operations. Thus, a defensive campaign can be fought with offensive battles, and in a defensive battle, we can employ our divisions offensively. Even in a defensive position awaiting the enemy assault, our bullets take the offensive. So the defensive form of war is not a simple shield, but a shield made up of well-directed blows.

2 ADVANTAGES OF DEFENSE

What is the object of defense? Preservation. It is easier to hold ground than take it. It follows that defense is easier than attack, assuming both sides have equal means. Just what is it that makes preservation and protection so much easier? It is the fact that time which is allowed to pass unused accumulates to the credit of the defender. He reaps where he did not sow. Any omission of attack—whether from bad judgment, fear, or indolence— accrues to the defenders' benefit. This saved Prussia from disaster more than once during the Seven Years War. It is a benefit rooted in the concept and object of defense: it is in the nature of all defensive action. In daily life, and especially in litigation (which so closely resembles war) it is summed up by the Latin proverb *beati sunt possidentes*. Another benefit, one that arises solely from the nature of war, derives from the advantage of position, which tends to favor the defense.

Having outlined these general concepts, we now turn to the substance.

Tactically, every engagement, large or small, is defensive if we leave the initiative to our opponent and await his appearance before our lines. From that moment on we can employ all offensive means without losing the advantages of the defensive—that is to say the advantages of waiting and the advantages of position. At the strategic level the campaign replaces the engagement and the theater of operations takes the place of the position. At the next stage, the war as a whole replaces the campaign, and the whole country the theater of operations. In both cases, defense remains the same as at the tactical level.

We have already indicated in general terms that defense is easier than attack. But defense has a passive purpose: *preservation*; and attack a positive one: *conquest*. The latter increases one's own capacity to wage war; the former does not. So in order to state the relationship precisely, we must say that *the defensive form of warfare is intrinsically stronger than the offensive*. This is the point we have been trying to make, for although it is implicit in the nature of the matter and experience has confirmed it again and again, it is at odds with prevalent opinion, which proves how ideas can be confused by superficial writers.

If defense is the stronger form of war, yet has a negative object, it follows that it should be used only so long as weakness compels, and be abandoned as soon as we are strong enough to pursue a positive object. When one has used defensive measures successfully, a more favorable balance of strength is usually created; thus, the natural course in war is to begin defensively and end by attacking. It would therefore contradict the very idea of war to regard defense as its final purpose, just as it would to regard the passive nature of defense not only as inherent in the whole but also in all its parts. In other words, a war in which victories were used only defensively without the intention of counterattacking would be as absurd as a battle in which the principle of absolute defense—passivity, that is—were to dictate every action. [. . .]

THE CULMINATING POINT

Success in attack results from the availability of superior strength, including of course both physical and moral. In the preceding chapter we pointed out how the force of an attack gradually diminishes; it is possible in the course of the attack for superiority to increase, but usually it will be reduced. The attacker is purchasing advantages that may become valuable at the peace table, but he must pay for them on the spot with his fighting forces. If the superior strength of the attack—which diminishes day by day—leads to peace, the object will have been attained. There are strategic attacks that have led directly to peace, but these are the minority. Most of them only lead up to the point where their remaining strength is just enough to maintain a defense and wait for peace. Beyond that point the scale turns and the reaction follows with a force that is usually much stronger than that of the original attack. This is what we mean by the culminating point of the attack. Since the object of the attack is the possession of the enemy's territory, it follows that the advance will continue until the attacker's superiority is exhausted; it is this that drives the offensive on toward its goal and can easily drive it further. If we remember how many factors contribute to an equation of forces, we will understand how difficult it is in some cases to determine which side has the upper hand. Often it is entirely a matter of the imagination.

What matters therefore is to detect the culminating point with discriminative judgment. We here come up against an apparent contradiction. If defense is more effective than attack, one would think that the latter could never lead too far; if the less effective form is strong enough the more effective form should be even stronger.

The Centre of Gravity

The aim of war should be what its very concept implies—to defeat the enemy. We take that basic proposition as our starting point. [. . .]

What the theorist has to say here is this: one must keep the dominant characteristics of both belligerents in mind. Out of these characteristics a certain center of gravity develops, the hub of all power and movement, on which everything depends. That is the point against which all our energies should be directed.

Small things always depend on great ones, unimportant on important, accidentals on essentials. This must guide our approach.

For Alexander, Gustavus Adolphus, Charles XII, and Frederick the Great, the center of gravity was their army. If the army had been destroyed, they would all have gone down in history as failures. In countries subject to domestic strife, the center of gravity is generally the capital. In small countries that rely on large ones, it is usually the army of their protector. Among alliances, it lies in the community of interest, and in popular uprisings it is the personalities of the leaders and public opinion. It is against these that our energies should be directed. If the enemy is thrown off balance, he must not be given time to recover. Blow after blow must be aimed in the same direction: the victor, in other words, must strike with all his strength and not just against a fraction of the enemy's. Not by taking things the easy way—

using superior strength to filch some province, preferring the security of this minor conquest to great success—but by constantly seeking out the center of his power, by daring all to win all, will one really defeat the enemy.

Still, no matter what the central feature of the enemy's power may be—the point on which your efforts must converge—the defeat and destruction of his fighting force remains the best way to begin, and in every case will be a very significant feature of the campaign.

Basing our comments on general experience, the acts we consider most important for the defeat of the enemy are the following:

1. Destruction of his army, if it is at all significant
2. Seizure of his capital if it is not only the center of administration but also that of social, professional, and political activity
3. Delivery of an effective blow against his principal ally if that ally is more powerful than he.

Up till now we have assumed—as is generally permissible—that the enemy is a single power. But having made the point that the defeat of the enemy consists in overcoming the resistance concentrated in his center of gravity, we must abandon this assumption and examine the case when there is more than one enemy to defeat.

If two or more states combine against another, the result is still politically speaking a *single* war. But this political unity is a matter of degree. The question is then whether each state is pursuing an independent interest and has its own independent means of doing so, or whether the interests and forces of most of the allies are subordinate to those of the leader. The more this is the case, the easier will it be to regard all our opponents as a single entity, hence all the easier to concentrate our principal enterprise into one great blow. If this is at all feasible it will be much the most effective means to victory.

I would, therefore, state it as a principle that if you can vanquish all your enemies by defeating one of them, that defeat must be the main objective in the war. In this one enemy we strike at the center of gravity of the entire conflict.

[From Carl von Clausewitz, *On War*, ed. and trans. by Michael Howard and Peter Paret (Princeton, NJ: Princeton University Press, 1976), 75, 86–7, 119–20, 357–8, 528, 595–7.]

BARON DE JOMINI

60 Strategy and Grand Tactics

Strategy embraces the following points, viz.:

1. The selection of the theater of war, and the discussion of the different combinations of which it admits.

2. The determination of the decisive points in these combinations, and the most favorable direction for operations.

3. The selection and establishment of the fixed base and of the zone of operations.

4. The selection of the objective point, whether offensive or defensive.

5. The strategic fronts, lines of defense, and fronts of operations.

6. The choice of lines of operations leading to the objective point or strategic front.

7. For a given operation, the best strategic line, and the different maneuvers necessary to embrace all possible cases.

8. The eventual bases of operations and the strategic reserves.

9. The marches of armies, considered as maneuvers.

10. The relation between the position of depots and the marches of the army.

11. Fortresses regarded as strategical means, as a refuge for an army, as an obstacle to its progress: the sieges to be made and to be covered.

12. Points for intrenched camps, *têtes de pont, &c.*

13. The diversions to be made, and the large detachments necessary.

These points are principally of importance in the determination of the first steps of a campaign; but there are other operations of a mixed nature, such as passages of streams, retreats, surprises, disembarkations, convoys, winter quarters, the execution of which belongs to tactics, the conception and arrangement to strategy.

The maneuvering of an army upon the battle-field, and the different formations of troops for attack, constitute Grand Tactics. Logistics is the art of moving armies. It comprises the order and details of marches and camps, and of quartering and supplying troops; in a word, it is the execution of strategical and tactical enterprises.

To repeat. Strategy is the art of making war upon the map, and comprehends the whole theater of operations. Grand Tactics is the art of posting troops upon the battle-field according to the accidents of the ground, of bringing them into action, and the art of fighting upon the ground, in contradistinction to planning upon a map. Its operations may extend over a field of ten or twelve miles in extent. Logistics comprises the means and arrangements which work out the plans of strategy and tactics. Strategy decides where to act; logistics brings the troops to this point; grand tactics decides the manner of execution and the employment of the troops.

It is true that many battles have been decided by strategic movements, and have been, indeed, but a succession of them; but this only occurs in the exceptional case of a dispersed army: for the general case of pitched battles the above definition holds good.

Grand Tactics, in addition to acts of local execution, relates to the following objects:

1. The choice of positions and defensive lines of battle.

2. The offensive in a defensive battle.

3. The different orders of battle, or the grand maneuvers proper for the attack of the enemy's line.

4. The collision of two armies on the march, or unexpected battles.

5. Surprises of armies in the open field.

6. The arrangements for leading troops into battle.

7. The attack of positions and intrenched camps.

8. *Coups de main.*

All other operations, such as relate to convoys, foraging-parties, skirmishes of advanced or rear guards, the attack of small posts, and any thing accomplished by a detachment or single division, may be regarded as details of war, and not included in the great operations.

The Fundamental Principle of War

It is proposed to show that there is one great principle underlying all the operations of war—a principle which must be followed in all good combinations. It is embraced in the following maxims:

1. To throw by strategic movements the mass of an army, successively, upon the decisive points of a theater of war, and also upon the communications of the enemy as much as possible without compromising one's own.

2. To maneuver to engage fractions of the hostile army with the bulk of one's forces.

3. On the battle-field, to throw the mass of the forces upon the decisive point, or upon that portion of the hostile line which it is of the first importance to overthrow.

4. To so arrange that these masses shall not only be thrown upon the decisive point, but that they shall engage at the proper times and with energy.

[From Baron de Jomini, *The Art of War*, trans. Capt. G. H. Wendell and Lt. W. P. Craighill (Philadelphia: J. B. Lippincott & Co., 1862; republished Westport: Greenwood Press, 1971), 68–70.]

NAPOLEON

61 **Maximes**

In war, only the commander-in-chief understands the importance of certain things and only he, through his will and his superior understanding, can vanquish and overcome all his difficulties.

A collective government has less simple ideas and takes longer to decide.

Do not hold a war council, but ask the opinion of everybody individually. [. . .]

The art of war consists of always having more forces than the enemy, even with a smaller army [of one's own], at the point where one attacks or at the point that is attacked; but that art cannot be learnt from books nor from drill, it is a form of conduct which in itself constitutes the genius of war.

The art of war is to deploy one's troops in such a way that they are everywhere at once. The art of troop deployment is the great art of war. Deploy your troops in such a way that, whatever the enemy does, you can always concentrate your troops in a few days.

Do not make a frontal attack on a position that you can seize by turning it.

Do not do what the enemy wants you to do, for the simple reason that he wishes it; avoid the battlefield which he has reconnoitred, studied, and even more the one he has fortified, and where he is entrenched.

What are the conditions of the superiority of an army? First, its organization; second, the officer's and the soldier's accustomedness to war; third, the self-confidence of everybody, in other words the bravery, patience, and all moral power that self-confidence gives.

The transition from defensive to offensive operation is one of the most delicate operations in war.

Above all, one must not leave a defensive line on which troops have reassembled and taken a rest, without a well-defined project which leaves no uncertainty about the ensuing operations. It would be a great misfortune to leave this line if one were later forced to fall back on it. In war, three-quarters [of what matters] is morale; the relative strength of troops only matters one-quarter.

In mountain warfare, the attacker is disadvantaged; even in an offensive war, the art consists in not having anything but defensive fights and in forcing the enemy to attack.

The loss of time in war is irreplaceable; the reasons one alleges are always bad, as operations only fail because of delays.

In the occupation of a country, the key positions have to be occupied, and from them mobile columns have to set out in pursuit of brigands. The experience of the Vendée shows that it is best to have mobile columns, distributed and multiplied everywhere, and not stationary corps.

The outcome of a battle is the result of an instant, of a thought; one comes together with differing mixtures [of forces], one engages, one fights for a certain time, the decisive moment comes, a moral spark flies and the smallest reserve accomplishes everything.

The principles of Caesar were the same as those of Hannibal: to keep one's forces united, avoid being vulnerable anywhere, move in rapidly on the important positions, draw on moral means, on the reputation of one's arms, on the fear one inspires and also on political means in order to maintain the loyalty of one's allies and the obedience of the conquered peoples.

Military genius is a heavenly gift, but the essential quality of a commander-in-chief is firmness of character and the determination to win at all costs.

Commanders-in-chief are guided by their own experiences or by genius. Tactics, developments, the science of the engineer and the artillery man can be learnt from treatises, almost like geometry; but the knowledge of the higher levels of war can only be obtained through experience and through the study of the wars and battles of the great commanders. Can one learn through grammar how to compose a song of the *Iliad*, a tragedy of Corneille?

Military science consists of first calculating all the odds, and then calculating precisely, almost mathematically, the part played by accident. One must not make a mistake with regard to this, where one decimal point more or less can change everything. This division of science and work can only be matched in the head of a genius, and it is necessary wherever there is creativity and, certainly, the greatest improvisation of the human mind is that which gives existence to something that does not exist. Therefore, accident always remains a mystery for mediocre minds while it becomes a reality for superior people. [...]

The art of war does not demand complicated manœuvres: the simplest are preferable; what is needed above all is common sense. Consequently, one does not understand how generals make mistakes: it is because they want to be clever. The most difficult thing is to divine the plans of the enemy, and to see what is reality in all the reports one receives. The rest requires nothing but common sense, it is like a boxing match: the more you deal out, the better it is. [...]

Remember these three things: concentration of forces, activeness, and firm resolve to go down in glory. These are the three great principles of military art which have always given me good fortune in all my operations. Death is nothing; but to live defeated and without glory, that is to die every day.

The entire art of war consists of a well-thought-out and extremely circumspect defence and of a daring and quick offence.

One has to be slow in deliberation and quick in execution.

The art of war is a simple art, consisting entirely of its execution: there is nothing vague; everything here is common sense, nothing is ideology.

It is not enough to win, one has to take advantage of this success.

At the beginning of a campaign, one has to consider well whether one should or should not advance; but if one has started the offensive, one has to keep it up until the end: quite apart from the military honour and the morale of the army which one loses in a retreat, and the courage which one gives to the enemy, retreats are more disastrous, cost more men and material than the bloodiest engagements, with the difference that in a battle the enemy loses about as much as you do, while during a retreat, you lose more than he loses.

With a few exceptions, victory is assured to the more numerous forces. The art of war is thus to have superior strength at the point where one wants to fight. If your army is smaller than that of the enemy, do not leave the enemy the time to concentrate his forces; surprise him while he is still moving; and by throwing yourself rapidly against the different corps which you have craftily isolated, combine your manœuvres in such a way as to be able to meet parts of his army with the entirety of your army. Thus, with an army half as large as that of the enemy, you will always be stronger than him on the battlefield.

From Napoléon, *Pensées politiques et sociales*, rassemblées par A. Danserre, (Paris: Flammarion, 1969), et Lébovici (ed.), *Comment faire la guerre* (1973); printed in Gérard Chaliand (ed.), *Anthologie Mondial de la Stratégie* (Paris: Robert Laffont, 1990), 785–8. Trans. Beatrice Heuser.

HELMUTH VON MOLTKE

62 **Doctrines of War**

The operative preparation of Battle

I WAR AND PEACE

Eternal peace is a dream and not even a beautiful one, while war is an element of God's world order. In war, the most noble virtues of man unfold, which would otherwise slumber and become extinct: courage and abstention, loyalty to one's duty and willingness to make the sacrifice of one's life; the experiences of war are a lasting influence, strengthening a man's ability for all future.

Yet who would deny that every war, even a victorious one, inflicts painful wounds on every people? For no conquest of land, no milliards can replace human lives and weigh heavier than the sorrow of the families; war is an overwhelming craft.

But in this world, who could escape from misfortune, from need? Are not both conditions of our earthly existence, according to the will of God? Need and misery are inescapable elements of the world order. What would have become of human society, if this harsh compulsion had not necessitated thinking and action! [. . .]

The wars of the present call entire peoples to arms, hardly a family is spared. The entire financial strength of the state is drawn in, and no seasonal change puts a limit to these ceaseless activities. It is the varying mood of the peoples, lust for annexation and revenge, the desire to draw close to peoples of the same tribe, dissatisfaction with the state of internal affairs, the activities of the parties, particularly of their spokesmen, which endanger peace. It is easier for an assembly to take the momentous decision to go to war, where nobody bears the full responsibility, than for a single person, however high his position, and one will more frequently find a peace-loving head of state than an assembly of wise men. Today it is no longer the cabinets alone who decide matters of war and peace and who lead the affairs of the peoples, but in many places it is the peoples themselves who lead cabinets. Thus an element has been introduced into politics which is completely unpredictable. [. . .] If a war were to erupt now, its duration and its end would be unpredictable. The largest powers in Europe would be going to war with each other, armed as never before; not one of them could be so totally defeated after one or two campaigns that they would actually admit defeat, that they would conclude peace despite the harsh conditions attached, and that they would not stand up again a year later, in order to continue the war. It could be a seven-year, a thirty-year war, and woe to him who sets fire to Europe, who puts the torch to the powder keg! . . .

Being prepared for war is thus the greatest guarantee for peace. With weak forces, with short-term enlisted armies, this aim cannot be reached; the fate of each nation depends on its own strength. An alliance is certainly of value, but even in everyday life it is little use relying on others for help. Our best insurance therefore lies in the excellence of our army.

We must not allow the inner quality of the army to be weakened, otherwise we will end up with militias. Wars conducted by militias characteristically last much longer, and for that reason demand more sacrifices of money and lives than all other wars. [. . .]

An army can never be a provisional affair, it cannot be improvised in weeks or months, it needs to be educated throughout long years, for the basis of any military organization is continuity and stability. The army is the prince of all the institutions of the country: it alone makes the existence of all the other institutions possible, all political and civic freedom, all creations of culture, finance, the state itself rise and fall with the army.

The better our forces on land and at sea are organized, the more comprehensively they are equipped, the readier they are for war, the more hope we have of protecting peace or of prevailing in an inevitable fight with honour and glory.

II WAR AND POLITICS

(a) *Mutual influence between politics and strategy.* War is the forceful action of peoples for the purpose of realizing and maintaining the policies of the state; it is the extreme means of acting out the will aiming at this, and while it lasts, it creates a situation in which international conventions are suspended between the warring factions. War is, as General von Clausewitz remarked, 'the continuation of politics by other means'. Politics can therefore unfortunately not be divorced from strategy: it uses war to obtain its ends, it influences the beginning and the end of war, retaining the right to raise the stakes or to make do with lesser achievements.

In view of this uncertainty [of the political aim], strategy can only focus on the highest obtainable goal which it can reach with whatever means are available to it. Strategy serves politics best by working for its aim, but by retaining maximum independence in the achievement of this aim. Politics should not interfere in operations. Thus General von Clausewitz commented in his tactical letters to Müffling:

The task and the right of the art of war *vis-à-vis* politics is mainly to prevent politics from demanding things which are against the nature of war, to prevent politics from making mistakes in the use of this instrument through lack of knowledge of its effects.

For the course of war is determined mainly by military considerations, while political considerations are only of avail if they do not ask for things that are military nonsense. In no case must the leader allow his operations to be influenced by politics *alone*; quite the contrary, he must keep his eye on the military success. It is of no concern to him how politics can subsequently use his victories or defeats: it is up to politics to exploit them. Where the head of state goes along on campaign, as is the case with us, the political and military demands are reconciled within his person.

(*b*) *Coalitions*   A coalition is marvellous as long as all interests of all members are the same. In reality, the interests of allies in all coalitions only converge up to a point; as soon as one of the allies has to make sacrifices for the achievement of the great common goal, one can no longer rely on the coalition, for coalitions will not easily understand that the great aims of a war cannot be reached without such partial sacrifices.

For this reason a mutual defence pact is at all times the least perfect form of mutual aid; it is worth only what each member on its own can give by way of aid. One thus cannot expect mere coalitions to do what is militarily most desirabe, but only what is advantageous for both parts of the coalition. Every strategic agreement of allied armies is thus a compromise which tries to take into account special interests; these can only be ruled out within a single, unified state.

(c) *Neutrality*   The direction of the borders of a neutral country are theoretically totally inconsequential. If it must not be attacked, it need not be militarily strong. The neutral country's length and situation are more important for the non-neutral states than for the neutral country itself. Thus until 1860 the neutrality of northern Savoy had more effect on Switzerland than on the Piedmont, and in 1870 Belgium's neutrality affected almost the entire Rhine province.

But in reality it becomes clear that every neutrality can potentially be disregarded, if this step does not lead to certain disadvantages to the attacker which outweight the advantages.

These disadvantages could lie in the resistance of the neutral state against aggression, and in the aid which it might be accorded by the guarantors of its neutrality. The state's own resistance is the most important factor, however, as foreign aid will only materialize to the extent that the direct interest of the guarantors is involved. [. . .]

Battle

I STRATEGY

Strategy is a system of expediencies. It is more than a science; it is the application of knowledge to practical life, the development of an original leading idea in response to constantly changing circumstances; it is the art of action under the pressure of the most difficult circumstances.

Strategy is the application of common sense to the conduct of war; its lessons do not much exceed the primary rules of common sense, and its value lies solely in its concrete application. What is needed is to take in the constantly changing situation at the right time and consequently to take the simplest and most natural action with firmness and circumspection. Thus war becomes an art, but one which is served by many sciences.

In war, as in art, there is no general norm; in both cases talent cannot be replaced by rules.

General dogmas or rules deduced from them or systems built upon them can therefore in no way have any practical value for strategy. Strategy is not like abstract sciences. Those have their fixed, defined truths on which one can construct arguments, from which one can make deductions. The square of the hypotenuse always equals the sum of the squares of both cathetes, that is always true, whether the right-angled triangle is large or small, whether it is pointed towards the east or towards the west.

Archduke Charles declared strategy to be a science, and tactics an art. He thought that the 'science of the supreme commander' should 'determine the development of military enterprises', while the art was to execute strategic plans.

General von Clausewitz, however, says that 'Strategy is the use of the battle for the purposes of the war' and indeed it is strategy which gives to tactics the means to strike and the likelihood to win through the leadership of the armies and their concentration on the battlefield. Yet strategy also uses the success of each battle and builds on it. The demands of strategy fall silent in the face of a tactical victory; strategy adapts to the new situation.

Strategy controls the means required by tactics in order to be ready at the right time in the right place.

The strategic aim determines the premeditated decision to engage in a battle. If this only arises from accidental encounter—as often happens—it is an act of tactics. Strategy leads the movement of the army for the *intended* battle; the form of its execution is determined by tactics. The former gives directives, the latter gives orders.

II VICTORY AND SUPERIORITY

1 *Quick Decisions*   The character of the modern conduct of war is determined by the quest for great and quick decisions. The mobilization of all the able-bodied, the size of the armies, the difficulties of feeding them, the expensiveness of the mobilized forces, the interruption of trade and commerce, industry and agriculture, and the armies' organized readiness to strike and the ease with which they are assembled—all this urges the quick termination of a war.

Smaller skirmishes only have a small influence on this state of affairs, but they make possible the main decision in battle and pave the way towards battle. [...]

2 *Victory [is] essential—superiority—initial deployment*   Victory in combat is the most important moment in war. It alone breaks the will of the enemy and forces him to submit himself to ours. It is not in general the conquest of a piece of land or of a strong point, but only the destruction of the enemy's forces which will be decisive. This is therefore the chief objective of the operation.

In all circumstances we must bring to battle whatever forces we can muster, for one can never have too much strength ready nor too much luck for a victory. In order to achieve it, we have to bring even the last battalion on to the battlefield. Many battles have been decided through troops which only reached the battlefield on the evening of the day of battle. [...]

If the concentrated forces of the still dispersed enemy should be larger than ours, we must not wait for him to concentrate his forces, but we must, if there is any chance at all of a partial success, attack with whatever forces we have available.

[From Helmuth von Moltke, *Moltkes Kriegslehren*, ed. Grosser Generalstab, iv: *Kriegslehren* (Berlin: Ernst Siegfried Mittler & Son, 1912), pt. 1, 1–14, pt. 3, 1–6. Trans. Beatrice Heuser.]

ARDANT DU PICQ

63   Moral Elements in Battle

When, in complete security, after dinner, in full physical and moral contentment, men consider war and battle they are animated by a noble ardor that has nothing in common with reality. How many of them, however, even at that moment, would be ready to risk their lives? But oblige them to march for days and weeks to arrive at the battle ground, and on the day of battle oblige them to wait minutes, hours, to deliver it. If they were honest they would testify how much the physical fatigue and the mental anguish that precede action have lowered their morale, how much less eager to fight they are than a month before, when they arose from the table in a generous mood.

Man's heart is as changeable as fortune. Man shrinks back, apprehends danger in any effort in which he does not foresee success. There are some isolated characters of an iron temper, who resist the tendency; but they are carried away by the great majority (Bismarck).

Examples show that if a withdrawal is forced, the army is discouraged and takes flight (Frederick). The brave heart does not change.

Real bravery, inspired by devotion to duty, does not know panic and is always the same. The bravery sprung from hot blood pleases the Frenchman more. He understands it, it appeals to his vanity; it is a characteristic of his nature. But it is passing; it fails him at times, especially when there is nothing for him to gain in doing his duty. [. . .]

What makes the soldier capable of obedience and direction in action, is the sence of discipline. This includes: respect for and confidence in his chiefs; confidence in his comrades and fear of their reproaches and retaliation if he abandons them in danger; his desire to go where others do without trembling more than they; in a word, the whole of esprit de corps. Organization only can produce these characteristics. Four men equal a lion.

Note the army organizations and tactical formations on paper are always determined from the mechanical point of view, neglecting the essential coefficient, that of morale. They are almost always wrong.

Esprit de corps is secured in war. But war becomes shorter and shorter and more and more violent. Consequently, secure esprit de corps in advance.

Mental acquaintanceship is not enough to make a good organization. A good general esprit is needed. All must work for battle and not merely live, quietly going through with drills without understanding their application. Once a man knows how to use his weapon and obey all commands there is needed only occasional drill to brush up those who have forgotten. Marches and battle maneuvers are what is needed. [. . .]

The effect of an army, of one organization on another, is at the same time material and moral. The material effect of an organization is in its power to destroy, the moral effect in the fear that it inspires.

In battle, two moral forces, even more than two material forces, are in conflict. The stronger conquers. The victor has often lost by fire more than the vanquished. Moral effect does not come entirely from destructive power, real and effective as it may be. It comes, above all, from its presumed, threatening power, present in the form of reserves threatening to renew the battle, of troops that appear on the flank, even of a determined frontal attack.

Material effect is greater as instruments are better (weapons, mounts, etc.), as the men know better how to use them, and as the men are more numerous and stronger, so that in case of success they can carry on longer.

With equal or even inferior power of destruction he will win who has the resolution to advance, who by his formations and maneuvers can continually threaten his adversary with a new phase of material action, who, in a word, has the moral ascendancy. Moral effect inspires fear. Fear must be changed to terror in order to vanquish.

When confidence is placed in superiority of material means, valuable as they are against an enemy at a distance, it may be betrayed by the actions of the enemy. If he closes with you in spite of your superiority in means of destruction, the morale of the enemy mounts with the loss of your confidence. His morale dominates yours. You flee. Entrenched troops give way in this manner.

At Pharsalus, Pompey and his army counted on a cavalry corps turning and taking Cæsar in the rear. In addition Pompey's army was twice as numerous. Cæsar parried the blow, and his enemy, who saw the failure of the means of action he counted on, was demoralized, beaten, lost fifteen thousand men put to the sword (while Cæsar lost only two hundred) and as many prisoners.

Even by advancing you affect the morale of the enemy. But your object is to dominate him and make him retreat before your ascendancy, and it is certain that everything that diminishes the enemy's morale adds to your resolution in advancing. Adopt then a formation which permits your destructive agency, your skirmishers, to help you throughout by their material action and to this degree diminish that of the enemy. [. . .]

In modern battle, which is delivered with combatants so far apart, man has come to have a horror of man. He comes to hand to hand fighting only to defend his body or if forced to it by some fortuitous encounter. More than that! It may be said that he seeks to catch the fugitive only for fear that he will turn and fight.

Guilbert says that shock actions are infinitely rare. Here, infinity is taken in its exact mathematical sense. Guilbert reduces to nothing, by deductions from practical examples, the mathematical theory of the shock of one massed body on another. Indeed the physical impulse is nothing. The moral impulse which estimates the attacker is everything. The moral impulse lies in the perception by the enemy of the resolution that animates you. They say that the battle of Amstetten was the only one in which a line actually waited for the shock of another line charging with the bayonets. Even then the Russians gave way before the moral and not before the physical impulse. They were already disconcerted, wavering, worried, hesitant, vacillating, when the blow fell. They waited long enough to receive bayonet thrusts, even blows with the rifle (in the back, as at Inkerman).

This done, they fled. He who calm and strong of heart awaits his enemy, has all the advantage of fire. But the moral impulse of the assailant demoralizes the assailed. He is frightened; he sets his sight no longer; he does not even aim his piece. His lines are broken without defense, unless indeed his cavalry, waiting halted, horsemen a meter apart and in two ranks, does not break first and destroy all formation.

With good troops on both sides, if an attack is not prepared, there is every reason to believe that it will fail. The attacking troops suffer more, materially, than the defenders. The latter are in better order, fresh, while the assailants are in disorder and already have suffered a loss of morale under a certain amount of punishment. The moral superiority given by the offensive movement may be more than compensated by the good order and integrity of the defenders, when the assailants have suffered losses. The slightest reaction by the defense may demoralize the attack. This is the secret of the success of the British infantry in Spain, and not their fire by rank, which was as ineffective with them as with us.

The more confidence one has in his methods of attack or defense, the more disconcerted he is to see them at some time incapable of stopping the enemy. The effect of the present improved fire arm is still limited, with the present organization and use of riflemen, to point blank ranges. It follows that bayonet charges (where bayonet thrusts never occur), otherwise attacks under fire, will have an increasing value, and that victory will be his who secures most order and determined dash. With these two qualities, too much neglected with us, with willingness, with intelligence enough to keep a firm hold on troops in immediate support, we may hope to take and to hold what we take. Do not then neglect destructive effort before using moral effect. Use skirmishers up to the last moment. Otherwise no attack can succeed. It is true it is haphazard fire, nevertheless it is effective because of its volume.

This moral effect must be a terrible thing. A body advances to meet another. The defender has only to remain calm, ready to aim, each man pitted against a man before him. The attacking body comes within deadly range. Whether or not it halts to fire, it will be a target for the other body which awaits it, calm, ready, sure of its effect. The whole first rank of the assailant falls, smashed. The remainder, little encouraged by their reception, disperse automatically or before the least indication of an advance on them. Is this what happens? Not at all! The moral effect of the assault worries the defenders. They fire in the air if at all. They disperse immediately before the assailants who are even encouraged by this fire now that it is over. It quickens them in order to avoid a second salvo.

It is said by those who fought them in Spain and at Waterloo that the British are capable of the necessary coolness. I doubt it nevertheless. After firing, they made swift attacks. If they had not, they might have fled. Anyhow the English are stolid folks, with little imagination, who try to be logical in all things. The French with their nervous irritability, their lively imagination, are incapable of such a defense.

[From Charles Ardant du Picq, *Battle Studies: Ancient and Modern*, trans. Col. John Greely and Major Robert Cotton (Harrisburg, Pa.: The Military Service Publishing Co., 1947), 118–29.]

JULIAN CORBETT

64 Command of the Sea

The object of naval warfare must always be directly or indirectly either to secure the command of the sea or to prevent the enemy from securing it.

The second part of the proposition should be noted with special care in order to exclude a habit of thought, which is one of the commonest sources of error in naval speculation. That error is the very general assumption that if one belligerent loses the command of the sea it passes at once to the other belligerent. The most cursory study of naval history is enough to reveal the falseness of such an assumption. It tells us that the most common situation in naval war is that neither side has the command; that the normal position is not a commanded sea, but an uncommanded sea. The mere assertion, which no one denies, that the object of naval warfare is to get command of the sea actually connotes the proposition that the command is normally in dispute. It is this state of dispute with which naval strategy is most nearly concerned, for when the command is lost or won pure naval strategy comes to an end.

This truth is so obvious that it would scarcely be worth mentioning were it not for the constant recurrence of such phrases as: 'If England were to lose command of the sea, it would be all over with her.' The fallacy of the idea is that it ignores the power of the strategical defensive. It assumes that if in the face of some extraordinary hostile coalition or through some extraordinary mischance we found ourselves without sufficient strength to keep the command, we should therefore be too weak to prevent the enemy getting it—a negation of the whole theory of war, which at least requires further support than it ever receives.

And not only is this assumption a negation of theory; it is a negation both of practical experience and of the expressed opinion of our greatest masters. We ourselves have used the defensive at sea with success, as under William the Third and in the War of American Independence, while in our long wars with France she habitually used it in such a way that sometimes for years, though we had a substantial preponderance, we could not get command, and for years were unable to carry out our war plan without serious interruption from her fleet.

So far from the defensive being a negligible factor at sea, or even the mere pestilent heresy it is generally represented, it is of course inherent in all war, and, as we have seen, the paramount questions of strategy both at sea and on land turn on the relative possibilities of offensive and defensive, and upon the relative proportions in which each should enter into our plan of war. At sea the most powerful and aggressively-minded belligerent can no more avoid his alternating periods of defence, which result from inevitable arrests of offensive action, than they can be avoided on land. The defensive, then, has to be considered; but before we are in a position to do so with profit, we have to proceed with our analysis of the phrase, 'Command of the Sea', and ascertain exactly what it is we mean by it in war.

In the first place, 'Command of the Sea' is not identical in its strategical conditions with the conquest of territory. You cannot argue from the one to the other, as has been too commonly done. Such phrases as the 'Conquest of water territory' and 'Making the enemy's coast our frontier' had their use and meaning in the mouths of those who framed them, but they are really little but rhetorical expressions founded on false analogy, and false analogy is not a secure basis for a theory of war.

The analogy is false for two reasons, both of which enter materially into the conduct of naval war. You cannot conquer sea because it is not susceptible of ownership, at least outside territorial waters. You cannot, as lawyers say, 'reduce it into possession', because you cannot exclude neutrals from it as you can from territory you conquer. In the second place, you cannot subsist your armed force upon it as you can upon enemy's territory. Clearly, then, to make deductions from an assumption that command of the sea is analogous to conquest of territory is unscientific, and certain to lead to error.

The only safe method is to inquire what it is we can secure for ourselves, and what it is we can deny the enemy by command of the sea. Now, if we exclude fishery rights, which are irrelevant to the present matter, the only right we or our enemy can have on the sea is the right of passage; in other words, the only positive value which the high seas have for national life is as a means of communication. For the active life of a nation such means may stand for much or it may stand for little, but to every maritime State it has some value. Consequently by denying an enemy this means of passage we check the movement of his national life at sea in the same kind of way that we check it on land by occupying his territory. So far the analogy holds good, but no further.

So much for the positive value which the sea has in national life. It has also a negative value. For not only is it a means of communication, but, unlike the means of communication ashore, it is also a barrier. By winning command of the sea we remove that barrier from our own path, thereby placing ourselves in position to exert direct military pressure upon the national life of our enemy ashore, while at the same time we solidify it against him and prevent his exerting direct military pressure upon ourselves.

Command of the sea, therefore, means nothing but the control of maritime communications, whether for commercial or military purposes. The object of naval warfare is the control of communications, and not, as in land warfare, the conquest of territory. The difference is fundamental. True, it is rightly said that strategy ashore is mainly a question of communications, but they are communications in another sense. The phrase refers to the communications of the army alone, and not to the wider communications which are part of the life of the nation.

But on land also there are communications of a kind which are essential to national life—the internal communications which connect the points of distribution. Here again we touch an analogy between the two kinds of war. Land warfare, as the most devoted adherents of the modern view admit, cannot attain its end by military victories alone. The destruction of your enemy's forces will not avail for certain unless you have in reserve sufficient force to complete the occupation of his inland communications and principal points of distribution. This power is the real fruit of victory, the power to strangle the whole national life. It is not until this is done that a high-spirited nation, whose whole heart is in the war, will consent to make peace and do your will. It is precisely in the same way that the command of the sea works towards peace, though of course in a far less coercive manner, against a continental State. By occupying her maritime communications and closing the points of distribution in which they terminate we destroy the national life afloat, and thereby check the vitality of that life ashore so far as the one is dependent on the other. Thus we see that so long as we retain the power and right to stop maritime communications, the analogy between command of the sea and the conquest of territory is in this aspect very close. And the analogy is of the utmost practical importance, for on it turns the most burning question of maritime war, which it will be well to deal with in this place.

[From Julian Corbett, *Some Principles of Maritime Strategy* (London: Longman, Green & Co., 1911), 91–5.]

GIULIO DOUHET

65 Command of the Air

The aeroplane has complete freedom of action and direction; it can fly to and from any point of the compass in the shortest time—in a straight line—by any route deemed expedient. Nothing man can do on the surface of the earth can interfere with a plane in flight, moving freely in the third dimension. All the influences which have conditioned and characterized warfare from the beginning are powerless to affect aerial action.

By virtue of this new weapon, the repercussions of war are no longer limited by the farthest artillery range of surface guns, but can be directly felt for hundreds and hundreds of miles over all the lands and seas of nations at war. No longer can areas exist in which life can be lived in safety and tranquillity, nor can the battlefield any longer be limited to actual combatants. On the contrary, the battlefield will be limited only by the boundaries of the nations at war, and all of their citizens will become combatants since all of them will be exposed to the aerial offensives of the enemy. There will be no distinction any longer between soldiers and civilians. The defences on land and sea will no longer serve to protect the country behind them; nor can victory or land or sea protect the people from enemy aerial attacks unless that victory ensures the destruction, by actual occupation of the enemy's territory, of all that gives life to his aerial forces. [. . .]

* * * * * *

Because of its independence of surface limitations and its superior speed—superior to any other known means of transportation—the aeroplane is the offensive weapon *par excellence*.

The greatest advantage of the offensive is having the initiative in planning operations—that is, being free to choose the point of attack and able to shift its maximum striking forces; whereas the enemy, on the defensive and not knowing the direction of the attack, is compelled to spread his forces thinly to cover all possible points of attack along his line of defence, relying upon being able to shift them in time to the sector actually attacked as soon as the intentions of the offensive are known. In that fact lies essentially the whole game of war tactics and strategy.

From this it is obvious that those nations which have the means to mass their forces rapidly and strike at whatever point they choose of the enemy's forces and supply lines are the nations which have the greatest potential offensive power. In the days when war was fought with small, light, fast-moving bodies of forces, it offered a wide field for tactical and strategic moves; but as the masses engaged grew larger, the playground diminished in size and the game became more restricted. During the [First] World War the masses involved were enormous, and extremely slow and heavy; as a consequence their movements were reduced to a minimum and the war as a whole became a direct, brutal clash between opposing forces.

The aeroplane, in contrast, can fly in any direction with equal facility and faster than any other means of conveyance. A plane based at point A, for example, is a potential threat to all surface points within a circle having A for its centre and a radius of hundreds of miles for its field of action. Planes based anywhere on the surface of this same circle can simultaneously converge in mass on point A. Therefore, an aerial force is a threat to all points within its radius of action, its units operating from their separate bases and converging in mass for the attack on the designated target faster than with any other means so far known. For this reason air power is a weapon superlatively adapted to offensive operations, because it strikes suddenly and gives the enemy no time to parry the blow by calling up reinforcements.

The striking power of the aeroplane is, in fact, so great that it results in a paradox: for its own protection it needs a greater striking force for defence than for attack. For example, let us suppose that the enemy has an air force with the offensive capacity of X. Even if its bases are scattered, such a force can easily concentrate its action, gradually or however it sees fit, on any number of objectives within its radius of action. To be exact, let us say that there are twenty of these objectives. In this case, in order to defend ourselves from *what force X can do*, we are obliged to station near each of these twenty objectives a defensive force corresponding to force X, in all twenty times as many planes as the enemy has. So that to defend ourselves we would need a minimum aerial force twenty times as large as the attacking force of the enemy—a solution of the problem which partakes of the absurd because the aeroplane is not adaptable to defence, being pre-eminently an offensive weapon.

* * * * * *

There is no practical way to prevent the enemy from attacking us with his air force except to destroy his air power before he has a chance to strike at us. It is now axiomatic—and has long been so—that coastlines are defended from naval attacks, not by dispersing ships and guns along their whole extent, but by holding the command of the seas; that is, by preventing the enemy from navigating. The surface of the earth is the coastline of the air. The conditions pertaining to both elements, the air and the sea, are analogous; so that the surface of the earth, both solid and liquid, should be defended from aerial attack, not by scattering guns and planes over its whole extent, but by preventing the enemy from flying. In other words, by 'achieving command of the air'.

This is the logical and rational concept which should be recognized, even for simple defence—namely to prevent the enemy from flying or from carrying out any aerial action at all.

Some conception of the magnitude aerial offensives may reach in the future is essential to an evaluation of the command of the air, a conception which the World War can clarify for us in part.

Aerial bombardment can certainly never hope to attain the accuracy of artillery fire; but this is an unimportant point because such accuracy is unnecessary. Except in unusual cases, the targets of artillery fire are designed to withstand just such fire; but the targets of aerial bombardment are ill-prepared to endure such onslaught. Bombing objectives should always be large; small targets are unimportant and do not merit our attention here.

The guiding principle of bombing actions should be this: *the objective must be destroyed completely in one attack, making further attack on the same target unnecessary.* Reaching an objective is an aerial operation which always involves a certain amount of risk and should be undertaken once only. The complete destruction of the objective has moral and material effects, the repercussions of which may be tremendous. To give us some idea of the extent of these repercussions, we need only envisage what would go on among the civilian population of congested cities once the enemy announced that he would bomb such centres relentlessly, making no distinction between military and non-military objectives.

In general, aerial offensives will be directed against such targets as peacetime industrial and commercial establishments; important buildings, private and public; transportation arteries and centres; and certain designated areas of civilian population as well. To destroy these targets three kinds of bombs are needed—explosive, incendiary, and poison-gas—apportioned as the situation may require. The explosives will demolish the target, the incendiaries set fire to it, and the poison-gas bombs prevent fire fighters from extinguishing the fires.

Gas attacks must be so planned as to leave the target permeated with gas which will last over a period of time, whole days indeed, a result which can be attained either by the quality of the gases used or by using bombs with varying delayed-action fuses. It is easy to see how the use of this method, even with limited supplies of explosive and incendiary bombs, could completely wreck large areas of population and their transit lines during crucial periods of time when such action might prove strategically invaluable.

* * * * * *

This offensive power, the possibility of which was not even dreamed of fifteen years ago, is increasing daily, precisely because the building and development of large, heavy planes goes on all the time. The same thing is true of new explosives, incendiaries, and especially poison gases. What could an army do faced with an offensive power like that, its lines of communication cut, its supply depots burned or blown up, its arsenals and auxiliaries destroyed? What could a navy do when it could no longer take refuge in its own ports, when its bases were burned or blown up, its arsenals and auxiliaries destroyed? How could a country go on living and working under this constant threat, oppressed by the nightmare of imminent destruction and death? How indeed! We should always keep in mind that aerial offensives can be directed not only against objectives of least physical resistance, but against those of least moral resistance as well. For instance, an infantry regiment in a shattered trench may still be capable of some resistance even after losing two-thirds of its effectives; but when the working personnel of a factory sees one of its machine shops destroyed, even with a minimum loss of life, it quickly breaks up and the plant ceases to function.

All this should be kept in mind when we wish to estimate the potential power of aerial offensives possible even to-day. To have command of the air means to be in a position to wield offensive power so great that it defies human imagination. It means to be able to cut an enemy's army and navy off from the bases of operation and nullify their chances of winning the war. It means complete protection of one's own country, the efficient operation of one's army and navy, and peace of mind to live and work in safety. In short, it means to be in a position *to win*. *To be defeated* in the air, on the other hand, is finally to be defeated and to be at the mercy of the enemy, with no chance at all of defending oneself, compelled to accept whatever terms he sees fit to dictate.

This is the meaning of the 'command of the air'.

[From Giulio Douhet, *The Command of the Air*, trans. Dino Ferrari (New York: Coward-McCann, 1942), 11–16.]

B. H. LIDDELL HART

66   The Indirect Approach

More and more clearly has the fact emerged that a direct approach to one's mental object, or physical objective, along the 'line of natural expectation' for the opponent, has ever tended to, and usually produced, negative results. The reason has been expressed scientifically by saying that while the strength of an enemy country lies outwardly in its numbers and resources, these are fundamentally dependent upon stability or 'equilibrium' of control, morale and supply. The former are but the flesh covering the framework of bones and ligaments.

To move along the line of natural expectation is to consolidate the opponent's equilibrium, and by stiffening it to augment his resisting power. In war as in wrestling the attempt to throw the opponent without loosening his foothold and balance can only result in self-exhaustion, increasing in disproportionate ratio to the effective strain put upon him. Victory by such a method can only be possible through an immense margin of superior strength in some form, and even so tends to lose decisiveness. In contrast, an examination of military history, not of one period but of its whole course, points to the fact that in all the decisive campaigns the dislocation of the enemy's psychological and physical balance has been the vital prelude to a successful attempt at his overthrow. This dislocation has been produced by a strategic indirect approach, intentional or fortuitous . . .

The art of the indirect approach can only be mastered, and its full scope appreciated, by study of and reflection upon the whole history of war. But we can at least crystallise the lessons into two simple maxims, one negative, the other positive. The first is that in the face of the overwhelming evidence of history no general is justified in launching his troops to a direct attack upon an enemy firmly in position. The second, that instead of seeking to upset the enemy's equilibrium by one's attack, it must be upset before a real attack is, or can be successfully, launched . . .

Mechanised forces, by their combination of speed and flexibility, offered the means of pursuing this dual action far more effectively than any army could do in the past.

[From Captain B. H. Liddell Hart, *Memoirs*, vol. 2 (London: Cassell, 1965), 162–5.]

F. O. MIKSCHE

67 Blitzkrieg

Two campaigns in Spain, one in Poland, two in France with a brief pause between them, one in the Balkans, and one in Libya—the methods of the Blitzkrieg have shown their value, where there are plenty of roads and few roads, open country or good cover or mountains, in the desert and even, with necessary adaptations, in the Arctic conditions of Norway. Let us make sure that these new methods of war, so thoroughly proved, are now equally thoroughly understood.

What are the principles of the Blitzkrieg and how should they be distinguished from the methods that they have defeated? In the first place the basic principle is that of infiltration, but of infiltration carried to new levels by the use of new material—infiltration motorized, that becomes so clearly a new method that we shall call it 'irruption'. Infiltration used to be a tactical method only, a way in which infantry moving forward, as slowly as men on their feet must always move, worked their way through weak points in the opponent's line. A classic example of infantry infiltration was Ludendorff's great attack of March 1918. This was infiltration as a tactic only, on a small scale. Strategically this attack was not modern infiltration; it was a break-through on a wide front. Strategically Ludendorff was not attempting to infiltrate with large forces through and behind his opponent, not trying to use these forces to fan out in every direction behind the lines that had been pierced. He was not attempting strategical irruption, which in those days had not become possible.

The new method of attack, the Blitzkrieg, is completely different from the old attempt, on classic Great War lines, to make a break-through. At Verdun or on the Somme or elsewhere the attempt to make a break-through involved attacks by infantry, other arms acting in support, over widely extended fronts. It was a wide pressure aiming at occupying slices of ground. This was the sort of attack that the Poles had expected, and the French. So did all other armies that accepted French military doctrine.

How were the Germans led to reject this form of attack, and develop instead the idea of piercing the positions of the defence on relatively narrow fronts? Where does the basic idea of the Blitzkrieg come from? It does not only come from the fact that the Germans saw, and saw first, the true characteristics of modern transport, the power of the petrol engine to concentrate masses of troops and material in a very short time on a couple of miles of front. This capacity of the new material of transport plays its part in the development of the Blitzkrieg, but here as in all other aspects of war doctrine is more important than equipment. The Blitzkrieg derives in its basic idea from the influence of von Schlieffen.

This great strategist infected the Germans with their immense respect for the Carthaginian victory at Cannae in 216 BC. References to this battle occur with monotonous regularity in all German military literature. This was a battle won by complete envelopment of the flanks, and later the rear, of the Roman Army. And Schlieffen taught the Germans to strive constantly to reach a decision on the enemy flanks or rear. The immense size of modern armies, filling the whole battlefield, makes it impossible to reach the flanks or rear of the enemy by simple manœuvre—the last attempt to do this which had any likelihood of success on the grand scale was Schlieffen's own plan for a move through Belgium and round Paris, which came to grief in the hands of smaller men in 1914. Since no modern army has open undefended flanks, the attacking force must create, by the form of its initial attack, the unprotected enemy flanks against which its main pressure will develop. The attacker must pierce, penetrate, before he can envelop a section past which his thrust has gone. This leads to the search for the weak point in any enemy disposition, and the search for ways of concentrating overwhelming force against this weak point. This search for the weak point and concentration against it is the chief characteristic of modern German methods, both on the scale of world strategy and in the tiny details of a tactical operation.

Modern defensive positions disposed in some depth are difficult to attack frontally, by infantry, even if these infantry are well trained in tactical infiltration. Therefore for success part of the attacking forces must be first brought, preferably in a motorized form, to the flank or rear of the defended position that they are to storm, because then they can more easily infiltrate into it, 'in reverse'. In this sense an irruption through the enemy's line must precede a more normal infiltration into it.

The problem for the German General Staff was how to use motorization and new weapons for the new form of break-through. They saw that motorization permitted a very rapid concentration to give local superiority, and that this local superiority need not be thinned out over forty or fifty miles of front but could be used to pierce a narrow gap. In most of their campaigns of this war the main weight of their offensive has been thrown on to a front of only a dozen miles or so. Why not? A dozen miles will contain a good road or two, and some open country across which tracked vehicles can move easily. Such a gap would not be wide enough for slow-moving masses of men and guns, who would jam within it, but it is wide enough for fast moving vehicles to pass through. And that is the aim.

But even in the creation of this gap the Germans normally do not choose to attack on the whole twelve-mile front at once. Pressure is likely to occur along the whole of the front attacked, as it may occur elsewhere to distract the enemy. But the real force of the attack is normally concentrated at perhaps three separate points; each attack will be on a front of only one and a half to two miles, and each may head in a direction divergent from the others. On these three tiny fronts the Panzer divisions concentrate so that they can break through to attack the defence zones, already opposing infiltration, from the flanks and rear.

Then the whole twelve-mile front is opened, so that the main German forces can pass through the breach; and the breach is continually enlarged by flank attack or attack from the rear against the enemy's defended zone.

Logically, the process is this: the aim is Cannae, the method irruption. Next stage in the argument: the aim is irruption, the method is concentration on a narrow front. But here comes in also a third stage in the argument, which should logically be interposed between concentration and irruption, as the method by which the concentrated forces achieve the piercing of the enemy's defences.

[From F. O. Miksche, *Blitzkrieg* (London: Faber, 1942), 50–3.]

68 **Soviet Strategy**

[T]he following definition of military strategy can be given:

Military strategy is a system of theoretical knowledge dealing with the laws of war as an armed conflict in the name of definite class interests. On the basis of military experience, military and political conditions, economic and morale potential, new means of conducting war, and the views of the potential opponent, strategy studies the conditions and the nature of future war, the methods for its preparation and conduct, the branches of the armed services and the basis for their strategic utilization, as well as the material and technological basis for war.

At the same time, it remains the area of practical activity of the higher military and political leadership of the supreme command and the higher headquarters pertaining to the art of preparing the country for war and the conduct of armed conflicts under concrete historical conditions.

The Content and Nature of Military Strategy Under Conditions of Modern Nuclear-Missile War. The technical development of means of warfare has considerable influence on the nature of war and military strategy.

The appearance of rockets with nuclear warheads radically changed previous concepts of the nature of war. The destructive potential of modern nuclear-missile warfare has no comparison with previous wars. Mass application of nuclear-missile weapons makes it possible within a very short time to incapacitate a country or a number of countries, even those with relatively large areas, well-developed economies, and populations numbering tens of millions.

There is an immeasurable increase in the spatial scope of modern warfare. An almost unlimited capacity to deliver nuclear weapons lends to modern warfare unlimited scope, so that the boundaries between the front line and the rear areas are erased, changing previous concepts of the theater of operations.

Military strategy under conditions of modern warfare becomes a strategy of deep nuclear-missile strikes in conjunction with operations of all branches of the armed forces in order to inflict a simultaneous defeat and destruction of the enemy's economic potential and armed forces throughout the whole depth of his territory, for the accomplishment of the war aims within a short time span.

In the light of this definition, a number of previous principles, norms, and rules, which had been considered definitive even as late as World Wars I and II, either are subjected to radical revision or lose their significance altogether.

The ancient and still existing principle of concentrating forces and weapons in the decisive sector requires a radically new approach. In previous wars, it was accomplished by concentration of manpower and equipment and by their increased density in a relatively limited sector of the land front; today this can be achieved by massed strikes of nuclear-rocket weapons.

Concentration of troops at the areas of break-through and formation of high troop densities in these relatively narrow front sectors, a technique employed as recently as World War II, is now fraught with grave consequences. Moreover, there is no longer a need for it, since continuous fronts have become a thing of the past and the concept of break-through has lost its significance. The most important thing is now not the direction of the main blow but the areas of maximum effort, since nuclear strikes can be simultaneously delivered in many directions at a number of points throughout the entire enemy territory. Great importance is also attached to the proper evaluation of objectives, the sequence and chronology of the strikes against them.

Under conditions of nuclear-missile warfare, the strategic principle of the economy of force appears in a new light. It is apparent that when the very outcome of the war depends largely on the extent and effectiveness of strikes at the very beginning of the war, it is hardly reasonable to count on utilizing the potential capabilities of a country and to reserve a large part of its forces for military operations during the subsequent periods of the war. An overwhelming majority of military theoreticians in the highly developed countries of the world are coming to this conclusion.

In the military strategy of previous wars, the principle of partial victory played an important part. It was considered irrefutable that a general victory in war consisted of a number of partial successes on various fronts and in various spheres of military activity. Modern strategic weapons, at the immediate disposal of the high commands, make it possible to achieve decisive results and at times even victory without utilizing the means and forces of the tactical and operational elements, and speak in favor of the theory that today partial successes can be determined by successes of a general strategic nature.

The changes introduced into strategy by new weapons affect not only the principles and rules of military strategy, but also basic strategic categories. Thus, the concept of a theater of military operations has changed completely. In the classic definition, a theater of military operations signified a territory or sea area in which direct military action took place. Its boundaries were determined by the range of weapons which, until World War II, rarely penetrated deep into the operational rear areas. Thus, the strategic rear area and the entire territory of the belligerent country beyond these boundaries were not part of the theater of operations.

The development of strategic long-range bomber aircraft, nuclear weapons, and, especially, intercontinental missiles significantly changed the concept of a theater of military operations. Now a theater of military operations may include the whole territory of a belligerent country or coalition, whole continents, large bodies of water, as well as extensive air and cosmic space. Thus, the zone of military operations today is not limited by the range of firepower, for the latter is almost unlimited; it may be restricted only by the location of strategic objectives.

Strategic offense and strategic defense as forms of strategic operations have, under conditions of nuclear-missile warfare, lost their previous significance. They played a major role when the main aims and tasks of war were achieved by ground troops—with the cooperation of aviation, and in coastal areas, of the navy—and the main basis of conducting war was land combat. Under conditions of nuclear-missile warfare, the achievement of the main aims of war will be accomplished by the strategic rocket forces, by means of the delivery of massed nuclear-rocket strikes. Land forces, with the aid of aviation, will perform important strategic operations: By means of extremely rapid offensive movements, they will conclusively annihilate the target enemy formations, occupy the enemy's territory, and prevent the enemy from invading his own territory. The strategic operations of other branches of the armed forces will consist of the following: The air defense forces will defend the country from nuclear strikes of the enemy; the navy will act in naval theaters of operations to destroy enemy naval forces and communications, and to defend its own communications as well as the coastal areas from attack by sea.

Offense and defense as forms of strategic operations can retain their significance in military operations of conventional forces in certain types of local wars, the probability of which cannot be excluded even under contemporary conditions.

Nuclear missiles have introduced substantial changes in the concept of strategic deployment of the armed forces. As it existed until World War II, strategic deployment was a complex of measures designed to screen, mobilize, concentrate, and deploy the armed forces in the theater of operations, according to a predetermined sequence and plan; this concept has now clearly become obsolete. Today, most of these measures can be accomplished beforehand, so that they need only be completed in a period of danger.

Thus, the new concept of strategic deployment is one of the establishment of strategic formations prior to the outbreak of war according to the war plan and to the conditions of its development. An important part is played by increased military preparedness of the armed forces.

Perfection of the means of delivery of nuclear weapons, their long range, and the ability rapidly to change the direction of nuclear attack from one target to another have drastically changed the concept of strategic maneuver. This was previously defined as the most favorable location of forces and weapons in a theater of operations or in a strategic direction; today, its essence apparently consists in the creation of favorable conditions through the switching and concentration of nuclear strikes aimed at solving the main problems and achieving the main objectives of war, as well as in the accomplishment of strategic results by all branches of the armed forces.

The accomplishment of strategic maneuver in the recent war was realized by moving large commands and units, by rail and motor transport, from one front or theater of operations to another. The high vulnerability of communications and the lack of time necessary for such regrouping will make these maneuvers difficult to accomplish and in a number of cases not expedient.

Consequently, strategic maneuver under conditions of nuclear-rocket warfare can be described as a transfer of effort from one strategic direction or objective to another, mainly by the fire of nuclear weapons. Maneuver in the old sense may be applied primarily within theaters of operation by the various branches of the armed forces, and primarily on an operational scale.

These basic principles and categories of military strategy confirm the applicability of those radical changes that are being introduced by the appearance of new weapons.

These are the general principles of military strategy that affect the concepts and position of strategy in military science, its content, and the changes in it produced by the appearance of nuclear-rocket weapons.

[From Marshal V. D. Sokolovsky (ed.), *Military Strategy: Soviet Doctrine and Concepts*, introd. Raymond Garthoff (London and Dunmow: Pall Mall Press, 1963), 13–17.]

A. BEAUFRE

69 A Strategy of Deterrence

I propose to set out here only those conclusions I consider basic. Although they may appear trite or bordering on the self-evident, I have a feeling that all too often they do not figure adequately in our concepts on strategy and international relations.

(1) The disproportionate dangers produced by nuclear weapons have now become such that it is very difficult to conceive of open war in the areas where a minimum of credibility still attaches to the use of nuclear weapons.

As a result, in these areas the role of armed forces, and in particular nuclear forces, must not be considered from the point of view of their possible employment in war, as has been our habit, but from that of the prevention of war, in other words of *deterrence*.

(2) This fundamental transformation in the character and influence of armaments entails an almost complete *reversal* of our concepts: the danger of destruction creates stability, too great stability recreates the danger (of war). So the subtle rules of a new game of international relationships begin

to emerge with increasing clarity: the object of the game is to maintain deterrent effect by a judicious admixture of danger and stability. It is a form of strategy, the *strategy of deterrence*.

(3) The essential feature of the strategy of deterrence [...] lies in the non-employment of nuclear weapons through judicious exploitation of the fact that they exist. Although deterrence cannot be classed as an operation of war, it is—contrary to some beliefs—neither policy nor diplomacy. It is a powerful instrument, *at the disposal of policy*: it is a strategy.

(4) Since, like any other strategy, it must be subordinate to policy, the strategy of deterrence can only produce meaningful solutions in the light of the political aim being pursued. As in any argument between the strategist and the politician, the strategist can do no more than emphasize the limits of his capabilities and recommend the solutions which appear to him the most favourable; it is for the politician to decide in the light of his wider spectrum of considerations.

(5) Since the strategy of deterrence does not make actual use of its weapons, technical developments play a less decisive role than in a war strategy. The technical qualities of weapons are of course important, but their psychological and political impact is so overriding that it largely outweighs the technical aspect; thus the French strategic force exerted an influence well before it was actually in existence. The strategy of deterrence is therefore far more abstract and ambiguous than the strategy of war. [...]

The problem has been to look for, and bring out into the open, some logical basis for the role to be allotted today to military forces, now that their use would appear to be generally restricted to the minor forms of warfare.

The logical basis would appear to a great extent to emerge from the essential distinction we have drawn between the forms of warfare for which preparations are made in order that they may be used, and those for which preparations are made in order to prevent them being used. The resulting train of thought should lead to the establishment of the principles governing a nuclear age defence doctrine; but with this goes the necessity to be prepared at any time to adapt oneself to very different types of action by preparing simultaneously for two types of war at opposite ends of the scale—limited conventional war and 'spasm' nuclear war.

These principles should help to give us back our confidence, all too often lacking in this field owing to the accumulation of contradictions and over-simplifications. The nuclear weapon has brought profound changes to the methods employed in the defence function but the function as such still has all its old importance. In fact, since the total strategy of deterrence is constantly in action, the defence function has also become a continuous operation instead of being restricted as in the old days to periods of serious crisis.

Let us hope that our military professionals will grasp this new truth and so come to realize that their day-to-day efforts have some meaning and value.

Looking further ahead than our present day problems, consideration of deterrence brings out certain major conclusions opening up a vista of new developments.

(1) An extraordinary transformation has taken place in the modern world; the cauldron is seething as a result of the impact of technology, the new White Man's magic, and of the collapse of the European World Empire; the 'Tiers Monde' is frantically Europeanizing itself and over everything tower the American and Russian giants. It is all in a state of flux.

Nevertheless at the same time the nuclear weapon introduces a completely new factor of stability. Wherever its influence extends the situation congeals, whereas outside its influence the pace of upheaval increases (Asia and Africa are on the move, but Berlin and Formosa are stagnant). One of the most important questions facing us is to find out whether in fact it is possible to extend nuclear stability to other zones and so put a brake on the more dangerous developments. It seems possible that such a prospect may open up through the machinery of multilateral deterrence, so far regarded from too narrow a point of view, that of fear and the interests of the two great nuclear powers.

(2) Another major conclusion is inescapable. We are in the midst of events, the evolution of which we have not so far been able to foresee, and in which all forecasts prove precarious. It is vital that we should know how we intend to bring some conscious influence to bear on the future. Irrespective of the philosophical or political line we choose to follow, we are therefore faced with the problem of the *manœuvre in time*. This would seem to be the essential role of modern strategy, just as the manœuvre in space was that of traditional strategy. [. . .]

Finally, as we have seen, nuclear deterrence perhaps opens up prospects on the nature of things.

The nuclear weapon is one of the products of science. Science has endowed man with powers far exceeding his capacity for foresight and wisdom. Yet in the magnitude of power is inherent its own limitation because of the dangers which go with it. Instead of acquiring wisdom through increased intelligence and a more lively conscience, wisdom is being taught us and forced upon us by material advances capable of bringing us to ruin.

So, as it develops, the world ought to be able to maintain a degree of balance in the fundamental and salutary antithesis between determinism and liberty, between man's power and his freedom of action.

[From A. Beaufre, *Deterrence and Strategy*, trans. Major-General R. H. Barry (London: Faber, 1965), 170–4. First published as *Dissuasion et Stratégie* (Paris: Armand Colin, 1964).]

70 **The Threat that Leaves Something to Chance**

It is typical of strategic threats that the punitive action—if the threat fails and has to be carried out—is painful or costly to both sides. The purpose is deterrence *ex ante*, not revenge *ex post*. Making a credible threat involves proving that one would have to carry out the threat, or creating incentives for oneself or incurring penalties that would make one evidently want to. The acknowledged purpose of stationing American troops in Europe as a 'trip wire' was to convince the Russians that war in Europe would involve the United States whether the Russians thought the United States wanted to be involved or not—that escape from the commitment was physically impossible.

As a rule, one must threaten that he *will* act, not that he *may* act, if the threat fails. To say that one *may* act is to say that one *may not*, and to say this is to confess that one has kept the power of decision—that one is not committed. To say only that one *may* carry out the threat, not that one certainly will, is to invite the opponent to guess whether one will prefer to punish himself and his opponent or to pass up the occasion. Furthermore, if one says that he may—not that he will—and the opponent fails to heed the threat, and the threatener chooses not to carry it out, he only confirms his opponent's belief that when he has a clear choice to act or to abstain he will choose to abstain (consoling himself that he was not caught bluffing because he never said that he would act for sure).

There are threats of this kind nevertheless that may be effective in spite of this loophole. They can work, however, only through a process that is a degree more complicated than firm commitment to certain fulfilment. Furthermore, they may arise inadvertently and may entail unintended behavior. For this reason they are less likely to be recognized and understood.

The key to these threats is that, though one may or may not carry them out if the threatened party fails to comply, *the final decision is not altogether under the threatener's control*. The threat is not quite of the form 'I may or may not, according as I choose', but, has an element of, 'I may or may not, and even I can't be altogether sure'.

Where does the uncertain element in the decision come from? It must come from somewhere outside of the threatener's control. Whether we call it 'chance', accident, third-party influence, imperfection in the machinery of decision, or just processes that we do not entirely understand, it is an ingredient in the situation that neither we nor the party we threaten can entirely control. An example is the threat of inadvertent war.

The Threat of Inadvertent War

The thought that general war might be initiated inadvertently—through some kind of accident, false alarm, or mechanical failure; through somebody's panic, madness, or mischief; through a misapprehension of enemy intentions or a correct apprehension of the enemy's misapprehension of ours—is not an attractive one. As a general rule one wants to keep such a likelihood to a minimum; and on the particular occasions when tension rises and strategic forces are put on extraordinary alert, when the incentive to react quickly is enhanced by the thought that the other side may strike first, it seems particularly important to safeguard against impetuous decision, errors of judgment, and suspicious or ambiguous modes of behavior. It seems likely that, for both human and mechanical reasons, the probability of inadvertent war rises with a crisis.

But is not this mechanism itself a kind of deterrent threat? Suppose the Russians observe that whenever they undertake aggressive action tension rises and this country gets into a sensitive condition of readiness for quick action. Suppose they believe what they have so frequently claimed—that an enhanced status for our retaliatory forces and for theirs may increase the danger of an accident or a false alarm, theirs or ours, or of some triggering incident, resulting in war. May they not perceive that the risk of all-out war, then, depends on their own behavior, rising when they aggress and intimidate, falling when they relax their pressure against other countries?

Notice that what rises—as far as *this* particular mechanism is concerned—is not the risk that the United States will *decide* on all-out war, but the risk that war will occur whether intended or not. Even if the Russians did not expect deliberate retaliation for the particular misbehavior they had in mind, they could still be uneasy about the possibility that their action might precipitate general war or initiate some dynamic process that could end only in massive war or massive Soviet withdrawal. They might not be confident that we and they could altogether foretell the consequences of our actions in an emergency, and keep the situation altogether under control.

Here is a threat—if a mechanism like this exists—that we *may* act massively, not that we certainly will. It could be most credible. Its credibility stems from the fact that the possibility of precipitating major war in response to Soviet aggression is not limited to the possibililty of our coolly deciding to attack; it therefore extends beyond the areas and the events for which a more deliberate threat is in force. It does not depend on our preferring to launch all-out war, or on our being committed to, in the event the Russians confront us with the *fait accompli* of a moderately aggressive move. The final decision is left to 'chance'. It is up to the Russians to estimate how successfully they and we can avoid precipitating war under the circumstances.

The threat—if we call this contingent-behavior mechanism a 'threat'—has some interesting features. It may exist whether we realize it or not. Even those who have doubted whether our massive-retaliation threat was a potent deterrent to *minor* aggression during the last several years, but are perplexed that the Russians have not engaged in more mischief than they have, can note that the threat we voiced was backed by an additional implicit threat that we might be triggered by Soviet actions in spite of ourselves. Furthermore, even if we prefer not to incur even a small probability of inadvertent war, and would not use this mechanism deliberately, the 'threat' in question may be a by-product of other actions that we have a powerful incentive to take. We may get this threat whether we like it or not when we (and the Russians) take precautions commensurate with a crisis; knowing this, the Russians may have to take the risk into account. Finally, the threat is not discredited even if the Russians accomplish their purpose without triggering war. If the Russians estimate that the chance of inadvertent war during a particular month rises from very small to not-so-small if they create a crisis, and they go ahead anyway, and no major war occurs, they still have little reason to suppose that their original estimate was wrong, and little reason to suppose that repetition would be less risky, any more than a person who survives a single play of Russian roulette should decide it isn't dangerous after all.

Limited War as a Generator of Risk

Limited war as a deterrent to aggression also requires interpretation as an action that enhances the *probability* of a greater war. If we ask how the Western forces in Europe are expected to deter a Russian attack or to resist it if it comes, the answer usually runs in terms of a sequence of *decisions*. In case of attack on a moderate scale, we could make the decision to fight limited war; it would not be a decision to proceed with mutual annihilation. If we can resist the Russians on a small scale, they must either give up the idea or themselves take a step upward on the scale of violence. At some point there is a discontinuous jump from limited war to general war, and we hope to confront *them* with that choice. If this is not the typical sequence of decisions envisaged, it at least seems typical in one respect: it involves *deliberate* decisions—decisions to take an action or to abstain from it, to initiate a war or not to, to step up the level of violence or not to, to respond to a challenge or not to.

But another interpretation can be put on limited war. The danger of all-out war is almost certainly increased by the occurrence of a limited war; it is almost certainly increased by an enlargement of limited war. This being so, the threat to engage in limited war has two parts. One is the threat to inflict costs directly on the other side, in casualties, expenditures, loss of territory, loss of face, or anything else. The second is the threat to expose the other party, together with one's self, to a heightened risk of general war.

Here again is a threat that all-out war *may* occur, not that it certainly will occur, if the other party engages in certain actions. Again, whether it does or does not occur is not a matter altogether controlled by the threatener. Just how all-out war would occur—just where the fault, initiative, or mis-understanding may occur—is not sure. Whatever it is that makes limited war between great powers a risky thing, the risk is a genuine one that neither side can altogether dispel if it wants to. The final decision, or the critical action that initiates an irreversible process, is not something that should necessarily be expected to be taken altogether deliberately. 'Chance' helps to decide whether general war occurs or not, with odds that are a matter of judgment based on the nature of the limited war and the context in which it occurs.

Why would one threaten limited war rather than all-out war to deter an attack? First, to threaten limited war—according to this analysis—is to threaten a risk of general war, not the certainty of it; it is consequently a lesser threat than the massively retaliatory threat and more appropriate to certain contingencies. Second, it has the advantage, in case the enemy misjudges our intentions or commitments, of an intermediate stage: we can *engage* in limited war, creating precisely the risk for both of us that we threatened to create, without thereby making general war the price we both pay for the enemy's mistaken judgment. We pay instead the lesser price of a risk of general war, a risk that the enemy can reduce by withdrawal or settlement.

Third, in case the enemy is irrational or impetuous, or we have mis-judged his motives or his commitments, or in case his aggressive action has gotten up too much momentum to stop, or his actions are being carried out by puppets or satellites that are beyond his immediate power to control, there is some prudence in threatening risk rather than certainty. If we threaten all-out war, thinking it not too late to stop him, and it is, we must either go ahead with it or have our threat discredited. But if we can threaten him with a one-in-twenty chance of all-out war in the event he proceeds, and he does proceed, we can hold our breath and have nineteen-to-one odds of getting off without general war. Of course, if we scale down the risk to us, we scale it down to him too; it may degrade the threat to put too much safety in it. But in cases where there is danger that we completely misjudge the enemy's commitment to an action, or completely misjudge his ability to control his own agents, allies, or commanders, the more moderate risk may deter anything that is still within his control.

[From Thomas Schelling, *The Strategy of Conflict* (New York: Oxford University Press, 1963), 187–92.]

Section F

Total War and the Great Powers

BRIAN HOLDEN REID AND LAWRENCE FREEDMAN

The significance of the new type of warfare which rocked Europe at the start of the nineteenth century has already been remarked upon in this volume. The consequence of this revolution is examined in the first extract from Geoffrey Parker (71). In the sixteenth and seventeenth centuries, states had placed more men with better equipment in the field than was possible in the armies of the later Middle Ages, but the administrative and financial burdens required to keep them there were enormous. The resources were such as to prolong the war, on a number of different fronts, but not to bring it to a decisive and complete victory. The object was attritional, even for commanders with the ardent spirit of a Gustavus Adolphus or a Marlborough. If this was a 'revolution' in military method it only served to confirm rather than break a strategic deadlock. According to Parker, by the late eighteenth century there were three 'transformations' which saw the culmination of the revolution: the use of light infantry, the spread of light artillery, and the introduction of a divisional organization which rendered strategy more flexible. These developments came together as a system of warfare in the Napoleonic period. It was to break down slowly under the influence of the Industrial Revolution in the nineteenth century, but by this time it had demonstrated the possibility of one state dominating the European heartland. It had also made overseas expansion possible, and allowed European states to gain bridgeheads on the coastal areas of indigenous empires in the Americas, Africa, and the Near East.

In 72 Ian Beckett describes how it was the ability of states to mobilize fully their economic resources which determined their ability to wage total war. He illustrates the ineluctable tendency over time to increase the volume of destructive force deployed in war. His essay should be read in conjunction with Geoffrey Best's discussion of attempts to put some limits on the conduct of land war before the end of the Second World War (74). It should also be read in the light of the discussion of strategy in the previous section, for here we can see the gradual realization of the doctrines of mass war as developed in the decades leading up to the First World War. In 75 Douglas Porch indicates that in practice doctrinal evolution is a complex process which (he notes in the part of his essay not reprinted here) reflects political and social pressures as well as purely military matters.

The attempts to avoid the devastating consequences of land war through the employment of naval and air power are assessed in the pieces by Colin Gray and David MacIsaac respectively (78 and 79). Both confirm that hopes for the use of either as an independent means to victory were limited. They were most effective when operating in support of a campaign on the ground. This is true even of air power as it has become more accurate and more lethal in the years since the Second World War. Even in the 1991 Gulf War (22), when full command of the air was achieved, the Iraqi will to fight was as much broken by the growing impotence of its land army as its means of sustenance was steadily destroyed and the troops left exposed to attack, as by the strikes geared to weakening the leadership's will and command structure. The extract on the 1944 Normandy landings (76) is included as a reminder that the key to victory does not necessarily depend on controlling the environment, on land, air, or sea, but that good intelligence and the manipulation of the information available to the other side (especially when it conforms with the enemy's prejudices) can be critical to victory. A similar point emerges in Michael Handel's discussion of surprise attack in the next section (92).

In the nuclear age there were natural questions with regard to the advisability of total war strategies, and that meant consideration of both the methods and the objectives of war. As is made clear in 80, there was an early recognition in the United States that the occupation of the Soviet Union was unlikely to be a feasible option in a future war. It would be one thing to limit Moscow's ability to extend its influence beyond state borders: quite another to seek to take over its state. In addition to the limitation on objectives there was a natural interest, when confronting the prospect of a nuclear holocaust, in considering the limitation of means. This was manifested most noisily in demands for nuclear disarmament, as if fewer arms would mean more peace, even though the logic of the nuclear age appeared to be that it was the quantity of arms and their individual destructive power which had induced a welcome caution in world leaders. In 81, Hedley Bull provides a classic critique of disarmament theory while at the same time making a case for a more modest effort—arms control—which could allow the two superpowers to co-operate in ensuring that the balance of terror did not get out of kilter.

In practice this sort of co-operation developed naturally as a result of the nuclear deadlock. Combined with the neatness of the division of Europe into the two ideologically opposed blocs and with eventual inertia, the European state system settled down into what came to be described as a 'long peace'. The durability of this arrangement and the stability with which it was associated meant that there were many who were disappointed when it came to its conclusion, not as a result of the sort of war which had marked the end of other periods in European history but through the collapse of the Communist economic and political system. To some (82) this created a grave risk of a return to a much more fluid state system, with the consequential risk of a clash of great powers. The first few years of the post-cold-war period gave little support to the view that the old Great Powers would suddenly unlearn their disposition towards peaceful coexistence with each other. It did confirm fears that in a Europe without the disciplines of the cold war, many ethnic disputes would bubble to the surface and lead to widespread violence and disorder. These conflicts did not fall naturally into the categories of warfare developed during the decades of Great Power conflict and the domination of total war concepts: they were more reminiscent of those that had hitherto been considered more applicable to the developing, post-colonial world.

GEOFFREY PARKER

71 The Military Revolution

Categorizing Frederick II of Prussia (1740–86) as an exponent of the traditional art of war, rather than as the initiator of a new one, is controversial. When Hans Delbrück argued the case in *The strategy of Pericles illuminated by the strategy of Frederick the Great* (published in 1890), he sparked off a furious debate that lasted for twenty years. But he was surely right, for Frederick's wars were still dynastic rather than national, and his strategy aimed at attrition rather than annihilation (because the king lacked the resources either to destroy his enemies or otherwise to impose his will on them). Furthermore, the size and composition of Frederick's armies were not much different from those of earlier rulers. During the Seven Years War (1756–63), Prussia's armed forces totalled about 150,000 men, rising to perhaps 200,000 in 1786; and, as in the continental armies of the seventeenth century, one-third of the men were normally foreigners. In few of Frederick's battles—which were numerous—did the king command more than 40,000 men, of whom up to 40 per cent might become casualties, even in victory. This appalling wastage was due to further improvements in firepower since the days of Marlborough. Speed, not accuracy, remained the supreme goal and so the length of musket barrels was reduced and drill was intensified until Frederick's musketeers, drawn up in three ranks, were able to equal the continuous fire once achieved by Maurice of Nassau's army drawn up in ten. At the battle of Leuthen, in 1757, some of the Prussian musketeers fired off 180 rounds at the enemy. But at such speed, and with such weapons, accuracy was impossible. The drill-books of the Prussian army contained no command for 'take aim' (the troops just fired straight ahead) and their guns, like the English 'Brown Bess', possessed no sights.

But these tactics of rapid fire at close range, with the consequent heavy losses of men, called for a far better supply of war materials than previous armies had enjoyed. In this lay Frederick's major military achievement. The Splitgerber and Daum arms factory at Postdam, for example, turned out 15,000 muskets a year in the 1740s, while the annual powder production of Prussia rose from 448,000 pounds in 1746 to 560,000 pounds in 1756. The commissariat placed contracts for munitions supply two years ahead so that, according to Frederick himself, 'the army never ran short of what it needed, even though we had some campaigns which cost us 40,000 muskets and 20,000 horses'. Food rations were also accumulated on a massive scale: by 1776 the military magazines of Berlin and Breslau alone contained 76,000 bushels of grain or flour—enough to feed an army of 60,000 men for two years. And finally, new uniforms of standard design were issued annually to every regiment by its own individual manufacturers, whose blue cloth 'though coarser, wears better and has a more decent appearance, when long worn, than the finest cloth manufactured in England or France'.

But the cost of all this was crippling. In human terms, the wars consumed too many men. The Prussian army may have been the fourth or fifth largest in Europe, and the largest of any European state *per capita*, but the Prussian population was only the thirteenth largest: almost a quarter of its young men were conscripted into the army, and the death of almost 180,000 of them during the Seven Years War—equivalent to a survival rate of only one in fifteen for those in the ranks when hostilities began in 1756—was as deleterious in demographic terms as the slaughter of the Thirty Years War had been to Sweden. [. . .] In financial terms, too, the cost was unacceptably high: 90 per cent of Frederick the Great's receipts were spent on war. It was enough to support an army of almost 200,000, but only by cutting corners: the currency was debased; contributions and plunder were ruthlessly extracted; no money was spent on curing wounded troops; and officers were not allowed to marry because Frederick could not afford to pay pensions to military widows.

The originality of Frederick's military system thus lay principally in his improvements in supply, which allowed him to move his armies relatively swiftly and in relatively good order (provided they did not stray too far from Prussian territory); and in the superior discipline of his troops, which allowed the king to direct surprise attacks under the noses of his enemies (manoeuvres which, in other armies, would have produced chaos). But it was still not enough to secure decisive victories. Frederick's only substantial gain by war was the capture of Silesia in 1741; after that, he became a staunch defender of the military status quo. In 1775 he wrote:

The ambitious should consider above all that armaments and military discipline being much the same throughout Europe, and alliances as a rule producing an equality of force between belligerent parties, all that princes can expect from the greatest advantages at present is to acquire, by accumulation of successes, either some small city on the frontier, or some territory which will not pay interest on the expenses of the war, and whose population does not even approach the number of citizens who perished in the campaigns.

Precisely the same sentiments, albeit less elegantly expressed, could have been written by almost any early modern statesman, for Frederick's Prussia (like its principal enemies) was not very different from the states of seventeenth-century Europe. Society was still rigidly hierarchical, with most wealth and power concentrated in the hands of the aristocracy; and armies naturally reflected this state of affairs—the officers of Frederick II, as of Louis XV, were all (or almost all) noblemen; the rank and file were all commoners; and up to half of them were foreigners, some of them even enlisted prisoners of war. Likewise the resources for financing war remained, for most eighteenth-century governments, similar to those of Philip II or Charles V; while the roads and transport available were also little better in most parts of Europe in 1750 than in 1550. Just as the middle decades of the eighteenth century represented the apogee of the *ancien régime*, so the same period saw the culmination of 'the military revolution'.

By the time of Frederick's death in 1786, however, the military system of early modern Europe was clearly changing. In the first place, new varieties of regular troops appeared: the light infantry and light cavalry. They first achieved prominence in 1740–1, when Frederick of Prussia's surprise attack on the Habsburg empire was halted with the aid of some 20,000 veterans from the military border with the Turks, in Hungary and Croatia. These lightly armed skirmishers, few of whom wore uniforms, were described by an English observer as:

fierce, undisciplined and subject to scarcely any military laws. They were attached to the house of Austria by prejudices and predilections of religion, manners and education, peculiar to themselves . . . A degree of primeval rudeness and simplicity characterizes them, totally unlike the spirit which animates the mercenary stipendiary of modern armies.

Their success against the best-trained regular troops in Europe came as a surprise (despite the fact that they had just withstood the Turks in 1737–9) and it caught the attention of other military leaders. In 1742–3 the king of Savoy, defending his mountainous state against the Bourbons, also made extensive use of irregular forces in the Alps; and in 1743 the maréchal de Saxe, who had once served in Hungary, introduced light infantry to the French army. Later, when the war was over and military commentators began to pick over the lessons and achievements to be digested, several reported favourably on the light troops and their tactics: the lord of La Croix in his *Treatise on small wars* of 1752, Turpin de Crissé in his *Essay on the art of war* of 1754, and the fifty or so other volumes on 'small wars' published in Europe between 1750 and 1800 all praised the 'light troops'. Some of these works were read attentively by British army officers and, when regular battalions went to America after 1755 to fight against the French and their Indian allies, they adopted in part the techniques of irregular warfare recommended by La Croix and Turpin. According to one officer in the colonies, troops there:

require no exercise but to be perfectly acquainted with the use of their arms, that is to load quick and hit the mark, and for military discipline but this one rule: if they are attacked by French and Indians to rush to all parts from where their fire comes.

Admittedly, not all the experts were convinced of the need for light troops. Even after Austrian hussars made a raid deep into Prussian territory in 1757 and (briefly) captured Berlin, Frederick the Great refused to follow suit. Instead, obsessed by the fear that his expensively trained infantry would seize every available opportunity to desert, he surrounded his camps with fences, avoided marches through forests, and even forbore to send out scouting parties more than 200 metres ahead of the army for fear that his men would run away. He viewed organized skirmishing merely as a licence to escape. But he was wrong: the 'light' infantry and cavalry had come to stay.

Another innovation of the War of the Austrian Succession (1740–8) was the organization of large armies into a number of self-sufficient units called divisions. Pierre de Bourcet's *Principles of mountain warfare*, composed in the 1760s, proposed that the ideal army should be made up of three separate columns, each of them one day's march (or less) distant from the others, so that the enemy should never know the point at which the force would concentrate and attack. The technique had worked well in the Franco-Spanish Alpine campaign against Savoy-Piedmont in 1744 (in which Bourcet served as a staff engineer officer), but it met with considerable opposition from the army establishment. Only in 1787–8 did the French adopt the division as the basic administrative unit, so that up to 12,000 infantry, cavalry and artillery units, together with engineers and other ancillary groups, were organized under a single commander and his staff. Divisional organization in the field, however, was harder to achieve (and did not become standard in France until 1796) because of the relative scarcity of the roads and maps which would allow a large army to disperse, coordinate its movements, and reassemble swiftly. Even in the Seven Years War, armies had managed to march off their maps, and suffered defeats through ignorance of topography. Not until the 1780s, with the enormous Josephine survey of all lands of the Austrian Habsburgs (in 5,400 sheets) and Cassini's massive cartographic survey of France, was the continental road network fully surveyed and thus made available to military planners and generals. And that road network was now more extensive and better maintained than ever before: bridges were regularly repaired and road surfaces were often paved; and if strategy called for a road where none existed, the expanding corps of engineers and pioneers in the service of most governments could soon build one, as the British army did in Scotland in the mid-eighteenth century—1,500 kilometres were constructed at a cost of £50 per kilometre. In some areas of the continent there was also a programme of canal-building specifically to carry vital war materials swiftly from the centres of production to the army's magazines.

These changes in the art of war in the later eighteenth century were accompanied by the creation, for the first time, of a powerful yet fully mobile field artillery. The guns of Louis XIV's day had been cast with the possibility in mind that they might, in case of need, be used against fortresses in sieges as well as against troops in battle: so their barrels were relatively long and thick, in order to withstand a heavy powder charge. But under Louis XV, attempts were made to produce shorter, lighter pieces that, although less useful in sieges, would be equally effective in the field. Under the enlightened direction of Jean Baptiste de Gribeauval, the calibres, carriages and equipment of the French artillery were standardized, and their parts were made interchangeable (thanks to the ability of industrial plants to mass-produce identical, precise and highly durable metalwork). At the same time, gunfounders in French service demonstrated that, with more accurate casting, the powder required for effective firing of cannon could be reduced by 50 per cent, making it possible to slim down gun barrels considerably, since the concussion was less. In the course of the 1750s and 60s, the weight of a French four-pounder field gun dropped from 1,300 pounds to only 600. At this weight, it could easily be drawn by only three horses (and handled by a mere eight men) and so could keep up even with the more mobile armies and divisions of the day.

These three transformations—the use of light troops and skirmishers; the introduction of divisions and a more mobile strategy; and the creation of a swift and powerful field artillery—were associated after 1793 with a further revolution in military manpower. Once again, the French led the way. The royal army in 1788–9, on the eve of the Revolution, stood at some 150,000 men. By August 1793 its paper strength had reached 645,000 and the celebrated *levée en masse* probably doubled this figure. By September 1794, the army of the Republic numbered, at least in theory, 1,169,000 men. Needless to say, reality sometimes lagged behind expectation. There was very high wastage among the recruits—probably only 730,000 men were actually with the colours in September 1794—and their equipment was often far inferior to that of the old royal army. For example, at first it proved impossible to clothe all the men in the same uniform, and some local authorities in 1793–4 were forced to order 'coats and trousers of the material that most closely resembles the "national blue" '; while others revived the pike for their recruits 'because it is the only appropriate weapon, given the short time available for instruction'. But such temporary problems were only to be expected, for no European state had ever attempted—let alone managed—to raise, equip and maintain an army of 730,000 men. In all, perhaps 3 million soldiers served in the armies of France between 1792 and 1815, providing her rulers with an almost irresistible concentration of force. In 1805, 176,000 French troops, with 286 field guns, moved through Germany on a 200-kilometre front; in 1812, the *Grande Armée* of 600,000 men, with 1,146 field guns, invaded Russia on a 400-kilometre front.

Here at last was an army large enough to break the stranglehold of the *trace italienne*. The French did not sweep aside the problems posed by bastioned fortifications; indeed, as at Torres Vedras in Portugal in 1810, a well-defended position could still paralyse a mighty army. But, for most of the time, the armies were now so mighty that there were enough men to allow commanders to encircle the enemy's strategic fortresses, to defend their own, and yet still be able to lead forces of unprecedented size into the field. This was clearly warfare on a totally different plane to anything previously seen in Europe. Napoleon's armies may have fought in much the same way as those of Frederick, Marlborough or Gustavus Adolphus; and Napoleon, marooned in Egypt in 1798–9, may have asked the Paris government to send him military histories of the Thirty Years War to read. But the scale of warfare was by then so totally transformed that it might be said that another 'military revolution' had occurred.

The evolution of naval warfare was roughly similar. The near-equilibrium of the three navies of north-west Europe in the later seventeenth century [. . .] was shattered in the later eighteenth because Britain forged ahead while the others did not. In 1789, there were perhaps 440 ships-of-the-line in Europe's navies, of which almost one-third (153) were British, all of them equipped with standard, mass-produced steel cannon. But by 1810, after almost twenty years of continuous war at sea, the Royal Navy comprised over 1,000 purpose-built warships (243 of them ships-of-the-line) with a total displacement of 861,000 tons and a complement of 142,000 men. These, too, represented an almost irresistible concentration of force, which could be applied anywhere in the world. It was from this position of overwhelming strength that Britannia could, and did, rule the waves.

However, these achievements in land and sea warfare represented another threshold beyond which, for several decades, European states could not pass. The concentration of such large armies and fleets strained to the limit the expanded economic, political and technological resources which had permitted their creation. Even the system of command and supply that had served to conquer Italy and Germany for *La Grande Nation* failed when it was applied to the larger armies required to invade Spain and Russia. Telegraph, railways, and breech-loading firearms were needed before armies larger than those favoured by Napoleon could operate effectively; and it required the iron-clad steamship to challenge effectively the supremacy of the Nelsonian ship-of-the-line. Not until then did the Europeans at last possess the means to subjugate those peoples who had so far escaped their embrace. In February 1841, on her way to Canton during the first Opium War, for example, the two pivot-mounted 32 pounders of the ironclad steamship *Nemesis* destroyed, in just one day, nine war-junks, five forts, two military stations and one shore battery. In 1854, at Sinop, the destruction of the Turkish navy by Russian ironclads opened the Ottoman empire to Western exploitation. And in 1863, a belated attempt by the Tokugawa government to exclude western warships from Japanese waters ended in catastrophic failure, with the Royal Navy closing in (despite a typhoon) to destroy all shipping and most dwellings at Kagoshima, while the French, Netherlands, American and British navies combined to silence the modern gun batteries in the straits of Shimonoseki. Meanwhile, at much the same time, the rapid-firing guns of the White Men swiftly and brutally overcame all resistance by the native tribes and nations of the American plains and the African interior.

The West had now indeed risen. In a way that few could have foreseen, the sustained preoccupation of the European states with fighting each other by land and sea had at length paid handsome dividends. Thanks above all to their military superiority, founded upon the military revolution of the sixteenth and seventeenth centuries, the Western nations had managed to create the first global hegemony in History.

[From Geoffrey Parker, *The Military Revolution: Military Innovation and the Rise of the West, 1500–1800* (Cambridge: Cambridge University Press, 1988), 147–54.]

IAN F. W. BECKETT

72 **Total War**

The emergence of total war

Traditionally, historians have described the late eighteenth century as a classic era of 'limited war', in which armies were relatively small in size and would manoeuvre with the intention of avoiding rather than engaging in battle. Campaigns would be designed to exhaust an opponent's economy by occupation in search of strictly limited political and dynastic aims. Societies as a whole would hardly be touched by the impact of war and, indeed, a prevailing bourgeois assumption that military activity was not the destiny of mankind ensured that trade flourished between states at war. Examples usually cited of the normality of social intercourse include Laurence Sterne's visit to Paris during the Seven Years War (1756–63) and the continuance of the Dover to Calais packet service for a year after France in 1778 had joined the United States in the American War of Independence (1774–83). Closer analysis, however, reveals that war between 1648 and 1789 was limited, in the words of John Childs, 'only when it was compared with the holocaust that had gone before and the new totality of the Napoleonic wars'. As surely as the Thirty Years War (1618–48) had devastated Germany, reducing its urban population by 33 per cent and its rural population by 45 per cent, so incipient warfare during the next 120 years laid waste much of central Europe and the Low Countries at regular intervals. Conventions applied by armies in relation to each other did not extend to civilian populations, as the French army's ravages in the Palatinate in 1688 and 1689 or both the Russian and Swedish armies' depredations in the Great Northern War (1700–21) well illustrate. In any case, for all their balletic appearance, battles were murderous affairs, the 'butcher's bill' at Malplaquet in 1709 of an estimated 36,000 casualties not being surpassed until the battle of Borodino in 1812. Borodino itself was then exceeded by the 127,000 casualties at the four day 'Battle of the Nations' at Leipzig in 1813. The cumulative effect of such conflict upon areas that were fought over was considerable. Equally, participation in five major wars between 1689 and 1783 was a major stimulus for English industry and trade at a crucial early stage in the world's first industrial revolution.

None the less, warfare was to become increasingly more total in its impact during the course of the nineteenth century, which can be taken as representing an extended transitional period. During the French Revolutionary and Napoleonic wars (1792–1815), the motive forces of nationalism and democracy combined to create a mass French citizen army through the introduction of universal male conscription. The success of this 'nation in arms' or 'armed horde' resulted in the example being emulated elsewhere, notably in Prussia. Although the concept of the nation in arms came under sustained attack after 1815 from monarchs and restored monarchs, who distrusted its social and political implications, the actual system of short-service conscription survived in Prussia. The military victories then won by Prussia in the German wars of unification of 1864, 1866 and 1870 and the ability of short-service conscription to produce large numbers of trained reserves upon mobilization encouraged European states—with the exception of Britain—to reintroduce Prussian-style conscription. Although the forms of universal service adopted were necessarily selective in practice, states were rapidly accepting the national birthrate as an index of military power. Moreover, the transformation wrought by the technological innovations of the industrial age, particularly the development of the railway, ensured that ever larger armies could be mobilized theoretically more quickly than hitherto and sustained in the field for far longer.

At the same time, industrialization dramatically increased the destructive capacity of armies by providing them with weapons of enhanced range, accuracy and rate of fire. By 1870, a firefight between opposing infantry, which might have been conducted at 60 yards range seventy years before, had now stretched to a possible 1,600 yards and a breechloading rifle such as the Prussian Dreyse now fired seven rounds for every one from a smoothbore musket of the Napoleonic era. By the 1880s and 1890s magazine rifles, quick-firing artillery and machine guns had all entered service with major European armies. Just before the First World War, most armies were also experimenting with aircraft, even if it appeared to require a considerable feat of imagination to conceive that airmen could offer any valuable intelligence while flying over the ground at speeds approaching 30 m.p.h. At sea, too, wood, sail and round shot had given way to iron and steel, steam and screw propellor, and shell, while mines, submarines and torpedoes all threatened the traditional supremacy of the capital ship.

Through the innate conservatism of European military and naval officer corps, the significance of much of the change that had taken place during the nineteenth century was misinterpreted. Contrary to popular belief, soldiers did recognize the problems inherent in crossing the so-called 'empty battlefield' in the face of modern firepower, but they believed mistakenly that they could solve the difficulty simply by closing with an enemy more rapidly. Moreover, the use of bayonet, lance and sabre implicit in this 'offensive spirit' ideally complemented traditional military ideals of honour and glory, which some feared devalued by the unwelcome intrusion of technology and professionalism into an overwhelmingly aristocratic occupation. While soldiers conspired to discount the more uncomfortable evidence of such conflicts as the American Civil War (1861–65), Franco-Prussian War (1870–71) and Russo-Japanese War (1904–5), civilians were equally seduced by the general trend in the later nineteenth century towards popular nationalism, imperialism, militarism and crude social Darwinism into a more ready acceptance of war and conflict as an appropriate test of nationhood and national virility. There were pacifists but, in 1914, it was nationalism and not inter-nationalism that triumphed across Europe. Similarly, a succession of international conferences, such as those at St Petersburg in 1868 or at the Hague in 1899 and 1907, failed to find a universal readiness among nation states to compromise their future freedom of manœuvre by accepting meaningful limitations on the actual conduct of war.

Wars between 1789 and 1914, while such developments were occurring, were hardly devoid of impact upon those societies that waged them. In the case of Britain, for example, the manpower problems experienced during the Crimean War (1854–56) were very similar to those encountered in the First World War, and losses sustained in the twenty years of almost continuous warfare between 1793 and 1815 were almost certainly proportionately higher in terms of men under arms than in the First World War. Military participation in Britain was also probably greater in proportion to the male population between 1793 and 1815, and it is at least arguable that the resulting social, economic and political upheaval in the immediate postwar period was of more significance for the future pattern of British society and democracy than developments in the aftermath of either of the world wars. Of course, the wars of German and Italian unification were of very limited duration, but they still had profound political consequences for Europe.

There was once a tendency to view the American Civil War largely in terms of its military developments and to focus upon such innovations as armoured trains, the first clash of armoured warships, the first loss of ships to mines and submarine torpedoes, the first extensive use of the telegraph, and so on. In fact, the largely amateur armies fought the war on the battlefield as if it were the last Napoleonic encounter rather than the 'first modern war' but it is now recognized widely that the war was truly modern in terms of its impact upon society. Both the northern states of the Union and the southern states of the Confederacy deployed large numbers of men in the field but, for the predominantly agricultural Confederacy, war also demanded efforts to create an industrial economy to challenge the far greater manufacturing potential of the North. It had become essential to outproduce as well as to outfight an opponent. Despite its efforts at industrialization, the mobilization of 75 per cent of its white male population, and unprecedented participation by white women and blacks in industry and agriculture, the Confederacy was doomed to defeat by the superiority of the North's numbers and resources. The inescapable logic of the attempt to create a war economy was the recognition that a society that sustained a war became as much a legitimate target for military action as an army that waged war on its behalf. Thus, in the autumn of 1864, Sheridan's Union forces swept down the southern 'bread basket' of the Shenandoah valley while Sherman's armies wrought equal destruction in cutting a swathe from Atlanta to the sea in November and December 1864 and through the Carolinas in the following months in a determination to expose the Confederacy to the 'hard hand of war'.

The world wars

Thus, there are sufficient examples of the way in which the impact of war upon society was increasing through the nineteenth century to suggest that the world wars should be regarded as a natural progression from earlier conflicts rather than as unique. But, of course, this is not to suggest that the impact of world war was not greater than that of earlier wars through the sheer scale of conflict enhancing the effect. Quite obviously, both world wars were global in scope, although both began as European conflicts. In the First World War, the Central Powers comprised Imperial Germany, Austria-Hungary, Ottoman Turkey (from October 1914) and Bulgaria (from October 1915), but the Allies eventually embraced twenty-two states including the major European powers of Britain, France, Imperial Russia and Italy (from May 1915) and their colonies and dependencies, and also Japan, the United States (from March 1917), Liberia (from August 1917) and Brazil (from October 1917). Similarly, the Second World War widened with the aggression of Germany, Italy (from June 1940 to September 1943) and Japan (from December 1941) bringing in the Soviet Union (from June 1941) and the United States (from December 1941), although the Soviet Union did not join in the war against Japan until August 1945. Successive German and Soviet occupation contributed to a bewildering proliferation of contradictory declarations of war by many eastern European states during the war, while, between February and March 1945, no less than ten states ranging from Peru to Saudi Arabia declared war on both Germany and Japan and a further two on Japan alone.

Total war therefore implies a far wider global conflict than previous wars and, while limited war suggests a degree of constraint, self-imposed or otherwise, total war implies a lack of constraint. In practice, total war was still a relative concept in both world wars since, as an absolute, it was unrealizable through a lack of instantaneously destructive weapons. Nevertheless, belligerents could not be accused of failing to attempt the absolute even if they were unable to mobilize all their resources at the same time and at the same point. In effect, they employed all the weapons they felt appropriate rather than all the weapons available in every case. The array and potential of weapons increased dramatically over previous wars. For example, in eight days before the opening of the British offensive on the Somme on the Western Front on 1 July 1916, British artillery fired 1.7 million shells at German positions. In fourteen days preceding the opening of the Passchendaele offensive on 31 July 1917, the British fired 4.2 million shells. In addition to the weight of shell, horrendous new weapons were introduced in search of an elusive breakthrough. Gas was first used on the Western Front at Langemarck near Ypres on 22 April 1915, although it had previously been used by the Germans at Bolimov on the Eastern Front, and, in July 1915, flamethrowers were used effectively for the first time by the Germans at Hooge near Ypres. In all, over 150,000 tons of varying gases were produced during the First World War and caused an estimated 1.2 million casualties, of which more than 91,000 proved fatal. Tanks were also introduced for the first time by the British on the Somme on 15 September 1916.

Although gas was not used in the Second World War other than in the context of Nazi genocide, its military use was pressed by a powerful military-industrial lobby in Germany. There were also considerable technological advances that further enhanced the destructive power of the belligerents. Paradoxically, the speed of the early German *Blitzkriegs* actually made these operations less costly in terms of casualties than trench warfare during the First World War but, equally, there was the development in the capacity to bring aerial destruction to civilian populations. Ultimately, Germany utilized its V1 and V2 rockets and the Allies, of course, dropped the first atomic weapons on Japan.

The conscious abandonment of most if not all restraints was paralleled by the wider war aims adopted by belligerents in total war. Limited dynastic aims had given way to sweeping territorial aggrandisement and the total destruction of states and of peoples. It could be argued in this respect that the necessary manipulation of the population of democratic states through propaganda and other means, in so far as this proved possible, in order to sustain the war effort introduced as great a push towards total war aims as the attempt by authoritarian or totalitarian states to impose their ideologies on others. Thus, on the one hand, the Germans pursued total domination in the Second World War, while Britain and the United States adopted a declaration of the need for the unconditional surrender of Germany at the Casablanca conference in January 1943. At Cairo in November and December 1943 Britain, the United States and nationalist China also agreed to strip Japan of all those overseas possessions taken by her forces since 1894.

Quite clearly, the participation of many states and their willingness to use extreme means to achieve wide aims resulted in destruction of life and property on an unprecedented scale compared with previous wars. In all, the First World War is thought to have resulted in 10 million dead and 20 million maimed or seriously wounded, leaving 5 million women widows and 9 million children orphans. The Second World War may have cost 30 million dead in Europe, although other estimates put Soviet losses alone at well over 20 million dead. Although figures for the First World War usually exclude an estimated 1.5 million Armenians exterminated by the Turks in 1915, those for the Second World War do include an estimated 5.9 million Jewish victims of Nazi genocide. Moreover, as many as 26 million people may have become displaced from their country of origin during the Second World War through forced transportation or other reasons: in Britain alone, which did not suffer such displacement, there were still 60 million changes of address during the Second World War. Compared with previous wars, also, civilians had become subject to sustained and deliberate attack to an unprecedented degree. During the First World War, some 1413 British civilians were killed by aerial attack, but, between 1939 and 1945, German bombers and rockets accounted for 51,509 civilian deaths in Britain. Hamburg suffered approximately 50,000 dead in a week in July and August 1943, and calculations of the loss of life at Dresden on a single night in February 1945 range from 35,000 to 135,000. In all, total German civilian losses to aerial bombardment may have been 593,000 during the Second World War. USAAF 'fire raids' on Japan caused an estimated 100,000 deaths in Tokyo on one night in March 1945, or approximately the same number of immediate deaths at both Hiroshima and Nagasaki combined in August 1945.

[From Colin McInnes and G. D. Sheffield (eds.), *Warfare in the Twentieth Century: Theory and Practice* (London: Unwin Hyman, 1988), 3–9.]

ANDREW LAMBERT

73 Crimean Illusions

The object of this article is to demonstrate that the 'Crimean War' so familiar to twentieth-century students of history has no historical reality; the conflict discussed under that label has been created by misguided and derivative scholarship. The very term 'Crimean War' is a later gloss, one that can be dated back to the 1890s, which developed from a concentration on the most newsworthy events of the war, rather than the intentions of the policymakers. The Crimea never held the central position in strategic decision-making that it has achieved in historical studies. The war did not begin or end in the Crimean Peninsula, it was not decided there, and the end of the sanguinary siege of Sevastopol on 9 September 1855 had little bearing on the Russian decision to accept the allied terms in March 1856. Furthermore the British and French never occupied the city of Sevastopol. Contemporary observers were well aware that the Crimean campaign was only a part of the wider Black Sea theatre, and of the vital linkage with the equally significant Baltic theatre. Insofar as allied military pressure had any bearing on Russia's decision to accept terms, that pressure came from the Royal Navy in the Baltic.

The accepted view of the war can be summarised briefly. Russia, reacting to French pressure on Turkey, made heavy-handed demands which amounted to a marked reduction in the independence of the Sultan in his own dominions. These were rejected by the Turks, which in turn forced Britain to support the Sultan in concert with France. Russia occupied the Danubian Principalities (modern day Romania) to coerce Turkey into accepting her terms. Britain and France sent their fleets to Besika Bay (just outside the Dardanelles) to support Turkey without providing Russia with a cause of war. When Russia refused to leave the Principalities, the western powers moved up to cover Constantinople. The Russian fleet then destroyed a Turkish squadron at Sinope on the southern shore of the Black Sea, forcing the allies to react. The allied ultimatum of 27 March 1854 demanded that Russia withdraw from the Principalities. Allied troops occupied the Gallipoli peninsula, before moving up to Constantinople and then on to Varna (on the coast of modern Bulgaria). Under pressure from Austria the Russian army withdrew from the Principalities without coming into contact with the allies. This secured Turkey's Danube Front, enabling the allies to invade the Crimea in September 1854. After a year-long siege, characterised by the heroism of the troops and the incompetence of their commanders and of the politicians at home, the city finally fell to an assault on 9 September 1855. Thereafter the war drew to an unsatisfactory close in January 1856, heavily influenced by an Austrian Ultimatum demanding that Russia accept the mild allied terms. The other campaigns, in Asia Minor, the Baltic, the White Sea and the Pacific, were of no significance. [. . .]

The Crisis that foreshadowed the Crimean War became a serious issue for the British government in March 1853, on receipt of the first reports of the mission of Prince Menshikov, the Russian Envoy to Constantinople. The Ministry of Lord Aberdeen, a coalition between the small Peelite Party and the Whig/Liberal Party, was particularly ill-suited to meet the situation. Aberdeen and his fellow Peelites feared and distrusted the new Emperor of France, Louis Napoleon III, while the Whigs considered Czar Nicholas I to be the personification of repression. As the resolution of the crisis required Britain to stand alongside one or other of these powers the debate was long, and often turbulent. The decision to support France was based more on her inability to overthrow Turkey than any faith in her motives.

In the 12 months before war broke out the First Lord of the Admiralty, the Peelite Sir James Graham, prepared two plans to take the war to Russia, gain the initiative and hopefully create a wider alliance to secure an early victory without a large-scale mobilisation of British forces. In the Black Sea he always looked to destroy Sevastopol, the Russian naval base, either by naval or amphibious attack. The operation was finally carried out largely as he had intended. However, where he envisaged a two week-long grand raid, the problems of allied command and the risks of the undertaking resulted in a year-long siege. In the other major theatre, the Baltic, Graham revived the plan set out by Lord Nelson after the Battle of Copenhagen, to attack the Russian battle-squadron based at Reval in April, before the ice that covers much of the Baltic during the winter had melted far enough to allow the ships to escape, or to be reinforced from the main base at Cronstadt. In the event the Russians withdrew their ships in the autumn of 1853. Graham consulted few of his colleagues in preparing these plans, and the Sevastopol strategy crept into the cabinet's thoughts by a process of osmosis rather than deliberation. [. . .]

Allied Strategy

Palmerston had a very clear conception of the long-term interests of Britain; he realised that Russia and the United States would be the real rival for British world power once they had harnessed their continental resources and made full use of the technology that Britain pioneered. To sustain British primacy he favoured exploiting the opportunity of 1854, and specifically the French alliance, to inflict a defeat on Russia that would set her back a generation or more. In 1861–63 a similar opportunity beckoned in the New World, but domestic and French support were not available, the real possibility of British intervention in the American Civil War was forestalled, although the vision remained. In fact both Russia and the United States were to suffer such damage that they did not threaten British interests until the end of the nineteenth century.

The decision to attack Sevastopol was the only major strategic decision taken by allied statesmen before the problems of the Crimean campaign began to dictate the direction of the war. Once ashore the allies could not leave until they had beaten the Russians. As a result the wider Black Sea theatre, including support for rebels in Georgia and Circassia and the Turkish Asian front, were given little attention. Essentially the allies elected to open their Black Sea campaign with a major raid. Their failure to carry out the original plan forced them to spend the winter outside Sevastopol, which had never been intended, and exposed the armies to the full rigour of a particularly harsh winter under canvas. When the British, and to a lesser extent French, public became aware of this it became politically imperative to secure an early improvement in the condition of the troops, and some dramatic results to deflect the widespread dissatisfaction with the conduct of the ministers. Lord Aberdeen's government fell in January 1855, to be replaced by many of the same ministers, partly shuffled into new offices, under Lord Palmerston, who was popularly believed to be the one man capable of 'winning' the war. In fact Palmerston's period as war premier proved particularly frustrating. He could not persuade his colleagues to enlarge on the Four Points, to facilitate the aggressive war against Russia that he really desired, and he had to accept an increasing degree of French direction of the war in the Crimea. The first problem reflected the weakness of his political position, the latter the weakness of the British army which was reduced to raising corps of mercenaries from Switzerland, Germany and Italy to supplement the slow recruitment of domestic troops.

French war aims were never identical to those of Britain. Louis Napoleon desired a quick victory to raise the prestige of his regime, and a European Congress to overthrow the Vienna settlement of 1815 and reestablish France as a dominant force in world politics. As the leader of a military power, who had used the army to seize power in 1851, Louis depended on the support of his generals. In consequence he was only interested in a military success in the Crimea. The French treated British concern over the fate of the Turkish fortress at Kars in Asia Minor, and the support of the Circassian rebels, as merely attempts to protect the routes to India, refusing to lend any support, or even to countenance the movement of the Turkish army in the Crimea to Asia Minor until after the fall of Sevastopol. With a curious irony, the fall of Sevastopol was brought about by a naval campaign that the French twice attempted to cancel.

The Fall of Sevastopol

Sevastopol was never surrounded by allied troops, the north side of the harbour was always open, and any number of troops and all types of supplies could be sent in by the main Russian army, which lay inland near Simpheropol. Whenever the allies pressed hard on Sevastopol the Russian field army would move onto the allied flank, at Balaclava and then Inkerman in late 1854, to force the British and French to stop the siege. This link between the Russian army and the fortress had been created by Prince Menshikov, the Russian Commander-in-Chief, who has generally been considered very unsatisfactory. Yet for nine months his strategy effectively kept the allies out of Sevastopol, and forced them to fight a campaign of attrition at the end of supply lines 3,000 miles long. Only the availability of steam shipping enabled the British and to a lesser extent the French to hang on through the severe winter, and then to build up a force of men and artillery that could win this battle. However, before any decisive moves could be made the allies had to break the link between the Russian field army and the city. Louis Napoleon and the French high command proposed taking the field to surround the city, but the allies never had sufficient troops to carry out such a plan.

Realising that the campaign had become a contest of strength rather than skill the British, particularly Sir James Graham, advocated an attack on Russian logistics. By occupying the Sea of Azov with a squadron of gunboats in May 1855 the British effectively cut off the Russian army from its main supply base in the basin of the River Don. Road transport, still drawn by horses and bullocks, could not replace the loss of water transport across the Sea of Azov, and the Russian army was forced to relinquish the defence of Sevastopol. In August the Russians staged a desperate frontal assault on strong allied defences, and only weeks later abandoned the city, after standing one last assault. However, having retreated across Sevastopol harbour they used the high northern shore to erect batteries that dominated the city, and prevented the allies from occupying it in safety. For the remainder of the war the two armies sat and watched one another across a deep moat, too exhausted and cautious to move.

Once Sevastopol had fallen allied attention switched to the wider theatre. The British were worried, with good cause in the event, for the Turkish-Asian border fortress of Kars, which surrendered on 23 November. Palmerston and others wanted to move the British army to Asia Minor in 1856, the French preferred to operate around Odessa. On 17 October 1855 an Anglo-French amphibious taskforce captured the Fortress at Kinburn, which covered the entrance to the River Bug, Russia's main transport route from the interior, and the site of her main shipyard, at Nicolaiev some 20 miles from the sea. The operation was noteworthy for the first use in combat of armour-plated warships, but was not followed up. After that the Black Sea theatre became quiet, the allies used the winter to ponder on their strategy, the Russians to reflect on the logistic and sanitary disaster that was rapidly reducing their army to a series of full hospitals and large burial details.

The Baltic Theatre

If there is any single aspect of the 'Crimean War' that stands in need of revision it is the importance of the Baltic Campaigns. Paul Kennedy was merely following a long line of scholars when he dismissed them as 'never very serious', in his latest book. Sir James Graham's prewar hopes for the Baltic were disappointed in March 1854 since there were no Russian ships at Reval, and the Swedish government was not interested in joining the allies. These two events were decisive for 1854, because the powerful British fleet of large battleships and cruisers did not have a single small gunboat or mortar vessel to carry the war to the Russian forts and harbours, and had no troops for amphibious operations. Graham had depended on Sweden for these resources. Without them he was forced to accept a French army, which was used to capture the fortress of Bomarsund in the Aland Islands, midway between Sweden and Russian Finland. To avoid the well-deserved criticism that should have been made of his policy Graham made a scapegoat of the Admiral Commanding the Fleet, Sir Charles Napier, at the time he was building the very gunboats and mortar vessels he had refused to prepare earlier in the year, when Napier requested them.

In 1855, while all attention was turned to Sevastopol, the Baltic fleet used its gunboats and mortar vessels to destroy the Russian dockyard at Sweaborg (outside modern Helsinki) in August. This success, added to that at Kinburn in October, pointed the way forward for the British government. With France increasingly looking for an early compromise peace, Palmerston had to find a major strategic move for early 1856 that would force Russia to concede his terms. Unable to rely on France, and lacking anything like the necessary number of troops for a military solution, he fell back, unwillingly, on the naval plan. In both Baltic campaigns an outstanding Naval Officer, Captain Bartholomew Sulivan had directed all the major operations, and minutely examined the Russian defences. He proposed using a large force of armoured batteries, mortar vessels and gunboats supported by rocket firing boats, the regular fleet and a large force of Royal Marines to bombard and capture the main Russian naval base at Cronstadt. Cronstadt was also the seaward defence of St Petersburg (modern Leningrad); if Cronstadt were captured the Russian capital would be open to allied attack. To carry out the attack, without the aid of France, the Royal Navy prepared the 'Great Armament of 1856' a force of 250 steam gunboats, 100 mortar vessels, 10 armoured batteries and numerous supporting craft to be ready for operations in April 1856. Only Britain had the industrial and financial strength required to carry out this programme in such a short space of time.

Why Russia Accepted the Allied Terms

In January 1856 the Russian Council of Ministers discussed the Austrian Ultimatum, which they realised was a mere gesture while the Austrian Army was in process of demobilising. They saw no real danger in the Black Sea theatre, but were very concerned by developments closer to home. The Russian economy had collapsed under the pressure of a strict British blockade. The only real friend left to the Russians, Prussia, was now urging them to accept terms, while Sweden had aligned herself with the allies in return for a guarantee of her territorial integrity and it was rumoured that she was now committed to joining the war. However, the catalyst for a year of disasters would be the capture of Cronstadt. After the fall of Sevastopol the great engineer General Totleben had been recalled to work on the island fortress and every effort was in progress. However, the technological superiority and boundless confidence of the Royal Navy gave them an edge that should have proved decisive. Rather than take the risk of defeat Russia accepted the humiliation of allied terms. In consequence the 'Great Armament' never reached the Baltic, let alone attacked Cronstadt.

One area where existing accounts are particularly faulty is in their appreciation of the long-term consequences of the 'Crimean War'. The defeat suffered by Russia forced her to abandon her dominant influence in central Europe. Within 15 years Prussia had used the power vacuum to create a unified Germany, and until the Red Army destroyed the Third Reich in 1945 Russia never recovered the position of 1853. Prince Albert celebrated the removal of Russian influence from Germany as the one great result of the war, George V and Kaiser Wilhelm II might well have reflected on the truth of that in the years after 1918. The war also highlighted the internal weakness of Russia. Economically backward, with almost all capital tied up in land and the labour force tied into the soil, it was impossible to create new industries, or raise fresh armies. The same Crown Council meeting that accepted the allied terms in January 1856 also agreed to the abolition of the status of serf. While it required another seven years to implement this decision it should be stressed that its origins lay in war and defeat, not liberal humanity.

The Great Armament for 1856 assembled at Spithead as the Peace Conference began to deliberate in Paris. The sheer size of the force was used by the British diplomats to silence any attempt by Russia to evade the allied terms. Influential neutrals were encouraged to inspect these mighty preparations, and reports were doubtless soon available in St Petersburg. Once the war was officially over the Baltic Fleet staged a triumphal Review, suitably enough on St George's Day 1856. The warning should have been clear to every major nation of the world. The Royal Navy had the power to destroy any naval arsenal and the fleet that sheltered inside. British seapower had reached its very zenith, unrivalled in strength, technical skill and experience. When Britain and Russia next came close to blows over Turkey, in 1877–79, Russia backed down. One British fleet lay off Constantinople, another was assembled at home for a campaign in the Baltic. British seapower was never the passive, defensive asset portrayed by twentieth-century commentators looking for the earliest possible period from which to date Britain's Imperial decline. By contrast it remained unrivalled as a sea control force and a means of amphibious power projection until the early years of the Second World War.

[From Andrew Lambert, 'The Crimean War, 1854–56: An Historical Illusion', *Modern History Review* (Nov. 1991), 11–14.]

GEOFFREY BEST

74 Restraints on Land War

[T]he Revolutionary and Napoleonic [wars] certainly witnessed a great quantity of the horrors and disasters which it is the object of the law of war to avert; yet the idea of the law of war was never seriously disputed or rejected; and the century which followed proved to be, in fact, its golden age, with the 1860s as its golden decade. That was when the converging streams of international humanitarian opinion, international law (developing very fast through the second half of the nineteenth century) and military modernization produced the three great landmarks of our modern Law of War. In 1863, United States Army General Order No. 100, *Instructions for the Government of Armies of the United States in the Field*, provided the first example of a manual for the conduct of war on land comprehensively attentive to the current state of customary law and the standards which a self-respecting civilized state should set for itself. Also known as 'Lieber's Code' (after the excellent German-born jurist who was principally responsible for it), it became the basis for all subsequent discussion and formulation through the next fifty years. In 1864 the first Geneva Convention, designed for the protection of the sick and wounded in land war, marked the great step forward of an international agreement signed by 'high contracting parties' for their common restraint and welfare. Four years later, in 1868, the St Petersburg Convention prohibited the use of certain types of missiles on the ground that belligerents were not unrestricted in their means of making war, and that therefore missiles of unnecessary nastiness could and should properly be outlawed.

From the 1860s to the First World War it was almost possible, perhaps, to measure the extent of the hold which the idea of restraint in war had on the public mind of Europe by the volume of clamour alleging the breaking or the neglect of it. This happy phase began with the Franco-Prussian War. The Prussians gave their opponents a propaganda opportunity they perhaps need not have given, and the French made the most of it. The world was soon more than adequately informed about German severity against French partisans and their civilian supporters; the *francs-tireurs* which then made such a stir in the world and continued to haunt the German military imagination through 1914. The world was also made fully aware of the German bombardments of Strasbourg, Peronne etc. and of course, climactically, Paris. These German excesses, if indeed they were such, which was arguable, were in areas of that customary law which by now was filling fat sections of the international law books. But when it came to breaches or neglects of the Geneva Convention, the first bit of international statute law, no one could doubt as to which of the two great powers was more at fault. The Germans took it seriously and observed it quite creditably. The French were doubly at fault, first, in not knowing much about it, and second, when they did wake up to its existence, by getting it wrong. [. . .]

The Geneva Convention and its governing idea thus came out of the Franco-Prussian war somewhat battered, and in Germany above all there was a great deal of indignation at the way the French had failed to understand and observe it, and the ways in which, as many Germans seemed to have felt, their conscientious observance of it under such circumstances had involved them in some disadvantages. But despite these mishaps, there was nothing here which could not be put right by improved legislation. The Red Cross from now on was a force to be reckoned with. Between 1871 and the 1914–18 war there was a positive vogue for it as a mixed philanthropic and patriotic venture in which the highest-born could engage without loss of status and in which civilians could do something war-related without much risk, to an extent which made some think that the age of chivalry (Burke's, not Froissart's) had returned.

No more extraordinary instance of this could be found than an incident during the war between Serbia and Bulgaria in late 1885. The Red Cross societies in each country sought supplies from the wealthier countries of Europe; those supplies were plentifully available and were routed towards them through Vienna. It was not difficult to transport them from Vienna to Belgrade but to get them to Sofia was a different question, the main lines from Vienna to Sofia running through Serbia! The Austrian Red Cross society, however, sought from King Milan of Serbia permission to send the supplies destined for Bulgaria through his territory. Permission was granted and the Red Cross materials were safely conducted to the Bulgarian outposts. The explanation of this episode must be as unusual as was the episode itself, because the Balkans were the last place in Europe (except perhaps the Iberian peninsula) in which, as a matter of historic fact, humanity in war was commonly expected or found. The episode nevertheless occurred and it fitted well with the mood of an epoch which supported internationalism and the peace movement and took pride in its spreading humanitarianism at the same time as its militarists, nationalists, and imperialists were egging on the first great arms race; an epoch which therefore not surprisingly culminated in the conferences at the Hague in 1899 and 1907 called Conferences for Peace and Disarmament but clearly more bent towards what Joseph Conrad, a curiously close observer of those doings, called the 'solemnly official recognition of the Earth as a House of Strife'. Much the same judgement on the ambivalent character of the Hague Conferences may be found in a remark made by a Japanese diplomat to a European one at that time. The 1899 Hague Conference was the first at which the Japanese were present as international equals of the European and American powers which had hitherto engrossed the making of international law. But by what title had Japan got there? 'We show ourselves at least your equals in scientific butchery, and at once we are admitted to your council tables as civilized men.' The Japanese diplomat seems to have been a bit worried about the moral character of the club his country had just joined.

[. . .] [T]he assembling of the laws of land war [. . .] was virtually completed between 1899 and 1907. Between then and the end of the Second World War, very little more was added. To the Hague Convention and Rules of those years, regarded as a code of combat law, nothing subsequently was added except the 1925 Geneva protocol on Gas Warfare. Indeed there was more movement in the Geneva line of explicitly humanitarian law. The 1864 convention which experience had shown to be unsatisfactory in several important respects was replaced by a better one in 1906 (better, anyway, from the soldier's point of view) and by other even better ones in 1929 when prisoners of war also became recognized as primary subjects of Red Cross concern. Such were the three levels of restraint at which the two world wars were supposed to be fought: the international conventions associated with the Hague and Geneva; the manuals of military conduct in which each armed service embodied the conventions and rules to which its Government had agreed, but which of course went far beyond them in scope and detail; and, what too often has been left out of account, the notions of the members of those armed services themselves about restraint, some of which worked for it and some of which clearly did not. [. . .]

Have the Geneva and Hague Conventions (taking them together, as we now may, as converging branches of international humanitarian law) proved worthwhile?

The first thing one observes as one surveys this body of law is the limitation of its scope; in particular that, until after 1945, very little of it was concerned with 'civilians'. Since 1945, it has become a commonplace that civilians are the category of persons most in need of whatever protection an up-dated law of war can offer; and it is towards that end that has been directed much of the thrust of the last ten years' intense activity in respect of the reaffirmation and development of the law of war. What happened to civilians earlier? And what happened by the end of the Second World War to create the ineffaceable impression that a more systematic regard for them was long overdue?

The theory about civilians from early days (i.e. since eighteenth-century writers began systematically to take note of them, in the age of 'limited wars') was that civilians were best kept right out of it. Wars, they maintained, were properly fought by 'armies'; by armed forces anyway, whether regulars or militiamen, raised by states for the special business of armed conflict and prudently controlled therein. No eighteenth-century government put arms into the hands of its subjects if it could help it. Just as it was desirable not to arm civilians, so to the mind of the eighteenth-century writers it was not necessary to harm them either. They rarely got in the way of the fighting unless they were unlucky enough to inhabit a village which became part of the battlefield or a fortified town which became besieged. Humanitarianism chimed in nicely with official self-interest to recommend the observance of a distinction between combatants and non-combatants. Non-combatants were of more value to all parties if they were allowed to carry on with their own business as peasants, traders, merchants etc. They were of more value to armies because you could get more out of a civilian populace by regulated requisitioning than by wasteful looting and vengeful destruction, which moreover was bad for discipline besides provoking resistance. Non-combatants were of more value to governments because their freedom and security kept in better shape the wealth-producing sectors of society upon whom governments and governing élites ultimately rested, whether they were winners or losers. Furthermore, there might not be much point in a victor's acquisition of territory which had been devastated and depopulated.

So the law of war in those formulative years of the eighteenth and early nineteenth centuries prescribed as fundamental that distinction between combatant and non-combatant which ever since has been a central part of it, and military practice then found it not too difficult to observe. This was because armies were so much smaller than they became after the French Revolution, because they were often under rigid and effective discipline, and because their systematic provisioning had become an expert and prominent if laborious part of the business of conducting military operations.

[From Geoffrey Best, 'Restraints on War by Land before 1945', in Michael Howard (ed.), *Restraints on War* (Oxford: Clarendon Press, 1977), 20–8.]

DOUGLAS PORCH

75 The Tactical Offensive in France

The tactical offensive was [. . .] aided [in the French Army] by the development of new techniques in modern warfare. It did not flourish, as historians would have it, in ignorance of those developments. General Fuller accused Foch of being a 'tactically demented Napoleon' and ignoring new developments in weaponry. 'Step by step,' he said, 'with a few variations, he follows Napoleon in the face of magazine rifles and quick-firing artillery as if they were the muskets and cannon of Jena and Freidland.' De La Gorce maintains the French 'ignored the firepower of modern armaments, and especially of heavy artillery and under-estimated the effectiveness of defensive tactics'. Liddell Hart said that: 'The new French philosophy, by its preoccupation with the moral element, had become more and more separated from the inseparable material factors.' But it was those very material factors that led to the logical evolution of the offensive. Armaments development required an almost constant reassessment of tactics. Colonel Langlois wrote:

The instability of the (tactical) regulations . . . results from the instability of our modern conditions. If formerly tactics changed every ten years, according to Napoleon, they change more frequently today, and the regulations must be constantly modified. This is a fact of life. However, the broader the terms in which the regulations are couched, the less the detail, the more durable they will be.

The republican doctrine of the offensive provided a durable tactical law. The only way to cope with the new technical developments despite poor French resources was to rely on the patriotic audacity of French soldiers.

Increased firepower was the most critical technical development in late nineteenth-century warfare. The modern rifle, machine gun and cannon compelled military pundits to re-think established tactical theory. Soldiers who once fought successfully in a relatively close order now had to spread out under fire or risk heavy casualities. With a greatly extended battlefield, officers and NCOs could no longer control or keep track of their men in combat. Simon feared that discipline would be the first casualty unless soldiers were fired by patriotic zeal:

When a company deploys a rank, on a 290-meter front . . . many will not hear orders. The men will no longer see their leaders. They have no-one in front to lead them, no-one behind to push them . . . Nothing is left to keep them moving forward but the individual will to conquer . . . History testifies that the soldiers who fight best when dispersed are those with the strongest patriotism and will to conquer, and the strongest devotion to their leaders and comrades. Soldiers without these feelings can be led into the attack only in relatively close formations . . . The more armaments are developed, the more dispersal becomes necessary and the more individual moral strength is needed.

General Langlois advocated the offensive for the same reasons: 'In any charge, direct commands are lost on fighting soldiers. It becomes every man for himself. A man's individual training and his moral health are therefore of paramount importance in modern combat.' General Bazaine-Hayter, Thirteenth Corps Commander, wrote in October 1906:

Firepower does not weaken the offensive spirit. Never forget that a defensive battle will seldom bring victory. However powerful weapons become, the victory will go to the offensive, which stimulates moral force, disconcerts the enemy and deprives him of his freedom of action.

The advantages of morale in the face of modern armaments were held to have been demonstrated in the Russo-Japanese War of 1905. The superior moral preparation of the Japanese soldiers had more than compensated for modern Russian armaments and those who maintained that the Boer War had put paid to the offensive were discredited. The devastating rifle fire of the Boer War was proof of exceptional Boer marksmanship, but more importantly revealed the sorry state of the British army—professional soldiers led by upper class officers. Joffre wrote later:

The Russo-Japanese War was a dazzling confirmation of General Langlois' view that the Boer War had not discredited the offensive. Under the direction of Foch, Lanrezac and Bourderiat, the young intellectual elite at the école de guerre now threw out the divisive old doctrine [the primacy of the defensive based on Franco-Prussian War experience]. But as always happens when established ideas are challenged, the value of the offensive was exaggerated by this group. People have referred to the 'mystique of the offensive'.

This is probably going too far. But it does demonstrate rather well the somewhat irrational character the cult of the offensive took after 1905.

Moral training was placed high for a second practical reason—the ever increasing superiority of German military strength. The French birthrate had dropped after 1870 so that by the turn of the century Germany's population was larger by fifteen million. France made prodigious efforts to overcome this deficiency in army terms, conscripting 5,620 men for each million inhabitants as compared to 4,120 per million in Germany. But in 1903 she was able to muster only 459,000 men and 25,000 officers to 621,000 men and 26,000 officers across the Vosges. With the approach of war, this situation worsened. The 1913 military law voted by the Reichstag gave the German army an almost two to one edge over the French, creating places for 42,000 officers and 112,000 NCOs to 29,000 officers and 48,000 NCOs in France. The long term projections were even more sobering: in 1932 Germany's military resources were estimated at 5,400,000 trained men, compared with a maximum of four million in France.

Although French military expenditure accounted for 36 per cent of the national budget, against only 20 per cent in Germany, in real terms the French investment fell far short of the German figure. Klotz, president of the parliamentary army committee, put the 1904 defence figures at 38,256,364 francs compared with the equivalent of 99,195,998 francs spent in Germany in the same year. General Langlois calculated in 1908 that Germany spent the equivalent of 1,770 francs per soldier while France spent only 914. 'This shows the efforts our eastern neighbours have made to equip and train their army . . . happily, we still have the moral emphasis which we must consider a headstart,' he said.

France therefore had to look for superiority in other spheres. 'To fight in dispersed order, a soldier must compensate for the lack of material support by a more solid moral preparation,' André wrote. 'We want an army which compensates numerical weakness with military quality,' Messimy stated in 1908. 'Neither numbers nor miraculous machines will determine victory', he said in 1913. 'This will go to soldiers with valour and "quality"—and by this I mean superior physical and moral endurance, offensive strength.' Patrice Mahon gauged that only drive could beat numbers: 'The truth', he said, 'is that the only possible way of overcoming Germany's more efficient mobilisation is to confront them with our offensive.' With these substantial material handicaps, France had to oppose mind to Germany's main. 'It is much more important to develop a conquering state of mind than to cavil about tactics,' Grandmaison concluded.

[From Douglas Porch, 'The French Army and the Spirit of the Offensive', in Brian Bond and Ian Roy (eds.), *War and Society* (London: Croom Helm, 1976), 135–7.]

STEPHEN E. AMBROSE

76 The Secrets of Overlord

On June 6, 1944, the United States, Britain, and Canada launched the largest force of warships in history across the English Channel. It escorted the largest concentration of troop transport vessels ever assembled, covered by the largest force of fighter and bomber aircraft ever brought together, preceded by a fleet of air transports that had carried tens of thousands of paratroopers and glider-borne troops to Normandy.

Not one German submarine, not one small boat, not one airplane, not one radar set, not one German anywhere detected this movement. As

General Walter Warlimont, deputy head of operations of the German Supreme Headquarters, later confessed, on the eve of Overlord the Wehrmacht leaders 'had not the slightest idea that the decisive event of the war was upon them'.

In World War I, surprise on a grand scale was seldom attempted and rarely achieved. In World War II, it was always sought and sometimes achieved—as with the Japanese attack on Pearl Harbor and the German invasion of Russia, both in 1941, and the German attack in the Ardennes in 1940 and again in 1944. One reason for this difference between the wars was that World War II commanders judged surprise to be more critical to victory than a preattack artillery bombardment. In the age of machine guns, other rapid-fire artillery, and land mines, the defenders could make almost any position virtually impregnable, no matter how heavy the pre-attack bombardment. Another reason for the increased emphasis on surprise was that the much greater mobility of World War II armed forces made surprise more feasible and more effective. Because of improvements in and more imaginative use of the internal-combustion engine (especially in tanks and trucks), the geographic area in which the conflict was fought was much larger in World War II. The preinvasion bombardment for Overlord, carried out by aircraft, was spread all across France and Belgium. It may have wasted a lot of bombs, but it also kept the Germans from discerning a pattern that would indicate the invasion site.

None of the surprises achieved in World War II was more complex, more difficult, more important, or more successful than Overlord. To fool Hitler and his generals in the battle of wits that preceded the attack, the Allies had to convince them not only that it was coming where it was not but also that the real thing was a feint. The first objective could be achieved by attacking in an unexpected, indeed illogical, place, and by maintaining total security about the plan. The second required convincing Hitler that the Allied invasion force was about twice as powerful as it actually was.

That there would be landings in France in the late spring of 1944 was universally known. Exactly where and when were the questions. To learn those secrets, the Germans maintained a huge intelligence organization that included spies inside Britain, air reconnaissance, monitoring of the British press and BBC, radio intercept stations, decoding experts, interrogation of Allied airmen shot down in Germany, research on Allied economies, and more.

The importance of surprise was obvious. In World War I it was judged that to have any chance at success, the attacking force had to outnumber the defenders by at least three to one. But in Overlord the attacking force of 175,000 men would be outnumbered by the Wehrmacht, even at the point of attack, and the overall figures (German troops in Western Europe versus Allied troops in the United Kingdom) showed a two-to-one German advantage. Doctrine in the German army was to meet an attack with an immediate counterattack. In this case, the Germans could move reinforcements to the battle much faster than the Allies, because they could bring them in by train, by truck, and on foot, while the Allies had to bring them in by ship. The Germans had storage and supply dumps all over France; the Allies had to bring every shell, every bullet, every drop of gasoline, every bandage across the Channel.

Allied intelligence worked up precise tables on the Germans' ability to move reinforcements into the battle area. The conclusion was that if the Germans correctly gauged Overlord as the main assault and marched immediately, within a month they could concentrate thirty-one divisions in the battle area, including nine panzer divisions. The Allies could not match that buildup rate.

In the face of these obstacles, the Allies managed to maintain a deception about their true intentions even after the battle began. How they did so is a remarkable story.

Thousands of men and women were involved, but perhaps the most important, and certainly the most dramatic, were the dozen or so members of BI(a), the counterespionage arm of MI5, the British internal-security agency. Using a variety of sources, such as code breaking and interrogation of captured agents, the British caught German spies as they parachuted into England or Scotland. Sir John Masterman, head of BI(a), evaluated each spy. Those he considered unsuitable were executed or imprisoned. The others were 'turned'—that is, made into double agents, who sent messages to German intelligence, the Abwehr, via radio, using Morse code. (Each spy had his own distinctive 'signature' in the way he used the code's dots and dashes, which was immediately recognizable by the German spy master receiving the message.) The British kept the double agents tap-tap-tapping, but only what they were told to send out.

This so-called Double-Cross operation, which had come into being in the dark days of 1940, managed to locate and turn every German spy in the United Kingdom, some two dozen in all. From the beginning the British had decided to aim it exclusively toward the moment when the Allies returned to France. Building up this asset over the years required feeding the Abwehr information through the spies that was authentic, new, and interesting, but either relatively valueless or something the Germans were bound to learn anyway. The idea was to make the agents trustworthy and valuable in the eyes of the Germans, then spring the trap on D Day, when the double agents would flood the Abwehr with false information.

The first part of the trap was to make the Germans think the attack was coming at the Pas de Calais. Since the Germans already anticipated that this was where the Allies would come ashore, it was necessary only to reinforce their preconceptions. The Pas de Calais was indeed the obvious choice. It was on the direct London–Ruhr–Berlin line. It was close to Antwerp, Europe's best port. Inland the terrain was flat, with few natural obstacles. At the Pas de Calais the Channel was at its narrowest, giving ships the shortest trip and British-based fighter aircraft much more time over the invasion area.

Because the Pas de Calais was the obvious choice, the Germans had their strongest fixed defenses there, backed up by the Fifteenth Army and a majority of the panzer divisions in France. Whether or not they succeeded in making the position impregnable we will never know, because the supreme Allied commander, Dwight D. Eisenhower, decided not to find out. He chose Normandy instead. Normandy had certain advantages, including the port of Cherbourg, the narrowness of the Cotentin Peninsula, access to the major road network at Caen, and proximity to the English ports of Southampton and Portsmouth. Normandy's greatest advantage, however, was that the Germans were certain to consider an attack there highly unlikely, because it would be an attack in the wrong direction: Instead of heading east, toward the German heartland, the Allies would be heading south into central France.

The second part of the trap was to make the Germans think, even after the attack began, that Normandy was a feint. Geography reinforced Eisenhower's choice of Normandy in meeting this requirement, too: If there were major Allied landings at the Pas de Calais, Hitler would not keep troops in Normandy for fear of their being cut off from Germany—but he might be persuaded to keep troops in the Pas de Calais following a landing in Normandy, as they would still stand between the Allied forces and Germany.

The deception plan, code-named Fortitude, was a joint venture, with British and American teams working together; it made full use of the Double-Cross system, dummy armies, fake radio traffic, and elaborate security precautions. In terms of the time, resources, and energy devoted to it, Fortitude was a tremendous undertaking. It had many elements, designed to make the Germans think the attack might come at the Biscay coast or in the Marseilles region or even in the Balkans. Most important were Fortitude North, which set up Norway as a target (the site of Hitler's U-boat bases, essential to his offensive operations), and Fortitude South, with the Pas de Calais as the target.

To get the Germans to look toward Norway, the Allies first had to convince them that Eisenhower had enough resources for a diversion or secondary attack. This was doubly difficult because of Ike's acute shortage of landing craft—it was touch and go as to whether there would be enough craft to carry five divisions ashore at Normandy as planned, much less spares for another attack. To make the Germans believe otherwise, the Allies had to create fictitious divisions and landing craft on a grand scale.

This was done chiefly with the Double-Cross system and through Allied radio signals.

The British Fourth Army, for example, stationed in Scotland and scheduled to invade Norway in mid-July, existed only on the airwaves. Early in 1944 some two dozen over-age British officers were sent to northernmost Scotland, where they spent the next months exchanging radio messages. They filled the air with an exact duplicate of the wireless traffic that accompanies the assembly of a real army, communicating in low-level and thus easily broken cipher. Together the messages created an impression of corps and division headquarters scattered all across Scotland: '80 Div. request 1,800 pairs of crampons, 1,800 pairs of ski bindings,' they read, or 'VII Corps requests the promised demonstrators in the Bilgeri method of climbing rock faces.' There was no 80th Division, no VII Corps.

The turned German spies meanwhile sent encoded radio messages to Hamburg and Berlin describing heavy train traffic in Scotland, new division patches seen on the streets of Edinburgh, and rumors among the troops about going to Norway. Wooden twin-engine 'bombers' began to appear on Scottish airfields. British commandos made some raids on the coast of Norway, pinpointing radar sites, picking up soil samples (ostensibly to test the suitability of beaches to support a landing), and in general trying to look like a preinvasion force.

The payoff was spectacular. By late spring, Hitler had thirteen army divisions in Norway (about 130,000 men under the German military system), along with 90,000 naval and 60,000 Luftwaffe personnel. In late May, Field Marshal Erwin Rommel finally persuaded Hitler to move five infantry divisions from Norway to France. They had started to load up and move out when the Abwehr passed on to Hitler another set of 'intercepted' messages about the threat to Norway. He canceled the movement order.

To paraphrase Winston Churchill, never in the history of warfare have so many been immobilized by so few.

Fortitude South was larger and more elaborate. It was based on the First US Army Group (FUSAG), stationed in and around Dover and threatening the Pas de Calais. It included radio traffic; inadequately camouflaged dummy landing craft in the ports of Ramsgate, Dover, and Hastings; fields packed with pâpier-maché tanks; and full use of the Double-Cross setup. The spies reported intense activity in and around Dover, including construction, troop movements, increased train traffic, and the like. They said that the phony oil dock at Dover, built by stagehands from Hollywood and the British film industry, was open and operating.

The capstone to Fortitude South was Ike's selection of General George S. Patton to command FUSAG. The Germans thought Patton the best commander in the Allied camp (a judgment with which Patton fully agreed, but which Eisenhower, unbeknownst to the Germans, did not) and expected him to lead the assault. Eisenhower, who was saving Patton for the exploitation phase of the campaign, used Patton's reputation and visibility to strengthen Fortitude South. The spies reported his arrival in England and his movements. FUSAG radio signals told the Germans of Patton's comings and goings and showed that he had taken a firm grip on his new command.

FUSAG contained real as well as notional divisions, corps, and armies. The FUSAG order of battle included the US Third Army, which was real but still in the United States; the British Fourth Army, which was imaginary; and the Canadian First Army, which was real and based in England. There were, in addition, supposedly fifty follow-up divisions in the United States, organized as the US Fourteenth Army—which was notional—awaiting shipment to the Pas de Calais after FUSAG established its beachhead. Many of the divisions in the Fourteenth Army were real and were actually assigned to General Omar Bradley's US First Army in southwest England.

Fortitude's success was measured by the German estimate of Allied strength. By June 1, the Germans believed that Eisenhower's entire command included eighty-nine divisions (of about 15,000 men each), when in fact he had forty-seven. They also thought he had sufficient landing craft to bring twenty divisions ashore in the first wave, when he would be lucky to manage five. Partly because they credited Ike with so much strength, and partly because it made such good military sense, the Germans believed that the real invasion would be preceded or followed by diversionary attacks and feints.

Security for Overlord was as important as deception. As Ike declared, 'Success or failure of coming operations depends upon whether the enemy can obtain advance information of an accurate nature.' To maintain security, in February he asked Churchill to move all civilians out of southernmost England. He feared there might be an undiscovered spy who could report the truth to the Abwehr. Churchill refused; he felt it was too much to ask of a war-weary population. A British officer on Ike's staff said it was all politics, and growled, 'If we fail, there won't be any more politics.'

Ike sent Churchill an eloquent plea, warning that it 'would go hard with our consciences if we were to feel, in later years, that by neglecting any security precaution we had compromised the success of these vital operations'. In late March, Churchill gave in; the civilians were put out of all coastal and training areas and kept out until months after D Day.

Eisenhower also persuaded a reluctant Churchill to impose a ban on privileged diplomatic communications from the United Kingdom. Ike said he regarded diplomatic pouches as 'the gravest risk to the security of our operations and to the lives of our sailors, soldiers, and airmen'. When Churchill imposed the ban, on April 17, foreign governments protested vigorously. This gave Hitler a useful clue to the timing of Overlord. He remarked in early May that 'the English have taken measures that they can sustain for only six to eight weeks'. When a West Point classmate of Ike's declared at the bar in Claridge's Hotel that D Day would be before June 15, and offered to take bets when challenged, Ike reduced him in rank and sent him home in disgrace. There was another flap a week later when a US Navy officer got drunk and revealed details of impending operations, including areas, strength, and dates. Ike wrote Chief of Staff George Marshall, 'I get so angry at the occurrence of such needless and additional hazards that I could cheerfully shoot the offender myself'. Instead, Ike sent the officer back to the States.

To check on how well security and deception were working, SHAEF (Supreme Headquarters Allied Expeditionary Force) had another asset, the Ultra system. This involved breaking the German code, Enigma, enabling SHAEF to read German radio signals. Thanks to Ultra, the British Joint Intelligence Committee was able to put together weekly summaries of 'German Appreciation of Allied Intentions in the West', one-or two-page overviews of where, when, and in what strength the Germans expected the attack. Week after week, the summaries gave Ike exactly the news he wanted to read: that the Germans were anticipating an attack on Norway, diversions in the south of France and in Normandy or the Bay of Biscay, and the main assault, with twenty or more divisions, against the Pas de Calais.

But Fortitude was an edifice built so delicately, precisely, and intricately that the removal of just one supporting column would bring the whole thing crashing down. On May 29, with D Day only about a week away, the summary included a chilling sentence: 'The recent trend of movement of German land forces towards the Cherbourg area tends to support the view that the Le Havre–Cherbourg area is regarded as a likely, and perhaps even the main, point of assault.'

Had there been a slip? Had the Germans somehow penetrated Fortitude?

The news got worse. The Germans, in fact, were increasing their defenses everywhere along the French coast. In mid-May the mighty Panzer Lehr Division began moving toward the Cotentin Peninsula, while the 21st Panzer Division, which had been with Rommel in North Africa and was his favorite, moved from Brittany to the Caen area—exactly the site where the British Second Army would be landing. More alarming, Ultra revealed that the German 91st Division, specialists in fighting paratroopers, and the German 6th Parachute Regiment had moved on May 29 into exactly the areas where the American airborne divisions were to land. And the German 352nd Division moved forward from St.-Lô to the coast, taking up a position overlooking Omaha Beach, where the US 1st Division was going to land.

Ike's air commander, British Air Chief Marshal Sir Trafford Leigh-Mallory, was so upset by this news that he recommended to Ike that the airdrops be canceled. Ike refused, but the German movements and Leigh-Mallory's reaction badly stretched his nerves.

Eisenhower did not, however, give up on Fortitude. At about midnight on June 5–6, even as Allied transport planes and ships began crossing the Channel for Normandy, the supreme commander played the ultimate note in the Fortitude concert: He had the spy the Germans trusted most, code-named Garbo—actually a resourceful spy for the British from the start—send a message in Morse code to the Abwehr giving away the secret. Garbo reported that Overlord was on the way, named some of the divisions involved, indicated when they had left Portsmouth, and predicted they would come ashore in Normandy at dawn.

The report had to be deciphered, read, evaluated, reenciphered, and transmitted to Hitler. Then Hitler's lackeys had to decide whether to wake him with the news. They did, but then the whole encoding and deciphering operation had to be reversed to get the word to the German forces in Normandy. By the time it arrived, the defenders could see for themselves—there were 6,000 planes overhead and 5,000 ships off the coast, and the first wave of troops was coming ashore.

In short, Garbo's report, the most accurate and important of the entire war, arrived too late to help the Germans. But it surely raised their opinion of Garbo—and this was vital. For now that Fortitude had helped the Allies get ashore, the question was, could the deception be kept alive long enough to let the Allies win the battle of the build-up that would follow?

Garbo was the key. On June 9 he sent a message to his spy master in Hamburg with a request that it be submitted urgently to the German high command. 'The present operation, though a large-scale assault, is diversionary in character,' Garbo stated flatly. 'Its object is to establish a strong bridgehead in order to draw the maximum of our [German] reserves into the area of the assault and to retain them there so as to leave another area exposed where the enemy could then attack with some prospect of success.' Citing the Allied order of battle as the Germans understood it, Garbo pointed out that Eisenhower had committed only a small number of his divisions and landing craft. He added that no FUSAG unit had taken part in the Normandy attack, nor was Patton there. Furthermore, 'the constant aerial bombardment which the sector of the Pas de Calais has been undergoing and the disposition of the enemy forces would indicate the imminence of the assault in this region which offers the shortest route to the final objective of the Anglo-Americans, Berlin.'

Within half a day, Garbo's message was in Hitler's hands. On the basis of it, the führer made a momentous decision, possibly the most important of the war. Rommel had persuaded Hitler to sent two Fifteenth Army panzer divisions to Normandy. The tanks had started their engines, the men were ready to go, when Hitler canceled the order. He wanted the armored units held in the Pas de Calais to defend against the main invasion. He also awarded the Iron Cross, second class, to Garbo. [. . .]

The deception went on. On June 13 another spy warned that an attack would take place in two or three days at Dieppe or Abbeville. A third spy reported that airborne divisions (wholly fictitious) would soon drop around Amiens. In late June a fourth agent, code-named Tate, said he had obtained the railway schedule for moving the FUSAG forces from their concentration areas to the embarkation ports, thus reinforcing from a new angle the imminence of the threat to the Pas de Calais. One Abwehr officer considered Tate's report so important that he said it 'could even decide the outcome of the war'. He was not far wrong.

The weekly intelligence summary on June 19 read: 'The Germans still believe the Allies capable of launching another amphibious operation. The Pas de Calais remains the expected area of attack. Fears of landings in Norway have been maintained.'

July 10: '[T]he enemy's fear of large-scale landings between the Seine and the Pas de Calais has not diminished. The second half of July is given as the probable time for this operation.'

July 24: 'There has been no considerable transfer of German forces from the Pas de Calais, which remains strongly garrisoned.'

By August 3, when Patton came onto the Continent with his U.S. Third Army, most German officers realized that Normandy was the real thing. By then, of course, it was too late. The Germans had kept hundreds of their best tanks and thousands of their finest fighting men (a total of fifteen divisions in France) out of this crucial battle in order to meet a threat that had always been imaginary.

[From Stephen E. Ambrose, 'The Secrets of Overlord', in Robert Cowley (ed.), *Experience of War* (New York: Norton & Co., 1992), 472–9.]

CHRISTOPHER THORNE

77 The Image of the Japanese

It might be argued that in modern, total war the wholesale branding of the foe is a common occurrence, as is the distortion of truth in general. But even the depiction during the First World War, for example, of the Germans as 'Huns' who had butchered Belgian civilians had not prevented a degree of fellow-feeling for the enemy troops from developing among British soldiers on the Western front. It had not created a situation akin to that in which Admiral William Halsey, one of the US Navy's outstanding commanders in the Pacific in the 1941–45 conflict, could regularly urge his men to kill more of the 'low monkeys' facing them and to make more 'monkey meat' thereby. During the Second World War itself, written propaganda, films and cartoons in the USA and Canada were directed in the main, where the struggle in Europe was concerned, against Hitler and Mussolini personally; but in the context of the Far Eastern struggle, they attacked the entire Japanese nation as evil animals. Americans and Canadians of German or Italian descent were for the most part not subjected to persecution; those of Japanese stock, on the other hand [. . .] were interned (and often well-nigh ruined in the process) on the basis of the conviction expressed by the commanding general of the western military zone in the United States when, in 1943, he was opposing their release: 'A Jap', declared General De Witt on that occasion, 'is a Jap.'

In Britain, also, whereas the Germans tended to be depicted publicly as a people who had been dragged down from a civilised condition by the evils of Nazism, the Japanese were commonly described, in the words of one study, 'in terms appropriate to a newly-discovered zoological species'. And if British attitudes towards this 'species' sometimes inclined towards 'amused contempt', they nevertheless embraced the frequent use of the analogue that Admiral Halsey was wont to employ and that was in virtually everyday use in America, Australia and New Zealand. It was to 'monkey men' that Harold Nicolson, for example (former diplomat and writer; a man about as far removed from Halsey in terms of personality as one could imagine), referred in his diary when sadly reflecting on the early victories of the Japanese.

It seems evident, in other words, that, to a large proportion of the white people involved, the war in the Far East was being waged against 'murderous little ape-men'; 'little men with devil faces and devil minds'. And for at least a substantial number, especially in Australia and the United States, the slogan (proclaimed on posters in the former country): 'We have always hated the Japanese', also appears to have reflected genuine sentiments, as did the belief at the end of the war (voiced by the Sydney *Daily Telegraph*, for example) that in order to render the enemy harmless one would have to 'lift across 2,000 years of backwardness . . . a mind which, below its surface understanding of the technical knowledge our civilisation has produced, is as barbaric as the savage who fights with a club and believes thunder in the voice of his God'. [. . .]

* * * * * *

Perceptions regarding the nature of the enemy were bound up, of course, with ideas concerning the nature and origins of the war itself. In this context it is interesting to note how change—usually unacknowledged—could take place once the fighting had actually begun. [. . .] [F]or example, Joseph Grew, the American Ambassador in Tokyo, had believed until late in the day that, as he wrote to one of his daughters in October 1941, the United States could 'pull through' the crisis with Japan without war coming about. Yet by the end of 1943 he was explaining the conflict in a series of public addresses as having been launched by 'gangster elements' in control of Japanese policy: men who had 'for a long time wanted war', who had 'held it back . . . [only] because they were not ready', and who were still (in September 1943) 'proposing to invade' the United States as the crucial step in their 'mission of conquest'. Likewise, the confidence before Pearl Harbor of the banker, Thomas Lamont, that the Japanese had no thought of attacking the USA had given place by September 1942 to the privately-expressed conviction that they had, in fact, entertained 'evil intent towards America for years'. The same shift occurred in the mind of Father James Drought, whose unofficial and counter-productive involvement in Japanese–American diplomtic exchanges in 1941 had been based in part on a firm belief in Tokyo's reasonableness and good faith, but who was declaring in 1942 (the words were his, though they were spoken by another) that the total destruction of the United States had 'always been the aim' of an enemy who embodied 'the deep, planned malice of an evil soul'.

This conviction that Japan had long prepared her assault against the West, and that fundamentally the war was one of survival, became widespread on the Allied side, both within official circles and among the publics at large. [. . .]

* * * * * *

Proposals for drastically punitive treatment to be meted out to the Japanese once they had been defeated were indeed, [. . .], not lacking within the ranks of the Allies. While the idea of the wholesale extermination of that nation appears to have appealed to a significant proportion of the American public, a representative of the US Navy who was a member of a State–War–Navy Coordinating Committee group in Washington that was making plans for post-war Japan likewise made clear his preference for 'the almost total elimination of the Japanese as a race'. If Queen Wilhelmina had earlier talked of 'drowning them like rats', Admiral Halsey only a shade less drastically now emphasised the need 'to make them impotent for all time to wage another war'. What Roosevelt, for his part, had in mind for a while at least was their enforced isolation within their home islands, in order that their congenital delinquency should not contaminate the process of bringing about more stable and peaceful conditions in the East through a programme of racial inter-breeding. Others, too, like the London *Daily Mail*, saw 'complete isolation from the rest of the world, as in a leper compound, unclean', as being the only suitable fate for what had been 'proved a sub-human race'.

To the very end of the war, and beyond, loud demands were also uttered in the West, not simply for the rooting out of Japan's militarism, but for the exemplary punishment of Emperor Hirohito, who was for the Sydney *Daily Telegraph* among many others 'the symbol of a barbarism we fought to expunge' and 'the core of the social system which begot [Japan's] ambition to rule the world and [her] assurance of racial superiority'. In the USA, polls taken in July and August 1945 showed roughly one-third of those questioned opting for Hirohito's immediate execution, about one-fifth for his imprisonment or exile, and only three to four per cent for his employment by the Allies. In Australia and New Zealand especially, the predominant conviction continued to be that Japan 'must be dealt with ruthlessly', and much unease and anger was to be occasioned in those two countries by the manner in which MacArthur and his American advisers approached their task when the occupation of Japan had actually begun: by their 'bewildering disposition', as one paper saw it, 'to treat the surrendering enemy with a clemency wholly out of keeping with the retribution that [their] crimes demand'. 'A people who can commit the outrages that the Japanese in their thousands everywhere have been responsible for,' the Wellington *Standard* was to argue in September 1945 (echoing in public what was also being urged in diplomatic and political circles), 'cannot be "re-educated" with sugar-coated pills. They must be made to taste the tang of corrective medicine.'

Yet even during the early days of the war there had been those in the West, especially in diplomatic circles and non-official 'foreign-policy communities', as they are sometimes termed, who had retained some hope in the post-war potential of what they saw as 'liberal' elements within Japanese politics, and/or believed that on grounds of *Realpolitik* Japan, while being disarmed, would have to be readmitted to the international community within a fairly short time of hostilities ending. John Emmerson, for example, had mentioned as a qualifying appendage to the main thrust of his State Department memoranda in January 1942

those in Japan who do not subscribe to the philosophy of life which has in recent years led their nation down a path of aggression and destruction of the rights of peoples. The future hope of Japan [he continued] will rest with new leaders and with a changed philosophy to arise when peace again prevails in the Pacific. And this can be accomplished through defeat of Japan's war effort and the inevitable repercussions in Japan and on the Japanese mind of such a defeat.

Other members of a small group of State Department officials who had experience of Japan—men such as Hugh Borton and Joseph Grew—were to contribute to this line of thought, in the face of much scepticism on the part of those Far Eastern Division colleagues whose expertise and primary concern were alike focused on China. And within the Office of War Information, Geoffrey Gorer, Ruth Benedict and others were to develop analyses of Japanese society that at least sought to move beyond facile stereotypes. In

British official circles, too, meanwhile—and with a more widespread concurrence within the Foreign Office—individuals like Sir George Sansom were arguing that, while Japan's record was 'certainly a discreditable one in many important respects', there was 'a better chance of her good behaviour if she [could] be invited to join the club and observe the rules instead of being blackballed'; that, now Japan's militants had 'had their fling' and had got the country into 'a disastrous mess', in due course an opportunity should arise 'for the liberal element (or as it would be more accurate to call them, the level-headed, worldly-wise element) to recover control'.

Indeed, by the final months of the war (and surely, in part at least, as a consequence of changed circumstances, preoccupations and requirements), the Japanese people as a whole were being described in some quarters in Washington in terms that suggested that they were an entirely different species from the nation whose deeply-ingrained propensity for militarism, dictatorship and xenophobia had been so carefully catalogued in 1942. Even the US Navy Department was emphasising by July 1945 that 'numerous Japanese' would be 'disposed to accept and assist in the development of democratic principles' once their Government had surrendered. In this particular respect, the American officials concerned were virtually isolated in terms of the Allied governments and peoples as a whole, for even their British counterparts retained an underlying distrust—even dislike—of the Japanese as a nation, just as they looked with much scepticism at American plans to 're-educate' the defeated enemy. (In many respects, this meant to Americanise them, just as China was to have been 'led into the twentieth century' and South Vietnam was to be the object of an exercise in 'nation-building'.)

The details of the policy debates that took place within and among Allied authorities on these matters as the war approached its close have been set out elsewhere by the present writer and others, and will not be repeated here. Should the Emperor, or at least the Throne, be retained? (Allied political warfare had taken care to steer around this particular topic.) How great was the possibility of social and political revolution—of a Communist revolution, perhaps—taking place in Japan in the aftermath of defeat, possibly fostered by those Japanese Marxists who (like their counterparts in the Korean Volunteer Army which fought alongside Mao's troops) had found refuge with the Yenan regime in China? Should the Allies occupy all of Japan, or only a few, key, strategic areas? Should a process of de-industrialisation, as well as of de-militarisation, be instituted, and how should the giant financial and manufacturing combines—the *zaibatsu*—be broken up? What role might the Soviet Union seek to play in the area? And so forth.

Discussions on such matters were often conducted with one eye on the need to avoid raising an outcry among one's own public by appearing unduly lenient towards a hated, or at the very least distrusted, foe. For

British ministers and officials there was also the additional handicap created by their own somewhat tardy approach to such issues, together with problems that arose from the importance of not giving ammunition to those Americans in and around official quarters (not least, those who attended the international gatherings of the Institute of Pacific Relations) who were wont to accuse Britain of 'favouring a soft peace toward Japan'. Above all, however, London found itself coming up against the determination in Washington that it was going to be American plans and American administrators that would shape the new Japan and make the Pacific safe for democracy. Overwhelmingly (and, although incorrectly, not without reason), opinion in the United States saw the Great Republic as having won the Far Eastern war single-handedly. Now it would win the peace.

[From Christopher Thorne, *The Far Eastern War: States and Societies, 1941–1945*
(London: Unwin Paperbacks, 1986), 129–38.]

COLIN GRAY

78   **The Strategy of Blockade**

If the financial exhaustion of an enemy is impracticable, it may be possible to achieve great strategic leverage by means of a maritime supply blockade—that is, denying continental enemies the materials necessary for the conduct of war. For example, by the late 1930s both the British and German governments regarded a supply blockade as the leading edge of the strategic effectiveness of sea power in its ability to influence the outcome of a war. This seemed to be a principal lesson of the Great War; moreover, Germany's small navy in the 1930s precluded for the near term all options but commerce raiding. In practice, Germany turned her back on the discredited notion of seeking military command at sea. For a while at least, Hitler and his admirals were determined not to repeat the errors in policy, grand strategy, and naval strategy committed in the early years of the century. In the case of Admiral Erich Raeder, however, it was the unexpected and very unwelcome circumstance of early war that most reduced his aspiration for the building of a balanced fleet that might challenge for command at sea. The Z (for *ziel*, or 'target') Plan fleet endorsed on January 29, 1939, envisaged an eight-year buildup to completion in 1948, hastily revised to 1946 at Hitler's insistence. The Z Plan rested on some significant, and significantly ridiculous, assumptions. Specifically, the plan required six to eight years of peace with Britain and assumed the availability of material resources and trained people. Moreover, the plan was drafted without regard for the disadvantages of German strategic geography, an oversight that agitated naval theorist Wolfgang Wegener. Furthermore, the fleet would be in a position to challenge the Royal Navy by 1946 or 1948 only if Britain neglected to take competitive corrective action against the blatant German menace in the North Sea.

The Royal Navy, though still faithful to the concept of a general maritime command, lacked for a worthy European opponent on the surface of the sea in the interwar years. The Jutland [battle] syndrome dominated a Royal Navy bereft of a European adversary with a large battlefleet. The next Jutland was expected to be waged with Japan east of the very incomplete fleet base at Singapore, not in the North Sea against Germany. A large body of British opinion in the 1930s was convinced that Germany's unexpected collapse in the fall of 1918 ultimately was traceable to the Allied economic blockade. If fight again she must, Britain was determined to return to a rather nostalgic and romanticized notion of its alleged traditional maritime way of war and until 1939 eschewed the kind of continental commitment that produced nearly 1 million British (Imperial) dead and 2 million wounded between 1914 and 1918. The supply blockade had been as unexpectedly effective in 1914–18 as it was overvalued in Britain in the late 1930s.

Nazi Germany was critically dependent on the foreign, including overseas, supply of raw materials. But her world leadership in chemicals enabled her to invent substitute substances that worked well enough, and diplomacy enlisted the Soviet Union as a secure rearward base of supply. Furthermore, the German Army and Air Force secured by force an all but continent-wide bank of resources. That same Army and Air Force, with naval assistance in Norway, changed the geostrategic terms of engagement for the German counterblockade of Britain. To be fair, British strategic planners early in 1939 could not have predicted many of these blockade-breaking steps. Most of the threats to seaborne commerce were discounted in Britain in the 1930s on the basis of her experience in foiling the surface raiders and U-boats in World War I, of confidence in ASDIC/sonar, and because of the understandable expectation that Germany would lack commerce-raiding bases on the open Atlantic. The leadership of Nazi Germany's *Kriegsmarine* entirely shared Britain's 1930s discounting of future submarine dangers to merchant shipping. Whereas Admiral Karl Dönitz insisted on April 13, 1939, that Germany required a U-boat force 300 strong in order to achieve 'decisive success' against Britain, Raeder's Z Plan promised only 162 (Atlantic-capable types) by 1948.

Prior to the industrial revolution and the age of mass warfare, the main purpose of a maritime blockade was to watch closely for the movement of enemy fighting ships. In war after war, the Royal Navy's blockade focused on Brest, Toulon, and Rochefort, with periodic need to add Antwerp/Flushing, Cadiz, Cartagena, Ferrol, and Corunna to the list of ports observed. The overriding objective of this naval blockade was the frustration of invasion designs. Blockade also ensured the maritime command necessary for the safe passage of British, and unsafe passage of enemy, seaborne trade. In addition, naval blockade provided strategic cover for British military expeditions on colonial or continental-peripheral ventures. Also, the blockade and actual interdiction of enemy shipping helped deny the enemy the revenue to finance military operations.

The strategic potential of supply blockade has varied widely with the differing vulnerabilities of states. Imperial Athens was as much at risk to the interruption of her seaborne supply of grain from the northern shores of the Black Sea as was twentieth-century Britain to the U-boat campaigns against her overseas food supply. In modern times, however, the efficacy of supply blockade has been the product of the interaction between the raw material needs of industrial war-making economies and—in the continental case—the closing of access to landward sources of supply. It was critical to the effectiveness of the British economic blockade of Germany twice in this century that the enemy should be besieged closely on land as well as by sea. The economic blockades of Germany were effected not only at sea but also to an important degree at source and with reference to German purchasing power. Economic warfare eventually became a total enterprise in both world wars. Allied and German agents sought to control, or at least to influence markedly, the direction of trade flows from neutral countries. Strategic geography was critical, as always. Even if German economic agents could corner some market on fertilizer in a South American country, that would avail them little if they could not arrange for safe transshipment to the Reich in German or neutral bottoms.

In the Cold War era, the Soviet Union, unlike the countries of preindustrial Europe, could not have been damaged strategically significantly by a maritime blockade directed toward the financial instrument of high policy, any more than could Napoleonic France, or later, Imperial or Nazi Germany. Supply blockade, on the other hand, peaked in its effectiveness as a strategic instrument in 1918 and again in 1944–45 against insular Japan, but it had also some noteworthy promise as a tool of war against the modern Soviet imperium. With reference to post-1945 conditions, the principal granaries of the world lay overseas from Eurasia, while even a conventional war in Eurasia would have wrought massive economic damage. It follows that a Soviet Union victorious on land in Eurasia would have had severe problems feeding an expanded and politically insecure empire.

The strategic effectiveness of maritime blockade of the supply of goods, and indeed of economic warfare broadly pursued, must depend on the political, social, economic, military, and geostrategic particulars of a specific case. Economic blockade has to be viewed, as must sea power, as an instrument of grand strategy for the conduct of conflict as a whole. Rarely will blockade be independently decisive. Absurdly optimistic claims for the strategic promise in economic sanctions surfaced yet again in late 1990–91 with the American debate over the prudent way to coerce Iraq to disgorge Kuwait. In permissive circumstances, however, the maritime blockade (and blockade at source) of overseas supply of critical materials can have massive multiplier effects generating strategic leverage in abundance. The leading example in modern history was the British blockade of Imperial Germany from 1914 to 1918. But even in that case the blockade worked only very slowly, necessarily by attrition, and as a contributor, a team player, to victory.

[From Colin Gray, *The Leverage of Sea Power* (New York: The Free Press, 1992), 36–9.]

DAVID MACISAAC

79 The Evolution of Air Power

Classical air strategy as it had evolved by 1939 met with some rude shocks in the course of the war itself. In its Douhetan formulation only two steps were required. The first was to win command of the air by destroying the enemy's air force on the ground by bombing his aircraft, bases, support facilities and factories. A second and decisive step would follow with the destruction by bombing of the enemy's industrial, governmental and population centres. The war proved more difficult. The destructive effects of bombing, both physically and psychologically, had been over-estimated; the prospects of air defence, both ground-based and airborne, proved hardier than they had appeared in a pre-radar age; and the dramatically effective employment of aircraft in support of surface forces could not be denied by the most zealous theorist of 'pure' air strategy.

Writing more than a decade after the war, the late Bernard Brodie addressed these matters.

Air power had a mighty vindication in World War II. But it was Mitchell's conception of it—'anything that flies'—rather than Douhet's that was vindicated. It was in tactical employment that success was most spectacular and that the air forces won the unqualified respect and admiration of the older services. By contrast, the purely strategic successes, however far-reaching in particular instances, were never completely convincing to uncommitted observers. Against Germany they came too late to have a clearly decisive effect; against Japan they were imposed on an enemy already prostrated by other forms of war.

Even General Carl A. Spaatz, senior commander of the US strategic air forces during the war, was ambivalent on the question of purely strategic successes. 'Because the last war saw the weapons of all services employed in profusion,' he wrote, 'one may argue the exact degree of contribution made by strategic bombing to the final decision.' In a now forgotten article in *Life*, he went on to assert that 'the war against Germany was fundamentally an infantry war supported by air power, much as the war against Japan was fundamentally a naval war supported by air'. Even the much heralded US Strategic Bombing Survey fudged the issue, declaring in its *Overall Report* (European War) that 'Allied air power was decisive in the war in western Europe'—a formulation that speaks to rather more than strategic bombing, leaves decisive undefined and geographically limits its intended scope.

And yet despite such readings of the air power lessons of the war, the USAF of the late 1940s and the 1950s set its sights squarely on 'the air-atomic mission'. Several reasons obtained, over few of which the airmen had any measure of control. Demobilisation to the point of disintegration of the military services was one, presidential budget decisions another, the emerging cold war with the Soviet Union yet another. Events in Czechoslovakia, Berlin, Russia (the atomic explosion of August 1949) and soon Korea—married to disappointments at Yalta and Potsdam and mixed with liberal doses of Stalinist-Leninist bombast—served to unhinge many in high places. The establishment of atomic, later nuclear, dominance over the Soviet Union was not a goal the airmen could have achieved without help from all the elements of the national government.

With severe restrictions governing the numbers of men, aircraft and weapons that would be made available, the presumably most dangerous eventuality, however unlikely, had to be prepared for first. And so, almost from its establishment in March 1946, the Strategic Air Command was given priority over the Air Defense Command and the Tactical Air Command. Several years would pass before the SAC's capabilities came to represent more than what now appears in retrospect to have been a hollow threat. Once they did, however, in the years roughly between 1957 and 1962, the SAC so thoroughly dominated the Air Force as a whole that other capabilities would prove difficult to revive.

The problem, to repeat, was not so much an inability to appreciate the multiple roles that air power could play as a 'co-operative permitter, expeditor, and force multiplier' across the full spectrum of warfare. Rather, it was how to mount the maximum amount of force so as to deter, and destroy if so ordered, any potential enemy bound on working its will against the United States, or so it seemed to the American air leaders of the late 1940s. A future historian might say that they succeeded beyond reason; that they became guilty of trying to make war fit a particular weapon rather than the other way round; that they were foolish to assume that a president would authorise the use of nuclear weapons in any but the most mortal of confrontations; that they had no reason to assume that future wars would be metropolitan wars between integrated societies built around vital centres; that they erred in equating deterrent capabilities with war-fighting capabilities, or at least in assuming the convertibility of the first into the second. A case can be made for all these arguments, but it is only fair to recall that the field of choice was narrower than some now assume; and that here, as in most affairs, the unforeseen and unintended consequences of decisions taken in the late 1940s were the most all-intrusive and long-lasting. [. . .]

In conclusion, one may recall briefly the essential elements of classical air power theory as it had evolved by 1945; and then list a number of serious conceptual challenges that theory has had difficulty incorporating over the past 40 years. From these the reader can then decide for himself where help is needed.

The classical theory would hold as follows: air power can exploit range, speed, altitude, and manoeuvrability better than can land or sea forces, and therefore must be allowed to operate independently of these forces. These characteristics of air power are most effectively realised when air power is controlled centrally and executed decentrally. The principal missions of air power are strategic offence and defence, air superiority, interdiction, airlift, reconnaissance, close air support and special operations. Although priorities in their application have undergone minor shifts in special circumstances, these principles and priorities have remained basically valid in the face of profound developments in technology, strategy and international relations.

Listed below are a few tendencies and questions that airmen have had difficulty with, some of them from long before 1945 but all of them notice-able since then. No priority is meant to be inferred from their order of appearance, nor does the writer expect his readers will agree with their selection.

—A prevailing tendency to magnify expected capabilities derived from designs still on the drawing boards. This was a problem well entrenched before the Second World War, to be sure. Its more modern offshoots include a tendency to view technology and its implied performance as the lynchpin of enemy capability, while relying for one's *own* security on prom-issory notes of what the R&D future portends—often at the expense of needed hedges against the war that might break out tomorrow morning. In some way related is the misplaced or at least questionable confidence that technical sophistication can offset numerical force deficiencies.

—A pattern of looking at the parts of the problem at the expense of the whole, a form of reductionism surely not limited to air theorists, but one evident since at least the strategic bombing campaigns of the Second World War.

—A tendency to confuse destruction with control, accounting in part for a transcendant faith in the efficacy of strategic bombing and, in less brutal circumstances as over Indochina in the 1960s, the error of allowing destruction to become the end rather than one of the means to the end.

—A prevailing tendency to emphasise the fire power role of air power at the expense of its other attributes, leading to extreme difficulty in understanding that technologically advanced weaponry and vastly superior fire power will not always be sufficient to produce victory.

—Difficulty in accepting the idea that air combat engagements, no matter how successful, *can*, depending on the nature of the conflict, the goals being sought, and the means applied, prove irrelevant to broader outcomes.

—A continuing tendency to emphasise the unique aspects of war in and from the air while neglecting the elements of continuity that mark all warfare. An example that is awkward to point out to airmen is that strong wills and conflicting opinions have almost always carried more weight than theory or doctrine; although on reflection that attribute may in fact be one element of continuity in all warfare!

Finally, it could well be that airmen will be forced by circumstances to give up their long-cherished hope for the establishment of an outlook, along with an attendant vocabulary, that will allow for some measure of purity in the concept of air power or 'war in the third dimension'. Advanced technology is today giving to all kinds of weapons the ability to strike targets from great distances, thereby blurring the former distinctions between land, sea, and air power. It could even be that the old concept of air power has become an outmoded construct that has outlived its usefulness. Michael Howard (and others) have argued that the technologies of nuclear bombs, ICBMs, satellite surveillance, etc. are making air power—at least at the strategic level—irrelevant as a useful tool for strategists. The strategic questions now are what should be attacked to fulfil the purpose of the war, and from what platform—air, sea, space or land—can this be done with the greatest effectiveness, efficiency and prospects of success?

[From David MacIsaac, 'The Evolution of Air Power since 1945: The American Experience', in R. A. Mason (ed.), *War in the Third Dimension: Essays in Contemporary Air Power* (London: Brassey's, 1986), 12–14, 30–1.]

80   US Objectives with Respect to Russia

There are two concepts of the relationship of national objectives to the factors of war and peace.

The first holds that national objectives be constant and should not be affected by changes in the country's situation as between war and peace; that they should be pursued constantly by means short of war or by war-like means, as the case may be. This concept was best expressed by

Clausewitz, who wrote that, 'War is a continuation of policy, intermingled with other means'.

The opposite concept is that which sees national objectives in peace and national objectives in war as essentially unrelated. According to this concept, the existence of a state of war creates its own specific political objectives, which generally supersede the normal peacetime objectives. This is the concept which has generally prevailed in this country. Basically, it was the concept which prevailed in the last war, where the winning of the war itself, as a military operation, was made the supreme objective of US policy, other considerations being subordinated to it.

In the case of American objectives with respect to Russia, it is clear that neither of these concepts can prevail entirely.

In the first place, this Government has been forced, for purposes of the political war now in progress, to consider more definite and militant objectives toward Russia even now, in time of peace, than it ever was called upon to formulate with respect either to Germany or Japan in advance of the actual hostilities with those countries.

Secondly, the experience of the past war has taught us the desirability of gearing our war effort to a clear and realistic concept of the long-term political objectives which we wish to achieve. This would be particularly important in the event of a war with the Soviet Union. We could hardly expect to conclude such a war with the same military and political finality as was the case in the recent war against Germany and Japan. Unless, therefore, it were clear to everyone that our objectives did not lie in military victory for its own sake, it might be hard for the US public to recognize what would in reality be a favorable issue of the conflict. The public might expect much more in the way of military finality than would be necessary, or even desirable, from the standpoint of the actual achievement of our objectives. If people were to get the idea that our objectives were unconditional surrender, total occupation and military government, on the patterns of Germany and Japan, they would naturally feel that anything short of these achievements was no real victory at all, and might fail to appreciate a really genuine and constructive settlement.

Finally, we must recognize that Soviet objectives themselves are almost constant. They are very little affected by changes from war to peace. For example, Soviet territorial aims with respect to eastern Europe, as they became apparent during the war, bore a strong similarity to the program which the Soviet Government was endeavoring to realize by measures short of war in 1939 and 1940, and in fact to certain of the strategic-political concepts which underlay Czarist policy before World War I. To meet a policy of such constancy, so stubbornly pursued through both war and peace, it is necessary that we oppose it with purposes no less constant and enduring. Broadly speaking, this lies in the nature of the relationship between the Soviet Union and the outside world, which is one of permanent antagonism and conflict, taking place sometimes within a framework of formal peace and at other times within the legal framework of war.

On the other hand, it is clear that a democracy cannot effect, as the totalitarian state sometimes does, a complete identification of its peacetime and wartime objectives. Its aversion to war as a method of foreign policy is so strong that it will inevitably be inclined to modify its objectives in peacetime, in the hope that they may be achieved without resort to arms. When this hope and this restraint are removed by the outbreak of war, as a result of the provocation of others, the irritation of democratic opinion generally demands either the formulation of further objectives, often of a punitive nature, which it would not have supported in time of peace, or the immediate realization of aims which it might otherwise have been prepared to pursue patiently, by gradual pressures, over the course of decades. It would therefore be unrealistic to suppose that the US Government could hope to proceed in time of war on the basis of exactly the same set of objectives, or at least with the same time-table for realization of objectives, which it would have in time of peace.

At the same time, it must be recognized that the smaller the gap between peacetime and wartime purposes, the greater the likelihood that a successful military effort will be politically successful as well. If objectives are really sound from the standpoint of national interest, they are worth consciously formulating and pursuing in war as in peace. Objectives which come into being as a consequence of wartime emotionalism are not apt to reflect a balanced concept of long-term national interest. For this reason, every effort should be made in government planning now, in advance of any outbreak of hostilities, to define our present peacetime objectives and our hypothetical wartime objectives with relation to Russia, and to reduce as far as possible the gap between them. [. . .]

1. The Impossibilities

Before entering into a discussion of what we *should* aim to achieve in a war with Russia, let us first be clear in our own minds about those things which we *could not hope* to achieve.

In the first place we must assume that it will not be profitable or practically feasible for us to occupy and take under our military administration the entire territory of the Soviet Union. This course is inhibited by the size of that territory, by the number of its inhabitants, by the differences of language and custom which separate its inhabitants from ourselves, and by the improbability that we would find any adequate apparatus of local authority through which we could work.

Secondly, and in consequence of this first admission, we must recognize that it is not likely that the Soviet leaders would surrender unconditionally to us. It is possible that Soviet power might disintegrate during the stress of an unsuccessful war, as did that of the tsar's regime during World War I. But even this is not likely. And if it did not so disintegrate, we could not be sure that we could eliminate it by any means short of an extravagant military effort designed to bring all of Russia under our control. We have before us in our experience with the Nazis an example of the stubbornness and tenacity with which a thoroughly ruthless and dictatorial regime can maintain its internal power even over a territory constantly shrinking as a consequence of military operations. The Soviet leaders would be capable of concluding a compromise peace, if pressed, and even one highly unfavorable to their own interests. But it is not likely that they would do anything, such as to surrender unconditionally, which would place themselves under the complete power of a hostile authority. Rather than do that, they would probably retire to the most remote village of Siberia and eventually perish, as Hitler did, under the guns of the enemy.

There is a strong possibility that if we were to take the utmost care, within limits of military feasibility, not to antagonize the Soviet people by military policies which would inflict inordinate hardship and cruelties upon them, there would be an extensive disintegration of Soviet power during the course of a war which progressed favorably from our standpoint. We would certainly be entirely justified in promoting such a disintegration with every means at our disposal. This does not mean, however, that we could be sure of achieving the complete overthrow of the Soviet regime, in the sense of the removal of its power over *all* the present territory of the Soviet Union.

Regardless of whether or not Soviet power endures on any of the present Soviet territory we cannot be sure of finding among the Russian people any other group of political leaders who would be entirely 'democratic' as we understand that term. [. . .]

All of the above indicates that we could not expect, in the aftermath of successful military operations in Russia, to create there an authority entirely submissive to our will or entirely expressive of our political ideals. We must reckon with the strong probability that we would have to continue to deal, in one degree or another, with Russian authorities of whom we will not entirely approve, who will have purposes different from ours, and whose views and desiderata we will be obliged to take into consideration whether we like them or not. In other words, we could not hope to achieve any total assertion of our will on Russian territory, as we have endeavored to do in Germany and in Japan. We must recognize that whatever settlement we finally achieve must be a *political* settlement, *politically* negotiated.

So much for the impossibilities. Now what would be our possible and desirable aims in the event of a war with Russia? [. . .]

2. The Retraction of Soviet Power

The first of our war aims must naturally be the destruction of Russian military influence and domination in areas contiguous to, but outside of, the borders of any Russian state.

Plainly, a successful prosecution of the war on our part would automatically achieve this effect throughout most, if not all, of the satellite area. A succession of military defeats to the Soviet forces would probably so undermine the authority of the communist regimes in the eastern European countries that most of them would be overthrown. Pockets might remain, in the form of political Tito-ism, i.e., residual communist regimes of a purely national and local character. These we could probably afford to by-pass. Without the might and authority of Russia behind them, they would be sure either to disappear with time or to evolve into normal national regimes with no more and no less of chauvinism and extremism than is customary to strong national governments in that area. We would of course insist on the cancellation of any formal traces of abnormal Russian power in that area, such as treaties of alliance, etc.

Beyond this, however, we have again the problem of *the extent to which we would wish Soviet borders modified as a result of a successful military action in our part: We must face frankly the fact that we cannot answer this question at this time.* The answer depends almost everywhere on the type of regime which would be left, in the wake of military operations, in the particular area in question. Should this regime be one which held out at least reasonably favorable prospects of observing the principles of liberalism in internal affairs and moderation in foreign policy, it might be possible to leave under its authority most, if not all, of the territories gained by the Soviet Union in the recent war. If, as is more probable, little dependence could be placed on the liberalism and moderation of a post-hostilities Russian authority, it might be necessary to alter these borders quite extensively. This must simply be chalked up as one of the questions which will have to be left open until the development of military and political events in Russia reveals to us the full nature of the post-war framework in which we will have to act.

We then have the question of the Soviet myth and of the ideological authority which the Soviet Government now exerts over people beyond the present satellite area. In the first instance, this will of course depend on the question of whether or not the present All-Union Communist Party continues to exert authority over any portion of the present Soviet territory, in the aftermath of another war. We have already seen that we cannot rule out this possibility. Should communist authority disappear, this question is automatically solved. It must be assumed, however, that in any event an unsuccessful issue of the war itself, from the Soviet standpoint, would probably deal a decisive blow to this form of the projection of Soviet power and influence.

However that may be, we must leave nothing to chance; and it should naturally be considered that one of our major war aims with respect to Russia would be *to destroy thoroughly the structure of relationships by which the leaders of the All-Union Communist Party have been able to exert moral and disciplinary authority over individual citizens, or groups of citizens, in countries not under communist control.*

3. The Alteration of the Russian Concepts of International Relations

Our next problem is again that of the concepts by which Russian policy would be governed in the aftermath of a war. How would we assure ourselves that Russian policy would henceforth be conducted along lines as close as possible to those which we have recognized above as desirable? This is the heart of the problem of our war aims with respect to Russia; and it cannot be given too serious attention.

In the first instance this is a problem of the future of Soviet power: that is, of the power of the communist party in the Soviet Union. This is an extremely intricate question. There is no simple answer to it. We have seen that while we would welcome, and even strive for, the complete disintegration and disappearance of Soviet power, we could not be sure of achieving this entirely. We could therefore view this as a maximum, but not a minimum, aim.

Assuming, then, that there might be a portion of Soviet territory on which we would find it expedient to tolerate the continued existence of Soviet power, upon the conclusion of military operations, what should be our relationship to it? Would we consent to deal with it at all? If so, what sort of terms would we be willing to make?

First of all, we may accept it as a foregone conclusion that we would not be prepared to conclude a full-fledged peace settlement and/or resume regular diplomatic relations with any regime in Russia dominated by any of the present Soviet leaders or persons sharing their cast of thought. We have had too bitter an experience, during the past fifteen years, with the effort to act as though normal relations were possible with such a regime; and if we should now be forced to resort to war to protect ourselves from the consequences of their policies and actions, our public would hardly be in a mood to forgive the Soviet leaders for having brought things to this pass, or to resume the attempt at normal collaboration.

On the other hand, if a communist regime were to remain on any portion of Soviet territory, upon the conclusion of military operations, we could not afford to ignore it entirely. It could not fail to be, within the limits of its own possibilities, a potential menace to the peace and stability of Russia itself and of the world. The least we could do would be to see to it that its possibilities for mischief were so limited that it could not do serious damage, and that we ourselves, or forces friendly to us, would retain all the necessary controls.

For this, two things would probably be necessary. The first would be the actual physical limitation of the power of such a residual Soviet regime to make war or to threaten and intimidate other nations or other Russian regimes. Should military operations lead to any drastic curtailment of the territory over which the communists held sway, particularly such a curtailment as would deprive them of key factors in the present military-industrial structure of the Soviet Union, this physical limitation would automatically flow from that. Should the territory under their control not be substantially diminished, the same result could be obtained by extensive destruction of important industrial and economic targets from the air. Possibly, both of these means might be required. However that may be,

we may definitely conclude that we could not consider our military operations successful if they left a communist regime in control of enough of the present military-industrial potential of the Soviet Union to enable them to wage war on comparable terms with any neighboring state or with any rival authority which might be set up on traditional Russian territory.

[From 'U.S. Objectives with Respect to Russia', NSC 20/1, 18 Aug. 1948, reps. in Thomas Etzold and John Lewis Gaddis, eds. *Containment: Documents on American Policy and Strategy, 1945–1950* (New York: Columbia University Press, 1978), 174–95.]

HEDLEY BULL

81 Disarmament and the Balance of Power

Disarmament is the reduction or abolition of armaments. The idea that the world is most secure when there is a *minimum* of armaments, the pursuit of the *maximum* disarmament, has been the central assumption of modern negotiations about arms control. The negotiations conducted under the auspices of the League of Nations between 1921 and 1934, and those under the auspices of the United Nations between 1946 and 1957 and in 1960, have had as their chief formal object the promotion of international security by a general reduction of armaments. Even in negotiations which have been concerned with limiting the further growth of armaments, rather than with reducing existing ones (as in the negotiations at the first Hague Conference in 1899, and in those which led to the Washington Naval Treaty of 1922), it was the idea of the desirability of the minimum armaments that provided the starting point. And where arms control negotiations have not been concerned with the quantity of armaments at all, but with regulating or controlling what should be done with them [. . .] these negotiations are regarded as important partly because they may set off a train of events which might result in a general reduction of armaments. [. . .]

[There have always been qualifications, but they] have not been seen as detracting from the principle that it is in the reduction of armaments that the contribution of arms control to international security lies. They have rather been seen as qualifications which have to be made so as to bring about the international agreement that can alone set the process of reduction of armaments in motion. Sovereign powers, it has been considered, will not agree to disarm unless they can retain internal security forces, unless a central authority or collective security system will protect them from attack, and unless at all stages in their disarmament there is a balance between their own strength and that of their opponents.

But the idea that security lies in the minimum of armaments cannot be accepted uncritically. In considering this idea, we must examine separately two of the forms it takes: the stronger form, that the abolition of armaments makes war physically impossible; and the weaker form, that the reduction of armaments makes war less likely.

The stronger form is a doctrine which has great popular appeal, because it promises a form of security which is absolute and independent of the continuance of favourable political conditions. It suggests a world in which states cannot make war, even if they want to. It has played an important part in Soviet disarmament policy. [. . .]

The objection is often made to proposals for 'total disarmament' [. . .] that such a thing is impracticable: that nations will not in fact agree to it. It is true that agreement among heavily armed and hostile nations to implement such a proposal is as near to inconceivable as anything can be in the realm of politics. It is true also that actual proposals for total disarmament [. . .] include the retention of internal security forces: forces which in authoritarian countries and countries with dissident overseas territories are often very powerful. [. . .]

The objection that proposals for it are impracticable, however, concedes too much to the idea of total disarmament. The objection to total disarmament is not that it is impracticable, but that there can be, in principle, nothing of the kind: the physical capacity for organized violence is inherent in human society. Even the most thoroughgoing disarmament treaty must leave nations with the capacity to wage war on a primitive level; and, moreover, with the capacity to raise this level, to re-establish what has been dis-established, to remember or to re- invent what has been laid aside. Thus there is no force in [. . .] [the] argument that 'total disarmament' will make war impossible in some sense in which lesser forms of disarmament will not: the physical possibility of war is not erased along with 'armaments'. Moreover, the most thoroughgoing disarmament treaty must leave some powers with a greater capacity for war than others: like lesser forms of disarmament, it must result in a definite ratio of military power. A nation's war potential does not reside merely in its 'armaments', but in the whole complex of its economic and demographic resources, strategic position, technological and industrial skill, military experience and ingenuity, morale, commitments and more besides: a fact which emerges nowhere more clearly than in negotiations for disarmament, when the negotiators attempt to reach agreement by reference to armaments and armed forces alone. The removal of 'armaments' does not disturb these other factors, but brings them further into play. [. . .]

No system of disarmament can abolish the physical capacity to wage war, and the idea of an absolute security from war emerging from such a system is an illusion. However, it is at least logically and physically possible that the art of war might be rendered primitive: by the abolition of sophisticated weapons and the decay of sophisticated military organization and technique. There may be a great difference between an international society in which sovereign powers are bristling with modern weapons and organized military forces, and one in which they are not: just as there is a great difference between a society in which gentlemen carry swords, and one in which they do not. There is nothing contrary to logic, or nature either, in the idea of an international society not only without such weapons and forces, but with habits, institutions, codes or taboos which could impede the will to utilize the physical capacity for war inherent in it. We should have the imagination and the vision to contemplate the possibility of such a world, to recognize that the political and military structure of the world could be radically different from what it is now. But we should recognize that a world which was radically different from our own in respect of the primitiveness and extent of its national armaments would also be radically different in many other ways. If nations were defenceless, there could hardly be a political order worthy of the name unless there were an armed, central authority: the abolition of national military power appears to entail the concentration of military power in a universal authority. If a universal authority or world government were to be established in any other way than by conquest, and if, once established, it were to maintain itself in any other way than by the constant suppression of dissidence, the bitter political conflicts which now divide the world would have to have subsided. In a world fundamentally different from our own in all these respects, and in other respects, the reduction of national armaments to a primitive level might have a place. But the world in which we now find ourselves is not such as this: nor is it within the power of any political authority or combination of authorities to being it about by *fiat*. The possession by sovereign powers of armaments and armed forces is not something extraneous to the structure of international society, something whose presence or absence does not affect other of its parts: it is, along with alliances, diplomacy and war, among its most central institutions. It is possible to conceive systems of world politics and political organization from which this institution is absent: but they are systems from which some of the most familiar and persistent landmarks of international experience are also absent; and which, though they might occur, cannot be legislated.

In a world such as our own it seems doubtful whether the reduction of national armaments to a primitive level, even if it could be brought about in isolation from other fundamental changes, would contribute to international security. It would carry within itself no guarantee that arms races would not be resumed. The resumption of an arms race from a primitive level, with its attendant circumstances of unpredictability and surprise, would be likely to lead to extreme instability in the balance of power, and might well produce greater insecurity than that attending a higher quantitative and qualitative level of armaments.

The weaker form of the doctrine of disarmament is that international security is enhanced when armaments are reduced to the lowest level that is practicable, given that there are limits to the reductions which the powers will entertain. This, rather than total disarmament, has been the formal object of most of the great multilateral disarmament negotiations: it may entail the abolition, rather than the reduction, of particular categories of armament, but falls short of the abolition of all categories. [. . .]

It is clear that if the objective of arms control were the economic one of reducing the resources devoted to armaments, it would have to comprise a reduction of armaments and armed forces, or, at all events, a reduction of expenditure on them. If, however, it is the objective of arms control to promote international security, it is far from clear that this is a matter of reducing the quantity of forces or weapons, or restricting the sums spent on them. If in fact there is no question of the elimination of forces and weapons, it is not to be assumed that the level of forces and weapons most favourable to international security is the lowest one. The claims of the reduction of armaments clash with those of the balance of power, and must be weighed against them.

In international society as we know it, security is not provided by the concentration of military power in an authority superior to sovereign states, but rests on a balance of power among them.

The existence of a military situation in which no one power or bloc is preponderant is a most precarious and uncertain source of security. The idea of the balance of power, like that of disarmament, rests on the abstraction of the military factor. If there is a military balance between opposed powers, such as to leave them alike without prospect of decisive victory, there is no guarantee that they will act in accordance with an appreciation of this balance or even that they will be aware that it exists. The inherent uncertainty that surrounds estimates of military power, the play of the contingent in military operations themselves, the inadequacy of intelligence and its frustration by counter-intelligence, the willingness of governments to take risks despite unfavourable odds, their frequent failure even to weigh up the odds, render peace something precarious even where the balance of power is most stable. Military balances, moreover, do not remain stable for long periods but are inherently temporary. The technological, economic, demographic, political and other ingredients that go to make up the military strength of each side are subject to constant change, as is the attitude of each side towards the existing balance, which it may find satisfactory and accept, or find unsatisfactory and seek to overthrow.

The unsettling effect of changes on the balance of power is mitigated by the practice of making adjustments in the system of alliances: changes in the diplomatic combinations of the Powers enable the balance among them to accommodate changes in the intrinsic strength of each of them. But the recourse to the adjustment of alliances does not exist for two blocs between whom the world is divided. If, as now, in strictly military terms, neither antagonist can substantially affect the balance by throwing the strength of further powers into the scales, this balance is determined by the efforts of each in the arms race: in the event of the swing of the balance towards one of them, there are no new worlds the other can call into being in order to redress it. Military balances which are unstable and fluctuating are notoriously corrosive of international security: they give rise, in the power with a temporary preponderance, to the counsel of preventive war. [. . .] Military balances have contributed to the avoidance of particular wars, but they are not a guarantee against war: on the contrary, war is one of the instruments by which the balance is maintained. The chief function of the balance of power in international society has not been to preserve peace, but to preserve the independence of sovereign states from the threat of domination, and to preserve the society of sovereign states from being transformed by conquest into a universal empire: to do these things, if necessary, by war.

But though it is no kind of panacea, the existence of a military balance between politically opposed powers and blocs is one of the chief factors making for peace and order among them. We shall be able to appreciate the importance of the balance of power if we consider carefully what, in the short run, the alternatives to it are. If—like the critics of the balance of power, from Richard Cobden to President Wilson to the present supporters of unilateral disarmament—we contrast the security provided by a military balance with that provided by some imagined political system that might arise in the long run, or with our image of some system that has occurred in the past, we shall be very conscious of its shortcomings. If we examine the present military balance alongside our image of a just and liberal world

government, or total disarmament, or free trade and universal brother-
hood, or the Roman peace, we must be impressed with its dangers. But if
we examine it alongside the alternatives to it that exist now, the alternatives that we by our action or inaction can bring about, we must form a very
different impression. The alternative to a stable balance of military power
is a preponderance of power, which is very much more dangerous. The
choice with which governments are in fact confronted is not that between
opting for the present structure of the world, and opting for some other
structure, but between attempting to maintain a balance of power, and
failing to do so. The balance of power is wrongly regarded as a synonym for
international anarchy; rightly regarded as something which mitigates an
anarchy which might otherwise be more rampant. It is not a panacea. But
it exists now; and among those forces which make for international security
and can be built upon by action that can be taken now it is one of the
strongest. [. . .]

The maintenance of balances of power is often fortuitous. The unilateral
action of the contending parties, from which for the most part they result,
is aimed at preponderance: the United States and the Soviet Union have
together brought about a balance but they would both prefer a preponderance. The most primitive kind of military balance arises in the absence of
any conscious pursuit of it, and without the contending parties being aware
of any mutual interest in the establishment or preservation of a balance.
Moreover, neither may be aware of any special interest of its own in such a
balance; nor may it comprehend the notion of a balance of power at all. In
principle a balance of power may occur in the absence even of that most
elementary notion of military policy, that the proper military strength of
the nation or the tribe should be determined by reference to the military
strength of surrounding nations or tribes: that the level of the nation's
military strength should be set by a standard which is not absolute, but
relative to the strength of others, whether greater than that of others, less
or the same. A balance of power might be no more than a moment of
deadlock in a war of annihilation.

Were the origins of balances of power so wholly fortuitous as this we
could not expect them to display much stability or tendency to persist.
However, the military policies of civilized nations are in general determined
by relative standards: the level of each nation's armed power is determined
at least in part by reference to the levels of armed power in other nations, or
at least with reference to beliefs about these levels. They are sometimes
directed, moreover, towards the achievement of some kind of balance in
strength with the nations with which they are in conflict, rather than towards the achievement of superiority over them. There is such a thing as
being content with a balance, such a thing as pursuing a balance not only by
frustrating the growth of the opponent's strength, but also by deliberately

restraining the inordinate growth of one's own. At least since the eighteenth century the idea that great powers should behave so as to preserve the balance of Europe has been a principle of state conduct. In the nineteenth century it was a central idea of the Concert of Europe that the maintenance of the balance of power should not be left to the operation of a hidden hand, but should be jointly pursued by the great powers in unison.

The chief means by which balances of power are maintained or upset are adjustments in armaments and alliances: a state may increase its military strength by increasing or improving its own armaments, or by gaining allies or depriving its opponents of them. In the nineteenth century, the attempt to maintain a balance by concerted international action was made through the adjustment of alliances and the adjustment of territorial boundaries, and not to any significant degree through international agreement about the character or the size of military forces and weapons: though agreement about territorial boundaries, settling as it did the distribution of military assets as important at that time as strategic position and population, may be regarded as a form of arms control. At the present time, however, the armaments competition plays a much more important part in determining the ratio of military power between the opposed blocs than does the competition for allies. If there were to be a stabilization of the military balance, it would have to be by the adjustment of armaments. Moreover, if it were to last for any length of time it would have to be by *arms control*. The uncontrolled arms race has fortuitously led the two opposed blocs in recent years into a system of balance at the strategic level which provides a modicum of security, including a balance of strategic nuclear power which gives a reasonable promise of preserving the peace through mutual deterrence. But there is no guarantee that, if the arms race remains uncontrolled, it will not lead the powers out of this situation of relative security as fortuitously as it led them into it. The nuclear stalemate will not maintain itself: if it is to persist, it will have to be maintained, and the joint consideration by the two military blocs of what cooperative measures they may take in order to see that it is appears to be one of the most likely sources of its maintenance.

[From Hedley Bull. *The Control of the Arms Race* (New York: Praeger, 1961), 31–9, 58–60.]

JOHN MEARSHEIMER

82 **Instability in Europe After the Cold War**

The profound changes now underway in Europe have been widely viewed as harbingers of a new age of peace. With the Cold War over, it is said, the threat of war that has hung over Europe for more than four decades is lifting. Swords can now be beaten into ploughshares; harmony can reign among the states and peoples of Europe. Central Europe, which long groaned under the massive forces of the two military blocs, can convert its military bases into industrial parks, playgrounds, and condominiums. Scholars of security affairs can stop their dreary quarrels over military doctrine and balance assessments, and turn their attention to finding ways to prevent global warming and preserve the ozone layer. European leaders can contemplate how to spend peace dividends. So goes the common view. [. . .]

[Under one] scenario [. . .] the Cold War comes to a complete end. The Soviet Union withdraws all of its forces from Eastern Europe, leaving the states in that region fully independent. Voices are thereupon raised in the United States, Britain, and Germany, arguing that American and British military forces in Germany have lost their principal *raison d'être*, and these forces are withdrawn from the Continent. NATO and the Warsaw Pact then dissolve; they may persist on paper, but each ceases to function as an alliance. As a result, the bipolar structure that has characterized Europe since the end of World War II is replaced by a multipolar structure. In essence, the Cold War we have known for almost half a century is over, and the postwar order in Europe is ended.

How would such a fundamental change affect the prospects for peace in Europe? Would it raise or lower the risk of war?

I argue that the prospects for major crises and war in Europe are likely to increase markedly if the Cold War ends and this scenario unfolds. The next decades in a Europe without the superpowers would probably not be as violent as the first 45 years of this century, but would probably be substantially more prone to violence than the past 45 years.

This pessimistic conclusion rests on the argument that the distribution and character of military power are the root causes of war and peace. Specifically, the absence of war in Europe since 1945 has been a consequence of three factors: the bipolar distribution of military power on the Continent; the rough military equality between the two states comprising the two poles in Europe, the United States and the Soviet Union; and the fact that each superpower was armed with a large nuclear arsenal. Domestic factors also affect the likelihood of war, and have helped cause the postwar peace. Most importantly, hyper-nationalism helped cause the two world wars, and the decline of nationalism in Europe since 1945 has contributed to the peacefulness of the postwar world. However, factors of military power have been most important in shaping past events, and will remain central in the future.

The departure of the superpowers from Central Europe would transform Europe from a bipolar to a multipolar system. Germany, France, Britain, and perhaps Italy would assume major power status; the Soviet Union would decline from superpower status but would remain a major European power, giving rise to a system of five major powers and a number of lesser powers. The resulting system would suffer the problems common to multi-polar systems, and would therefore be more prone to instability. Power inequities could also appear; if so, stability would be undermined further.

The departure of the superpowers would also remove the large nuclear arsenals they now maintain in Central Europe. This would remove the pacifying effect that these weapons have had on European politics. Four principal scenarios are possible. Under the first scenario, Europe would become nuclear-free, thus eliminating a central pillar of order in the Cold War era. Under the second scenario, the European states do not expand their arsenals to compensate for the departure of the superpowers' wea-pons. In a third scenario, nuclear proliferation takes place, but is misman-aged; no steps are taken to dampen the many dangers inherent in the proliferation process. All three of these scenarios would raise serious risks of war.

In the fourth and least dangerous scenario, nuclear weapons proliferate in Europe, but the process is well-managed by the current nuclear powers. They take steps to deter preventive strikes on emerging nuclear powers, to set boundaries on the proliferation process by extending security umbrellas over the neighbors of emerging nuclear powers, to help emerging nuclear powers build secure deterrent forces, and to discourage them from de-ploying counterforce systems that threaten their neighbors' deterrents. This outcome probably provides the best hope for maintaining peace in Europe. However, it would still be more dangerous than the world of 1945–90. Moreover, it is not likely that proliferation would be well-man-aged.

Three counter-arguments might be advanced against this pessimistic set of predictions of Europe's future. The first argument holds that the peace will be preserved by the effects of the liberal international economic order that has evolved since World War II. The second rests on the observation that liberal democracies very seldom fight wars against each other, and holds that the past spread of democracy in Europe has bolstered peace, and that the ongoing democratization of Eastern Europe makes war still less likely. The third argument maintains that Europeans have learned from their disastrous experiences in this century that war, whether conventional or nuclear, is so costly that it is no longer a sensible option for states. [. . .]

But the theories behind these arguments are flawed [. . .]; hence their prediction of peace in a multipolar Europe is flawed as well. [. . .]

Three policy prescriptions are in order.

First, the United States should encourage the limited and carefully man-aged proliferation of nuclear weapons in Europe. The best hope for avoid-ing war in post-Cold War Europe is nuclear deterrence; hence some nuclear proliferation is necessary to compensate for the withdrawal of the Soviet and American nuclear arsenals from Central Europe. Ideally [. . .] nuclear weapons would spread to Germany, but to no other state.

Second, Britain and the United States, as well as the Continental states, will have to balance actively and efficiently against any emerging aggressor to offset the ganging up and bullying problems that are sure to arise in post-Cold War Europe. Balancing in a multipolar system, however, is usually a problem-ridden enterprise, either because of geography or because of significant coordination problems. Nevertheless, two steps can be taken to maximize the prospects of efficient balancing.

The initial measure concerns Britain and the United States, the two prospective balancing states that, physically separated from the Continent, may thus conclude that they have little interest in what happens there. They would then be abandoning their responsibilities and, more importantly, their interests as off-shore balancers. Both states' failure to balance against Germany before the two world wars made war more likely in each case. It is essential for peace in Europe that they not repeat their past mistakes, but instead remain actively involved in maintaining the balance of power in Europe.

Specifically, both states must maintain military forces that can be deployed to the Continent to balance against states that threaten to start a war. To do this they must also socialize their publics to support a policy of continued Continental commitment. Support for such a commitment will be more difficult to mobilize than in the past, because its principal purpose would be to preserve peace, rather than to prevent an imminent hegemony, and the latter is a simpler goal to explain publicly. Moreover, it is the basic nature of states to focus on maximizing relative power, not on bolstering stability, so this prescription asks them to take on an unaccustomed task. Nevertheless, the British and American stake in peace is real, especially since there is a sure risk that a European war might involve large-scale use of nuclear weapons. It should therefore be possible for both countries to lead their publics to recognize this interest and support policies that protect it.

The other measure concerns American attitudes and actions toward the Soviet Union. The Soviets may eventually return to their past expansionism and threaten to upset the status quo. If so, we are back to the Cold War; the West should respond as quickly and efficiently as it did the first time. However, if the Soviets adhere to status quo policies, Soviet power could play a key role in balancing against Germany and in maintaining order in Eastern Europe. It is important that, in those cases where the Soviets are acting in a balancing capacity, the United States recognize this, cooperate with its former adversary, and not let residual distrust from the Cold War interfere with the balancing process.

Third, a concerted effort should be made to keep hyper-nationalism at bay, especially in Eastern Europe. This powerful force has deep roots in

Europe and has contributed to the outbreak of past European conflicts. Nationalism has been contained during the Cold War, but it is likely to reemerge once Soviet and American forces leave the heart of Europe. It will be a force for trouble unless it is curbed. The teaching of honest national history is especially important, since the teaching of false chauvinist history is the main vehicle for spreading virulent nationalism. States that teach a dishonestly self-exculpating or self-glorifying history should be publicly criticized and sanctioned.

On this count it is especially important that relations between Germany and its neighbors be handled carefully. Many Germans rightly feel that Germany has behaved very responsibly for 45 years, and has made an honest effort to remember and make amends for an ugly period of its past. Therefore, Germans quickly tire of lectures from foreigners demanding that they apologize once again for crimes committed before most of the current German population was born. On the other hand, peoples who have suffered at the hands of the Germans cannot forget their enormous suffering, and inevitably ask for repeated assurance that the past will not be repeated. This dialogue has the potential to spiral into mutual recriminations that could spark a renewed sense of persecution among Germans, and with it, a rebirth of German-nationalism. It is therefore incumbent on all parties in this discourse to proceed with understanding and respect for one another's feelings and experience. Specifically, others should not ask today's Germans to apologize for crimes they did not commit, but Germans must understand that others' ceaseless demands for reassurance have a legitimate basis in history, and should view these demands with patience and understanding.

None of these tasks will be easy to accomplish. In fact, I expect that the bulk of my prescriptions will not be followed; most run contrary to powerful strains of domestic American and European opinion, and to the basic nature of state behavior. Moreover, even if they are followed, this will not guarantee the peace in Europe. If the Cold War is truly behind us, the stability of the past 45 years is not likely to be seen again in the coming decades.

[From John Mearsheimer, 'Back to the Future: Instability in Europe After the Cold War', *International Security*, 15/1 (Summer 1990), 141–4, 190–2.]

Limited War and Developing Countries

MARTIN NAVIAS AND TIM MOREMAN

For tens of centuries warfare in the regions which we now loosely describe as the Third World was fought in the main by forces with equivalent types of weapons, logistical arrangements, and control systems. While there were as many differences in armaments as there were armies, and variations in forms of military organization as there were societies, the qualitative gap between contending forces was never as profound as that between the expanding European powers and local inhabitants. It was this which provided one of the major themes of colonial warfare up until the 1930s and accounted for the cheap and easy victories of the European states. The determination to combat and overcome this disparity of force at a later stage encouraged modern day guerrilla warfare theory and practice. Then, having won their independence, many Third World countries began to take advantage of the industrial capabilities of the developed world in order to acquire sophisticated conventional arsenals and, where possible, weapons of mass destruction. In this way they sought to close the gap between the firepower of the developing and developed worlds.

Colonial warfare in the developing world represented a distinct genre of military operations during the nineteenth and twentieth centuries. The succession of imperial campaigns fought in Africa and Asia included wars of conquest, pacification, punitive expeditions, and wars of competition between European powers for territory. The acquisition of empires brought with it a constant legacy of warfare in which European racial and social Darwinist ideas coloured the use of force. Military power was ruthlessly exploited to bring comparatively poorly armed and politically weak indigenous societies to their knees in one-sided and bloody campaigns. The ruthless destruction of lives, property, and crops revealed the emergence of total warfare for the local people however limited an affair it might be for the invaders.

The role of both civil and military technology was decisive in the expansion and consolidation of European empires. The employment of quinine, steam gunboats, railways, the telegraph, and the breech-loading rifle enabled small European armies to dominate the battlefield. The machine-gun became the symbol of European superiority and was employed with devastating effect. Hilaire Belloc observed that 'whatever happens we have got the Maxim gun and they have not'.

The impact of modern weapons was devastating against opponents employing mass shock tactics in open terrain. At Omdurman in 1898 11,000 Mahdist warriors were destroyed by massed machine-guns, breech-loading rifles, and artillery before they could reach close-quarters with British and Egyptian troops. Against better armed opponents who employed more sophisticated tactics the situation could be reversed, and during the campaigns on the North-West Frontier of India in 1897–8 and in South Africa in 1899 British troops were often unable to locate and engage their dispersed opponents and suffered heavily in result.

The environment was often a greater threat to the colonial armies than the foe. Indeed, colonial warfare was dominated by the debilitating effects of nature on European troops as imperial armies operated in areas where the effects of disease, the nature of the terrain, the lack of supplies and of reliable intelligence often hamstrung the conduct of operations. European armies were thus forced to seek a decisive tactical engagement before climate, disease, and precarious logistics brought an end to the campaign.

The conduct of 'small wars' required the development and utilization of military skills, organization, and training among troops far different from that required for 'civilised' warfare in Europe. This conflict between the military requirements of the two was never fully resolved. The tactics and lessons derived from one 'small war' were seldom applicable to another and accounted sometimes for European defeats at the hands of local populations employing tactics adapted to the terrain that nullified the superiority in small arms. Charles Callwell developed the first detailed handbook on the conduct of colonial warfare (83), and this served as the manual for the British army engaged in colonial war until the 1930s.

The division of Africa and Asia between the European powers at the end of the First World War brought an end to the era of 'small wars'. The consolidation and defence of imperial possessions became the predominant concern and for this a purely military response to colonial warfare was ill-suited. The military was forced to work closely with the civil authorities in a subordinate role to exploit and control colonial possessions in Africa and Asia against nationalist and revolutionary movements, rioting, and communal disturbances. Policing rather than conventional military operations characterized this period. Major-General C. W. Gwynn evolved a number of principles for regulating the use of the army in imperial policing (84).

The ideas of Gwynn and the efforts of colonial authorities to contain local discontent met with some successes and seemed adequate for a short while. However, already by the outbreak of the Second World War growing local restiveness had helped serve notice to the European powers that colonial control would require increasing numbers of men, material, and political will-power in order to maintain imperial rule.

By the end of the Second World War the colonial powers had been weakened both economically and politically. Retention of overseas possessions by continuing military technological dominance was challenged by local leaders employing the methods of guerrilla warfare, and seeking to exploit their own geographical and demographic advantages.

Yet, as Walter Laqueur notes in his major historical and comparative study (87), this form of warfare is neither a twentieth-century nor a Third World phenomenon but one that since biblical times has been employed by weaker forces to harry and wear down superior enemies. What was novel about twentieth-century guerrilla war was not only its application to revolutionary anti-colonial efforts but the emergence of a fully fledged doctrine claiming universal applicability.

In China, Mao Tse-tung recognized that against technologically superior forces any effort to force an immediately decisive conventional battle would be suicidal (86). This, after all, had long been the fate of Third World armies in combat against colonial troops. For success to be achieved by the less developed society it was necessary on one level to subordinate military operations to political struggle and, on another level, to exploit the advantages of both space and time.

Political struggle involves the mobilization of the population resources for the guerrillas and against the enemy. The mobilized population would, as Mao puts it, be the sea in which the guerrilla fish would swim. It would provide food, shelter, and intelligence for the roving guerrilla bands while, at the same time, the political mobilization process would ensure that the authority and residual legitimacy of the colonial power be steadily undermined.

This could never be a rapid process, but neither on the military level were the guerrillas seeking quick solutions. The tactic was to exploit the environment (be that the mountains or the jungles) in which the technological superiority of the enemy could not be brought to bear and in which the guerrilla would seek tactical advantages, attacking and retreating when opportunities availed and necessities demanded. Over time, guerrilla base areas would enlarge, enemy losses would mount, and enemy will to fight would be sapped. Then and only then, Mao argues, could the guerrillas begin to engage in the final conventional phase of fighting.[1] The interview with General Giap (88) provides a valuable insight into the strategic thinking behind a man who can claim major victories against France and the United States following a comparable approach to Mao.

Throughout the developing world, guerrilla operations helped undermine European and American power and encouraged the move towards

---

[1] For an alternative model, based on Fidel Castro's campaign against the Batista regime in Cuba, see Che Guevara, *Guerrilla Warfare* (Harmondsworth: Pelican Books, 1969).

independence especially amongst Asian and African states. With few exceptions, European and American militaries had great difficulties in mastering this form of combat. And, as Mao had predicted, their populations generally had little stomach for long-drawn-out campaigns with few clear-cut results and constant streams of casualties. Significantly, termination of the imperial presence did not lead to the end of guerrilla warfare, and this very successful method of fighting continued to be employed—with equally destructive results—in many domestic and regional Third World disputes. Even as late as 1983 the United States could still get caught by taking sides in a messy civil war (89). Ten years later, the same problems emerged in Somalia.

For the Americans, the concept of limited war had never really been intended to apply to these sort of conflicts. Their purpose was to use it in conventional campaigns waged against enemies backed by the Soviet Union but in circumstances in which both Moscow and Washington had a stake in preventing the extension of the conflict or escalation into total war. As can be seen in the extract from Robert Osgood's seminal work on limited war, based largely on the Korean experience (90), the concern of proponents of this sort of warfare was to prevent a total war mentality leading the United States to fail to reach a satisfactory deal which preserved essential interests without running unnecessary risks. The alternative approach was exemplified by the famous statement of General MacArthur, the American commander of the United Nations forces in Korea, that there was 'no substitute for victory'.

The unusual features of Korea, at least until the 1991 Gulf War, turned out to be the United Nations backing and the largely conventional character of its operations. In the case of Vietnam, part of the frustration of the United States Army was that the enemy only rarely took it on in open battle. Others, who looked for example at Britain's successful counter-insurgency campaign in Malaysia, recognized that the answer might be found in an approach which concentrated more on the 'hearts and minds' of the Vietnamese (91). This experience led Osgood to reappraise his own confidence in a limited war strategy (93).

The wars of national liberation resulted in independence but not in peace. The newly sovereign states were from the start beset by problems of political legitimacy, economic development, and territorial sovereignty. Until the late 1980s they were also caught up in the midst of superpower competition with the result that not only were there major causes of conflict, but there existed patrons ready to supply weaponry with which to prosecute these wars.

While in the 1950s and 1960s the major weapons suppliers to the Third World—such as the US, USSR, and the European states—tended to transfer second-rate items, by the 1980s the quality of weaponry transferred was sometimes on a par with that to be found in the industrialized world's arsenals. It is therefore not surprising that conflicts in the Third World have been characterized by an increasing level of destructiveness. Andrew Pierre (94) was one of the first political scientists in the early 1980s to begin to assess the phenomenon of the international arms trade in terms of its influence on shifting patterns of regional and global politics. He notes that the transfer of arms was a very important contributing factor in the emergence of new regional powers and that it had a crucial impact on power balances and on regional stability. Pierre emphasizes that arms sales constitute a form of power redistribution in North–South relations, and that 'The diffusion of defense capabilities contributes at the same time to the erosion of the early postwar system of imperial or hegemonic roles formerly played by the major powers around the globe'. He argues that the diffusion of this technology would ultimately lead to the former colonial powers losing their ability to control and influence former colonial regions.

While during the 1991 Gulf War the allies were still able to brush aside the assembled Iraqi forces without great difficulty, it should not be forgotten that this was only after the assembly of a force of half a million men and the investment of billions of dollars—a very far cry from the scope and scale of foreign intervention in the developing world during the previous century.

The integration of sophisticated weaponry into Third World armies had, of course, long preceded the 1991 Gulf War. By the 1970s and 1980s a number of states in the developing world had superior quantities (and in some instances a better quality) of weaponry than most NATO and Warsaw Pact armies. More significantly, wars in South Asia, Southern Africa, and especially the Middle East demonstrated that developing countries were well adept at integrating imported sophisticated conventional technologies into their armed forces and employing them on a vast scale (92). The wars between India and Pakistan, Israel and its neighbours, and Iran and Iraq proved testing grounds for weaponry, doctrine, and tactics, and both NATO and Warsaw Pact analysts—who, after all, had little opportunity for direct experience with their tools of trade—showed a very keen interest in the role of military technology in the Third World.

The search by developing states to expand their military and political power has also over the past three decades taken on an even more dangerous turn with efforts to acquire weapons of mass destruction—nuclear, chemical, and biological munitions. With these weapons the destructive capabilities of a number of Third World states have increased immeasurably and the consequences are already being felt domestically, regionally, and internationally. Now, not only will power projection into parts of the Third World be potentially more expensive, but, theoretically at least, a growing number of developing countries have the option of doing great damage in the industrialized world itself. Fear in the industrialized world about the implications of proliferation for their own well-being has thus ensured that the issue of the spread of weapons of mass destruction has emerged as a key element in North–South relations.

With the industrialized world intent upon stifling proliferation efforts, development programmes are usually conducted in great secrecy. Consequently, unlike the field of guerrilla warfare, there is yet to emerge a substantial literature on non-conventional weaponry by Third World authors. Most of the material tends to be from western sources and much of it is American.

Kenneth Waltz took a provocative view of the proliferation process (95). More, argues Waltz, may in fact be better and focusing attention on the destructive effects of nuclear weapons obscures the potential benefits of proliferation. Indeed, he believes that 'Nuclear weapons and an appropriate doctrine for their use may make it possible to approach the defensive–deterrent ideal, a condition that would cause the chances of war to dwindle'. Waltz's position, however, remains a decidedly minority one and few analysts would now agree that proliferation has many positive benefits.[1]

The collapse of superpower conflict has helped unleash a variety of nationalistic, ethnic, and religious forces within the developing world which seem to augur ill for the prospects for regional peace and stability. These forces are of course nothing new, but it is their increasing ability to do damage to themselves and to others outside their immediate regions that underlines the importance of Third World security for international security. As noted in the previous section, the sort of wars familiar in the Third World are now to be found in Europe. In the final two extracts Martin Van Creveld and Lawrence Freedman (96, 97) consider the implications of this development.

---

[1] For a contrary view, see Lewis A. Dunn, *Containing Nuclear Proliferation*, Adelphi Paper No. 263 (London: IISS, Winter 1991).

83 Small Wars

Small war is a term which has come largely into use of late years, and which is admittedly somewhat difficult to define. Practically it may be said to include all campaigns other than those where both the opposing sides consist of regular troops. It comprises the expeditions against savages and semi-civilised races by disciplined soldiers, it comprises campaigns undertaken to suppress rebellions and guerilla warfare in all parts of the world where organized armies are struggling against opponents who will not meet them in the open field, and it thus obviously covers operations very varying in their scope and in their conditions.

The expression 'small war' has in reality no particular connection with the scale on which any campaign may be carried out; it is simply used to denote, in default of a better, operations of regular armies against irregular, or comparatively speaking irregular, forces. For instance, the struggle in 1894–95 between Japan and China might, although very large forces were placed in the field on both sides, from the purely military point of view almost be described as a small war; for the operations on land were conducted between a highly trained, armed, organized, and disciplined army on one side, and by forces on the other side which, though numerically formidable, could not possibly be described as regular troops in the proper sense of the word. Small wars include the partisan warfare which usually arises when trained soldiers are employed in the quelling of sedition and of insurrections in civilised countries; they include campaigns of conquest when a Great Power adds the territory of barbarous races to its possessions; and they include punitive expeditions against tribes bordering upon distant colonies. The suppression of the Indian Mutiny and the Anglo-French campaign on the Peiho, the British operations against the Egyptian army in 1882, and the desultory warfare of the United States troops against the nomad Red Indians, the Spanish invasion of Morocco in 1859, and the pacification of Upper Burma, can all alike be classed under the category of small wars. Whenever a regular army finds itself engaged upon hostilities against irregular forces, or forces which in their armament, their organization, and their discipline are palpably inferior to it, the conditions of the campaign become distinct from the conditions of modern regular warfare, and it is with hostilities of this nature that this volume proposes to deal.
[. . .]

The teachings of great masters of the art of war, and the experience gained from campaigns of modern date in America and on the continent of Europe, have established certain principles and precedents which form the groundwork of the system of regular warfare of to-day. Certain rules of conduct exist which are universally accepted. Strategy and tactics alike are in great campaigns governed, in most respects, by a code from which it is perilous to depart. But the conditions of small wars are so diversified, the enemy's mode of fighting is often so peculiar, and the theatres of operations present such singular features, that irregular warfare must generally be carried out on a method totally different from the stereotyped system. The art of war, as generally understood, must be modified to suit the circumstances of each particular case. The conduct of small wars is in fact in certain respects an art by itself, diverging widely from what is adapted to the conditions of regular warfare, but not so widely that there are not in all its branches points which permit comparisons to be established. [. . .]

Tactics necessarily depend largely on armament, and while the weapons which regular troops take into the field have vastly improved in the last 40 years, it must be remembered that the arms of the enemy have also improved. Even savages, who a few years ago would have defended themselves with bows and arrows, are often found now-a-days with breech-loading rifles—the constant smuggling of arms into their territories, which the various Powers concerned seem wholly unable to suppress, promises that small wars of the future may involve very difficult operations.

[From Colonel C. E. Callwell, *Small Wars: Their Principles and Practice* (London: HMSO, 1906), 21–4.]

CHARLES W. GWYNN

84 Imperial Policing

[T]he police duties of the Army [. . .] may be roughly grouped in three categories, though in the course of events an incident may pass from one category to another. In the first category are small wars: deliberate campaigns with a definite military objective, but undertaken with the ultimate object of establishing civil control. The conduct of such wars differs in no respect from defensive or punitive wars undertaken to check external aggression. No limitations are placed on the amount of force which can legitimately be exercised, and the Army is free to employ all the weapons the nature of the terrain permits. Such campaigns are clearly a purely military responsibility. They involve operations of a military character for which the Army receives training, and there is an extensive literature dealing with their conduct in all its aspects. I have not, therefore, included any example of this type.

The second category [. . .] includes cases when the normal civil control does not exist, or has broken down to such an extent that the Army becomes the main agent for the maintenance of or for the restoration of order. To a greater or less degree it is then vested with responsibility for the action to be taken. In certain cases, as when martial law is proclaimed, the civil authority abdicates its position temporarily and is superseded by military government in the area proclaimed. More commonly, responsibility is shared between the two authorities in giving effect to measures required to restore control. Special powers which they do not ordinarily possess may be given to military officers; but in any case they are required on their own responsibility to take such action as the necessity of the situation demands.—To the third category belong those occasions when the civil power continues to exercise undivided control but finds the police forces on which it normally relies insufficient. In such cases the Army is employed 'in aid of the civil power' and its responsibility goes little further than for the methods the troops adopt to give effect to the directions of the civil magistrate.—In both these latter categories the Army is bound to exercise the minimum force required to attain its object.

Of these three categories of police duties, it is the second which has become of special importance in modern times. In the Victorian era, when the Empire was in process of expansion, small wars were of frequent occurrence and at that time might well have been considered the Army's principal police task. Now that civil control has been established in practically all parts of the Empire, small wars are of less frequent occurrence, and when they do occur, are generally defensive or punitive operations to protect our frontier regions from aggression. But the civil control which has been established still rests on insecure foundations; the edifice in some cases is liable to collapse and to require rebuilding. In others where the structure appeared to be secure it has developed weaknesses. The principal police task of the Army is no longer to prepare the way for civil control, but to restore it when it collapses or shows signs of collapse. Subversive movements take many forms and are of varying intensity; but even when armed rebellion occurs, it presents a very different military problem from that of a deliberate small-war campaign. There is an absence of a definite objective, and conditions are those of guerrilla warfare, in which elusive rebel bands must be hunted down, and protective measures are needed to deprive them of opportunities. The admixture of rebels with a neutral or loyal element of the population adds to the difficulties of the task. Excessive severity may antagonise this element, add to the number of the rebels, and leave a lasting feeling of resentment and bitterness. On the other hand, the power and resolution of the Government forces must be displayed. Anything which can be interpreted as weakness encourages those who are sitting on the fence to keep on good terms with the rebels.

[From Major-General Sir Charles Gwynn, *Imperial Policing* (London: Macmillan, 1934), 3–5.]

L. J. SHADWELL

85 Savage Warfare

I will now deal very briefly with some of the main points in which all savage, or non-European warfare, differs from that of civilized people. Few non-civilized nations possess ordnance, and, therefore, one's own artillery can come into action at much shorter ranges than would otherwise be the case; and there is not the same necessity for massing or concentrating the guns.

No savage nation, as far as I am aware, employs second and third lines of troops, either in the attack or the defence, and consequently, if the first line—which contains every available man—is defeated, the enemy has no general reserve to bring up to cover his retreat or make a counter attack. Once such a foe has been defeated no rearguard is formed to cover a retreat, and the loss of *morale* is infinitely greater than in a European force.

In attacking an Asiatic foe in position, a flank attack may be separated from a frontal attack to a much greater extent than would be safe in European warfare. In the former case the enemy never has either the reserve of troops in hand, nor the generalship to contain or hold back one attack with a comparatively small force, and fall in overwhelming strength on the other; as Napoleon did at Austerlitz, and Wellington at Salamanca.

Lastly, on account of the advantages which civilized troops possess over savage or semi-barbarous foes, owing to the power of discipline and of better weapons, and to the possession of artillery and machine-guns, a well-handled European force can resist or attack with every chance of success a much greater force of savages or semi-barbarians than it could of disciplined Europeans.

These appear the main respects in which a European force has the advantage over a savage or semi-barbarous force, though, doubtless, many other points of superiority will readily suggest themselves to the reader. [. . .]

The Soudanese warrior as he existed in the days of El Teb and Tamai, the Ghazi fanatic we have so often encountered on the North-Western frontier of India, and the Zulu of Ulundi, are individuals for whom death had no terrors at all, and who, regardless of losses amongst their comrades and their own wounds, charged recklessly home. In the Soudan and in the Zulu campaign our forces were fighting a nation of individuals of this character.

On the frontier the Ghazi has formed only a percentage of the opposing force; and with the remainder of the tribe, valour is generally, as with Europeans, mingled with discretion. But when excited by the prowess of their Ghazi brethren, or elated by success, they are resolute and bold; and if hopeful of victory, or when temporarily excited by a fanatical preacher to expect a safe conduct to Paradise in case of death, their daring and courage is of the most reckless description.

A frontier tribesman can live for days on the grain he carries with him, and other savages on a few dates; consequently no necessity exists for them to cover a line of communications. So nimble of foot, too, are they in their grass shoes, and so conversant with every goat-track in their mountains, that they can retreat in any direction. This extraordinary mobility enables them to attack from any direction quite unexpectedly, and to disperse and disappear as rapidly as they came. For this reason the rear of a European force is as much exposed to attack as its front or flanks; and as the line of communications can be cut at almost any point, not only have the various depôts on the line of communications to be very strongly fortified, but all convoys moving along the road must be well guarded, and hills commanding the road held by pickets.

Troops or convoys moving in the dusk render themselves liable to annihilation, for a savage foe can see in the dark far better than a European, can approach noiselessly unseen, and attack simultaneously from all sides.

Whereas some savages are so inexperienced in the use of firearms, and so reckless that they prefer to trust to shock tactics and to their spears, the Pathan, and more especially the Afridi, is as skilled a marksman as could be found in the world. His rifle is to him the joy of his life. He has been brought up to use firearms from boyhood; and has probably been engaged from early manhood in trying to shoot one or more kinsmen or fellow-tribesmen with whom he has a blood feud. Frequently he has served in the Indian Army and learnt all that a musketry instructor can teach him; so that, when our troops are halted or in camp, he has a target to fire at which he can hardly miss. On the other hand, his dirty garments are so indistinguishable from the surrounding rocks, and he moves about with such agility, that he is comparatively safe.

So great again is his ferocity and his love for bloodshed that, with two or three comrades, he will lie concealed for hours in the hope of cutting up and mutilating some unarmed straggler or follower, or, better still, shooting some armed man and possessing himself of a rifle which is worth its weight in silver. So little does he think of the future that the loss of his house, his store of grain, and his fodder, is as nothing to the young Afridi, when compared with the present delight of murder and plunder; and he well knows that, were his tribe to combine and meet us in open fight, our discipline and armament would prevail, whereas his guerilla tactics offer him personally the maximum chance of plunder and success with the minimum of risk.

[From Captain L. J. Shadwell, *Lockhart's Advance through Tirah* (London: W. Thacker & Co., 1898), 100–5.]

86 Mao's Military Principles

War and politics

... 'War is the continuation of politics'; in this sense war is politics and war itself is a political action; there has not been a single war since ancient times that did not bear a political character. The Anti-Japanese War is a revolutionary war waged by the whole Chinese nation. Victory in this war is inseparable from the over-all policy of persistently carrying on our war of resistance and maintaining the united front. It is inseparable from the mobilization of all the people in the nation, from political principles such as unity of officers and men, unity of the army and the people, and the disintegration of the enemy forces, from the implementation of the united-front policy; from cultural mobilization, and from efforts to win the support of international forces and of the people of the enemy's country. In short, war cannot be separated from politics. Any tendency among the anti-Japanese soldiers to belittle politics, to isolate war from it, and to make war an absolute, is erroneous and must be corrected.

But war has its special characteristics and in this sense it is not identical with politics. 'War is a special political technique for the realization of certain political objectives.' When politics has developed to a certain stage beyond which it cannot proceed by the usual means, war is made to sweep away the obstacles in the way of politics. For instance, the semi-independent status of China has been an obstacle to the political development of Japanese imperialism, and so Japan started her war of aggression to sweep away that impediment. . . . It can therefore be said that politics is bloodless war, while war is the politics of bloodshed . . .

Such a gigantic national revolutionary war as ours cannot succeed without universal and thoroughgoing political mobilization. China was greatly remiss in failing to undertake anti-Japanese political mobilization before the war of resistance. By this, she lost a move to the enemy. Even after the war of resistance began, political mobilization had been far from universal, let alone thoroughgoing. News about the war reached the great majority of the people through the enemy's shelling and air bombing. That also constituted a kind of mobilization, but it was done by the enemy, not by ourselves. People in remote regions who cannot hear the guns lead a tranquil life even now. This situation must be changed, otherwise there can be no victory for our life-and-death struggle. We must not again fail to make the move against our enemy; on the contrary, we must fully exploit this move to vanquish him. Such a move is of the highest significance, in fact a matter of paramount importance, whereas our inferiority in things like weapons is but secondary. With the common people of the whole country mobilized, we shall create a vast sea of humanity in which the enemy will be swallowed up, obtain relief for our shortage in arms and other things, and secure the prerequisites to overcome every difficulty in the war. In order to achieve victory, we must persistently carry on the war of resistance, maintain the united front, and keep up the protracted war. But none of these can be separated from the mobilization of the common people. To aim at attaining victory while neglecting political mobilization means 'trying to drive one's chariot southward by heading northward', a step that would inevitably forfeit victory . . .

There are those who feel that it is hardly conceivable for a guerrilla unit to exist for a long period behind the enemy lines. This is a viewpoint based on ignorance of the relations between the army and the people. The popular masses are like water, and the army is like a fish. How then can it be said that when there is water, a fish will have difficulty in preserving its existence? An army which fails to maintain good discipline gets into opposition with the popular masses, and thus by its own actions dries up the water. In this case, it naturally cannot continue to exist. All guerrilla units must thoroughly understand this principle. [. . .]

Every communist must understand this truth: Political power grows out of the barrel of a gun. Our principle is that the Party commands the gun; the gun shall never be allowed to command the Party. But it is also true that with the gun at our disposal we can really build up the Party organizations; the Eighth Route Army has built up a powerful Party organization in North China. We can also rear cadres and create schools, culture and mass movements. Everything in Yenan has been built up by means of the gun. Anything can grow out of the barrel of the gun. Viewed from the Marxist theory of the state, the army is the chief component of the political power of a state. Whoever wants to seize and hold on to political power must have a strong army. Some people have ridiculed us as advocates of the 'theory of the omnipotence of war'; yes, we are, we are advocates of the theory of the omnipotence of revolutionary war. This is not a bad thing, it is good and it is Marxist. With the help of guns, the Russian communists brought about socialism. We want to bring about a democratic republic. Experience in the class struggle of the era of imperialism teaches us that the working class and the toiling masses cannot defeat the armed bourgeois and landlord except by the power of the gun; in this sense we can even say that the whole world can be remoulded only with the gun. As advocates of the abolition of war, we do not desire war; but war can only be abolished through war—in order to get rid of the gun, we must first grasp it in hand.

The military principles for defeating Chiang Kai-shek

. . . Our principles of operation are:

1. To attack dispersed, isolated enemy forces first; to attack concentrated, strong enemy forces later.

2. To take small and medium cities and extensive rural areas first; to take big cities later.

3. To make the wiping out of the enemy's effective strength our main objective, rather than the holding or seizure of a city or place. Holding or seizing a city or place is the outcome of wiping out the enemy's effective strength, and often a city or place can be held only after it has changed hands a number of times.

4. In every battle, to concentrate an absolutely superior force (two, three, four, and sometimes even five or six times the enemy's strength), to encircle the enemy forces completely, to strive to wipe them out thoroughly and not let any escape from the net. In special circumstances, to deal crushing blows to the enemy, that is, to concentrate all our strength on a frontal attack and also to attack one or both of his flanks, with the aim of wiping out one part and routing another, so that our army can swiftly move its troops to smash other enemy forces. To avoid battles of attrition in which we lose more than we gain or only break even. In this way, although we are inferior as a whole (in terms of numbers), we are absolutely superior in every part and every specific campaign, and this ensures victory in the campaign. As time goes on, we shall become superior as a whole and eventually wipe out the enemy.

5. To fight no battle unprepared, to fight no battle if we are not sure of victory; to try to be well prepared for each battle, to make every effort to ensure victory in the prevailing conditions.

6. To give full play to our style of fighting—courage in battle, no fear of sacrifice or fatigue, and continuous fighting (that is, fighting successive battles in a short time without rest).

7. To wipe out the enemy through mobile warfare, at the same time paying attention to the tactics of positional attack and capturing fortified enemy points and cities.

8. With regard to attacking cities, resolutely to seize all weakly defended fortified enemy points and cities. To seize at opportune moments all moderately defended fortified enemy points and cities if circumstances permit. As for strongly defended fortified enemy points and cities, to wait until conditions are ripe and then take them.

9. To replenish our strength with all the arms and most of the personnel captured from the enemy. Our army's main sources of manpower and *matériel* are at the front.

10. To make good use of the intervals between campaigns to rest, train, and consolidate our troops. In general, periods of rest, training, and con-

solidation should not be very long, and the enemy should so far as possible be permitted no breathing space.

[From Stuart R. Schram, *The Political Thought of Mao Tse-tung* (Harmondsworth: Pelican Books, 1969), 286–92.]

WALTER LAQUEUR

87 The Character of Guerrilla Warfare

The multiple 'objective' and 'subjective' factors involved in guerrilla warfare and their complicated interaction rule out all-embracing formulas and explanations that are scientific, in the sense that they have predictive value. To recognize these limitations is not to deny that certain patterns are common to many guerrilla movements and that a study of these patterns could be of help in understanding why guerrilla wars have occurred in some conditions but not in others, and why some have succeeded and others have failed. The following attempt to summarize experience is concerned with probabilities not certainties.

1. The geographical milieu has always been of importance. Guerrilla movements have usually preferred regions that are not easily accessible (such as mountain ranges, forests, jungles, swamps) in which they are difficult to locate, and in which the enemy cannot deploy his full strength. Such areas are ideal in the early period of guerrilla warfare, during the period of consolidation, and they retain their uses later on as hideouts in a period of danger. In such areas the guerrillas will be relatively unmolested, but at the same time there are obvious drawbacks. If the enemy has to undergo the hardships of a mountain climate, the guerrillas, too, will have to suffer. It is difficult to obtain food and other supplies in distant, sparsely populated areas. Restricting their operations to these regions the guerrillas will be safe but they will be ineffective, for they will be able to harass only isolated enemy outposts, they will not be in a position to hit at the main lines of communication and they will lose contact with the 'masses'. Thus the ideal guerrilla territory while relatively inaccessible should be located not too far from cities and villages. Of late, topographical conditions have lost some of their erstwhile importance. On the whole it has become easier for the antiguerrilla forces to locate the rebels. Furthermore, with the rapid progress of urbanization, the countryside has lost much of its original political importance. The village cannot encircle the city if the majority of the population resides in urban areas. For this reason, and for some others, the main scene of guerrilla operations has shifted from the countryside to the city in predominantly urban societies, with a simultaneous shift in strategy from hiding in nature to finding cover in town.

Guerrilla movements need bases and they cannot operate without a steady flow of supplies. Ideally a sanctuary should be on foreign territory outside the reach of the antiguerrilla forces. Bases are needed for guerrilla units to recover from their battles, to reorganize for new campaigns and for a great many other purposes. While movement is one of the cardinal principles of guerrilla tactics a guerrilla unit is not a *perpetuum mobile*. The main drawback of a base is that it offers a fixed target for enemy attack. Thus guerrillas may be compelled to change their bases from time to time, unless they have established 'liberated zones' which the enemy, with his resources overextended, can no longer destroy. The question of supply was not of decisive importance before the nineteenth century, when guerrillas (as regular armies) lived off the land, when weapons were unsophisticated and could be locally manufactured. The more complicated the arms, the greater the guerrillas' dependence on supply routes, frequently from abroad. There are but two cases in recent history in which major guerrilla armies survived and expanded without outside supply of arms—China and Yugoslavia. But this was exceptional in that these guerrilla armies came into being during a general war that offered many opportunities of acquiring arms. The decisive victories of Mao's army and of Tito's partisans came only after they had the opportunity of rearming themselves from outside sources.

2. The etiology of guerrilla wars shows that it very often occurs in areas in which such wars have occurred before. [. . .] Furthermore, there are cultural traditions favoring or militating against large-scale political violence. Beyond a certain stage of cultural development it is difficult for a guerrilla movement to gain mass support. Neither the middle class nor workers and peasants in civilized countries feel sufficient enthusiasm to 'go to the mountains' even at a time of grave crisis. What Engels wrote in 1870—that our tradition gives only barbarians the right of real self-defense and that civilized nations fight according to established etiquette—is *a fortiori* true now. Even in the case of foreign invasion and occupation the great majority of the population in a civilized country will not engage in a war risking total destruction.

3. To this extent there is a (negative) correlation between guerrilla warfare and the degree of economic development. There have been few peasant guerrilla wars in modern times in which acute agrarian demands constituted the central issue (Mexico, the Philippines). On the other hand, in many more countries the peasantry has been the main reservoir of manpower for guerrilla armies led by nonpeasant elites. The breakdown of traditional peasant society under the pressure of capitalist development, absentee landlordism, demographic pressure, falling prices for agricultural produce, natural catastrophes and other misfortunes have created in many Asian countries (and to a lesser extent in Africa and Latin America) conditions in which there has been great sympathy among poor peasants, land-

less laborers, but also middle peasants for popular movements promising land to the landless, even if this promise was not the immediate issue in the war. The difficulty facing the guerrilla leaders has always been to harness this revolutionary potential on a nationwide basis in view of the traditional reluctance of peasants to fight outside their neighborhood. This could mostly be achieved only in the framework of a national struggle transcending the parochial framework such as a war against a foreign enemy (China, Algeria).

4. Throughout the nineteenth and twentieth centuries there have been three main species of guerrilla wars. They have been directed against foreign occupants, either in the framework of a general war or after the defeat of the regular army and against colonial rule. Secondly, guerrilla warfare has been the favorite tactic of separatist, minority movements fighting the central government (the Vendée, IMRO, IRA, ELF, the Basques, the Kurds, the FLQ, etc.). And thirdly, guerrilla warfare against native incumbents has been the rule in Latin America and in a few other countries (Burma, Thailand, etc.). But the national, patriotic element has always been heavily emphasized even if domestic rulers were the target; they were attacked as foreign hirelings by the true patriots fighting for national unity and independence. In China, Vietnam, Yugoslavia, Albania, Greece, the Philippines and Malaya partisan units were established to fight foreign occupants but they became civil war forces with the end of the general war. Throughout the nineteenth century the achievement of national independence has been the traditional goal of guerrilla movements; more recently social and economic programs have featured prominently. But the patriotic appeal has always played a more important role than social-revolutionary propaganda. Castro's war was fought for the overthrow of Batista's tyranny; most Latin American guerrilla movements have stressed general reform programs rather than clearly defined socialist-Communist slogans in their fight against domestic contenders. As the outcome of these wars show, guerrillas succeed with much greater ease against foreign domination than against native incumbents.

5. The character of guerrilla war has undergone profound changes during the last two centuries, but so has regular war on the one hand, and the technique of revolution on the other. However, there is no justification for regarding modern guerrilla warfare (or 'people's war', or revolutionary insurgency) as an entirely new phenomenon which has little connection with the guerrilla wars of former periods. Organization (the role of the political party) and propaganda play an infinitely more important role in present day guerrilla war than in the past, and it is of course true that in some Third World countries guerrilla war is merely one stage in the struggle for power. Guerrilla war was never 'apolitical', it was always nationalist in character and became national-revolutionary in an age of

revolution. Too much importance has been attributed to the use of Marxist-Leninist verbiage on the part of Third World liberation movements. This has led Western observers to interpret their progress either in terms of a worldwide Communist conspiracy or as a great new liberating promise. While the common denominator of most of these Third World movements is anti-imperialism and the rejection of the capitalist form of modernization, the ideology guiding them is a mixture of agrarian populism and radical nationalism (with 'nationalism' and 'socialism' often interchangeable). Such political movements have certain similarities with European Communism (dictatorship, the role of the monolithic party) but on a deeper level of analysis they are as distant from socialism as from liberal capitalism. Elsewhere the basic inspiration for guerrilla warfare has been sectarian-separatist (religious-tribal) with revolutionary ideology as a concession to prevailing intellectual fashions and modes of expression.

6. The leadership of nineteenth- and early twentieth-century guerrilla movements was usually in the hands of men of the people (Mina, the Empecinado, Andreas Hofer, Zapata, the Boer leaders, the IMRO). In backward countries they were traditionally led by tribal chiefs or religious dignitaries. More recently they have become, by and large, the preserve of young intellectuals or semi-intellectuals; this refers particularly to Latin America and Africa with only a very few exceptions (Fabio Vasquez, Samora Machel).

The social origin of the twentieth-century guerrilla elite in Latin America and also in Asia and the more backward European countries is usually middle class, especially the administrative stratum (the 'lower mandarins') which has no independent means of its own. Equally frustrated by their own limited prospects and the real or imaginary plight of their country, they have opted for revolutionary violence, the transformation of an old-fashioned, ineffective autocracy into a more modern, more effective and by necessity also more despotic regime. To seize power, the civilian intelligentsia transforms itself into the military leadership. A formula of this kind does not apply to every single guerrilla movement, even less to all of its leaders; nor does it do justice to the idealistic motivation of leading guerrilla cadres. But in historical perspective this has been the political function of radical guerrilla movements. [. . .]

7. Social composition: Attention has been drawn to the fact that peasants traditionally constituted the most important mass basis of guerrilla movements, but conditions varied considerably from country to country even in the nineteenth century and there have been further changes since. [. . .] Usually the smaller the guerrilla army, the larger the middle-class element. This applies above all to the Cuban revolution and the various urban guerrilla groups such as the Tupamaros. Women have participated in almost all guerrilla movements. They have been most prominent in the small urban guerrilla groups (West Germany, the US) and in Korea (more than a

quarter of their total force). Available data are insufficient to establish whether the occupation of insurgents reflects the occupational pattern of the population as a whole. This may have been the case in some countries (Philippines, Algeria) but not in others (Latin America). A poll taken by the French during the first Vietnam war showed that almost fifty percent of their prisoners were classified as 'petty bourgeois', and in African guerrilla movements, too, the urban petty bourgeoisie was apparently represented far above their share in the population. The small urban guerrilla movements are preponderantly constituted of students, or recent students, the IRA being the one major exception.

8. The motives that have induced men and women to join guerrilla bands are manifold. Historically, patriotism has been the single most important factor—the occupation of the homeland by foreigners, the resentment directed against the colonial power—often accompanied by personal grievances (humiliation, material deprivation, brutalities committed by the occupying forces). Secessionist guerrilla movements have based their appeal on the discrimination against and the persecution of ethnic or religious minorities. Guerrilla movements fighting domestic contenders stress obvious political or social grievances such as the struggle against tyranny, unequal distribution of income, government inefficiency, corruption and 'betrayal', and, generally speaking, the 'antipopular character of the ruling clique'. Land hunger, high interest rates (Philippines), the encroachment by the *haciendados* on Indian land (Mexico) have been important factors in predominantly agrarian societies. On top of these causes there has been a multiplicity of personal reasons ranging from a developed social conscience to boredom, the thirst for adventure and the romanticism of guerrilla life to personal ambition—the expectation of bettering oneself socially or of reaching a position of power and influence. The dynamic character of guerrilla movements has always exerted a powerful attraction of young idealists—the prospect of activity, of responsibility for one's fellows, of fighting with equally enthusiastic comrades for the national and social liberation of the homeland. As Maguire wrote seventy years ago and Denis Davydov well before him, a partisan must be a kind of military Byron, his enterprise requires a romantic imagination. What induces guerrillas to stay on is above all *esprit de corps*, loyalty to his commander and fellow soldiers. The feeling of togetherness and team spirit seems to be more important than ideological indoctrination. Guerrilla warfare usually opens larger vistas to personal initiative and daring than regular warfare; it has been said that slavish imitation produces good military tailors but not guerrilla leaders. But the motives are by no means all idealistic; guerrilla war is an excellent outlet for personal aggression, it provides opportunities for settling accounts with one's enemies, and conveys a great sense of power to those hitherto powerless. [. . .] There is a tendency not just to employ violence

but to glorify it; in this respect there are parallels between modern guerrilla movements and Fascism. Guerrilla warfare and, *a fortiori*, urban terror implant a pattern of dictatorial practices and brutality that perpetuates itself. Graduates of the school of violent action do not turn into practitioners of democracy and apostles of humanism after victory.

9. Organization, propaganda and terror have always been essential parts of guerrilla warfare, but their importance has greatly increased over the years and the techniques have been refined. Organization implies the existence of a political party or movement or at least a noncombatant fringe, semilegal or underground, providing assistance to the guerrillas—money, intelligence and special services. [. . .]

Propaganda is of particular importance in civil wars when the majority of the population, as is often the case, takes a neutral, passive attitude in the struggle between incumbents and insurgents. The apathy of the majority usually favors the guerrillas more than their enemies. No guerrilla movement has obtained its objectives solely through propaganda; equally none has succeeded by terrorism alone.

Terror is used as a deliberate strategy to demoralize the government by disrupting its control, to demonstrate one's own strength and to frighten collaborators. More Greeks were killed by EOKA than British soldiers, more Arabs than Jews in the Arab rebellion of 1936–1939, more Africans than white people by the Mau Mau. The terrorist element has been more pronounced in some guerrilla movements than in others; in 'urban guerrillaism' it is the predominant mode of the armed struggle, in China and Cuba it was used more sparingly than in Vietnam, Algeria or in Greece. While few guerrilla movements have been opposed in principle to terror, some, for strategic reasons, have only seldom applied it because they thought it tactically ineffective or because they feared that it would antagonize large sections of the population. It is impossible to generalize about the efficacy of terror as a weapon; it has succeeded in some conditions and failed in others. It was used with considerable effect in Vietnam and Algeria; elsewhere, notably in Greece and in various Latin American countries, it had the opposite effect. Much depends on the selection of targets, how easy it is to intimidate political opponents, whether it is just a question of 'liquidating' a few enemies, or whether the political power of the incumbents is widely diffused. Guerrilla war has been defined by insurgents and counterinsurgents alike as the struggle for the support of the majority of the people. No guerrilla movement can possibly survive and expand against an overwhelmingly hostile population. But in the light of historical experience the measure of active popular support required by a guerrilla movement need not be exaggerated.

10. The techniques and organizational forms of guerrilla warfare have varied enormously from country to country according to terrain, size and

density of population, political constellation, etc. Thus, quite obviously, guerrilla units in small countries have normally been small whereas in big countries they have been large. In some countries guerrilla units gradually transformed themselves into regular army regiments and divisions (Greece) and yet failed, in others they won the war though they never outgrew the guerrilla stage (Cuba) or despite the fact that militarily they were beaten (Algeria). In some guerrilla movements the personality of the leader has been of decisive importance. One need recall only Shamyl and Abd el-Kader in the nineteenth century; the same goes for more recent guerrilla wars (Tito, Castro, Grivas). On other occasions personalities have been of little consequence; the fact that the French captured some of the leaders of the Algerian rebellion did not decisively influence the subsequent course of the war. The leaders of the Vietnam Communists were expendable, Mao probably was not.

There are, by definition, no *Blitzkrieg* victories in guerrilla war, yet some campaigns succeeded within a relatively short period (two years) whereas others continued, on and off, for decades. Some involved a great deal of fighting, resulting in great losses, others were, on the whole, unbloody (Cuba, Africa). There has been a tendency to explain the defeats of guerrilla movements by referring to their strategic errors. Thus the Greek Communists have been blamed for their premature decision to adopt regular army tactics, and the Huks for not carrying the war to the cities. But this does not explain why other guerrillas succeeded, despite the fact that they made even graver mistakes. Success or failure of a guerrilla movement depends not only on its own courage, wisdom and determination but equally on objective conditions and, last but not least, on the tenacity and aptitude of the enemy. [. . .]

11. Urban terrorism in various forms has existed throughout history; during the past decade it has become more frequent than rural guerrilla warfare. Some modern guerrilla movements were predominantly city-based; for instance, the IRA, EOKA, IZL and the Stern Gang, others were part urban (Algeria). Neither the nineteenth-century anarchists nor the Russian pre-revolutionary terrorists regarded themselves as guerrillas; their assassinations were largely symbolic acts of 'punishment' meted out to individual members of the forces of oppression—they were not usually part of an overall strategy. Whereas guerrilla operations are mainly directed against the armed forces of the enemy and the security services, as well as installations of strategic importance, modern urban terror is less discriminate in the choice of its targets. Operations such as bank robberies, hijackings, kidnappings, and, of course, assassinations are expected to create a general climate of insecurity. Such actions are always carried out by small groups of people; an urban guerrilla group cannot grow beyond a certain limit because the risk of detection increases with the growth in numbers. A

successful urban guerrilla war is possible only if the strength of the establishment has deteriorated to the point where armed bands can move about in the city. Such a state of affairs has occurred only on very rare occasions and it has never lasted for any length of time, leading within a few days either to the victory of the insurgents or the incumbents. The normal use of 'urban guerrilla' is a euphemism for urban terrorism which has a negative public relations image. Thus the Tupamaros always advised their members to dissociate themselves from 'traditional terrorism' and only a few fringe groups (Marighela, Baader-Meinhof) openly advocated terror. Urban terrorism can undermine a weak government, or even act as the catalyst of a general insurgency but it is not an instrument for the seizure of power. Urban terrorists cannot normally establish 'liberated zones'; their operations may catch headlines but they cannot conduct mass propaganda nor build up a political organization. Despite the fact that modern society has become more vulnerable than in the past to attacks and disruptions of this kind, urban terrorism is politically ineffective, except when carried out in the framework of the overall strategy of a political movement, usually sectarian or separatist in character, with an already existing mass basis.

12. Guerrilla movements have frequently been beset by internal strife, within their own ranks or between rival groups. Internal dissension has been caused by quarrels about the strategy to be pursued (China, Greece) or by the conflicting ambitions of individual leaders (Frelimo, Columbia). The rivalry between the political and the military leadership, unless these were identical, has also been a frequent cause of friction.

[From Walter Laqueur, *Guerrilla: A Historical and Critical Study* (London: Weidenfeld & Nicolson, 1977), 393–404.]

STANLEY KARNOW

88 General Giap on Dien Bien Phu and Tet

Ho[1] offered to remain affiliated with France, but the French rebuffed his compromise, and war broke out in 1946. Giap preserved his teams and built up popular sympathy. By late 1949, the Chinese Communists had conquered China and begun to send him heavy weapons, which enabled him to enlarge his guerrilla bands into battalions, regiments, and ultimately divisions. Giap opened the path into Vietnam for Chinese arms shipments by destroying the French border posts in a series of lightning attacks.

Stunned, France sent out its most distinguished general: Jean de Lattre de Tassigny. Giap gallantly announced that the Vietminh now faced 'an adver-

---

[1] Ho Chi Minh, first leader of North Vietnam.

sary worthy of its steel'. But de Lattre died of cancer amid plans for an ambitious French offensive. Both sides sparred for the next three years as Gen. Henri Navarre, now the French commander, forecast victory in a statement that would be his unofficial epitaph: 'We see it clearly—like light at the end of the tunnel.'

By 1953 Ho was considering negotiations with France. But he knew he had to win on the battlefield to win at the conference table. The arena would be Dien Bien Phu, which was to equal Waterloo and Gettysburg among the great battles of history.

'At first I had no idea where—or even whether—the battle would take place,' he recalled. Then, a veteran recounting his war, he reconstructed the scene by moving the cups and saucers around the coffee table in front of us.

Navarre, ordered to defend nearby Laos, chose the site by placing his best battalions at Dien Bien Phu, a distant valley not far from the Laotian border in northwest Vietnam—never imagining that Giap would fight there. He misjudged badly.

Giap brought a huge force into the area. His troops marched for weeks, carrying supplies on bicycles and their backs through jungles and over mountains. But no task was tougher than deploying the cannon that China had furnished them. Relying on sheer muscle, they dragged the howitzers up the hills above the French positions. 'It was difficult, *n'est-ce pas*, very difficult,' Giap recollected, adding that only truly 'motivated' men could have performed such a feat.

He planned to launch his attack on Jan. 25, 1954, and at first heeded his Chinese military advisers, who proposed 'human wave' assaults of the kind their forces had staged against the Americans in Korea. But, after a sleepless night, he concluded that it would be suicidal to hurl his troops against the deeply entrenched French, with their tanks and aircraft. His tone rose dramatically as he told me: 'Suddenly I postponed the operation. My staff was confused, but no matter. I was in command, and I demanded absolute obedience—*sans discussion, sans explication!*'

Giap rescheduled the attack for March, and directed his men to creep toward the French through a maze of tunnels as his cannon pounded them from the heights above the valley. The battle dragged on for nearly two months and, one by one, the French positions fell.

At the time, President Dwight D. Eisenhower weighed and rejected the idea of United States air strikes. What if he had intervened? 'We would have had problems,' Giap allowed, 'but the outcome would have been the same. The battlefield was too big for effective bombing.'

The French surrendered on May 7, the day an international conference met in Geneva to seek an end to the war. The Vietminh failed to transform the battlefield victory into a full diplomatic victory. Under Soviet and

Chinese pressure, its negotiators accepted a divided Vietnam pending a nationwide election to be held in 1956. Giap would only say that 'we could have gained more'. [...]

By late 1967, [...] Giap [...] faced a hard choice. The half-million United States troops then in Vietnam were chewing up his forces, and his hopes of an early victory seemed dim. But, as he wrote at the time, the Americans were stretched 'as taut as a bowstring' and could not defend the entire country. He also detected growing antiwar feeling in the United States and rising unrest in South Vietnam's urban areas. Thus he gambled on a campaign that would break the deadlock. Later known as the Tet offensive of 1968, it would be a coordinated assault against South Vietnam's cities.

'For us, *vous savez*, there is never a single strategy,' Giap explained. 'Ours is always a synthesis, simultaneously military, political, and diplomatic—which is why, quite clearly, the offensive had multiple objectives. We foresaw uprisings in the cities. But above all, we wanted to show the Americans that we were not exhausted, that we could attack their arsenals, communications, elite units, even their headquarters, the brains behind the war. And we wanted to project the war into the homes of America's families, because we knew that most of them had nothing against us. In short, we sought a decisive victory that would persuade America to renounce the war.'

Giap prefaced the drive in late 1967 with a diversion, striking a string of American garrisons in the Vietnamese highlands. Johnson, who viewed Giap's siege of Khe Sanh as a replay of his showdown against the French, pledged Westmoreland to hold the base—saying, 'I don't want any damn Dinbinphoo.' The Communist troops, bombed by B-52's, took ghastly losses. But Giap had lured the American forces away from the populated coast.

On the night of Jan. 31, 1968, the Lunar New Year, some 70,000 Communist soldiers attacked South Vietnam's cities. A suicide squad stormed into the United States Embassy compound in Saigon, and American troops fought for weeks to rescue Hue. The televised scenes shocked the American public, which was already souring on the war. His ratings plummeting as antiwar sentiment spread, Johnson abandoned the race for re-election. Vietnam, coupled with civil rights protests, threw America into turmoil.

Looking back, Giap maintains that Tet was a 'victory' that showed 'our discipline, strength, and ardor'. But, he admits, it was not 'decisive'. Another seven years of war lay ahead and, he concedes, they were 'difficult'. Still, he added with typical bravado, 'no obstacle, nothing the Americans could do, would stop us in the long run'. This was a reality, he emphasized, that Westmoreland failed to perceive. 'He was a cultivated soldier who had read many military texts', Giap said. 'Yet he committed an error following the Tet offensive, when he requested another 206,000 troops. He could have put in 300,000, even 400,000 more men. It would have made no difference.'

But the aftermath of Tet was bleak for the Communists. According to one of Giap's aides, their casualties during the drive had been 'devastating'. American bombing of the South Vietnamese countryside further crippled their forces as their peasant supporters fled to urban refugee camps. They were also ravaged by the Phoenix program, devised by the CIA to destroy their rural sanctuaries. The Communist structure retreated to Cambodia, where it was again uprooted by President Richard M. Nixon's incursion in 1970.

As Nixon withdrew United States troops, however, Giap had only to wait until he faced the inept Saigon army. The climax, he figured, would involve big units. Early in 1972, he staged a massive offensive intended to improve Hanoi's hand for the final negotiations. It failed as American aircraft crushed his divisions. But Nixon, eager for peace before the United States Presidential election in November, compromised on a cease-fire. Signed in January 1973, it would gradually erode. The Communists rolled into Saigon two years later.

'I was delirious with joy,' Giap said. 'I flew there immediately, and inspected the South Vietnamese army's headquarters, with its modern American equipment. It had all been useless. The human factor had been decisive!'

[From Stanley Karnow, 'An Interview with General Giap', *New York Times Magazine*, 24 June 1990, 131–5.]

JOHN MACKINLAY

89 **The Failure of the Multi-National Force: Lebanon, 1983–4**

The success of a peacekeeping force in maintaining an interpositional presence relies on its acceptance by each of the opponent parties and not on the deterrent military power of the interpositional force itself being greater than that of the sum of the opposing factions; for the latter activity cannot be defined as peacekeeping in the currently accepted meaning of that word. The problem with MNF 2 was that it did not have the required degree of mutual consent for its activities to operate as a recognized peace force. It was also bound by its mandate to support only one side of the civil war. Added to this, the contributing nations represented a very narrow slice of the international community and lacked worldwide credibility. There were therefore several political reasons why the hostage effect of placing an MNF peacekeeper between the hostile forces around Beirut was unlikely to have much impact. Since the protection and recognition normally enjoyed by a peacekeeping force would not operate in this case, it was inevitable that some other form of authority would be required. However, there were also problems in its capacity to deter; the MNF's collective strength was diminished by its federal style of organization, and even had they operated together the contingents did not equal the sum of all the warring factions. So they had neither the recognition accorded to a properly constituted peacekeeping force nor the military power to operate in an interventionist role.

The MNF did, however, have a considerable offensive capability. The three major contingents had air-strike and naval gunfire support available to them. The US Marines had a platoon of M60 tanks, and each force had armoured reconnaissance vehicles which could be used to great effect against an unsophisticated enemy. The French and the American contingents also had close-support artillery and mortar weapons. This fire power was used in three ways: first, on a fairly large scale to support LAF operations; secondly, to carry out reprisals after the 23 October bombings;[1] and thirdly, to return fire against individual weapon systems which were interdicting the MNF compounds. Supporting the LAF and carrying out the 23 October reprisals were the result of political decisions; the return-fire role was delegated to military commanders to decide.

Because military commanders were generally more in touch with the local situation than their political masters at home, this last category of the use of force was carried out in accordance with the principles of minimum force. The purpose in this case was to protect the soldiers in the compounds from the gratuitous attacks which were occurring throughout the area without becoming drawn into local fire fights. Certainly in the case of the US Marines there were scrupulously defined conditions for returning indirect fire, which set out to warn the attacker first of all that his position was known before fire was returned by a counter-bombardment weapon similar in size to that of the attacker's. There were not many cases of the US Marines using indirect fire weapons in this role, because the attackers usually stopped firing once they realized that their fire was about to be effectively returned.

However, in the case of reprisals and support for the LAF [Lebanese Armed Forces], the use of fire power was not so effective. In the latter instance the ostensible reason for the use of United States naval gunfire to support the LAF at Suq al Gharb was that the Druze attackers would, if successful, soon have been in a position to threaten the MNF bases in Beirut. The proposal to use gunfire support was initiated from Beirut by Robert McFarlane's staff, but the decision to fire was taken in Washington

---

[1] This refers to the attack on US and French barracks in Beirut by driving bomb-laden trucks into them, causing substantial casualties.

at NSC level. The local US Marines commander advised against becoming involved in this way but was overruled. Because the Druze had been the dominating military force in the area for some time prior to 19 September and remained there after the incident, it is hard to maintain that the gunfire turned the tide of events on the ground in any significant way. Robert Fisk of *The Times* noted that the greater part of the shells failed to hit Druze military installations, and this observation is reinforced by the US Marines historian Eric Hammel.

However, although the military effect was small, the political impact was considerable. For American constituencies it was a satisfactory display of the use of their naval power in the firm execution of a national foreign initiative. But in Lebanon it gave the kiss of death to any hopes the MNF, in particular the American contingent, may have had of remaining impartial. The use of force as a reprisal against the October bombings also had a negative effect. As mentioned earlier, the American and French intelligence agencies were not immediately able to find the real identity or motive of the individuals from the group styling itself as the Islamic Jihad who were responsible for the 23 October bombings; they were referred to as the 'truck bombers' until the end of the MNF operation. It is doubtful whether the reprisal raids carried out by French and United States aircraft could have succeeded in destroying many, or indeed any, members of the Islamic Jihad; what they did, however, was provoke the intense hatred of the factions that were hit during these raids and also directly involve the Syrians in the spiral of violence. [. . .]

The situation in Beirut required the military forces there to operate in an internal security role and as peacekeepers. The French, Italian and British contingents all had experience in both. Each European army had a fairly long-standing commitment to a UN peacekeeping force, the British to UNFICYP and the French and Italians to UNIFIL. The European troops also had some experience of an internal security threat in their own country—in the British case, Northern Ireland. Although Beirut was different in many respects from both their previous UN and internal security roles, they had sufficient experience in low-intensity operations to adapt themselves to the changeable situation in Beirut. It was noticeable in the city that when these contingents conducted 'green line patrols' during the honeymoon period they were relaxed in the streets where they could afford to relax and alert when the situation demanded alertness. The Italians and British in particular had an easy manner with the local people, and on the whole the conduct of their hard-profile troops was appropriate to the situation and produced a warm and co-operative response from the citizens.

The US Marines on the other hand regarded themselves as trained only for general war and had no experience of UN peacekeeping or low-intensity operations. There were no grey shades in their appreciation of Beirut;

there were only good guys and bad guys. Unlike the European contingents the Marines rotated frequently and never seemed to develop much familiarity with the locals or the other contingents. Eric Hammel describes some of the incidents which took place between the Marines and the locals which illustrate a gaucherie and naïvety which a longer experience in the city would have erased. As a result their presence in the streets was less relaxed and more intimidating towards the local people. The Marines moved in large AMTRAC vehicles which were clumsy in traffic. Their operational area also reflected the absolutist approach; troops were dug into sandbagged positions and bunkers, and when not on duty slept in tents. This attitude did not produce a good effect with the locals and made the Marines in particular a target for gratuitous attacks by the local cowboys. The Europeans also had the advantage of language experience. The French diplomatic and military staff had an abundance of Arabic speakers and were fortunate to have a French-speaking environment at the co-ordinating conferences arranged by the Lebanese army staff. The Italians were fairly careful to appoint staff with recent UNIFIL experience in key posts. They also had no problem with language. Even in the British contingent the Ambassador, Sir David Roberts, was a fluent French and Arabic speaker, and the military commander on deployment was a French linguist. The United States contingent, however, appeared to have made little effort to anticipate the requirements for French and Arabic in its diplomatic and military staff. It could be construed from this that the Americans did not place much value on communication either with the locals at unit level or at the liaison and co-ordination conferences at Lebanese government level.

[From John MacKinlay, *The Peacekeepers: An Assessment of Peacekeeping Operations at the Arab–Israeli Interface* (London: Unwin Hyman, 1989), 106–11.]

ROBERT E. OSGOOD

90 **Limited War and Korea**

Communist Aggression and American Intervention

The Korean War is the single most significant event in the development of American postwar strategy. When the full history of the cold war is written, it may loom as one of the truly decisive events that shaped the pattern of war and politics in our era. [. . .]

In retrospect [. . .] nothing seems more logical than the shift of the main thrust of Communist expansion from an era of relative Western strength, where expansion entailed large risks of total war, to an area of great vulnerability and weakness, where the West had scarcely applied the strategy of containment, where the risks of total war were minimized, and where neither local resistance nor massive retaliation was an effective deterrent. [...]

The trouble with our action in Korea was not that we intervened in the war—which was necessary from the standpoint of containment—or that we intervened under the aegis of the United Nations—which probably facilitated more than it hampered the achievement of American objectives—but, rather, that our eagerness to represent American intervention as an altruistic act of pure collective security tended to obscure the underlying basis of *Realpolitik* without which intervention, regardless of UN sanction, would have been unjustified.

It is natural that nations should justify their actions on the highest possible grounds, especially when they must endure the sacrifices of war; but the danger in this is that they may lose sight of the peculiar circumstances of self-interest which enable them to claim those grounds and that, consequently, they will lack a consistent basis of action under circumstances in which the same happy coincidence of idealism and self-interest does not exist. Clearly, some quite special circumstances enabled the United States to fight the Korean War in the name of the United Nations.

In the first place, the Republic of Korea had been established by free elections held under UN supervision and had been recognized by the United Nations as the lawful government in the area south of the thirty-eighth parallel. In the second place, the Communists chose an overt attack on the Republic of Korea, so that the UN's special obligations as well as its charter were directly violated. In the third place, soon after the North Korean attack the Security Council was able to pass a resolution calling for an immediate end to the fighting and the assistance of all members in restoring peace, which would not have been possible without the Soviet delegate's absence during Russia's boycott of the UN.

In the Korean War, as in the Greek civil war, the problem of containment was obscured by broader and more palatable motives for intervention, which happened to correspond to the dictates of American security. In the urge to envision American resistance to Communist aggression on the highest moral plane, it was easy to overlook the power-political basis of our action and to overgeneralize its determining objectives. In this way we somewhat misled ourselves as to the true basis of our interests. One might have concluded from the announcement of the Truman Doctrine that the United States had adopted a policy of helping free peoples to resist totalitarian aggression, but Secretary Acheson had had to explain that it all depended on how the circumstances affected American interests. Similarly, one might have inferred from official explanations of American intervention in the Korean War that the United States would henceforth resist Communist aggression according to the collective will of peace-loving nations, as manifested in the councils of the UN. But a moment's reflection would indicate that neither resistance to aggression nor the collective will of peace-loving nations would always correspond with America's security interests in containing the Communist sphere; and it would be folly to suppose that the United States should always resist aggression, regardless of the consequences.

Would we have intervened in Korea if the South Koreans instead of the North Koreans had struck across the thirty-eighth parallel? If so, we certainly would not have intervened in behalf of the Communists or under the auspices of the United Nations. Moreover, aside from the special circumstances that permitted the United States to obtain UN sanction for its intervention and despite a desire to check a chain of aggression in the interests of international peace, one must suppose that American leaders would have foregone intervention if intervention had not been practicable from the standpoint of American interests. One circumstance that made intervention practicable in Korea was the existence of a clear-cut act of military aggression. Another was the fact that a large part of the American ground and air force in the Pacific area was stationed near the scene of action, in Japan. But certainly one could not count upon these fortunate circumstances recurring in future Communist aggressions.

The Korean War raised grave problems concerning the methods of containing lesser aggressions by limited war. These problems could not be resolved in terms of the general goals of defeating aggression and upholding collective security. They were strategic problems—the problems of managing national power according to an over-all plan for achieving security objectives. They would have to be appraised in the light of concrete military and political circumstances bearing upon America's power position. But the strategic lessons of the Korean War were partially concealed by the nation's instinctive depreciation of containment and its attempt to reconcile intervention in a limited war with the traditional image of the United States as a crusader above power politics. [. . .]

The administration's position was from first to last dedicated to keeping the war in Korea limited. Whether or not it conducted the war in the most effective manner, there can be no doubt that it was impressed with the need for limiting the ends and means of warfare and that it succeeded in this endeavor.

The overriding consideration that led the administration to limit the war in Korea was the fear of provoking Russian intervention and bringing about a third world war. As President Truman has written, 'Every decision I made in connection with the Korean conflict had this one aim in mind: to prevent a third world war and the terrible destruction it would bring to the civilized world. This meant that we should not do anything that would provide the excuse to the Soviets and plunge the free nations into full-scale all-out war.' From the beginning of the war the Truman administration believed that the North Korean invasion was a Russian maneuver, and it operated largely on the prevailing assumption among its counsels that the Kremlin was probing the West's positions on the Communist periphery in order to discover and exploit weak points. However, at the same time, it could never entirely abandon the fear, which was especially strong at the outset of the war, that the invasion might really be part of a Russian plan to distract the United States preliminary to a general assault on the non-Communist world. It was determined not to fall into this trap by offering the Russians the slightest pretext for direct intervention.

A second decisive consideration was the fear of overcommitment, of allowing the war in Korea to expand to such an extent as to render the United States incapable of meeting aggression in any of a half-dozen other potential trouble-spots. The administration was not only keenly conscious of the danger of depleting the defense of western Europe and thereby encouraging major aggression in that vital area; it was also apprehensive of a Russian attack on Japan and of pressure of a more limited nature on Berlin, Yugoslavia, Iran, and Indochina. President Truman assumed from the first that, whether or not the Korean War was the immediate prelude to a general assault, the Kremlin aimed to destroy America's capacity to meet her principal adversary by drawing her into military conflicts with a satellite in Asia. Therefore, he believed that 'we could not afford to squander our reawakening strength as long as that enemy was not committed in the field but only pulling the strings behind the scenes'. This reasoning was in accord with the Central Intelligence Agency's estimate that 'the Russians were not themselves willing to go to war but that they wanted to involve us as heavily as possible in Asia so that they might gain a free hand in Europe'. It was also consistent with the assumption, which the President and his advisers had considered from the outbreak of the war, that the Russians might be merely probing the West's defenses, as in Iran, Greece, and Berlin, but did not intend the action in Korea as a prelude to total war.

Beyond these two determining considerations in limiting the war, the administration was also restrained by its relations with other nations. It was particularly anxious to maintain unity with America's European allies; and it believed that unity required a certain deference to their wishes—as in the case of forbidding air pursuit over the Yalu—in order to allay their fear of a total war. However, the decisive limitations which the American government placed upon the conduct of the war seem to have arisen from considerations affecting the United States directly, rather than from solicitude for allied sensibilities.

In order to avoid precipitating a third world war or overcommitting American resources in Korea the administration explicitly limited its political objectives and endeavored to keep military means and political objectives in proportion as the circumstances of the war changed. The principal restrictions it imposed upon military operations entailed confining both air and ground action to the Korean peninsula, withholding the employment of Chinese Nationalist troops, and rejecting measures, like the blockade of the Chinese mainland, which in the opinion of the Joint Chiefs of Staff carried a risk of expanding the war disproportionate to the possible military advantages. [. . .]

One can hardly overestimate the importance of the United States achievement in containing the Communist attack on South Korea without precipitating total war. By this achievement the nation went a long way toward demonstrating that it could successfully resist direct military aggression locally by limited war in the secondary strategic areas, where a demonstrated capacity for local resistance was the only effective deterrent to Communist military expansion. As a result, the United States placed itself in a much stronger position to contain the Communist sphere of control than if it had stood passively aside and fretfully watched the Communists swallow Korea. If it had stood aside, one can scarcely doubt that Peking and the Kremlin would have been encouraged to engineer other attacks at vulnerable points along the Sino-Soviet periphery. In any event, the resulting blow to America's prestige might have fatally weakened the NATO coalition. It would certainly have encouraged neutralism in Japan and Germany and a massive swing to the Communist bloc throughout the defenseless areas of Asia. Unfortunately, by fighting a limited war in Korea the United States incurred serious internal schisms that weakened the national will to fight future limited wars. Yet this penalty was incidental to the main achievement, and it was mild compared to the turmoil and confusion, the cross-purposes and the extremism, that would have attended passive acquiescence in a blatant Communist aggression that the United States might have halted.

However, granting the American achievement in Korea, we must still wonder whether it was sufficient, whether we could have achieved much more at a tolerable cost. By repelling the Communist aggression through limited war we struck an effective blow for containment; but by leaving the Communists in control of North Korea we incurred some serious liabilities. We permitted the Chinese to gain great prestige throughout the vulnerable populations and wavering governments of Asia, while we raised serious doubts in the minds of those peoples about our ability to defend them. At the same time, we committed ourselves to defend a strategically profitless area under difficult circumstances, and we left a thorn in our Pacific flank; for the Communists, who have flagrantly disregarded the truce restrictions in Korea, could at any time force us to live up to our commitment. (This same disadvantage would exist if we had unified Korea, since Communist forces beyond the border would still hold a sword over the peninsula, but the problem of creating local defensive strength would be eased consider-

ably.) In addition, we incurred the vexing liability of restraining an impetuous South Korean government led by an aging patriot whose whole life has
revolved about the consuming ambition to unify Korea.

[From R. E. Osgood, *Limited War: The Challenge to American Security* (Chicago: Chicago
University Press, 1957), 163–79.]

RICHARD A. HUNT

91 Pacification and Attrition in Vietnam

The introduction of US ground forces in South Vietnam in 1965 did more
than involve the United States Army in land combat in Southeast Asia. US
troops, relying on lavish use of artillery, tactical air support, and sweeps by
heavily armed and mechanized units, changed the style and scale of combat
in the area. The US strategy of attrition by actively seeking out and destroying enemy formations was at odds with the tactics and philosophy of
South Vietnam's pacification program—Saigon's effort to bring security,
economic development and responsive government to the countryside.
Attrition offered a convenient way to measure success in the short run by
counting the number of enemy who were put out of action. Hence, the
dynamics of attrition mitigated against static, population control missions
and encouraged American commanders to actively pursue their adversary.
Attrition was not designed to achieve an outright military victory, nor to
resolve the political issues of the war. It had two basic purposes: (1) to
prevent South Vietnam's military defeat at the hands of the Viet Cong and
North Vietnamese; and (2) to convince the communists that they could not
afford to win, to diminish their warmaking capacity, and thus make the
cost of their continuing the war against South Vietnam prohibitive.

The focus on attrition of the Viet Cong through conventional combat
operations meant the underlying political issues of the war were overlooked. The struggle in South Vietnam was between rival groups of Vietnamese, and the principal enemy goal was to subvert the authority of the
government in the settlements of the countryside and to supplant Saigon's
officials with persons loyal to or members of the Viet Cong—a broad term
that encompassed both political and military communist elements. The
contrasts between the two strategies—pacification and attrition—were
seen very clearly at the province level. [. . .]

Viewed from the perspective of the village and the province, the attrition
strategy of the United States was not the most effective or appropriate
response to the insurgency rending South Vietnam in the 1960s. General
Westmoreland developed attrition to prevent by conventional military
means the defeat of South Vietnam in 1965. Given the communists' access

to sanctuaries, attrition as employed in Vietnam was not designed to secure a military victory in the conventional sense, but rather to make it impossible for the other side to win and thus deter them from continuing. If the North Vietnamese and Viet Cong had intended in 1965 to cut South Vietnam in half, defeat Saigon's forces, and capture the cities, then attrition succeeded, for none of those things happened as long as US air and ground forces fought in South Vietnam. However, if the other side's intentions were political and more modest, namely, to set in place a communist infrastructure while undermining the local government nominally in charge and weakening South Vietnam's military, then attrition was ill-suited. There is another possibility. The introduction of US ground forces might have caused the communists to modify their immediate objectives and postpone the completion of their timetable.

Although the exact intentions of the communists in 1965–1966 are still far from clear, their conduct of the war, save for the major, conventional offensives they set in motion in 1968, 1972, and 1975, was consistent. They fought a war without frontlines and deliberately concentrated their attacks on their weakest foe, the territorial forces. That pattern held true not just for the war against the Americans but for the Viet Minh's struggle against the French as well.

The consistency of that pattern underscores the weakness of attrition in a political war. It points as well to a more appropriate response on the part of the US government: devoting more funds and material to arming, equipping, and training South Vietnamese forces to fight a war unlike any that the US Army had in its recent past fought—a war without fronts. In other words, the so-called 'Vietnamization' program that began in 1967 and received wide publicity during the tenure of Westmoreland's successor, General Creighton W. Abrams, should have started even earlier. In addition, Washington should have devoted more resources and better management in support of the pacification program; it was both vital and a uniquely Vietnamese responsibility. Unified management of US support and a build-up of manpower and money for pacification came in 1967; not until early 1969 was their effect visible. According to HES reports, which are useful mainly as indicators of aggregate, long-term trends, the percentage of the South Vietnamese population living in secure or relatively secure settlements improved from 42 percent in December 1967 to over 79 percent in January 1969. That change also reflected a decline in VC capability over that period. Nevertheless, it is not clear if Washington had begun the Vietnamization program and improved support of pacification earlier than it did that South Vietnam's fate would have been different. After all, it was up to the South Vietnamese to build a cohesive political community, subdue its foe on the battlefield and in the villages, and protect its people from terrorism. US arms, equipment, economic assistance, and technical advice (military as well as nonmilitary) could not serve indefinitely as proxies for the Saigon government's own achievements in providing security and a better life for its citizens and establishing a bulwark against the North Vietnamese.

Certainly, Long An and Hau Nghia were more hostile to the Saigon government and more difficult to pacify than most provinces in the country, but the very severity of the situation in those troubled areas starkly illuminated the central issue of the war for the South Vietnamese side: the performance of the government and its forces. The danger to Hau Nghia, Long An, and the rest of South Vietnam in the 1960s was less a military defeat at the hands of the North Vietnamese, however real that possibility was in 1965, than a continuation of internal political and military problems. Why the South Vietnamese government failed to improve and reform despite serious threats to its existence and the repeated efforts of American officials is perhaps the basic question of the war and one that cannot be explored fully in a short essay. Part of the answer was Washington's concern for South Vietnam's sovereignty. In no aspect of the war did US officials command or control the South Vietnamese military or government, however strong or pervasive American influence was. For the United States to take charge of South Vietnam's affairs would have most likely resulted in greater efficiency, but would have exposed Washington to well-founded charges of neocolonialism. Another part of the answer stems from the decision in 1965 to use US soldiers to keep the Saigon government afloat. The United States' commitment of forces to fight the North Vietnamese and Viet Cong and money to support the economy of South Vietnam had a profound effect. Because we were so deeply involved, we could not afford to leave and let our allies fail. Because we could not let them fail, we lost leverage in forcing them to improve. Americanizing the war lowered the incentives for the South Vietnamese to make fundamental political changes or prosecute the war with vigor. Sending US forces also diverted attention from the village political war to the sparsely populated areas of South Vietnam where most of the search and destroy operations of the attrition strategy took place.

The gravest danger to the Republic of Vietnam in the long run was the unabated spread of unresponsive and corrupt government administration, poor civilian and military leadership, and lackluster indigenous forces. Those factors directly contributed to the inability of successive governments in Saigon to gain the political commitment of the peasantry, or to preempt the appeal or loosen the hold of the Viet Cong on the villagers. Without solving its internal problems, the Saigon government was apt to last as long as US forces remained in South Vietnam and thus made it unlikely that the North Vietnamese would win a military victory.

[From Richard A. Hunt, 'Strategies at War: Pacification and Attrition in Vietnam', in Richard A. Hunt and Richard H. Schultz, Jr. (eds.), *Lessons from an Unconventional War* (New York: Pergamon Press, 1982), 23–4, 43–5.]

MICHAEL HANDEL

92 Surprise in October 1973

An obvious although important lesson in strategic and military surprise is that the weaker side has a very strong incentive to compensate for his weakness by resorting to the use of strategem and surprise as a force multiplier. The powerful, stronger side conversely lacks the incentive to resort to surprise and thus not only sacrifices an important military advantage but also plays into his enemy's hands. We shall see below how this simple but often forgotten lesson appears again and again in our story. [...]

By 1973, experience had taught the Arab countries that strategic surprise was a key element in military success. Earlier, the Arabs had been confident that their overwhelming numerical military superiority guaranteed an easy victory; no effort was made to conceal their preparations for war. In contrast, their plans for attack in 1973 were made under the strictest secrecy and concealed by elaborate deception; great efforts were made to maintain a facade of routine activities.

From Arab reports, it is clear that the *planning* and *timing* of the attack were meticulous. Early October was chosen as the best time to attack for a variety of reasons. In the first place, the autumn climate was most suitable for the attacking forces. Secondly, it coincided with the Jewish high holidays—on the assumption that the Israeli level of alert would be lower, that more than the usual number of soldiers would be on leave, and that the closure of all businesses on the day of atonement would slow down Israeli mobilization. A third factor was the approach of Israeli elections in early November, which diverted the attention of Israeli leaders from security matters and foreign affairs to domestic affairs and political campaigning. Furthermore, in 1973 the holiest of the Arab holidays—Ramadan—fell in October; and it was hoped the Israelis would assume that no Moslem country would initiate a war during that month. (So far as is known, this last ruse did not have any effect on Israeli intelligence estimates.)

Purportedly in preparation for the well-advertised war games that were to begin in early October, the Egyptians and Syrians readied their troops over a period of four months. This undoubtedly misled Israeli intelligence, creating an opportunity for the Arabs to concentrate their troops without starting an international crisis. When Israeli intelligence grasped the real intent of the troop concentrations, it was too late for Israel to muster sufficient political and military counterpressure by belatedly activating its own mobilization process. On the morning of October 6, when Israeli intelligence concluded that the Syrian-Egyptian war games were only a ruse, much valuable warning time had been lost. The government had always been promised a warning time of at least 48 to 76 hours, but in October 1973, it was cut to 12–16 hours, which did not allow a full-scale mobilization. To maintain secrecy for as long as possible, Egyptian and Syrian soldiers were not told—until the attack itself—that their war games were the first phase of a real war.

Other deception plans included, for example, the demobilization of 20,000 Egyptian soldiers 48 hours before the war and the spreading of rumors over a long period of time concerning the shortage of spare parts for Soviet military equipment, the low maintenance level of Egyptian antiaircraft batteries, and other indications about the low level of preparedness for war and the weakness of Egyptian and Syrian material capabilities. On the political level, Egyptian Foreign Minister Zayat arrived in the United States at the end of September 1973 to reactivate Washington as a mediator and to give peace another chance. At the last moment, the attention of Israeli decision-makers was drawn to a Palestinian terrorist action in Vienna, which Syrian intelligence claimed to have planned.

Major General Hassan el Badri calls the Egyptian deception plan 'an overwhelming success' that 'misled foreign intelligence service bodies including the CIA, as well as Israeli intelligence'. Yet it seems the only part that was truly effective was the 'war games'. Otherwise, the Egyptians simply added noise to a system already overloaded with contradictory information. While the attack was indeed devastating, it was technically only a partial surprise. When it began, partial mobilization had already been declared and Israeli troops were supposed to be fully alerted.

The Egyptians and Syrians surprised the Israeli Army not only in the timing of their attack but also in two other important areas, namely in technology and in their military doctrine and goals. The effectiveness of some of the Arab coalition's weapons—in particular Soviet antiaircraft missiles, antitank missiles, bridging equipment, and night fighting equipment—came as a great surprise to Israeli troops on the battlefield. Both Arab armies had introduced these new weapons on a *massive scale*—the condition necessary for making a powerful impact with new weapons systems. Moreover, the effectiveness of the new weapons enabled Egypt and Syria to design a new military doctrine which proved to be more appropriate for the quality of their manpower. Some of the Israeli doctrine's greatest advantages were neutralized; and the Israeli troops, initially thrown off balance, lost a number of important battles. By the time adequate countertactics had been improvised, the Israelis had suffered heavy material losses, lost ground that had to be regained, and suffered a blow to their morale and self-confidence.

The innovative Egyptian doctrine was strategically offensive but tactically defensive. It was the opposite of the Israeli military doctrine which was strategically defensive, but highly offensive on the tactical level. The

Egyptians were able to develop such a modern version of Wellington's tactics only because of new weapons that gave the defense the advantage. The highly effective and mobile antiaircraft missiles (the SAM-6, and the infantry-fired SAM-7) combined with the deadly rapid-firing ZS4-23-4 anti-aircraft guns, imposed considerable limits on the performance of the Israeli Air Force; and the Soviet antitank missiles (the SAGGER and SWATTER) again combined with the RPG-7 and hand-held short-range infantry non-guided type of bazooka blunted, at least for the first few days, the offensive superiority of the Israeli armor.

In the years preceding the war, Israeli intelligence *had* obtained all the technical data on the performance of the newly acquired Egyptian and Syrian weapons. This information was duly passed along to the Israeli armed forces on all levels but was not taken seriously. Neither Israeli intelligence nor the general staff and various branches foresaw the impact those weapons would have on the battlefield, and they failed to recognize the new tactical opportunities that were created. In short, they did not see that the pendulum in the development of modern weapons had swung in favor of the defense. As a result, no effort was made to modify the Israeli military doctrine accordingly. The Israelis made a mistake that can be found in many other failures to anticipate a surprise attack: they projected their own military doctrine on the enemy. The cardinal assumption of the Israeli doctrine was that without air superiority or at least parity, one could not expect to win a war; furthermore, the offensive power of the tank dominated the battlefield on the ground. In both types of warfare the Israelis had a big advantage over their adversaries. Through the projection of their own reasoning on their adversaries, the Israelis felt that since the Egyptians and Syrians had no chance of winning the war militarily, they would not consider taking military action until their air power and the performance of their tank crews had been improved. To all this the Israelis added one more projection: their first defeat would also be the last one, so they would never dare to start a war they did not expect to win. The Israelis therefore incorrectly assumed that the Egyptians and Syrians would not open a war in which they would lose, particularly because of the 1967 debacle and what the Israelis perceived as the Egyptian defeat in the war of attrition.

Assumptions of symmetry are dangerous. While the Israelis were thinking positively, their enemies were thinking negatively. The Arabs set limited goals rather than a clear-cut military victory, and did not plan to achieve air superiority or to defeat Israeli tanks in huge tank battles. Instead, new technology enabled them to limit Israeli air superiority from the ground and blunt Israeli tank power with infantry. Significantly, Egypt and Syria could lose the war on the battlefield and win it politically (as they did), a strategy which was never open to, or feasible for, the Israelis.

This was a case in which there was no doubt concerning the adversaries' intentions. The Israelis had always assumed that whenever the neighboring Arab states had the capability to attack—they would. The Israelis' major mistake was to focus on the Egyptian and Syrian capabilities. Having concluded that the Arabs did not have the capabilities to wage a full-scale war, the Israelis believed that this would, in the short run, also affect their intentions. Had the Israelis instead focused more attention on Arab political intentions, they might have more seriously considered the possibility of a limited war or of a total war whose outcome was uncertain.

There are other important explanations for Israel's surprise and the decision not to preempt when the government became aware of the Arabs' plans in the last hours before the war broke out. Confident of their superior capabilities, top Israel commanders overestimated the defensive value of the Suez Canal and the Golan Heights on the one hand, and underestimated Arab capabilities on the other. They misjudged the impact that leaving the first move to their adversaries would have on their own plans. This weakened their incentive to preempt (although the Israeli Air Force was prepared to stage a preemptive attack at around 12:00 noon). As it turned out, knowledge of the timing of the attack did not prevent many other, no less damaging surprises from occurring in terms of the attackers' methods, doctrines, and new weapons. The Israeli high command temporarily lost control over the direction and pace of the battle, and could not implement its original plans, while the rate of attrition of manpower and matériel was much higher than anticipated.

There were, however, *political reasons* that reduced the incentives to preempt. Having been branded as aggressors and occupiers following the Six Day War, the Israelis were reluctant to risk this again. After preempting, it would be impossible to prove that the enemy had indeed been poised to attack. Moreover, since there is never a one hundred percent certainty that the enemy will attack—only a higher or lower probability—the Israelis were afraid that a preemptive attack would be a self-fulfilling prophecy. The Israeli government warned the Egyptian and Syrian governments, through the United States, not to attack. Israel naively thought that the Arabs would cancel their plans when they realized that they had lost the element of surprise as far as timing was concerned. A partial alert and mobilization in Israel, known to the Egyptians and Syrians, was to imply that there was no use in beginning a war, since Israel was ready to defend itself. An earlier partial alert and mobilization declared by the Israelis in May 1973 had *not* ended in conflict. Prime Minister Golda Meir and Defense Minister Dayan later admitted that the Israeli government decided not to preempt for fear of losing the backing of the United States, Israel's only ally. American officials (Henry Kissinger in particular) had threatened to withdraw American support if Israel attacked first.

The propensity to use strategic surprise is directly related to the general stability of a regional system. In an unstable system such as the Middle East, conflicting political, religious, and ethnic interests combined with a highly militarized system continue to provide a powerful incentive to resort to surprise attack. The military experience of nations in the area has demonstrated that a successful surprise attack can be the key to victory, sometimes even to the future of a nation. It is therefore to be expected that in the future, strategic surprises, such as the recent Iraqi attack on Iran, will recur more frequently in the Middle East than in any other region.

> [From Michael Handel, 'Crisis and Surprise in Three Arab–Israeli Wars', in Klaus Knorr and Patrick Morgan (eds.), *Strategic Military Surprise* (New Brunswick: Transaction Books, 1983), 113, 136–40.]

ROBERT E. OSGOOD

93 The Reappraisal of Limited War

One of the most significant developments in international politics since World War II is the change of attitude towards armed force in the advanced Western countries. Between the two world wars total warfare was commonly viewed as virtually the only kind of warfare relevant to military preparedness and strategy. In such a war victory would depend on destroying in the most thorough way the enemy's capability and will to fight. But in the cold war quite a different view has become widespread—the view that the principal objective of military policies is the avoidance of general war and the limitation and control of lesser wars according to political ends short of traditional military victory. One aspect of this change of attitude is the great attention devoted to limited war strategy and preparedness in the United States, especially in the last ten or twelve years.

To an extent that must amaze early proponents of limited war, who sought to overcome the formidable antipathy toward the concept during the Korean War and the Eisenhower–Dulles Administration, the rationale of limited war has gained widespread acceptance in the United States and, to a somewhat lesser degree, in allied countries. In the 1960s the United States went far in implementing the concept with strategies, weapons, and organization. Among research, academic and military analysts the concept of limited war inspired a great outpouring of strategic doctrine. In the Kennedy Administration limited war became official doctrine and achieved something approaching popularity. [. . .]

The concept and practice of limited war are as old as war itself; but the consciousness of limited war as a distinct kind of warfare, with its own theory and doctrine, has emerged most markedly in contrast and reaction to three major wars, waged between several major states, in behalf of popular national and ideological goals, by means of mass conscription and massive firepower: the Napoleonic Wars, World War I, and World War II. The contemporary interest in limited war springs partly from a determination to avoid World War III.

The relevance of limited war to contemporary international politics is manifest in the occurrence of more than fifty internationally significant local wars of various kinds since World War II, while there have been no general wars, and the armed forces of the most powerful states have come no closer to fighting each other than the American–Soviet confrontation in the Cuban missile crisis of 1962. The great majority of these wars, however, did not directly involve a nuclear or even a major power; most of them were insurgent or civil wars, none of them (except the Hungarian intervention in 1956) was fought between advanced industrial states or on the territory of an advanced state. They were limited, as before World War II, by such factors as the restricted fighting capacity of the belligerents, the one-sided nature of the contest, or the inherent limits of internal war. With the diffusion of power and intensification of local conflicts, such wars in the Third World may become an increasingly disturbing element in international politics, if only because they could involve major powers. But the kinds of wars that have occasioned the systematic concern with strategies and weapons of limited war are wars that the United States fought, that might have expanded into much wider and more violent conflicts, but that remained limited because the United States and its adversaries deliberately refrained from conducting military operations with their full capacities. Equally important, the concern has arisen from the desire to deter or limit hypothetical wars that have not occurred—especially wars that might have resulted from limited aggressions impinging on America's vital interests abroad.

The detailed elaboration of a strategic doctrine of limited war, the formulation of specific plans for carrying out this doctrine, and the combined efforts of government, the military establishment, and private analysts and publicists to translate the doctrine into particular weapons and forces are developments peculiar to the nuclear age. They are products of the profound fear of nuclear war and the belief that the limitation of war must be carefully contrived, rather than left to inherent limitations upon military capabilities. But they are also products of American foreign policy in a particular period of history. Reappraising limited-war strategy as, in part, a function of American policy in the cold war will help us to distinguish between those aspects of limited-war thinking that are obsolescent or of only transitory relevance, because they reflect vanishing or short-run circumstances, and those that are likely to remain valid or become increasingly relevant, because they reflect fundamental conditions or significant international developments.

On the most general grounds the conception of limited war surely remains relevant—indeed, imperative. On grounds of morality and expediency alike, it is essential that states—especially nuclear states—systematically endeavour to control and limit the use of force where force is unavoidable. The fact that American public officials and spokesmen now generally take this for granted, while little over a decade ago high government officials commonly asserted that once war occurs it has no limits save those determined by the capacity to gain a military victory, must be regarded as a major and, hopefully, lasting triumph of reason over viscera. [. . .]

It is significant how weak and ineffectual American 'all-or-nothing' sentiment has been in the Vietnamese as compared to the Korean war. The idea of the United States confining itself to a limited war, which was novel and antithetical in Korea, has been widely taken for granted in Vietnam. Indeed, the most influential American critics have urged more, not less, stringent restrictions on combat despite the fact that the danger of nuclear war or of Chinese or Russian intervention never seemed nearly as great as in Korea. Those (including some prominent conservative Senators and Congressmen) who took the position that the United States ought either to escalate the war drastically in order to win it or else disengage, clearly preferred the latter course. But their frustration did not manifest a general rejection of the conception of limited war but only opposition to the particular way of applying that conception in Vietnam.

Thus the popular disaffection with the Vietnamese war does not indicate a reversion to pre-Korean attitudes toward limited war. Rather, it indicates serious questioning of the premises about the utility of limited war as an instrument of American policy, the premises that originally moved the proponents of limited-war strategy and that underlay the original confidence of the Kennedy Administration in America's power to cope with local Communist incursions of all kinds. In Vietnam the deliberate limitation of war has been accepted by Americans simply from the standpoint of keeping the war from expanding, or from the standpoint of de-escalating it, whereas in Korea the desire to keep the war limited had to contend with a strong sentiment to win it for the sake of containment. In Korea the principal motive for limitation was the fear that an expanding war might lead to general war with China or nuclear war with the Soviet Union, but in Vietnam the limits were motivated as much by the sense that the political objective was not sufficiently promising to warrant the costs of expansion. This change of emphasis reflects more than the unpopularity of the war in Vietnam. It also reflects the domestication, as it were, of limited war—that is, of the deliberate, calculated restriction of the ends and means of fighting—as an operational concept in American foreign policy.

Some of the reasons for the strength of sentiment for keeping the war limited, however, bear upon the political question of whether to intervene in local wars at all. They suggest that the specific lessons about the strategy and constraints of limited war that one might derive from Vietnam are likely to be less important than the war's impact on the political premises that underlay American intervention.

The political premises that Vietnam has called into question are more profound, yet more limited, and at the same time less explicit than the sentiment embodied in the popular refrain 'no more Vietnams'. If Vietnam exerts a fundamental impact on American policy with respect to limited-war interventions, it will not be merely because of the national determination to avoid future Vietnams and to restrict American commitments to a scope more compatible with American power and the will to use it. The whole history of the expansion of American commitments and involvements is pervaded with the longing to avoid new commitments and involvements. Yet a succession of unanticipated crises and wars has led the nation to contravene that longing. Sometimes the desire to avoid the repetition of unpleasant involvements had only led to a further extension of commitments, which in turn has led to further involvements. That is what happened when the Eisenhower–Dulles Administration formed deterrent alliances (including SEATO) to avoid another Korean war.

The reason for this contradiction is not really a sublimated national longing for power—at least not power for its own sake—but rather the nation's persistent pursuit of a policy of containment, which under the prevailing international conditions has repeatedly confronted it with predicaments in which the least objectionable course has seemed to be the exercise and extension, rather than the abstention or retraction, of American power. If a fundamental change in America's use of limited-war strategy as an instrument of policy takes place, it will be because the premises of containment are no longer convincing to the nation and Vietnam has acted as the catalyst to enforce this realization.

[From Robert E. Osgood, 'The Reappraisal of Limited War', in Alastair Buchan (ed.), *Problems of Modern Strategy* (London: Chatto & Windus, 1970), 92–5, 112–14.]

ANDREW PIERRE

94   The Impact of Arms Sales

Arms sales have become, in recent years, a crucial dimension of international affairs. They are now major strands in the warp and woof of world politics. Arms sales are far more than an economic occurrence, a military relationship, or an arms control challenge—*arms sales are foreign policy writ large*.

The dramatic expansion in arms sales to the developing world during the 1970s is by now widely known. Less clear is what judgement to make of this important phenomenon.

To some observers, the arms delivered feed local arms races, create or enhance regional instabilities, make any war that occurs more violent or destructive, and increase the tendency for outside powers to be drawn in. The arms received are often seen as unnecessary to the true needs of the purchasing country and as a wasteful diversion of scarce economic re-sources. The remedy often proposed is drastic curtailment of arms sales, with tight international controls as the best means for achieving this.

To others, the recent increase in arms sales is no cause for particular concern. Sovereign nations have every right to the weapons that they deem necessary. By giving or selling arms the supplier country acquires political influence or friendship. It receives economic benefits. Regional peace and stability may be advanced rather than hindered by the transfer of arms. In any case, there is little that can be done about the international trade in arms. If one country does not sell the weapons, some other state will be only too happy to oblige. Accordingly, seeking international restraints is a will-o'-the-wisp.

Neither judgment is fully right or wrong. In order to be better under-stood, the arms trade phenomenon must be viewed in the wider context of the transformations under way in world politics.

Arms sales must be seen, essentially, in *political* terms. The world is undergoing a diffusion of power—political, economic, and military—from the industrialized, developed states to the Third World and the so-called Fourth World (poor and without oil). The acquisition of conventional arms, often sophisticated and usually in far greater quantities than the recipient state previously had, is a critical element of that diffusion.

Arms are a major contributing factor to the emergence of regional powers such as Israel, Brazil, South Africa, or, until recently, Iran; their purchase makes a deep impact upon regional balances and local stability. The diffusion of defense capabilities contributes at the same time to the erosion of the early postwar system of imperial or hegemonic roles former-ly played by the major powers around the globe. Thus the superpowers, and even the medium-sized powers such as Britain and France, are losing the ability to 'control' or influence events in their former colonies or zones of special influence. And the transfer of conventional arms is only one element of the diffusion of military power. Another, of prime importance, is the trend toward nuclear proliferation. As we shall see, the relationship between the two is intricate and complex.

Arms sales must also be seen in the context of North–South issues. They constitute a form of redistribution of power whose significance in certain cases may be equal to or greater than that of some of the well-recognized economic forms. Certainly the withholding or granting of arms can have a great political and psychological impact. Arms transfers can also be a form of transfer of technology; an increasing number of states do not want the weapons fresh out of the crate but the technology that will enable them to build, or 'co-produce', them at home.

Finally, arms sales remain a key element of the continuing East-West competition. Indeed, they may now be the prime instrument available to the Soviet Union, and a significant one for the United States, in their rivalry for the allegiance of much of the world. The condition of mutual deterrence at the nuclear level, and the risk that a conventional conflict could quickly or uncontrollably escalate to the nuclear level, make a direct military confrontation between the two superpowers unlikely—hence the tendency toward competition by 'proxy' in the Third World, with the superpowers supporting friendly states or regimes, or (in the case of the Communist states) assisting 'movements of national liberation'. Sometimes alliances and the identification of 'friends' alter quickly, as happened in the Horn of Africa where the Soviet Union initially supported Somalia with arms and the United States supported Ethiopia, only to see their respective roles reversed. A contributing factor to the emerging importance of arms transfers as an instrument of the East–West competition has been the relative decline of ideology as an element in the continuing struggle, because of the diminishing attractiveness of both the United States and the Soviet Union as models. Yet another factor has been the declining size and role of economic and developmental assistance. Both the United States and the Soviet Union now give less in economic assistance than the value of their arms sales.

Arms do not of themselves lead to war. The causes of war are manifold and complex, but the underlying roots are usually found in political, economic, territorial, or ideological competition. Yet arms sent into a region may exacerbate tensions, spur an arms race, and make it more likely that, as Clausewitz taught us, war will emerge as the continuation of politics by other means. Once war has started, the existence of large and sophisticated stocks of weapons may make the conflict more violent and destructive. And if the arms have been acquired from abroad, often with the establishment of a resupply relationship and sometimes including the presence of technical advisers from the producing country, they may have a tendency to draw the supplier into the conflict. Yet these undesirable developments need not be inevitable. Arms may deter aggression, restore a local imbalance, and generally enhance stability. All depends upon the specifics of the case and the perceptions that exist about it.

Nevertheless, the people of the world can take little comfort from the trend toward a higher level of global armaments. Total world military expenditures have grown from $100 billion in 1960 to $500 billion in 1980.

Measured in constant prices this is an increase of 80 percent. The rise in arms spending in the developing world has been especially acute. Since 1960 military expenditures in the Third World have risen over fourfold (in constant prices), while those in developed countries have gone up a more modest 48 percent.

[From Andrew Pierre, *The Global Politics of Arms Sales* (Princeton: Princeton University Press, 1982), 3–5.]

KENNETH WALTZ

95 Nuclear Weapons: More May Be Better

Countries more readily run the risks of war when defeat, if it comes, is distant and is expected to bring only limited damage. Given such expectations, leaders do not have to be insane to sound the trumpet and urge their people to be bold and courageous in the pursuit of victory. The outcome of battles and the course of campaigns are hard to foresee because so many things affect them, including the shifting allegiance and determination of alliance members. Predicting the result of conventional wars has proved difficult.

Uncertainty about outcomes does not work decisively against the fighting of wars in conventional worlds. Countries armed with conventional weapons go to war knowing that even in defeat their suffering will be limited. Calculations about nuclear war are differently made. Nuclear worlds call for and encourage a different kind of reasoning. If countries armed with nuclear weapons go to war, they do so knowing that their suffering may be unlimited. Of course, it also may not be. But that is not the kind of uncertainty that encourages anyone to use force. In a conventional world, one is uncertain about winning or losing. In a nuclear world, one is uncertain about surviving or being annihilated. If force is used and not kept within limits, catastrophe will result. That prediction is easy to make because it does not require close estimates of opposing forces. The number of one's cities that can be severely damaged is at least equal to the number of strategic warheads an adversary can deliver. Variations of number mean little within wide ranges. The expected effect of the deterrent achieves an easy clarity because wide margins of error in estimates of probable damage do not matter. Do we expect to lose one city or two, two cities or ten? When these are the pertinent questions, we stop thinking about running risks and start worrying about how to avoid them. In a conventional world, deterrent threats are ineffective because the damage threatened is distant, limited, and problematic. Nuclear weapons make military miscalculations difficult and politically pertinent prediction easy. [. . .]

Lesser nuclear states, with choices tightly constrained by scarcity of resources, may be forced to make choices that NATO has avoided, to choose nuclear defence or nuclear deterrence rather than planning to fight a conventional war on a large scale and to use nuclear weapons only when conventional defences are breaking. Increased reliance on nuclear defence would decrease the credibility of nuclear deterrence. That would be acceptable if a nuclear defence were seen to be unassailable. An unassailable defence is fully dissuasive. Dissuasion is what is wanted whether by defence or by deterrence.

The likelihood of war decreases as deterrent and defensive capabilities increase. Whatever the number of nuclear states, a nuclear world is tolerable if those states are able to send convincing deterrent messages: It is useless to attempt to conquer because you will be severely punished. A nuclear world becomes even more tolerable if states are able to send convincing defensive messages: It is useless to attempt to conquer because you cannot. Nuclear weapons and an appropriate doctrine for their use may make it possible to approach the defensive–deterrent ideal, a condition that would cause the chances of war to dwindle. Concentrating attention on the destructive power of nuclear weapons has obscured the important benefits they promise to states trying to coexist in a self-help world.

[From Kenneth Waltz, *The Spread of Nuclear Weapons: Move May Be Better*, Adelphi Paper No. 171 (London: IISS, 1977), 6–7.]

MARTIN VAN CREVELD

96   The Future of Low-Intensity War

[T]he application of strategy in its classical sense to low-intensity conflict has always been problematic. Even as Jomini wrote his *Précis des grandes operations de guerre*, Spanish guerrillas were showing that it was perfectly possible to wage war—and a very savage war at that—on a small scale. Many of those involved were illiterate peasants as well as women, children, and priests. Probably they had never even heard of strategy, which, as Tolstoy points out in *War and Peace*, was a newfangled notion with a sophisticated ring to it. Confronted by the most powerful conventional armed forces that the world had ever seen, the insurgents made do without 'armies', campaigns, battles, bases, objectives, external and internal lines, *points d'appui*, or even territorial units clearly separated by a line on a map.

Though guerrilla warfare has not always been successful, from that day to ours the lesson that strategy is irrelevant to it has been repeated a thousand times. Mao spoke of guerrillas as fish swimming in the 'sea' of the surrounding population, the point of the analogy being precisely that the sea does not have features that distinguish one part from another. Similarly in Vietnam, the Americans discovered that strategy, as taught at staff and war colleges, was inadequate for understanding 'a war without fronts', let alone for successfully waging it. Seen in this light, the geographical bias of strategy, as understood from Jomini through Moltke to Liddell Hart, stands out clearly; which also explains why the latter in particular does not cite a single example from the Middle Ages, when warfare in many ways resembled modern low-intensity conflict. In short, such conflict is to conventional warfare what the Einsteinian world-view is to the Newtonian.

If low-intensity conflict is indeed the wave of the future, then strategy in the classical sense will disappear—indeed many would say that already today it is little more than an exercise in make-believe whose relevance is limited to the war games played by general staffs. Like the domain to which it belongs—conventional war—strategy has been caught in a vise between nuclear weapons on the one hand and low-intensity conflict on the other. Nuclear weapons work against geographical distinctions of any kind: in the future, if armed forces—and, most probably, the political units by whom they are fielded—are to survive and fight in earnest, they will have to become intermingled with each other and with the civilian population. Low-intensity conflict will ensure that, once they are intermingled, battles will be replaced by skirmishes, bombings, and massacres. The place of lines of communications will be taken by short, covert approaches of a temporary nature. Bases will be replaced by hideous and dumps, large geographical objectives by the kind of population-control that is achieved by a mixture of propaganda and terror.

The spread of sporadic small-scale war will cause regular armed forces themselves to change form, shrink in size, and wither away. As they do, much of the day-to-day burden of defending society against the threat of low-intensity conflict will be transferred to the booming security business; and indeed the time may come when the organizations that comprise that business will, like the *condottieri* of old, take over the state. Meanwhile, and as has already happened in Lebanon and in many other countries, the need to combat low-intensity conflict will cause regular forces to degenerate into police forces or, in case the struggle lasts for very long, mere armed gangs. Though most present-day militia still put on something resembling a uniform when it suits their purpose, over time uniforms will probably be replaced by mere insignia in the shape of sashes, armbands, and the like. Their wearers will not amount to armies as we understand the term.

Again, a special chapter in the conduct of future war is formed by the weapons it will employ. The invention of strategy late in the eighteenth century took place at the very time when the crew-operated weapons that had long dominated siege-warfare were also beginning to govern operations in the field. Though this coincidence is seldom noted, it is probably not accidental. From the mid-nineteenth century on, the trend away from individual weapons and toward large, crew-operated ones has been one of the dominant themes of modern warfare. The majority were designed principally for use against each other *en rase campagne*, as the saying went. Many of the most powerful, such as tanks, are really unsuitable for anything else; where people and their dwellings are present—in other words, where there is something to fight *about*—they only become entangled. Alternatively, the purpose of many of the most powerful weapons has been to attack objectives deep in the rear. In the case of heavy bombers and ballistic missiles, their inability to pinpoint targets meant that they could only be used when no friendly forces were expected to be within a radius of many miles.

Today, even third-rate powers are acquiring weapons whose reach is practically unlimited, and that are able to reach any point in the territory of any conceivable enemy. Based on recent advances in electronics, other weapons are sufficiently powerful to drench the battlefield in fire and also to blast a concentrated opposition to smithereens. However, most systems—including in particular heavy artillery, missiles, and aircraft—still are not sufficiently accurate to make much of an impression on any enemy who is extremely dispersed, or indistinguishable from the civilian environment, or intermingled with friendly forces. Because of this fact, intermingling with enemy forces, mixing with the civilian population, and extreme dispersion have become the normal practice in low-intensity conflicts. If countless instances from Vietnam to Nicaragua and from Lebanon to Afghanistan have any lesson to offer, surely it is that the most advanced weapons have simply not been relevant to them. This is because, as experience shows, any good they can do is more than balanced by the damage inflicted on the environment, and their own insatiable demands for supply and maintenance.

[From Martin Van Creveld, *The Transformation of War* (New York: The Free Press, 1991), 206–8.]

LAWRENCE FREEDMAN

97   Weak States and the West

At the start of this decade the cold war formally ended with a warm surrender. Surviving over forty years of intense superpower antagonism without a conflagration was cause enough for collective relief. That it could be settled so gracefully led to an even more optimistic thought: the great powers had been civilized. If they now understood that it was imperative to resolve differences without recourse to violence then surely lesser powers would follow. The tide of history had turned decisively against total war.

Not against all war, of course. Nasty civil wars and intercommunal violence would continue, and even the occasional clash involving Third World countries. Perhaps the leading states would feel obliged to impose some order as 'peace-keepers'. Nonetheless, when Mikhail Gorbachev let the Iron Curtain be drawn back, the West seemed destined to take over the East—in economic and philosophical if not political terms. Thereafter, no other group of states could begin to challenge its international pre-eminence. In such circumstances there seemed little reason to fear the sort of war which had in the past threatened the world's equilibrium.

By definition, total wars are unlimited in their scope. In the nuclear age this became a terrifying prospect but it was bad enough before, when millions were left dead and whole societies devastated. Even before the Berlin Wall came down, the idea that wars of such obvious folly were unlikely to recur was already well-established. Indeed Western defence policy depended on this idea, for it posed the choice to the Soviet Union of accepting the status quo or risking a nuclear holocaust. There was much debate as to whether the NATO countries would ever implement such a threat. Fortunately, Moscow was not inclined to see if it was all bluff. The consequences of miscalculation were so stark as to overwhelm any attempt to make a case for war.

Meanwhile the cold war itself had simplified international politics. Facing the common threat of Communism, most of the old 'great powers' were banded together in alliance, which in turn created the conditions for ever-closer economic and political co-operation. So successful was this process that it is now unthinkable for France and Germany to renew their traditional antagonism. This is rightly celebrated as one of the triumphs of the European Community.

The relative economic success of the Western bloc at first blunted and then reversed Communism's ideological challenge. With no claims to legit-imacy the Soviet bloc collapsed of its own accord, pushed aside by force of example rather than force of arms. With a Western-oriented leadership in place, co-operation could be substituted for conflict. This was the great hope at the start of 1990. If the leading states now realized that there was nothing worth fighting each other about, it was time to cash the 'peace dividend'.

As for lesser conflicts, the remedy was to be found in reinforcing the institutional mechanisms which could calm disputes and resolve them through reason and good sense, drawing strength from diplomatic consen-sus reinforced by economic carrots and sticks.

In its most naïve form the euphoria lasted but a few months. In the summer of 1990 came the Gulf crisis and then the massive military operation mounted to liberate Kuwait. Yet there was still a hopeful reading of the Gulf War, popularized at the time by President Bush with his promise of a 'New World Order'.

Bush presented the response to Iraqi aggression as an opportunity to set the tone for the future conduct of international affairs, by convincing aggressors everywhere that they would not be allowed to hold on to ill-gotten gains. A constructive relationship between the United States and the Soviet Union would make it possible to realize all those hopes for an effective collective security arrangement which had been raised by the foundation of the United Nations, as the Second World War drew to a close, only to be dashed by the onset of the cold war.

In retrospect Iraq provided an ideal test case. The crudity of Saddam Hussein's defiance left him politically isolated while the balance of forces made the eventual result certain (though not the eventual cost). The test was passed and yet more optimistic conclusions drawn. A coalition could be put together under the authority of the United Nations. Major powers showed that they not only knew not to fight each other but could also wage war to uphold basic international norms without being tempted to conquer the enemy and occupy his territory. Brute force was still required, but at least its application could be tailored. In Desert Storm, care was taken to avoid hurting civilians and property. Targets were chosen with prudence and attacked with precision. Gloomy predictions of massive casualties and destruction all round were not realized.

When that phoney peace was over

The subsequent tests of this idea of a working collective security system have been more severe and offer a less comforting model for the future of warfare. Most difficult of all have been the upheavals within the former Yugoslavia, but a pointer was provided by the rebellion inside Iraq following the liberation of Kuwait. Thus far the major powers have still sought to meet these tests through the United Nations but the record is at best mixed. In such cases there is no risk of total war: the problem is less one of scale than of complexity and duration. The trigger is more likely to be intercommunal violence or the break-up of a state than the crude occupation of one state by another.

The prototypical conflict now is a function of a weak state. States are weak because of the fragile nature of the civil society upon which they have been built, their undeveloped institutional structures, which are often unable to contain and channel political tensions, and their problems of poverty and economic adjustment. These weaknesses can lead to breakdowns of law and order, to secessionist movements, to outright civil war. The most susceptible states combine structural weaknesses with a regime which is inherently divisive in representing only one part of the community.

The proliferation of weak states is a natural result of the expansion of the international community following decolonization. The UN began with 50 members: at the last count it had 183. This process has now almost run its course with the collapse of the Russian Empire.

Even here there could be grounds for optimism. Decolonization naturally loosened the ties between the erstwhile 'great powers' and many parts of the world. So not only are colonial wars anachronistic—with no inhabitable territory left over which would-be imperialists might scramble—but 'wars of national liberation' are also a rarity. There may be continuing tussles over the composition and constitutional form of the new states; but, unlike the early years of the twentieth century, the leading states show little interest in aggrandizement through courting particular factions. Post-Communist Europe has not been scoured by rival alliances looking for new recruits.

The leading—largely Western—states have, of course, important interests in what goes on beyond their own neighbourhoods. But only rarely can these be truly described as 'strategic'. Before one superpower would watch closely who was befriending the other, even in regions in which it had no other obvious stake. Now, there are still interests which are described as 'vital' relating to trade and raw materials, especially oil, but even these can appear to be less substantial than supposed on close examination. Narrowly national incentives that justify the resort to armed force are becoming few and far between.

Confused spectators

In the absence of pressing strategic imperatives, traditional concepts of international order would have suggested that the leading states could now relax and busy themselves with peaceful pursuits. The old order stressed state rights, which extended from opposition to armed aggression to adherence to non-interference in internal affairs; but this has been undermined through the steady elevation of minority and human rights.

During the years of decolonization, as new states came into being on the basis of arbitrary boundaries left over from imperial days, it was recognized that the safest course was to stick with them, for once challenges began they would never stop. The Organisation of African Unity made this an absolute rule. When Communist decolonization began in Europe the initial instinct was to follow the same rule, but this had been unhinged by an equal and now apparently ascendant regard for the contrary principle of self-determination—even in circumstances where it is extraordinarily difficult to see how it could realistically lead to viable statehood, or when its satisfaction would inevitably raise exactly the same demand from a group which might fear becoming a disadvantaged minority within this new state. Multinational states are now assumed to be inherently unstable and the idea of the 'melting pot' dubious and even racist, in the presumption of assimilation into a dominant culture.

In the West—in part prompted by the mass media's global and prying character—there is growing distaste with the idea of turning a 'blind eye' to crude forms of repression and persecution for the sake of a quiet life. When moral imperatives drive foreign policy there is always a risk of double standards and counter-productive intervention. While the principle of the inviolability of established borders remains sacrosanct it is in practice increasingly difficult to sustain once it is accepted that a minority subject to unacceptable oppression has the right to its own state.

The West thus views the world with a general lack of pressing strategic interest combined with a confused moral interest. Systematic repression, ethnic cleansing, and images of violent internal wars may affront them without directly affecting them. In which case, the question of meeting unambiguous challenges to the high standards of political behaviour poses fundamental questions of international responsibility.

Thus, however bitter for those consumed by its violence, the troubles of many weak states may be of no international consequence if they have little effect on the state system as a whole. Disputes well away from the main political centres are unlikely to excite the active participation of leading states. This is likely to come about only when a major principle is clearly at stake and this is combined with a degree of real concern over the practical consequences of a conflict left to its own devices.

Chaos might spread as a result of a crisis within a relatively large country or one with a sensitive location, or through a series of conflicts with distinctive origins beginning to combine. An ethnic group might appear in a politically influential position on one side of a border while as a victim on the other. Risks could develop to resident foreign nationals and sources of raw materials. Fears could grow of economic dislocation and mass emigration.

Determining the point at which a gathering disorder is getting too close for comfort and action is needed may be a fine judgement. The interest is likely to be in containment rather than resolution: if little can be done to stop the fighting, at least it must not spread. Thus, at least in their early stages, even conflicts in which there is a potential international interest may attract only slight outside attention. In the absence of direct threats the West will naturally be reluctant to become entangled in the deadly quarrels of others. Yet if nothing is done about these quarrels, there could be a rising tide of instability.

If the Western states acquire a reputation for hesitation when it comes to intervention, then weak states which feel vulnerable to external threat must look to stronger local powers to protect them. On this new basis new alliances may start to form, creating—as did alliances in the past—a mechanism by which conflicts might spread.

Moreover if the West is unable and unwilling to take decisive military action, it is natural that the vulnerable will take steps to defend themselves (and that potential predators will prepare to exploit their vulnerability). There has already been a substantial diffusion of military power from the advanced to the developing world, by means of the arms trade, and this shows every sign of continuing. Thirty years ago the gap between the military capabilities of the two was immense. Resisting Iraqi threats to Kuwait in 1961 involved a relatively small-scale response from Britain: in 1991 it involved a massive multinational operation.

The bitter bantam-weights

The Gulf War certainly demonstrated that in a regular fight the United States and its allies remain the heavyweight champions. They can overwhelm all-comers, even those which have squandered vast resources on military assets, and can use their material advantages such as information technology and air power in such a way as to minimize casualties to themselves and deliver knockout blows to the enemy.

The vast majority of wars do not come into the heavyweight range, but are distinguished more by their duration and bitterness than their weaponry. In a way they become more amenable to Western intervention when they do develop into straightforward clashes between regular forces. Civil wars, involving irregular fighters and skirmishes in the streets, with political confusion rife and good intelligence at a premium, present an appalling prospect to outsiders. Decisive victories are few and far between. Even success can mean a long-term commitment of troops to sustain an uneasy peace.

The West is also uneasily aware that its advantages might be neutralized through the proliferation of nuclear weapons. There is not going to be a rush to take on states with nuclear, chemical, biological, or ballistic missile stocks. As we saw in the Gulf, this threat—so long as it is non-nuclear—may not be overriding but it will raise the requirements for intervention. Another unnerving possibility is the further development of ecological warfare, threatening oil spills, the emptying of chemical plants into rivers, or the blasting of dams, and even of nuclear reactors. During the Gulf War just a hint of what is now a rather traditional form of terrorism—namely attacks on airliners—was sufficient to prompt a mass cancellation of travel plans around the world.

Nor has the West completely sorted out its relations with its old adversaries. The problems of turning Russia and the Ukraine into effective democracies and functioning economies are formidable. China has not lost its capacity to row with its neighbours. The long-term intentions of countries such as North Korea and Iran are uncertain. If any of these countries start to see force as a suitable means of resolving their dilemmas, then the international community could well find itself facing a challenge that would make Iraq's seizure of Kuwait seem quite modest by comparison.

The future of war is often taken to be simply a function of new technologies. There are certainly growing opportunities for precision warfare emerging as a result of the information revolution, just as the transformation of warfare in the nineteenth century reflected the revolutions in transport and industrialization. Yet it is difficult to conduct precision warfare in imprecise situations. As much as by technology, war has been influenced by the changing character of the state system, including colonization and the rise of mass society, and then by decolonization and the integration of trade and finance in the West. As the cold war closed, commentators spoke of a period of transition to a new international order, as stable as before but somehow more just. It was presumed that things would settle down for the forseeable future. But in a state system so complex and diverse, and with such inequalities in wealth and territory, stability is no more than a fond hope. Things will never settle down, and that is why we are unlikely to be able to stop worrying about war.

[From Lawrence Freedman, 'Weak States and the West: the Future Surveyed', *The Economist*, 11 September, 1993, 42–4.]

Select Bibliography

General

ARON, RAYMOND, *On War* (New York: W. W. Norton, 1968).
BUCHAN, ALASTAIR, *War in Modern Society* (London: Fontana, 1966).
DYER, GWYNNE, *War* (London: The Bodley Head, 1985).
HINDE, ROBERT, *The Institution of War* (London: Macmillan, 1991).
HOWARD, MICHAEL, *The Causes of Wars* (London: Temple Smith, 1983).
JONES, ARCHER, *The Art of War in the Western World* (London: Harrap, 1988).
KEEGAN, JOHN, *A History of Warfare* (London: Hutchinson, 1993)
MCINNES, COLIN, and SHEFFIELD, G. D. (eds.), *Warfare in the Twentieth Century: Theory and Practice* (London: Unwin Hyman, 1988).
MCNEILL, WILLIAM H., *The Pursuit of Power* (Oxford: Blackwell, 1983)
MIDLARSKY, MANUS, (ed.), *Handbook of War Studies* (Boston, Unwin Hyman, 1989).
OSTERUD, OYVIND, (ed.), *Studies of War and Peace* (Oslo: Norwegian University Press, 1983).

The Experience of War

BAYNHAM, HENRY, *From the Lower Deck: The Navy 1700–1840* (London: Arrow Books, 1972).
COWLEY, ROBERT (ed.), *Experience of War* (New York: Norton & Co., 1992).
MCGUFFIE, R. H. (ed.), *Rank and File: The Common Soldier at Peace and War 1642– 1914* (London: Hutchinson & Co., 1964).

Theories of War

BLAINEY, GEOFFREY, *The Causes of War* (Basingstoke: Macmillan, 1988).
CEADEL, MARTIN, *Thinking about Peace and War* (Oxford: Oxford University Press, 1987).
GILPIN, ROBERT, *War and Change in World Politics* (Cambridge: Cambridge University Press, 1983).
WALTZ, KENNETH, *Man, The State and War: A Theoretical Analysis* (New York: Columbia University Press, 1960).
WOLFERS, ARNOLD, *Discord and Collaboration* (Baltimore: John Hopkins University Press, 1962).
WRIGHT, QUINCY, *A Study of War* abridged by Louise Leonard Wright, (Chicago: The University of Chicago Press, 1966).

The Sociology of War

BOND, BRIAN and ROY, IAN (eds.), *War and Society* (London: Croom Helm, 1976).
EDMONDS, M. *Armed Services and Society* (Leicester: Leicester University Press, 1988).

FINER, S. E., *The Man on Horseback: The Role of the Military in Politics*, 2nd edn. (Boulder, Colo.: Westview Press, 1988).

HUNTINGTON, S. P., *The Soldier and the State* (Cambridge, Mass.: Harvard University Press, 1957).

MARSHALL, S. L. A., *Men Against Fire* (New York: William Morrow, 1947).

MOSKOS C., and WOOD, F. R., *The Military: More Than Just a Job?* (London: Brassey's, 1988).

PERLMUTTER, A., *The Military and Politics in Modern Times* (New Haven: Yale University Press, 1977).

SHAW, M., *Post Military Society: Militarism, Demilitarisation and War at the end of the Twentieth Century* (Oxford: Polity Press, 1991).

The Ethics of War

CALVOCORESSI, PETER, *Nuremberg: The Facts, the Law and the Consequences* (London: Chatto & Windus, 1947).

DONELAN, MICHAEL, *Elements of International Political Theory* (Oxford: Clarendon Press, 1990).

FOTION, NICHOLAS, and ELFSTROM, GERARD, *Military Ethics* (London: Routledge, 1986).

KUPER, LEO, *Genocide: Its Political Use in the Twentieth Century* (Harmondsworth: Penguin, 1981).

PASKINS, BARRIE, and DOCKRILL, MICHAEL, *The Ethics of War* (London: Duckworth, 1979).

SIMS, NICHOLAS (ed.), *Explorations in Ethics and International relations* (London: Croom Helm, 1981).

ROWE, PETER, *Defence: The Legal Implications* (London: Brassey's, 1987).

WALZER, MICHAEL, *Just and Unjust Wars* (Harmondsworth: Penguin, 1980).

Strategists and Strategy

BOND, BRIAN, *Liddell Hart: A Study of his Military Thought*, (London: Cassell, 1977).

GUEVARA, CHE, *Guerrilla Warfare* (Harmondsworth: Pelican Books, 1969).

EARLE, EDWARD MEAD (ed.), *Makers of Modern Strategy* (Princeton: Princeton University Press, 1943; repr. 1971).

FREEDMAN, LAWRENCE, *The Evolution of Nuclear Strategy*, 2nd edn. (London: Macmillan, 1989).

GADDIS, JOHN, *The Long Peace: Inquiries into the History of the Cold War* (New York: Oxford University Press, 1987).

KAPLAN, FRED, *The Wizards of Armageddon* (New York: Simon & Schuster, 1983).

LIDDELL HART, B. H. *Strategy: The Indirect Approach* (London: Faber, 1968).

LUTTWAK, EDWARD, *Strategy: The Logic of War and Peace* (Cambridge, Mass.: Harvard University Press, 1987).

PARET, PETER (ed.), *Makers of Modern Strategy* (Princeton: Princeton University Press, 1985).

REID, BRIAN HOLDEN, *J. F. C. Fuller, Military Thinker*, (London: MacMillan, 1987).

SCHELLING, THOMAS, *Arms and Influence* (New Haven: Yale University Press, 1966).

Biographical Notes

AMBROSE, STEPHEN E.: Professor of History at the University of New Orleans.

DU PICQ ARDANT, CHARLES: (1821–70) French military officer who rose to rank of colonel. Killed in action in 1870 during Franco-Prussian war.

ARENDT, HANNAH: (1906–75) Philosopher. Contributed many ideas to modern politics, including a seminal theory of the origins of totalitarianism.

ARON, RAYMOND: (1905–83) Prominent French sociologist and political philosopher.

BEAUFRE, ANDRE: (1902–75) French strategist and military officer who served in Indochina, Algeria, Suez, and in NATO.

BECKETT, IAN F. W.: Senior Lecturer, Department of War Studies, Royal Military Academy, Sandhurst.

BEST, GEOFFREY: Former Professor of History, University of Sussex, Brighton.

BROWN, SEYOM: Professor of International Relations at Brandeis University, Waltham, Mass.

BULL, HEDLEY: (1932–85) Formerly Montagu Burton Professor of International Relations, University of Oxford.

CALLWELL, MAJOR-GENERAL CHARLES EDWARD: (1859–1928) British military theorist, journalist and writer who served in India, Afghanistan, and during First World War.

CEADEL, MARTIN: Tutor in Politics and Fellow of New College, Oxford.

CLAUSEWITZ, CARL VON: (1780–1831) Prussian officer who fought against Napoleon and later as military adviser in Russian forces, before becoming administrative director of Prussia's General Military School.

COHEN, SAUL B.: Professor Emeritus of Geography at City University, New York.

CORBETT, JULIAN: (1854–1922) Naval historian who taught at Royal Naval College, Greenwich, and later at Oxford University.

DANDEKER, CHRISTOPHER: Senior Lecturer in War Studies, King's College, London.

DOCKRILL, MICHAEL: Reader in War Studies, King's College, London.

DOYLE, MICHAEL W.: Professor of Political Science, Johns Hopkins University, Baltimore, Md.

DOUHET, GIULIO: (1869–1921) Italian artillery officer who served in Italy's first air-force unit and enthusiast for air power. Reached rank of general.

ELSHTAIN, JEAN: Professor of Political Science, University of Massachusetts, Amherst.

FREEDMAN, LAWRENCE: Professor of War Studies, King's College, London.

GIDDENS, ANTHONY: Professor of Sociology, University of Cambridge, and Fellow of King's College, Cambridge.

GILPIN, ROBERT: Professor of Political Science at Princeton University, Princeton, NJ.

GRAY, COLIN: Professor of Politics, University of Hull.

GWYNN, MAJOR-GENERAL SIR CHARLES WILLIAM: (1870–1963) British army officer. Commandant, Staff College, Camberley, 1926–30.

HANDEL, MICHAEL: Professor of National Security Affairs, US Naval War College, Newport, Rhode Island.

HARE, JOHN E.: Professor of Philosophy, Lehigh University, Pennsylvania.

HARRISSON, TOM: (1911–76) Director of Mass Observation Archive and Professor at University of Sussex.

HASTINGS, MAX: Military historian and journalist, currently editor of *Daily Telegraph*.

HEUSER, BEATRICE: Lecturer in War Studies, King's College, London.

HOWARD, MICHAEL: Former Professor of War Studies, King's College, London, and Regius Professor of Modern History, University of Oxford. President of International Institute for Strategic Studies.

HUNT, RICHARD: Historian at US Center of Military History, Carlisle Barracks, Pennsylvania.

IBN, KHALDUN (1332–1406): Prominent Muslim historian, jurist, and scholar.

JANOWITZ, MORRIS: (1919–88) Former Professor at the Department of Sociology, University of Chicago, and founder of the Inter-University Seminar on Armed Forces and Society.

JOMINI, ANTOINE HENRI, BARON dE: (1779–1869): Swiss who fought for Napoleon. Became Counsellor of the Tsar during the Crimean War.

JOYNT, CAREY B.: Professor of International Relations, Lehigh University, Pennsylvania.

KARNOW, STANLEY: Author who has written extensively on Asia.

KARSH, EFRAIM: Reader in War Studies, King's College, London.

LAMBERT, ANDREW: Lecturer in War Studies, King's College, London.

LAQUEUR, WALTER: Director of the Institute of Contemporary History.

LENIN, VLADIMIR ILYICH: (1870–1924) Russian revolutionary who led the 1917 revolution and became first leader of the Soviet Union.

LIDDELL HART, BASIL: (1895–1970), Infantry officer in First World War who became influential journalist and military historian.

MACISAAC, DAVID: Associate Director, Air Power Research Institute, Air University.

MACKINLAY, JOHN: Specialist on peace-keeping. Currently at Brown University, Providence, RI.

MANIGART, PHILIPPE: Military sociologist, Royal Military Academy of the Belgian Armed Forces.

MEARSHEIMER, JOHN: Professor of Political Science, University of Chicago.

MIKSCHE, FERDINAND OTTO: (1910–70) Austrian by birth, became French military officer and then Professor of Tactics at the Portuguese Military Staff College.

MIDDLEBROOK, MARTIN: Military historian, Fellow of the Royal Historical Society.

MOLTKE, HELMUTH VON: (1800–91) Chief of the Prussian General Staff from 1857.

MOREMAN, TIM: Temporary Lecturer in War Studies, King's College, London.

MORGENTHAU, HANS: Former Professor of Political Science and Modern History, University of Chicago.

MOSKOS, CHARLES C.: Professor of Sociology, NorthWestern University, Evanston, Ill.

NAPOLEON I (1769–1821): First Consul of France from 1799, Emperor from 1804. Deposed in 1814, returned in 1815, when finally defeated at Waterloo.

NAVIAS, MARTIN: Lecturer in War Studies, King's College, London.

O'BRIEN, WILLIAM V.: Professor of Government, Georgetown University, Washington DC.

OSGOOD, ROBERT E.: Formerly Professor of International Relations, Princeton University, Princeton, NJ.

OWEN, WILFRED: Poet. Saw active service on the western front in First World War from 1916. Killed in action 1918.

PARKER, GEOFFREY: Professor of History, University of Illinois, Urbana-Champaign.

PASKINS, BARRIE: Senior Lecturer in War Studies, King's College, London.

PIERRE, ANDREW: Currently Senior Research Fellow at the Carnegie Foundation for International Peace, Washington DC.

PORCH, DOUGLAS: Mark W. Clark Professor of History, The Citadel, Charleston, South Carolina.

POWNALL, LT.-GEN. SIR HENRY: Vice-Chief of the Imperial General Staff, Chief of Staff in South East Asia Command in Second World War.

READ, HERBERT: Saw active service on the western front in First World War. Survived to become influential art critic.

REID, BRIAN HOLDEN: Senior Lecturer in War Studies, King's College, London, and Resident Historian at the Staff College, Camberley.

ROMMEL, FIELD MARSHAL ERWIN: (1891–1944) German military leader in Second World War, made his name as Commander of Afrika Corps.

SCHELLING, THOMAS: Economist who became Professor of Political Economy at Harvard and Director of Harvard's Center for International Affairs.

SHILS, EDWARD: Former Professor of Sociology, University of Chicago.

SOKOLOVSKY, VASSILY DANILOVICH: (1897–1968) Joined Red Army in 1918 and became Inspector General in the Ministry of Defence, where he presided over authoritative work on Soviet military doctrine.

STEWART, N. KINZER: Former member of US Army Research Institute for the Behavioral and Social Sciences.

THORNE, CHRISTOPHER: Former Professor of History, University of Sussex, Brighton.

TSE TUNG, MAO: (1893–1976) Founder of the Chinese Communist Party and leader of China from 1949.

VAGTS, A: American writer on militarism.

VAN CREVELD, MARTIN: Professor of Military History at Hebrew University of Jerusalem.

WALTZ, KENNETH: Professor of Political Science at the University of California, Berkeley.

WALZER, MICHAEL: Professor of Government, Harvard University.

WARNKE, PAUL C.: Lawyer who served in Johnson and Carter administrations, as head of the Arms Control and Disarmament Agency under the latter.

WHITE, JOHN: Reader in American History, University of Hull.

WIGHT, MARTIN: (1913–72) Formerly Professor of History at Sussex University, Brighton.

WRIGHT, QUINCY: Formerly Professor of International Law and International Relations at the University of Virginia.

YODER, JOHN: Mennonite theologian who has written extensively on Christian pacifism.

Acknowledgements

AKIZUKI, TATSUICHIRO, from *Nagasaki 1945*, ed. and with an introduction by Gordon Honeycombe (Quartet Books, 1981).

AMBROSE, STEPHEN, 'The Secrets of Overlord', in Robert Cowley (ed.), *Experience of War* (Reprinted by permission of W. W. Norton & Co., Inc.).

The American Council of Warsaw Jews and American Friends of Polish Jews, 'The End of the Warsaw Ghetto', from *The Extermination of 500,000 Jews in the Warsaw Ghetto* (New York, 1944).

ARENDT, HANNAH, from *Eichmann in Jerusalem*, © Hannah Arendt, 1963. Reprinted by permission of Laurence Pollinger Ltd., and Viking Penguin Inc.

ARON, RAYMOND, from *Peace and War: A Theory of International Relations*. Copyright © Doubleday & Company Inc., 1981.

BAREA, ARTURO, 'A Spanish Republican Official at the Siege of Madrid . . .', from *The Forging of a Rebel* (David-Poynter, 1972).

BAYNHAM, HENRY, 'Jack Nastyface', from *From the Lower Deck: The Navy 1700–1840* (Arrow Books, 1972).

BEAUFRÉ, ANDRÉ, from *Deterrence and Strategy* (*Dissuasion et Strategie*, Paris, 1964). Reprinted by permission of Armand Colin Editeur.

BECKETT, IAN, 'Total War', in *Warfare in the Twentieth Century: Theory and Practice*, ed. Colin McInnes and G. D. Sheffield (Unwin Hyman, 1988).

BEST, GEOFFREY, from 'Restraints on War by Land before 1945', in *Restraints on War*, ed. Michael Howard, © OUP 1979. Reprinted by permission of Oxford University Press.

BOROVIK, ARTYON, from *The Hidden War: A Russian Journalist's Account of the Soviet War in Afghanistan* (1991). Reprinted by permission of Faber & Faber Ltd., and Atlantic Monthly Press, New York.

BROWN, SEYOM, from *The Causes and Prevention of War*, © 1987. Reprinted with permission of St Martin's Press Incorporated.

BULL, HEDLEY, from *The Control of the Arms Race* (Praeger Publishers, 1961).

CEADEL, MARTIN, from *Thinking About Peace and War* (1987). Reprinted by permission of Oxford University Press.

VON CLAUSEWITZ, CARL, from *On War*, ed. and trans. Michael Howard and Peter Paret (Princeton University Press, 1976). © 1976 Princeton University Press.

CODY, ED, 'Covering Grenada', in William Schneider (ed.), *The Military and the Media*, The Keck Center for International Studies, July 1984.

COHEN, SAUL B., from *Geography and Politics in a World Divided* (New York: Oxford University Press, 1975)

VAN CREVELD, MARTIN, from *The Transformation of War*, © 1991 by Martin van Creveld. Reprinted by permission of The Free Press, a Division of Macmillan, Inc.

DANDEKER, C., 'The Bureaucratization of Force', from *Surveillance, Power and Modernity* (Polity Press, 1990). Reprinted by permission of Blackwell Publishers.

DOUHET, GIULIO, from *The Command of the Air*, trans. Dino Ferrari (New York: Coward-McCann, 1942).

DOYLE, MICHAEL, 'Kant, Liberal Legacies and Foreign Affairs', *Philosophy and Public Affairs*, Vol. 12, No. 3 (Summer 1983), © 1983 by Princeton University Press. Used with permission.

ELSHTAIN, JEAN, from *Women and War*, © Jean Elshtain 1987.

ETZOLD THOMAS, and GADDIS, JOHN LEWIS, 'U.S. Objectives with Respect to Russia', from *Containment: Documents on American Policy and Strategy, 1945–1950* (Columbia University Press, 1978).

FREEDMAN, LAWRENCE, and KARSH, EFRAIM, from *The Gulf Conflict, 1990–1991: Diplomacy and War in the New World Order* (1993). Reprinted by permission of Faber & Faber Ltd. and Princeton University Press.

GIDDENS, A., 'States and Military Power in Social Theory', from *The Nation State and Violence* (Polity Press, 1985). Reprinted by permission of Blackwell Publishers.

GILPIN, ROBERT, extract from *War and Change in World Politics* (1983). Reprinted by permission of Cambridge University Press.

GRAY, COLIN S., from *The Leverage of Sea Power*. © 1992 by Colin S. Gray. Reprinted by permission of The Free Press, a Division of Macmillan, Inc.

HARE J. E. and JOYNT, CAREY B., from *Ethics and International Affairs* (Macmillan, 1982).

HARRISSON, TOM, from *Living Through the Blitz* (Collins, 1976).

HASTINGS, MAX, from *The Korean War* (Michael Joseph, 1987), © Romadata, 1987. Reprinted by permission of Michael Joseph Ltd., and Curtis Brown Ltd.

HOWARD, MICHAEL, 'The Forgotten Dimensions of Strategy', reprinted in *The Causes of Wars* (London: Temple Smith).

JANEKOVIC, VANESSA VASIC, 'Beyond the Detention Camps', *War Report*, Bulletin of the Institute for War and Peace Reporting, October 1992.

JANOWITZ, MORRIS, from *The Professional Soldier: A Social and Political Portrait*. © 1960, 1971 by The Free Press. Reprinted by permission of The Free Press, a Division of Macmillan, Inc.

KARNOW, STANLEY, from 'An Interview with General Giap', *New York Times Magazine*, 24 June 1990. © 1990 by the New York Times Company.

KENNEDY, JOHN F., from a Tape of the Executive Committee, 27 October 1962, John F. Kennedy Library, transcribed by McGeorge Bundy, September 1987.

KHALDUN, IBN, from *The Muqaddimah: An Introduction to History*, trans. from the Arabic by Franz Rosenthal, ed. and abridged by N. J. Daood (Princeton University Press, 1967). © 1967 Princeton University Press.

LAMBERT, ANDREW, from 'The Crimean War, 1854–56: An Historical Illusion?', *Modern History Review*, Nov. 1991. Reprinted by permission of Philip Allan Publishers Ltd.

LAQUEUR, WALTER, from *Guerrilla: A Historical and Critical Study* (1977). Reprinted by permission of George Weidenfeld & Nicolson Ltd.

LENIN, V. I., from *Marxism and the Science of War*, by Bernard Semmel (New York: Oxford University Press, 1981).

LIDDELL-HART, B. H., extracts from *Memoirs*, 2 vols. (Cassell, 1967); from *The Rommel Papers* (Collins, 1963).

LOEHR, DAVIDSON, from 'To Care Without Judging', *The University of Chicago Magazine*, Spring 1985. © Davidson Loehr, 1985.

LUTTWAK, EDWARD, reprinted by permission of the publishers from *Strategy: The Logic of War and Peace*, Cambridge, Mass.: Harvard University Press, copyright © 1987 by The President and Fellows of Harvard College.

MCGUFFIE, R. H. (ed.), 'A French Infantryman at Waterloo . . .'; 'A Union–Confederate infantry skirmish at Gettysburg . . .' and 'A British Soldier fighting the Mahdis in the Sudan . . .', all from *Rank and File: The Common Soldier at Peace and War 1642–1914* (Hutchinson, 1964).

MACINTYRE, DONALD, from *U-Boat Killer* (Weidenfeld, 1956).

MAC ISAAC, DAVID, 'The Evolution of Air Power', in R. A. Mason (ed.), *War in the Third Dimension: Essays in Contemporary Air Power* (Brassey's, 1986).

MACKINLAY, JOHN, from *The Peacekeepers: An Assessment of Peacekeeping Operations at the Arab–Israeli Interface* (Unwin Hyman, 1989).

MANIGART, P., from 'The Decline of Mass Armed Forces in Belgium', *Forum*, Vol. 9 (1990), 37–64.

MIDDLEBROOK, MARTIN, from *The Fight for the 'Malvinas': The Argentine Forces in the Falklands War* (Viking, 1989), © Martin Middlebrook, 1989; from *Operation Corporate: The Falklands War, 1982* (Viking, 1985), © Martin Middlebrook, 1985. Reprinted by permission of Penguin Books Ltd.

MIKSCHE, F. O., from *Blitzkrieg* (1942). Reprinted by permission of Faber & Faber Ltd., and Random House, Inc., New York.

MORGENTHAU, HANS, from *Politics Among Nations*, 5/e by Hans Morgenthau, © 1948, 1954, 1960, 1967, 1972 by Alfred A. Knopf, Inc. Reprinted by permission of the publisher.

MOSKOS, C., 'Armed Forces in a Warless Society', *Forum*, Vol. 13, (1992), 3–10.

O' BRIEN, W. V., from *War: The Conduct of Just and Limited War* (Praeger Publishers, 1981).

PARKER, GEOFFREY, from *The Military Revolution: Military Innovation and the Rise of the West 1500–1800*. Reprinted by permission of Cambridge University Press.

PASKINS, BARRY, from *Exploration in Ethics and International Relations*, ed. Nicholas Sims (Croom Helm, London, 1981).

DU PICQ, COLONEL ARDANT, from *Battle Studies: Ancient and Modern*, trans. John Greely and Robert Cotton (The Military Service Publishing Co., 1947).

POWNALL, HENRY, from *Chief of Staff: The Diaries of Lieutenant-General Sir Henry Pownall*, Vol. 1: 1933–1940; 2 vols. (1972). Reprinted by permission of Leo Cooper.

from *Private War of Seaman Stumpf: The Unique Diaries of a Young German in the Great War* (Leslie Frewin, 1969).

REID BRIAN HOLDEN and WHITE, JOHN, 'A Mob of Stragglers and Cowards: Desertion from the Union and Confederate Armies, 1861–65'. Reprinted by permission from the eighth issue, number one of *The Journal of Strategic Studies*, published by Frank Cass & Co. Ltd., London. Copyright Frank Cass & Co. Ltd.

SCHELLING, THOMAS, extracts from *The Strategy of Conflict* (New York: Oxford University Press, 1963).

SCHRAM, STUART R., from *The Political Thought of Mao Tse Tung* (Phaidon Press Ltd.).

SHILS E., and JANOWITZ, M., 'Cohesion and Disintegration in the Wehrmacht in World War II', *Public Opinion Quarterly*, Vol. 12 (Summer 1948), 314–15. Reprinted by permission of the University of Chicago Press.

SOKOLOVSKY, MARSHAL, V.D., from *Military Strategy: Soviet Doctrine and Concepts.* © Frederick A. Praeger, Inc., 1963.

STEWART, N. KINZER, 'Military Cohesion', from *Mates and Muchachos: Unit Cohesion in the Falklands/Malvinas War* (Brassey's, 1991).

THORNE, CHRISTOPHER, from *The Far Eastern War: States and Societies, 1941–1945* (Unwin Paperbacks, 1986).

TRIPP, MILES, from *The Eighth Passenger: A Flight of Recollection and Discovery: A Documentary Account of a World War Two Bomber Crew* (Macmillan, 1985).

U.S. News and World Report, 'The Start of Desert Storm', from *Triumph Without Victory: The Unreported History of the Persian Gulf War* (Times Books, 1992).

VAGTS, ALFRED, from *A History of Militarism, Civilian and Military* (Harry N. Abrams, Inc.).

WALTZ, KENNETH, from *Man, the State and War: A Theoretical Analysis* (Columbia University Press, 1960).

WALZER, MICHAEL, from *Just and Unjust Wars* (Basic Books, Inc.).

WARNKE, PAUL, 'Vietnam and Nuremburg', from Peter D. Trooboff (ed.), *Law and Responsibility in Warfare.* © 1975 by The University of North Carolina Press. Used by permission of the author and publisher.

WIGHT, MARTIN, from *Power Politics*, ed. Hedley Bull and Carsten Holbraad. © Leicester University, 1979.

WRIGHT, QUINCY, 'Definitions of War', from *A Study of War*, abridged by Louise Leonard Wright. © The University of Chicago Press, 1967. Reprinted by permission of the publisher.

YODER, JOHN HOWARD, from *Nevertheless: The Varieties and Shortcomings of Religious Pacifism* (Scottdale, Pa.: Herald Press, 1992). Used with permission.

Any errors or omissions in the above list are entirely unintentional. If notified the publisher will be pleased to rectify these at the earliest opportunity.

Index